T0382443

"In *Truth and Transparency*, Alan Chen and Justin Marceau provide an insightful and thorough examination of the social and legal issues raised by undercover investigations. Chen and Marceau demonstrate that undercover investigations are a crucial element of the information-generation ecosystem that undergirds our society and our democracy, used in contexts far beyond the familiar ones of journalism and law enforcement. They closely examine the difficult moral and ethical issues raised by such investigations, which are after all based on deliberate lies, and they also carefully dissect the complex constitutional questions that arise when government officials seek to suppress such investigations. *Truth and Transparency* is an essential contribution to ongoing debates about the morality and legality of undercover investigations, and is a must-read for anyone with an interest in how, and how well, our society creates public awareness of lies and deceptions."

**Ashutosh Bhagwat, University of California, Davis School of Law**

"This timely, important, and fascinating book explores the legal, ethical, social, and technological dimensions of undercover investigations. Authors Chen and Marceau document the critical role undercover investigations play in uncovering abuses of power and galvanizing reform, analyze the ethical and legal constraints on such investigations, and expertly explain why blanket bans on such investigations, which often target deception or nonconsensual video recording, violate the Free Speech Clause of the First Amendment to the US Constitution. Anyone who cares about accountability in the public sphere should read this well-written and meticulously researched study."

**Lyrissa Lidsky, UF Levin College of Law**

"In *Truth and Transparency*, Alan Chen and Justin Marceau argue that undercover investigations and the right to record matters of public concern are vital to an informed public in a democratic society. They explain when the First Amendment should protect investigations and recordings and, conversely, when privacy interests should prevail. This is a comprehensive look at an important method of newsgathering in the digital age."

**Jack M. Balkin, Yale Law School**

"In this remarkable and important book, Chen and Marceau take a deep dive into the history, legality, ethics, and social significance of undercover investigations. Readers will learn of, among other things, journalism's evolving relationship to undercover investigations; the crucial role that such investigations have played throughout American history; social and legal backlash against undercover investigations; and First Amendment defenses against legislation that seeks to stymie such investigations. Above all, Chen and Marceau make a powerful case that undercover investigations – and the inconvenient truths that they expose –matter."

**Heidi Kitrosser, Northwestern University Pritzker School of Law**

"Marceau and Chen provide a crucial service with this book: bringing together a tight, persuasive, and empirically supported case for the role and value of undercover investigations as a uniquely powerful source of facts, upon which movements are built. This book can bring a new perspective for all audiences, but might be especially useful as a historical education and a guidebook for animal protection advocates or anyone else working in a social justice field."

**Cheryl Leahy, Executive Director, Animal Outlook**

"*Truth and Transparency* is the most original and comprehensive study of undercover investigations ever written. Chen and Marceau draw from history, ethics, law, policy, technology, and social science to provide their readers with a rich and insightful analysis of this provocative and paradoxical practice, wherein investigators engage in deception to uncover the truth about the behavior of powerful actors, both public and private. In so doing, the authors deliver a compelling evidence-based defense of the value of undercover investigations to a healthy democracy."

**Helen Norton, University of Colorado School of Law**

# TRUTH AND TRANSPARENCY

Undercover investigators have been celebrated as critical conduits of political speech and essential protectors of transparency. They have also been derided as intrusive and spy-like, inconsistent with private property rights, and morally or ethically questionable. In *Truth and Transparency*, Alan K. Chen and Justin Marceau rigorously examine this duality and seek to provide a socio-legal context for understanding these varying views. The book concretely defines undercover investigations, distinguishes the practice from investigative journalism and whistleblowing, and provides a comprehensive legal history. Chapters explore the public need for investigations and the rights of investigators, paying close attention to the types of investigations that fall beyond the scope of constitutional protection. The book also provides concrete empirical evidence of the broad, bipartisan support for undercover investigations and champions the practice as an essential component of the transparency our democracy needs to thrive.

ALAN K. CHEN is the Thompson G. Marsh Law Alumni Professor at the University of Denver Sturm College of Law. He is the coauthor of *Free Speech beyond Words: The Surprising Reach of the First Amendment* (2017) and has published numerous scholarly articles in leading national law journals.

JUSTIN MARCEAU is the Brooks Institute Professor of Law at the University of Denver Sturm College of Law. He is the author of *Beyond Cages* (2019) and a coeditor with Lori Gruen of *Carceral Logics: Human Incarceration and Animal Captivity* (2022). Marceau has worked with investigators, filmmakers, and journalists on cases and legal projects relating to undercover investigations.

# Truth and Transparency

## UNDERCOVER INVESTIGATIONS IN THE TWENTY-FIRST CENTURY

**ALAN K. CHEN**

University of Denver Sturm College of Law

**JUSTIN MARCEAU**

University of Denver Sturm College of Law

Shaftesbury Road, Cambridge CB2 8EA, United Kingdom

One Liberty Plaza, 20th Floor, New York, NY 10006, USA

477 Williamstown Road, Port Melbourne, VIC 3207, Australia

314–321, 3rd Floor, Plot 3, Splendor Forum, Jasola District Centre, New Delhi – 110025, India

103 Penang Road, #05–06/07, Visioncrest Commercial, Singapore 238467

Cambridge University Press is part of Cambridge University Press & Assessment, a department of the University of Cambridge.

We share the University's mission to contribute to society through the pursuit of education, learning and research at the highest international levels of excellence.

www.cambridge.org
Information on this title: www.cambridge.org/9781108485999

DOI: 10.1017/9781108622981

First published 2023

*A catalogue record for this publication is available from the British Library*

*A Cataloging-in-Publication data record for this book is available from the Library of Congress*

ISBN 978-1-108-48599-9 Hardback
ISBN 978-1-108-72542-2 Paperback

Cambridge University Press & Assessment has no responsibility for the persistence or accuracy of URLs for external or third-party internet websites referred to in this publication and does not guarantee that any content on such websites is, or will remain, accurate or appropriate.

*We dedicate this book to undercover investigators around the world who work to expose uncomfortable truths for the public good.*

# Contents

# Tables

# Preface

As this book goes to print, we find ourselves in troubling times with respect to truth, transparency, and democracy. Democracy as a form of government is under attack in other nations, and even in the United States. American culture seems to be transforming before our very eyes, with the country divided not only over ideological beliefs, but also about the very notion of truth. Fundamental changes in the economic structure of the news industry have weakened the press significantly, and have at least in the sphere of television news spawned broadcasting stations that do not even pretend to be objective in their coverage, catering to partisan audiences hungry for validation of their priors rather than information. These problems are exacerbated by entities both domestic and foreign that intentionally circulate fake news stories for the purpose of fomenting distrust and accomplishing political goals. And either as part of or because of some of these changes, Americans' faith in institutions has been on a steady decline.

There are no silver bullets or easy solutions to this web of problems facing modern democracy. But perhaps one key to addressing some of these concerns is to promote the gathering and dissemination of truthful information, of verifiable facts. With strong mistrust of government and increasingly partisan reactions to seemingly every issue, we think that new sources of knowledge and information that can help inform the public about the state of the world are ever more important. We don't think that transparency will magically restore faith in our governing institutions or republic, but we believe that at some level facts still matter. At the very least, facts provide the foundation upon which policy debates can be built. The facts may not always (or even usually) change minds, but they are, as Hannah Arendt has noted, more stubborn than opinions, and thus provide a grounded truth for debate and advocacy. This book is about one tool that can address information deficiencies and produce factual evidence: the use of undercover investigations to uncover and expose facts that can inform public discourse; promote debate about law, ethics, and morality; and perhaps even lead to social and legal reform.

As we explore in great detail in the chapters to come, an undercover investigation is an action by an individual or group of individuals to secure information, through the use of a couple of key tactics, from a business, institution, or individual that would otherwise be hidden from the public eye. First, and perhaps paradoxically, undercover investigations frequently begin with a lie told (or an omission used) to obtain the truth. To gain access to information, an investigator typically will have to either affirmatively misrepresent or mislead by omission the investigator's true identity and motive to the subject of the investigation. The investigator may use deception, for example, by applying for and obtaining a job with the investigation's target, to gain access to private property and be in a place to gather information about activities that take place behind closed doors. Second, these investigations often involve the documenting of information through various electronic media, from photography to audio recording to video recording, all of which take place without the consent of the persons being recorded.

At the outset of this project, we want to candidly admit that many readers will recoil at the idea of instrumentally using lies or nonconsensual recording as tools of investigation. Often these undercover investigations are characterized as dangerous threats to personal privacy and property rights. But as we conceive of undercover investigations, they should be limited to efforts to gain access to information that is in the public's interest to know (in contrast with, say, a private vendetta or prurient interest in spying on another's most intimate private moments). An investigation exposing physical abuse by staff at an elementary school, for example, is materially different from efforts to, say, spy on children in the school restrooms. Furthermore, we think that, following the best practices, investigations should be used only when they are necessary to obtain information sought that would otherwise be difficult, if not impossible, to discover.

Readers might immediately think that our description of undercover investigations is familiar in the context of "sting" operations by government law enforcement agents or undercover work carried out by investigative journalists. And those are, in fact, two important contexts in which such investigations take place. But investigations also serve important social and political functions in other contexts, including civil rights enforcement, union organizing, and political activism, as we explain in Chapter 1.

Perhaps undercover investigations have spread to these less familiar contexts precisely because they are so effective. In fact, it is safe to assume that without the key features of deception and nonconsensual recording, undercover investigations could not take place, or at least would be much less successful. Video evidence of corruption by a politician or abuse of power by a public figure is markedly different from hearsay evidence, or even firsthand, written accounts. In this era of media skepticism, without tangible evidence the subjects of an investigation will often argue that the claims are lies and fake news. But the efficacy of undercover investigations also makes them controversial. As a result, in the current climate, there have been efforts to shut down undercover investigations by threatening investigators with criminal punishment or with expensive civil lawsuits that subject them to potentially huge jury awards.

This book presents a comprehensive treatment of undercover investigations from a number of different perspectives. Chapter 1[1] sets out an overview of the topic, describing the many contexts in which undercover investigations have been conducted and produced benefits, as well as the important types of information they have revealed to the public. It also lays out what we believe to be the social and political conditions and institutional failures that have led us to the point when undercover investigations play a particularly important contemporary role in the ecosphere of information gathering. It concludes with a discussion of some of the legal and social impediments to carrying out undercover investigations – something of a backlash that is currently taking place.

Chapter 2 explores the history of undercover investigations in professional journalism and the factors that have influenced when such investigations have been more accepted and when the mainstream press has spurned them. This discussion necessarily draws us into a debate over the professional ethics of journalism and how they might apply to address concerns about undercover investigations. From this debate, we argue for a normative position grounded in utilitarianism, but there are other ethical perspectives worth considering.

In Chapter 3, we turn to the beginning of our legal and constitutional discussion, examining in greater detail the use of investigative deceptions, lies and omissions used to gain access to property, people, and information that are the focus of an investigation. Here, we contend that Free Speech Clause of the First Amendment should apply to government attempts to shut down undercover investigations.

---

[1] The material in this book builds on, expands, and updates material from several of our previously published law review articles: Alan K. Chen & Justin Marceau, *High Value Lies, Ugly Truths, and the First Amendment*, 69 VAND. L. REV. 1435 (2015); Justin Marceau & Alan K. Chen, *Free Speech and Democracy in the Video Age*, 116 COLUM. L. REV. 991 (2016); Alan K. Chen & Justin Marceau, *Developing a Taxonomy of Lies under the First Amendment*, 89 U. COLO. L. REV. 655 (2018); Alan K. Chen, *Cheap Speech Creation*, 54 U.C. DAVIS L. REV. 2405 (2021). Some portions of those articles are excerpted throughout the book with the generous permission of the *Vanderbilt Law Review*, the *Columbia Law Review*, the *University of Colorado Law Review*, and the *U.C. Davis Law Review*. Also, to be fully transparent, we disclose that we served as plaintiffs' counsel in several cases that we discuss throughout this book. Those case are Animal Legal Def. Fund v. Reynolds, 591 F.Supp.3d 397 (S.D. Iowa 2022), *appeal docketed*, No. 22-1830 (8th Cir. 2022); Animal Legal Def. Fund v. Kelly, 9 F.4th 1219 (10th Cir. 2021), *cert. denied*, 142 S. Ct. 2647 (2022); Animal Legal Def. Fund v. Reynolds, 8 F.4th 781 (8th Cir. 2021); Animal Legal Def. Fund v. Vaught, 8 F.4th 714 (8th Cir. 2021) (recently dismissed on remand to the district court); People for the Ethical Treatment of Animals, Inc. v. Stein, 60 F.4th 815, (4th Cir. 2023); Animal Legal Def. Fund v. Wasden, 878 F.3d 1184 (9th Cir. 2018) (including the district court cases, which are under the name of Animal Legal Def. Fund v. Otter); Animal Legal Def. Fund v. Herbert, 263 F. Supp. 3d 1193 (D. Utah 2017); and Ketcham v. U.S. Nat'l Park Serv., No. 16-CV-00017-SWS, 2016 WL 4269037 (D. Wyo. Feb. 5, 2016).

Exploring the doctrinal foundations of this claim, we suggest that to the extent investigative deceptions cause any harms to the targets of undercover investigations, they do not constitute the type of tangible harm that justifies the removal of the First Amendment's protection from these lies. Put simply, a lie should not be deemed unprotected speech simply because it exposes the entity investigated to ridicule, political scrutiny, or public condemnation. Indeed, lies used to gain access should be protected precisely because they expose matters of public concern.

Next, in Chapter 4, we discuss the legal and constitutional implications of government efforts to prohibit nonconsensual video recordings as part of undercover investigations. Here, we argue that under First Amendment theory and doctrine, the act of video recording is an act of expression or, at the very least, conduct that constitutes an essential precursor to speech. Accordingly, we assert that nonconsensual video recording, even on private property, should be protected by the First Amendment. We would limit the right to record, however, in a few important ways. First, it should apply only to those who are lawfully present in the place where they engage in the recording (even if that lawful presence is the result of investigative deceptions). Second, if the recording is done on private property without the consent of the investigation's subjects, the conduct recorded must be of public concern. With these important limitations in place, we suggest that any concerns about interference with property or privacy rights are substantially diminished. Chapter 4, as well as Chapter 3, contains a detailed analysis of the existing legal landscape as well as a careful look at the potential future developments in these areas of law.

Chapter 5 addresses the implications of emerging new technologies for the right to record. Here, we assert that the technological advances that have made it even more possible to conduct an undercover investigation enhance the free speech arguments for protecting such expressive activity, which involves a key component of expression: the creation of speech. Advances in technology have brought us ever shrinking video recording equipment, drones, and computer data scraping programs, tools that undoubtedly enhance undercover investigations. But new technologies can also generate new social problems, so we address the implications for the potential dangers of such technologies and how such concerns may be minimized without undercutting the effective use of undercover investigations.

Much of the material we cover in this book starts with an important assumption: undercover investigations *matter*. That is, they produce information that is valuable to public discourse, democratic debate, and promotes legal and social reforms. In Chapter 6, we take on that assumption through some important, original empirical research. Though earlier studies have examined whether whistleblowers and investigative journalism in general (not just undercover investigations) influence public opinion in a meaningful way, no one has ever published any studies asking what our study examines: whether public perception of the value of undercover investigations varies by the political ideology of the audience, the investigator, or the target of the investigation, or by the type of wrongdoing exposed by the investigation. The reason this is important is that we view undercover investigations as a public good from a macro perspective – the revelation of hidden facts feeds the information ecosphere in a positive way because more information is generally better than less. However, if investigations preach only to the converted, if they persuade only people who are predisposed to agree with the perspective of the investigator, then they are much less consequential. Our study shows, however, that there appears to be widespread acceptance of the value of undercover investigations even where they reveal things that contradict the audience's ideological perspective. In an era of hyper-politicization, a good faith belief in the value of undercover investigations appears to be a bipartisan value. These findings should give pause to legislators considering laws that would criminalize or otherwise prohibit undercover investigations, and they provide a glimmer of hope about the role that transparency plays in preserving our democracy.

Finally, we finish with a brief Conclusion, in which we summarize our conclusions and findings and suggest how they might shape future public debate, legislative policy, and judicial decisions about undercover investigations in the United States. Despite what we began with, which is a world in something of a disarray when it comes to truth, transparency, and democracy, we believe that there is promise emerging from this discord. Undercover investigations have been a critical form of information gathering for well over a hundred years. Whether conducted by government officials, civil rights advocates, union organizers, journalists (both professional and "citizen"), or political activists, these investigations provide a window into truth by revealing information that would otherwise not come to the public's attention. This information can lead to the enforcement of civil and criminal laws; promote political activism; inform public discourse over political, social, and moral issues; and may even promote reform.

# Acknowledgments

We are immensely grateful to Rebecca Aviel, RonNell Andersen Jones, Ashutosh Bhagwat, Joseph Blocher, David Dana, Michael Dorf, Angela Fernandez, Chris Green, Sam Kamin, Margot Kaminski, Jane Kirtley, Christina Koningisor, Tamara Kuennen, Doug Kysar, Camille Labchuk, Nancy Leong, Spencer Livingstone, Jonathan Lovvorn, Toni Massaro, Scott Memmel, Janice Nadler, Helen Norton, Scott Phillips, Blake Reid, Derigan Silver, Kristin Stilt, Leana Stormont, Matthew Strugar, Sonja West, and Steven Zansberg for their thoughtful comments and suggestions throughout the life of this project. We thank Matt Gallaway and his team for another smooth book production cycle with the Cambridge University Press. The empirical research for this book was made possible by grants provided by the Brooks Institute for Animal Rights Law and Policy.

Several of our excellent students at the University of Denver Sturm College of Law provided superb research assistance in support of this book: Richard Barahona, Caroline Brown, Chase Helseth, Molly Kokesh, Laura Martinez, and Jennifer Regier. We also received extraordinarily helpful institutional support from our Dean, Bruce Smith; Animal Law Program Manager Jessica Beaulieu; and Madeline Cohen, Catherine Dunn, and Michelle Penn, professional librarians at the Sturm College of Law.

1

# An Overview of Undercover Investigations in Journalism and Political Activism

In the late 1880s, abortion was illegal in Illinois and persons could face several years in prison for performing an abortion. During this time, a new class of women was trying to break into journalism. Known as "girl stunt reporters," these daring writers took dangerous undercover assignments and told stories in the first person as a means of exposing corruption and illegality. They frequently also published under pseudonyms. One such reporter, whose byline was "Girl Reporter," wrote a series of articles detailing the availability, cost, and process for arranging an abortion in Chicago in a series of front-page stories for the conservative publication the *Chicago Times*. The initial installments on the topic seem to have been driven by the anonymous author's interest in exposing what she perceived as the sort of scoundrel who would perform an abortion in contravention of the law.

The project spurred a long-raging debate among the public about the legality and morality of abortion, and the author herself conveyed to her readers a confusing disorientation about the practices she used for her undercover investigations: "I found that I was beginning to be somewhat of an adept at deceit and this rather startled me.... I began to be suspicious of myself. I have talked so much of my pretended [pregnancy] to the doctors that I now and then permitted my thoughts to wander and drift into the channels where it had been wading through the day."[1] And just as with muckrakers like Upton Sinclair who are much more well known, due no doubt in part to the fact that they were not writing under pseudonyms, the motives of this undercover investigator shifted somewhat over time. Late in her deception when a doctor would sternly refuse her request, she wrote of her feelings, "Don't prate of virtue to me. I am as good as the rest of the world only less lucky."

---

[1] Kim Todd, *These Women Reporters Went Undercover to Get the Most Important Scoops of Their Day*, SMITHSONIAN (Nov. 2016), www.smithsonianmag.com/history/women-reporters-undercover-most-important-scoops-day-180960775/.

Undercover investigations have always raised morally complicated questions about the propriety of deception, the relevance of one's prying motives, and the use of invasive investigative techniques and technology to document their findings. More recently, these investigations have also faced legal impediments, including statutes prohibiting certain types of undercover investigations or investigations in certain industries. This book comprehensively examines the history, social practices, institutions, and law relating to undercover investigations that obtain and document information that furthers the public interest. The investigators can be government agents, professional journalists, citizen journalists, political activists, or even individual citizens acting on their own. The targets of such investigations are typically powerful institutions, such as government entities and large corporations.

Such investigations have a long and storied history in the United States, stretching back to at least the late nineteenth century, and have often informed the public about critical facts that previously had been obscured from scrutiny. The facts they have uncovered are believed by some to have made a dramatic impact on law and policy, spurred the contemplation of and discussion about important social and moral questions, and generally led to a more transparent society. But they have also been sometimes fraught with controversy because of questions about whether they exceed legal or ethical boundaries or infringe on the valued property and privacy rights of their targets.

This duality – the investigator as simultaneously a hero and a villain – colors the history of undercover investigations. At times or among some groups, undercover investigators are celebrated as positive catalysts for law reform. By others and at other points in history, investigators are viewed as scofflaws, privacy-invaders, and agenda-driven miscreants. The very same tactics might be celebrated in one context, and derided in others. For politicians and ideologically driven groups, the varying reactions to investigations often appear to be motivated by a desire to insulate from scrutiny the causes they support. An investigation of corruption among police officers or abuse within jails might be celebrated by progressives, while the same people might object strenuously to an undercover investigation of Planned Parenthood or of persons involved with the Black Lives Matter movement.

Our original empirical research detailed in Chapter 6 tends to show that the public at large, unlike political entities or those directly impacted by an investigation, tend to support undercover investigations across all party lines and contexts. Still, creating a set of neutral legal principles governing the right to limit and carry out investigations is of critical importance if one hopes to avoid whipsaw-like treatment of investigators that varies depending on partisan political interests and other historical contingencies. Yet, notwithstanding the critical role of such investigations in our democracy and the risk of ideological drift in this field, undercover investigations have not previously received nearly the same level of scholarly examination as other mechanisms of transparency and speech.

This book is about law, but it is also about much more than that. It also examines the social conditions, institutions, and other actors that make up what might be called the "information-gathering ecosystem" or "newsgathering ecosystem." It is about professional journalists and citizen journalists. Examples are drawn from the work of political activists on both the left and the right. It is about the capacity of the individual and the internet to take on powerful institutions of government and the private sector and inform public discourse.

In this chapter, we provide an overview of the topic, which is developed in more detail in the subsequent chapters. We begin with a description of what we mean by "undercover investigations," followed by some historical context to trace the origins of this type of investigative work in the United States over time. Second, we situate the topic of undercover investigations within the set of broader social practices and institutions (government, the news media, political and law reform organizations, and the corporate private sector) that comprise the information-gathering ecosystem and the social conditions under which the need for such investigations is most likely to be important. Third, we examine emerging legal, structural, and political impediments to undercover investigations that have arisen in contemporary times. Finally, we provide an overview of the existing background of American law that governs the practices of undercover investigations.

## 1.1 HISTORY AND DEFINITION

This is a book examining the sociolegal history of undercover investigations. Yet, defining the scope of this field can be challenging, so we begin with some examples of different types of undercover investigations as background for our discussion.

### 1.1.1 *Investigative Journalists*

Perhaps the context in which most people would be familiar with undercover investigations is journalism. Though as we shall see later, the relationship between the journalism profession and *deception*-based investigations has been uneasy and inconsistent, there are numerous historical and contemporary examples of such investigations that have revealed to the public important information that has sparked public debate and perhaps led to legislative or other types of reforms. We begin with several early examples.[2]

---

[2]  Professor Brooke Kroeger has provided two valuable, comprehensive sources for researching undercover reporting – first, in her book, UNDERCOVER REPORTING: THE TRUTH ABOUT DECEPTION (2012) (KROEGER, UNDERCOVER REPORTING); and second, in an online repository collecting and publishing examples of this type of journalism. *Deception for Journalism's Sake: A Database*, NYU, https://undercover.hosting.nyu.edu/s/undercover-reporting/page/about (last visited Nov. 2, 2022).

Actively obscuring one's identity was a necessity for not only journalists but also political activists, who undertook to investigate and expose the grim realities of slavery prior to the Civil War.[3] Several reporters for the *New York Tribune* pursued this project in the years leading up to the war. In 1852, James Redpath, a journalist and abolitionist, was able to get hired by Southern newspapers so that he could spend time in the South to build trust with local communities and have a pretense for gathering information about the conditions of enslaved persons, which he would then write about in the form of letters to the *Tribune* under a pseudonym. These firsthand accounts were published under a feature called "The Facts of Slavery," to inform Northern readers about the abhorrent conditions of slavery. Similar methods were used by Albert Deane Richardson for the same newspaper in 1858. In another example, from 1859, *New York Tribune* reporter Mortimer Thompson, writing under a pen name, attended what was then one of the largest auctions of enslaved persons in the United States in Savannah, Georgia, so he could report about it to members of the general public.[4] A flavor of his reporting can be gleaned from the sub-headline "HUMAN FEELINGS OF NO ACCOUNT."

Thompson's story explicitly states that had he identified himself as a reporter, he would not have been welcome. Instead, he walked around with a pencil and auction catalogue, so that people would believe him to be one of the buyers of enslaved persons. Another *Tribune* reporter, Henry S. Olcott, went undercover to provide news coverage of the execution of abolitionist John Brown on December 2, 1859. The *Tribune* correspondent initially assigned to that area had fled town out of fear of being discovered by Southerners hostile to his stories, which were being published under a pseudonym. To gain access, Olcott joined a regiment assigned to guard Brown's body, but had to hide from people in the area who might be able to identify him as a New York journalist.

One of the most famous undercover investigations in US history was undertaken by the intrepid journalist Nellie Bly, who is often classified as one of the aforementioned "girl stunt reporters."[5] Born Elizabeth Jane "Pink" Cochran in 1864, Bly's career began when, as an emerging young journalist trying to break into a heavily male-dominated field, she found her first writing job with the *Pittsburgh Dispatch*, where she first acquired her pen name. There, she wrote columns mostly focused on women's issues, but eventually became dissatisfied with the limitations of that assignment. She left the *Dispatch* in 1887, and met with several newspaper editors in New York City to find employment, with her primary hope being to secure a position with the *New York World*, which had been recently bought by Joseph

---

[3]   These accounts are described in KROEGER, UNDERCOVER REPORTING, *supra* note 2, at 16–28.
[4]   Q. K. Philander Doesticks, *American Civilization Illustrated: A Great Slave Auction*, N.Y. TRIBUNE (Mar. 5, 1859), https://undercover.hosting.nyu.edu/files/original/7d937ea8eab0c4cbf372e60ca 9abb029274d7b3a.pdf.
[5]   The Bly narrative is drawn from NELLIE BLY, TEN DAYS IN A MAD-HOUSE (1887); BROOKE KROEGER, NELLIE BLY: DAREDEVIL, REPORTER, FEMINIST (1994); and Todd, *supra* note 1.

Pulitzer. She is believed to have snuck her way into the newspaper's offices, and promptly proposed a number of story ideas to Colonel John Cockerill, chief editor at the *World*. Instead, Cockerill commissioned her to undertake an investigative assignment. At the time, there had been reports about questionable treatment of residents at Blackwell's Island Insane Asylum for Women. Either Cockerill or Pulitzer (it is unclear which) suggested that Bly pretend that she was "insane" and get herself committed to the asylum to observe the conditions firsthand.

Bly gladly took on the challenge. Interestingly, she met with a local prosecutor before going undercover to ensure that she had immunity from any prosecution for her conduct during the investigation. She changed her clothing, appearance, and behavior to pose as a person subject to commitment and checked into a boarding house under the name Nellie Brown. While there, she proceeded to act erratically. That act was apparently convincing, for after only one night in the house, the police were called and Bly was brought before a judge, who sent her to Bellevue Hospital for an evaluation. Thereafter, she was quickly transferred to the Blackwell women's asylum, where she spent about ten days, before the newspaper sent in its lawyer to secure Bly's discharge. What followed was Bly's lengthy exposé about her experiences, first published in the pages of the *World* in October 1887, and later in her book, *Ten Days in a Madhouse*. Bly's story reported the deplorable conditions she discovered. Among the things she described were abusive and violent staff, fire hazards, severely cold temperatures, unsanitary practices, terrible food, and the treatment of foreign-born women who were not mentally ill but had been committed because others, including the asylum's staff, could not understand them and assumed them to require treatment. The results of her stories, besides promoting sales of the *World*, are somewhat unclear. A grand jury was convened to investigate the asylum, but there is no evidence that it led to any concrete actions. The government increased the asylum's budget, but that may have been in the works even prior to her reporting.

Perhaps the largest impact of Bly's investigation was on journalism itself. Though the techniques of undercover reporting were well established by this time, Bly is sometimes credited with the invention of what was at first labeled "stunt" or "immersion" journalism. Today, those terms appear to have a more negative connotation and are frequently used to describe a journalist who is not engaged in undercover reporting, but instead "becomes a guinea pig, attempting some masochistic or outrageous challenge in an attempt to prove a point or provide a first-hand experiential account."[6] But the impact of Bly's undercover investigation seems to be pretty clear. Following the success of the asylum investigation, Bly doggedly pursued numerous undercover investigations that she would write about for the *World*,

---

[6]  Zach Schonfeld, *Are We Living in a Golden Age of Stunt Journalism?*, Newsweek (July 25, 2016), www.newsweek.com/2016/09/02/are-we-living-golden-age-stunt-journalism-or-just-embar rassment-480508.html.

including posing as a maid to expose questionable practices by local employment agencies, pretending to be an unwed mother to identify a baby trafficking network, and getting hired at a paper box factory to report on the horrible working conditions, to name just a few. Moreover, she inspired other journalists, especially female reporters such as Nell Nelson, Annie Laurie, Eva Gay, and Nora Marks, to use similar deception-based techniques to gather and report important news.

Nearly twenty years after Bly's blockbuster journalism debut, Upton Sinclair also used deception to investigate wrongdoing in the Chicago meatpacking industry as he gathered material for his novel, *The Jungle*.[7] Sinclair's project initially began as an effort to reveal poor treatment of employees in this industry. According to some accounts, Sinclair did not have to affirmatively misrepresent himself, but instead was able to move around at the meatpacking facilities by disguising himself as a worker. As he described it in his autobiography, "I would wander about the yards, and my friends would risk their jobs to show me what I wanted to see. I was not much better dressed than the workers, and found that by the simple device of carrying a dinner pail I could go anywhere." However, one of his biographers reports that the clothes and dinner pail were not quite enough and that Sinclair gained access "armed with a few simple lies appropriate to the area in which he was investigating."[8] To prevent himself from being detected, he also had to be careful about his method of documentation. He had to remember the details of what he learned during working hours and then write his notes down once he returned to his living quarters. He had no other tool to document his findings.

Though published in novel form rather than as journalism, Sinclair's undercover investigation exposed the powerful meatpacking industry to close public scrutiny. At the time, livestock production was the country's largest industry and was becoming important to an increasingly globalized international market. The industry's reputation was important to preserving public and consumer trust, and meatpacking companies tried to do so through public relations efforts. As one Sinclair biographer observed, "The packers were wiser about public relations than most businessmen of that era, arranging Potemkin village tours to carefully manicured parts of their plants and advertising their own virtues lavishly."[9] It was a quintessential example of a

---

7   UPTON SINCLAIR, THE JUNGLE (1906). The Sinclair narrative is drawn from UPTON SINCLAIR, THE AUTOBIOGRAPHY OF UPTON SINCLAIR (1962); LEON HARRIS, UPTON SINCLAIR: AMERICAN REBEL (1975); THE MUCKRAKERS (Arthur Weinberg & Lila Weinberg eds., 2001); ANTHONY ARTHUR, RADICAL INNOCENT: UPTON SINCLAIR (2006). Although this book focuses on undercover investigations in the United States, it should be noted that the American author Jack London engaged in an investigation of living conditions in London's East End using an approach similar to Sinclair's. That investigation resulted in the publication of London's book, THE PEOPLE OF THE ABYSS in 1903, just a few years before publication of THE JUNGLE. KROEGER, UNDERCOVER REPORTING, *supra* note 2, at 77–83.
8   HARRIS, *supra* note 7, at 70 (emphasis added). In her work, Kroeger raises some doubts about exactly how secret Sinclair kept his activities. KROEGER, UNDERCOVER REPORTING, *supra* note 2, at 87–89.
9   HARRIS, *supra* note 7, at 69.

public deception through faux transparency; everything was readied for the tour so as to obscure the reality and ensure public trust. Notably, over 100 years later, the agricultural industry continues to offer these Potemkin village tours.[10] The lack of transparency combined with affirmative efforts to falsely construct a reassuring public narrative are precisely the type of practices by powerful institutions that underscore the need for undercover investigations.

The public reaction to Sinclair's work was profound and concrete. *The Jungle* became a best seller. It inspired President Theodore Roosevelt to send investigators to confirm Sinclair's reports. And Sinclair's work is frequently credited with prompting Congress to enact two major pieces of reform legislation, the Federal Meat Inspection Act and the Pure Food and Drug Act,[11] which remain in effect today.

The type of undercover investigation pioneered and made famous by Bly and Sinclair became a popular and widespread practice in journalism throughout the Progressive Era, and more of these accounts are reported in Chapter 2. But the state of journalism began to shift in the first half of the twentieth century. As one commentator noted, "Investigative work between 1917 and 1950 split into two camps: one continuing the muckraking zeal for reform, pushed by an ideological bent that bordered on socialism; the other evolving into an objective, mainstream version recognizable by today's standards."[12]

By most historical accounts, there seems to be a lull in undercover investigations, or at least in high-profile ones that received national attention, from the mid-twentieth century until the 1970s. During the 1970s, numerous examples of the type of deception-based investigations pioneered by Bly, Sinclair, and others can be identified. Among these are the work covering the Watergate scandal by *Washington Post* reporters Bob Woodward and Carl Bernstein, who may have used deception in communicating with sources to enhance the possibility that those sources would be forthcoming with information, though their deception may have been more through omissions than by affirmative lies.[13]

Later that same decade, *Chicago Sun-Times* reporters Zay Smith and Pam Zekman, working alongside a representative from a local nonprofit government reform group, teamed up to build one of the most elaborate undercover reporting facades ever, when they and their team opened and operated the Mirage Tavern on

---

[10] Mark Bittman, *Banned from the Barn*, N.Y. TIMES (July 5, 2011), https://opinionator.blogs.nytimes.com/2011/07/05/banned-from-the-barn/.

[11] Pub. L. No. 59-242, 34 Stat. 1260 (1906) (codified as amended at 21 U.S.C. §§ 601–695); Pub. L. No. 59-384, 34 Stat. 768 (1906) (codified as amended at 21 U.S.C. §§ 301–399f).

[12] JAMES L. AUCOIN, THE EVOLUTION OF AMERICAN INVESTIGATIVE JOURNALISM 33 (2005).

[13] CARL BERNSTEIN & BOB WOODWARD, ALL THE PRESIDENT'S MEN 250 (1974) ("They had dodged, evaded, misrepresented, suggested and intimidated, but they had not lied outright"). It is difficult to find a definitive account or discussion of whether Woodward and Bernstein ever engaged in affirmative deception to investigate the Watergate scandal. This question is discussed a little further in Chapter 2.

the South Side of Chicago.[14] Through this deception, they obtained and reported on corruption among the ranks of the city's health and safety inspectors, who took bribes for not reporting code violations. Their twenty-five-part series in the *Sun-Times* informed the public in detail about this misconduct, and also led to multiple criminal indictments and key statutory reforms.

Another illustration of deception-based undercover journalism, one that we will return to throughout this book, is the 1992 investigation of the Food Lion grocery store chain conducted by two reporters from the ABC News program Primetime Live. The reporters used résumés with false identities, addresses, and references to gain employment with two different Food Lion stores. After they were hired, they used hidden video cameras to document and confirm what their sources had initially reported to ABC News, which was that Food Lion's food handling practices were highly unsanitary and probably violated several laws. The broadcast included, for example, videotape that appeared to show Food Lion employees repackaging and redating fish that had passed the expiration date, grinding expired beef with fresh beef, and applying barbeque sauce to chicken past its expiration date in order to mask the smell and sell it as if it were fresh in the gourmet food section. The program included statements by former Food Lion employees alleging even more serious mishandling of meat at Food Lion stores across several states.

In the late 1990s, writer and researcher Barbara Ehrenreich set out to examine the plight of the working poor in the United States by traveling around the country applying for low-wage jobs. This resulted in the publication of her acclaimed book, *Nickel and Dimed: On (Not) Getting By in America*.[15] At the book's outset, she described how she was able to maintain her subterfuge so that she could obtain jobs without raising suspicion that she was not who she said she was. As she described it,

> There was also the problem of how to present myself to potential employers and, in particular, how to explain my dismal lack of relevant job experience. The truth, or at least a drastically stripped-down version thereof, seemed easiest: I described myself to interviewers as a divorced homemaker reentering the workforce after many years, which is true as far as it goes. Sometimes, though not always, I would throw in a few housecleaning jobs, citing as references former housemates and a friend in Key West whom I have at least helped with after-dinner cleanups now and then. Job application forms also want to know about education, and here I figured the Ph.D. would be no help at all, might even lead employers to suspect that I was an alcoholic washout or worse. So I confined myself to three years of college, listing my real-life alma mater. No one ever questioned my background, as it turned out, and only one employer out of several dozen bothered to check my references. When, on one occasion, an exceptionally chatty interviewer asked about

[14] Pamela Zekman & Zay N. Smith, *Our Bar Uncovers Payoffs, Tax Gyps*, CHI. SUN-TIMES (Jan. 8, 1978), https://undercover.hosting.nyu.edu/files/original/efb2fe975245467d38b9bc5360526e ceco6co7o2.pdf.

[15] BARBARA EHRENREICH, NICKEL AND DIMED: ON (NOT) GETTING BY IN AMERICA (2001).

hobbies, I said "writing" and she seemed to find nothing strange about this, although the job she was offering could have been performed perfectly well by an illiterate. There was always, of course, the difference that only I knew – that I wasn't working for the money, I was doing research for an article and later a book.[16]

More recently, in 2007, Ken Silverstein, a *Harper's Magazine* editor, set out to do a story on how much Washington lobbyists promise to their foreign government clients. Silverstein represented himself as the head of the Maldon Group, supposedly a collection of private investors who were exporters of natural gas from Turkmenistan, which had a government regime that he described as "Stalinist."[17] The purported goal of hiring a lobbying firm was to show American policymakers that the reforms being undertaken by the Turkmeni government were real, which would help increase the chance of the Maldon Group's business success. To support his scheme, Silverstein took what he called "minimal preparations."

> I printed up some Maldon Group business cards, giving myself the name "Kenneth Case" and giving the firm an address at a large office building in London, on Cavendish Square. I purchased a cell phone with a London number. I had a website created for The Maldon Group [–] just a home page with contact information [–] and an email account for myself. Then, in mid-February, soon after Berdymukhamedov's ascent, I began contacting various lobbying firms by email, introducing my firm and explaining that we were eager to improve relations between the "newly-elected government of Turkmenistan" and the United States. We required the services of a firm, I said, that could quickly enact a "strategic communications" plan to help us. I hoped that the firms might be willing to meet with me at the end of the month, during a trip I had planned to Washington.[18]

The fiction worked like a charm, and Silverstein set meetings with two powerful DC lobbying firms. As he described it in a later opinion essay, what he found and reported was that

> In exchange for fees of up to $1.5 million a year, they offered to send congressional delegations to Turkmenistan and write and plant opinion pieces in newspapers under the names of academics and think-tank experts they would recruit. They even offered to set up supposedly "independent" media events in Washington that would promote Turkmenistan (the agenda and speakers would actually be determined by the lobbyists). All this, [they] promised, could be done quietly and unobtrusively, because the law that regulates foreign lobbyists is so flimsy that the firms would be required to reveal little information in their public disclosure forms.[19]

---

[16] *Id.* at 5.
[17] Ken Silverstein, *Their Men in Washington: Undercover with D.C.'s Lobbyists for Hire*, HARPER'S BAZAAR, July 1, 2007, at 53.
[18] *Id.*
[19] Ken Silverstein, *Undercover, under Fire*, L.A. TIMES (June 30, 2007), https://www.latimes.com/la-oe-silverstein30jun30-story.html.

Rather than being praised for exposing the unsavory underbelly of foreign nationals' lobbying of the United States government, Silverstein was taken to task by, of course, the targets of his investigation, but also by other journalists, for engaging in what they called unethical behavior. As one of his most vocal critics, *Washington Post* reporter Howard Kurtz wrote: "no matter how good the story, lying to get it raises as many questions about journalists as their subjects."[20]

In just the past decade, Shane Bauer, a journalist for *Mother Jones* magazine, has published two exposés based on his experiences working undercover with a para-military militia group at the nation's southern border and as a private prison guard.[21] Chris Ketcham posed as a hunter and went undercover to report on a wolf and coyote killing contest in Idaho, where he quickly learned that armor-piercing ammunition is preferred because "[u]nlike soft lead-tipped bullets, which mush-room inside the body cavity and kill quickly," an armor-piercing bullet quickly exits the body and forces the animal to suffer: "It will bleed out slowly, run a mile or so in terrified panic, and collapse," a seasoned hunter explained to him.[22]

This list of successful undercover journalistic investigations goes on and on. As we discuss in Chapter 2, journalism using investigative deceptions has gone in and out of favor both within the journalism community and among the general public, and remains controversial. Yet its real-world impact is generally assumed.[23]

### 1.1.2 *Civil Rights Testers*

In March 1978, Sylvia Coleman and R. Kent Willis asked representatives of Havens Realty Corporation whether they had any available rental properties in suburban Richmond, Virginia.[24] On three different occasions within a ten-day period, Coleman was told that no apartments were available, while Willis was informed

---

[20] Howard Kurtz, *Undercover Journalism*, WASH. POST (June 25, 2007), www.washingtonpost .com/wp-dyn/content/blog/2007/06/25/BL2007062500353.html.

[21] Shane Bauer, *My Four Months as a Private Prison Guard*, MOTHER JONES (July/Aug. 2016), www.motherjones.com/politics/2016/06/cca-private-prisons-corrections-corporation-inmates-investigation-bauer/; Shane Bauer, *I Went Undercover with a Border Militia. Here's What I Saw*, MOTHER JONES (Nov./Dec. 2016), www.motherjones.com/politics/2016/10/undercover-border-militia-immigration-bauer/.

[22] Christopher Ketcham, *How to Kill a Wolf : An Undercover Report from the Idaho Coyote and Wolf Derby*, VICE (Mar. 13, 2014), www.vice.com/en_us/article/qbee5d/how-to-kill-a-wolf-0000259-v21n3.

[23] For some international examples of deception-based investigations, see SHA, *10 Most Courageous Undercover Journalists*, CAREER NEWS INSIDER (Nov. 9, 2012), www .careernewsinsider.com/10-most-courageous-undercover-journalists/.

[24] Facts from this investigation are drawn from Havens Realty Corp. v. Coleman, 455 U.S. 363 (1982), in which the Supreme Court held that testers have legal standing to sue discriminatory property managers under the federal Fair Housing Act even if they did not intend to rent the properties in question.

the opposite. Coleman is Black; Willis is white. Neither Coleman nor Willis had any intention of renting an apartment. Rather, they were acting as testers, posing as real renters to investigate racial steering, a form of housing discrimination in which persons discourage potential buyers or renters from pursuing housing opportunities because of the latter's race. Along with a fair housing organization, Coleman and Willis sued Havens for violating the Fair Housing Act of 1968 (FHA), which prohibits various forms of race, sex, religion, and national origin discrimination in the sale or rental of housing.

As with other violations of law, housing discrimination can be difficult to detect. This is particularly true of racial steering, which is conduct through which persons discourage potential buyers or renters from pursuing housing opportunities on a discriminatory basis. A person who represents to another person "because of race" or other protected category that "any dwelling is not available for inspection, sale, or rental when such dwelling is in fact so available" violates the FHA.[25]

To detect these violations, civil rights testers, like undercover journalists, must hide their true identities and motives by pretending to be actual consumers seeking services. In the case of fair housing testers, a false identity is even prepared, so that testers of different races have similar fabricated incomes, credit histories, and other backgrounds. If the testers are otherwise identical, their differential treatment is highly likely to be based on race alone. This is a technique called "paired testing," which uses regression analysis to rule out other variables as having influenced the targets' discriminatory acts. As one organization describes it, "testers simulate ordinary housing transactions for the purpose of obtaining credible and objective information about housing practices."[26] This same organization also authorizes testers, where lawful, to use hidden audio and video recorders to document their conversations with the investigation targets, but they also are encouraged to take careful notes.[27]

It is not just civil rights organizations that engage in testing. The Department of Justice runs its own fair housing testing program,[28] while the Department of Housing and Urban Development, authorized by Congress, created a Fair Housing Initiatives Program that allocates funds to nonprofit organizations for testing.[29] While federal regulations define who can become a tester, they do not (and realistically could not) prohibit testers from engaging in deception about their identities, which is central to the testing protocol.

---

[25]  42 U.S.C. § 3604(d).
[26]  Fair Housing Justice Center, Guide for Fair Housing Testers 6 (2012).
[27]  *Id.* at 19, 31–34.
[28]  *Fair Housing Testing Program*, U.S. Dep't of Just., www.justice.gov/crt/fair-housing-testing-program-1 (last visited Oct. 31, 2022).
[29]  42 U.S.C. § 3616a.

Moreover, civil rights testing is not limited to housing discrimination. Over the past half century, civil rights testing has been used extensively to identify race discrimination across a wide range of contexts, including hotels and restaurants, taxis and ride-sharing services, employment, retail stores, and government services, to name a few.[30] Nonprofits support litigation and activism by actively recruiting testers.[31] Testing has moved beyond race and is used to smoke out discrimination based on national origin, familial status, disability, gender, sexual orientation, and transgender or gender-nonconforming status.[32] Indeed, civil rights testing has become a central part of advocacy aimed at detecting and remedying discriminatory practices.

Long before anyone dreamed up civil rights testing, others also used deception to investigate racial injustices. As we have already described, journalists around the time of the Civil War assumed false identities to report about the conditions of slavery and the events of the war. Another fascinating example arose during the early twentieth century, when Walter F. White, a representative of the National Association for the Advancement of Colored People (NAACP) posed as a white man to investigate lynchings and other incidents of racial violence against Black people in the southern United States.[33] White, who was Black[34] but had blonde hair, blue eyes, and white skin, was easily able to "pass" as a white person during these investigations, which uncovered and documented these acts of violence in reports for the NAACP. His investigations led to national exposure of incidents of racial violence, including the Tulsa Race massacre.[35] In the early 1920s, White even made inroads into infiltrating the Ku Klux Klan, efforts that eventually led to press accounts on White's investigation indicating that the Klan was still active long after the Civil War, which many public officials had denied.[36] White eventually went on to become the chief executive of the NAACP.

---

[30] Robert B. Duncan & Karl M. F. Lockhart, *The Washington Lawyers' Committee's Fifty-Year Battle for Racial Equality in Places of Public Accommodation*, 62 How. L.J. 73 (2018).

[31] *Become a Tester*, EQUAL RTS. CTR., https://equalrightscenter.org/become-a-tester/ (last visited Oct. 31, 2022).

[32] *Fair Housing Testing Program, supra* note 28 (race, national origin, disability, and familial status); Molovinsky v. Fair Emp. Council of Greater Wash., Inc., 683 A.2d 142 (D.C. 1996) (gender); Jamie Langowski et al., *Transcending Prejudice: Gender Identity and Expression-Based Discrimination in the Metro Boston Rental Housing Market*, 29 YALE J.L. & FEMINISM 321 (2018) (transgender and gender-nonconforming people); EQUAL RIGHTS CENTER, BEHIND CLOSED DOORS: A TESTING INVESTIGATION INTO BIAS AGAINST LGBT JOB APPLICANTS IN VIRGINIA (2019) (sexual orientation).

[33] A. J. BAIME, WHITE LIES: THE DOUBLE LIFE OF WALTER F. WHITE AND AMERICA'S DARKEST SECRET (2022).

[34] Toward the end of his life, some people claimed that White was actually a white man after all, and that his greatest deception had been fooling the NAACP and others to believe he was Black, though there has never been a definitive resolution of this dispute. *Id.* at 303, 320.

[35] *Id.* at 84–89.

[36] *Id.* at 80–83.

### 1.1.3 *Animal Rights Investigators*

It has been said that the best thing animal agriculture has going for it is that most families are two or three generations removed from the mess and gore that is involved when animals are killed and processed for human use. Timothy Pachirat's compelling 2012 book, *Every Twelve Seconds*, documents the human and nonhuman animal suffering that he discovered while working undercover in a Nebraska slaughterhouse. Pachirat explores in detail what he calls the "politics of sight" in a slaughterhouse, noting that the facilities are constructed so that no single worker sees the entire killing and handling process; the facilities are separated with dividers and walls so that the process is divided into discrete, rote acts. Transparency is anathema to the modern factory farm, even from within the farm itself.[37]

For groups interested in promoting better legal protections for animals, the lack of transparency creates a stifling advocacy barrier. How can someone understand what preceded the cellophane-wrapped pork chop for sale at their local market when industrial slaughter is hidden from the public eye? Not surprisingly, then, though certainly not without controversy, groups and individuals have used a variety of tactics to expose the conditions present on factory farms. In 2020 during the COVID-19 pandemic, many farms were engaging in "depopulating" projects, or the mass killing of animals that had become unprofitable to keep due to decreasing consumer demand for meat. Glenn Greenwald, a Pulitzer prize–winning journalist, was provided video footage from cameras that were left at Iowa's largest pig farm, which revealed that the farm was using a "cruel and excruciating method to kill thousands of pigs."[38] Describing the video footage, Greenwald notes that Iowa Select Farm adopted the mass-extermination method known as "ventilation shut-down," which means that the pigs are killed "by sealing off all airways to their barns and inserting steam into them, intensifying the heat and humidity inside and leaving them to die overnight" of hyperthermia. The video reveals that "Most pigs – though not all – die after hours of suffering from a combination of being suffocated and roasted to death."

The work of animal rights investigators has unquestionably had a measurable impact on government policy, criminal prosecutions, and public opinion. One of the most significant animal investigations was done by Humane Society of the United States (HSUS) at the Westland/Hallmark slaughterhouse in Chino,

---

[37] There are exceptions. Pachirat himself is working on research examining a factory farm that doubles as an amusement park where guests pay money and buy souvenirs at a large facility that mass produces animal products for consumption. *See* FAIR OAKS FARMS, https://fofarms.com/ (last visited Nov. 4, 2022). In general, however, industry has been at the forefront of advocating for greater secrecy and less transparency.

[38] Glenn Greenwald, *Hidden Video and Whistleblower Reveal Gruesome Mass-Extermination Method for Iowa Pigs Amid Pandemic*, THE INTERCEPT (May 29, 2020), https://theintercept.com/2020/05/29/pigs-factory-farms-ventilation-shutdown-coronavirus/.

California, in 2008. The video footage from that investigation showed workers "kicking cows, ramming them with the blades of a forklift, jabbing them in the eyes, applying painful electrical shocks, and even torturing them with a hose and water in attempts to force sick or injured animals to walk to slaughter."[39] The disclosures resulted in significant government actions, including criminal prosecutions of some slaughterhouse employees, the adoption of new California laws to prevent animal cruelty, a beef recall that is reported to be the largest ever in the United States, and a $500 million judgment under the False Claims Act.[40]

### 1.1.4 *False Claims Act*

Another context in which undercover investigations can have substantial value is in accessing information that is the basis of claims under the False Claims Act (FCA), a federal statute that establishes a private cause of action that can be brought by individuals who reveal fraud against the federal government and can yield sizable financial awards.[41] Claims may be brought by the United States but also by "relators" pursuing qui tam actions on behalf of the government and who may recover a portion of the proceeds of the litigation if it is successful. Though the FCA was enacted primarily to encourage whistleblowers to come forward with evidence of fraud against the federal government, critics have argued that it is increasingly invoked not by insiders but by people and organizations that have financial or political goals unrelated to the primary purposes of the law. But these are not mutually exclusive functions.

Turning again to the animal agriculture industry, the HSUS's undercover investigation of the Westland/Hallmark meat company's facilities not only provided a basis for reforming the law and securing criminal convictions, but also led to an FCA claim against the company. HSUS filed a qui tam claim against Westland/Hallmark and the United States government intervened. The underlying claim was that the agricultural company, which was party to 140 contracts with the federal government to supply meat for the child nutrition programs, defrauded the government by selling meat that it claimed was processed in establishments that complied with specific federal health and safety standards, including humane handling of cattle that prevented needless suffering. Westland/Hallmark's certification that its facilities met this standard was fraudulent, but the only way that this was discovered in the

---

[39] *Modern Animal Farming*, VEGAN OUTREACH, https://veganoutreach.org/modernfarms-archive/ (last visited Nov. 4, 2022).

[40] *Jailed Chino Slaughterhouse Ex-Employee Says Abusive Tactics Ordered by a Superior*, THE PRESS-ENTERPRISE (Mar. 1, 2008), www.pressenterprise.com/2008/03/01/jailed-chino-slaughter house-ex-employee-says-abusive-tactics-ordered-by-a-superior/; United States' Second Amended Complaint in Intervention & Demand for Jury Trial, United States ex rel. Humane Society of the United States v. Westland/Hallmark Meat Company, et al., No. EDCV 08-0221 VAP (OPx) (C.D. Cal.) (Dec. 15, 2010) (False Claims Act suit); Nat'l Meat Ass'n v. Harris, 565 U.S. 452, 458 (2012) (describing beef recall and California law).

[41] 31 U.S.C. § 3730.

first place was through HSUS's undercover investigation. Thus, investigative deceptions can, in the right circumstances, lead to evidence supporting FCA claims.[42]

### 1.1.5 *Union "Salting"*

In 2009, as the recession was beginning to wane, James Walsh began working with Unite Here, one of the largest service unions in the United States.[43] After interviewing with a union representative, James became a union "salt." At the time, Unite Here was actively recruiting young progressive activists to volunteer with them and had an estimated 200 salts working in the local casino industry. James moved to Florida and applied for jobs with several nonunion racetrack casinos, ultimately securing a job as a buffet server, and later as a bartender. The casinos hired him, not knowing that his intent was to get to know some employees and identify candidates who could lead an organizing movement within the workplace. He performed his job duties well, which he viewed as the best way to avoid detection. To document his findings, James carried small notebooks, wrote down notes on paper receipts, and emailed himself information he had learned. Although Florida is a two-party consent state,[44] on one occasion he tried to use a hidden tape recorder to memorialize what management had said to him. Eventually, the casinos identified several of the salts, including James, and fired them, though ostensibly not because of their organizing work.

Salting represents another context in which investigative deception not only is effectively used but is also recognized as lawful. As James's story tells us, salting is when union organizers apply for and accept jobs with nonunion employers for the purpose of organizing its workers to form a union.[45] While some "salts" work openly, covert salts apply for jobs with nonunion employers while intentionally falsifying their employment applications, including omitting their work histories and connections with unions. And they engage in that deception for the specific purpose of enhancing the possibility that they will be hired. Sometimes the unions actually hire salts, who are then working for the union and for the employer; in other cases, such as James's, they are volunteers.

---

[42] *See supra* note 40.

[43] These accounts are drawn from Walsh's book, PLAYING AGAINST THE HOUSE: THE DRAMATIC WORLD OF AN UNDERCOVER UNION ORGANIZER (2016), and from a story and interview about his work. James D. Walsh, *The Double Life of an Undercover Union Organizer*, INTELLIGENCER (Feb. 19, 2016), https://nymag.com/intelligencer/2016/02/what-its-like-tobea-salt-for-the-unions .html; Bourree Lam, *Life as an Undercover Union Organizer*, THE ATLANTIC (Mar. 21, 2016), www.theatlantic.com/business/archive/2016/03/undercover-union-organizer/474387/.

[44] Two-party consent laws, which are present in 12 states as of 2022 according to the Digital Media Project, require that all parties to a conversation consent before an audio recording of the conversation is permitted. Although our focus in Chapter 4 is on video recording, the speech protections we elucidate apply with equal force to restrictions on audio recording. In fact, recording a video that includes audio would run afoul of most if not all of the existing two-party consent laws. There is no principled reason to believe that the First Amendment applies with less force to an audio recording or an audiovisual recording than to a video or visual recording.

[45] For an overview of the practice of salting, see James L. Fox, *"Salting" the Construction Industry*, 24 WM. MITCHELL L. REV. 681 (1998).

Although it is not the intention of salts to continue working for the targeted employer after they have completed their organizing work, they are recognized by the National Labor Relations Board as employees, and therefore benefit from prohibitions against unfair labor practices.[46] While on the job, covert salts communicate with other workers to help mobilize them and encourage them to form a union. Like other undercover investigators, though their purpose is to organize workers, salts are obligated under law to perform their work duties and must obey valid work rules.

Earlier generations of union activists also used deception to access workplaces. Around the same time that Walter White was conducting undercover investigations for the NAACP, Roger Baldwin, who would later help found the American Civil Liberties Union (ACLU), served as a "labor spy" to report on the working conditions in the steel industry.[47] He would engage in work during the day and document his observations later. "In the evenings he recorded the presence of morale problems, inefficient scab labor, and general problems in the production line."[48] As with other undercover investigations, Baldwin publicly exposed things that would otherwise have been hidden behind steel mill walls.

### 1.1.6 *Government Investigators and "Stings"*

On January 8, 1980, Congressman Richard Kelly arrived at a Washington, DC, townhouse he believed to be owned by Abdul Enterprises, which was actually a fake company set up by the Federal Bureau of Investigation as part of an elaborate undercover sting to root out political corruption and organized crime known as "Abscam."[49] FBI agents posing as officials of Abdul Enterprises had led Kelly to believe they needed his help as a member of Congress to introduce private immigration legislation to assist them in the event of political upheaval in Iran, where they were supposedly citizens. In exchange, they would pay Kelly $25,000. Kelly agreed, but tried to avoid any direct implication in the bribery by dealing through representatives. But after one of the undercover agents suggested to Kelly that he should receive the bribe directly to avoid having witnesses to the transaction, Kelly agreed to deal with them directly. The FBI had set up secret video recording equipment in the townhouse from which they were able to tape Kelly stuffing the cash into his suit pockets. Kelly, along with several other members of Congress and some local officials, was later convicted of corruption charges based on the operation.

[46] N.L.R.B. v. Town & Country Elec., Inc., 516 U.S. 85 (1995).
[47] ROBERT C. COTTRELL, ROGER NASH BALDWIN AND THE AMERICAN CIVIL LIBERTIES UNION 108–10 (2000).
[48] *Id.* at 110.
[49] The facts described in this narrative are from United States v. Kelly, 707 F.2d 1460 (D.C. Cir. 1983).

Abscam is perhaps the highest profile example of a significant law enforcement investigative tool: the undercover "sting." In these operations, government agents create scenarios for their targets based on lies and misrepresentations, particularly about the agents' identities. Officers pretend to be drug dealers, prostitutes, terrorists, or other players in a criminal enterprise to gain access to evidence of wrongdoing, often leading to criminal charges and convictions. As in journalism, there are debates about the ethics of such techniques (the trial judge in Congressman Kelly's case initially threw out his conviction because he concluded that the FBI's conduct was so outrageous that it violated Kelly's due process rights). But there is a long history of law enforcement lying to further criminal investigations and it has played a role in some of the most important prosecutions in US history.

Indeed, the federal courts not only have frequently upheld but also have praised the value of law enforcement stings. As one federal appeals court wrote in the context of an undercover investigation relating to insurance fraud, "[i]f total honesty by the police were to be constitutionally required, most undercover work would be effectively thwarted."[50] Furthermore, though there are specific limitations on law enforcement stings, including the rule against entrapment, the Supreme Court has sanctioned the use of deception in a wide range of contexts, including securing confessions without an attorney present, securing a confession without providing Miranda warnings, and obtaining access to conversations or private property based on false claims of friendship or business.[51] A secret told to a "false friend" does not enjoy any protection in the eyes of the Supreme Court.

But undercover law enforcement investigations bring risks of abuse as well. Between 1956 and 1971 the FBI operated a Counter Intelligence Program (infamously known as COINTELPRO), which was designed to infiltrate, disrupt, and discredit leftist organizations, particularly the Communist Party.[52] The operation targeted the work of Dr. Martin Luther King, Jr., the Black Panthers, and many others deemed subversive.

After retiring from the FBI, special agent Cril Payne wrote a memoir documenting his similar work infiltrating a leftist student group known as the Weather Underground.[53] Payne, a conservative Texas lawyer, describes how he grew a beard, pretended to be interested in the leftist ideologies of the group, and even started a relationship with one of the female activists in the group. If the FBI had wanted to search an activist's home or even just listen in on their private phone calls, a warrant would have been required. But Payne's deceptive entry and feigned romantic interest in the woman did not implicate the Constitution no matter how many

---

[50] Brokers' Choice of Am., Inc. v. NBC Universal, Inc., 757 F.3d 1125, 1146 (10th Cir. 2014).
[51] Hoffa v. United States, 385 U.S. 293, 303 (1966); Katz v. United States, 389 U.S. 347, 351 (1967); United States v. White, 401 U.S. 745, 749 (1971).
[52] COINTELPRO, Fed. Bureau of Investigation, https://vault.fbi.gov/cointel-pro (last visited Oct. 31, 2022).
[53] Cril Payne, Deep Cover: An FBI Agent Infiltrates the Radical Underground (1979).

private secrets he obtained through his lies. This was true even though the woman being investigated eventually became pregnant and was persuaded by Payne to get an abortion.[54] It would be a serious oversight to ignore the reality that the sociolegal history of deception-based investigations has frequently included rather unsavory tactics against persons on the political left.

### 1.1.7 *A Definition Drawn from Commonalities*

Several features link these otherwise vastly different undercover investigations. Many of the investigations we highlight involve the investigator engaging in some form of deception toward the investigation's target, either affirmatively misrepresenting the investigator's identity, background, and motives or at least omitting information that would cause the target to turn them away. Second, the investigation uses the deception or other tactic to access private property, information, or people. Third, the investigations reveal conduct that is unlawful, unethical, or immoral, or other-wise a matter of considerable public interest. Fourth, all of these investigations involve documenting the information discovered, whether by handwritten notes made while the investigator cannot be observed or by using hidden digital recording equipment, such as cameras, audio recorders, or video recorders. Finally, in each case the investigation's targets seek to keep the information that is sought from public scrutiny, thus making the information difficult if not impossible to obtain without an undercover investigation.

## 1.2 SOCIAL PRACTICES, SOCIAL CONDITIONS, AND INSTITUTIONS

Throughout this book, we stress that undercover investigations, like other social practices, do not exist in a vacuum. Rather, the emergence of these investigative techniques is in part a response to weaknesses in the infrastructure of speech and information in our society, and are therefore deeply historically contingent. Some of these factors are legal, but others relate more to structural, political, and social conditions. We contend that undercover investigations become central to the information-gathering ecosphere when, and because of failures of public policy, critical information is kept secret from the public. Indeed, the significance of any particular undercover investigation is inversely related to the public transparency of the events exposed. If certain information is readily available to the public through other means, or if the information sought is merely embarrassing or entertaining, an investigation into such matters is less valuable, and should probably enjoy fewer legal protections. On the other hand, the greater the secrecy and the more relevant the information to public debate, the potentially more valuable the undercover investigation.

---

[54] *Id.* at 262–66, 274.

We maintain that our contemporary environment, for reasons described below, is one in which undercover investigations are of critical importance to promoting free speech. We break this discussion down into two major categories. First, current social conditions make it increasingly difficult for the public to gain access to information that informs public discourse on a wide range of issues. Second, structural institutional failures have depressed the quality and quantity of efforts to acquire information and keep state and private institutions in check.

### 1.2.1 *Social Conditions*

Undercover investigations are a natural reaction to secrecy and non-transparency in powerful institutions. Investigators and those who sponsor them are always on the outside looking in. There may be a well-founded reason to suspect that an institution is engaged in unlawful, unethical, or otherwise unsavory practices, but few traditional avenues to gaining access to relevant information. As we elaborate on throughout this book, this type of transparency in government is essential to fulfilling one of the First Amendment's most critical purposes, promoting an effective, functioning democracy. And this is no less true with respect to the accountability of large corporate interests.

With regard to government institutions, lack of transparency substantially undermines accountability and makes it difficult to engage in political transformation through the electoral process. That process, of course, is plagued by dysfunctions almost too large to tally, whether we are talking about inequality in the electoral process through economic disparities and the ability of the very wealthy to donate and spend on political campaigns, the numerous impediments to voting imposed by governments keen to retain their political power, or, at the presidential level, the distortions of the Electoral College, which grants disproportionate power to voters who reside in less populous states.

But our democracy is equally threatened by an ecosystem that discourages the open and unfiltered disclosure of information from powerful institutions. To be sure, there are other, more formal ways than undercover investigations to gather information through structured legal processes. If the target of an investigation is a private corporation, those monitoring its behavior may be able to look to mandatory disclosures required by federal and state law. Disclosure requirements are narrowly circumscribed, however, and corporations have strong incentives to hide critical information. As one scholar has observed, "disclosure documents today are written by corporate lawyers in formalized language to protect the corporation from liability rather than to provide the investor with meaningful information."[55] Other critical information of great public interest may see the light of day from a beneficent

---

[55] Susanna Kim Ripken, *The Dangers and Drawbacks of the Disclosure Antidote: Toward a More Substantive Approach to Securities Regulation*, 58 BAYLOR L. REV. 139, 186 (2006).

insider. But while there are many examples of brave whistleblowers who have revealed information, the truth is that people who engage in this conduct are at significant risk for employment termination and maybe even criminal charges.

Consider the fate of Lt. Colonel Vindman, who testified about a phone call between President Donald Trump and foreign officials during Trump's first impeachment proceedings. No one, including the White House, has ever pointed to lies or misstatements made by Vindman. To the contrary, the released phone transcripts strongly corroborate Vindman's testimony. And yet a decorated officer was pressured into early retirement when he was removed from his position and threatened with undesirable assignments and non-promotions. This was the unfortunate outcome for a whistleblower who, according to President Trump's former Chief of Staff, did nothing wrong and acted just as he was trained.[56]

A third way to acquire information about corporate behavior is through lawsuits. In the American legal system, litigation provides parties with the opportunity to acquire information from opposing parties through the process of discovery, which entails formal requests for written answers to interrogatories, for production of relevant documents, and for admissions of certain facts. But before formal discovery may be commenced, the party who is suing must progress to a certain point in the litigation past the initial pleading stage, and the Supreme Court has made it increasingly difficult for plaintiffs who have not pled sufficiently specific information to survive a motion to dismiss the case prior to the discovery process.[57] This puts plaintiffs trying to sue powerful corporate entities or government officials in a bit of a Catch-22 position: they cannot succeed in acquiring information from a corporation unless their lawsuit has reached a certain stage of the litigation process, but they are unlikely to reach that stage unless they have already acquired enough information on which to base their legal claims. This means that claims of corporate malfeasance or government discrimination will be dismissed by trial judges prior to discovery unless the plaintiffs already have access to substantial information to verify their allegations of misconduct through other, informal channels.

Like private businesses, government entities are sometimes required by law to disclose certain information to the public, but like corporations, their incentives to be completely transparent may be limited. Beyond mandatory disclosure laws, if the investigative target is a federal, state, or local government entity, a person or organization who suspects unlawful or unethical behavior may try to acquire

---

[56] Michael S. Schmidt, *Vindman, Key Figure in Trump Impeachment, Alleges Retaliation in Lawsuit*, N.Y. TIMES (Feb. 2, 2022), www.nytimes.com/2022/02/02/us/politics/alexander-vind man-trump-lawsuit.html.

[57] In two cases decided over a decade ago, the Supreme Court established law making it more difficult for plaintiffs filing claims in federal court to adequately plead their complaint, meaning that they need to provide more than conclusory factual statements and must detail a facially plausible claim, or their suits will be dismissed at a very early stage of litigation. *See* Bell Atl. Corp. v. Twombly, 550 U.S. 544 (2007); Ashcroft v. Iqbal, 556 U.S. 662 (2009).

information from that entity through the federal Freedom of Information Act (FOIA)[58] or the applicable state law requiring disclosure of public records. These are laudable, but imperfect, statutory mechanisms to promote information gathering through a structured bureaucratic process.

To its supporters, FOIA is an essential structural component for a functioning democracy, even if it alone cannot address all information problems.[59] It allows any person (even a non-US citizen) to make a request to an entity of the federal government to produce documents; the requester does not have to provide a specific justification for the request; agency denials of requests are subject to de novo judicial review; and FOIA requests have sometimes led to revelations of information crucial to public discourse and government accountability.[60]

Yet legal scholars have produced a persistent barrage of critiques of FOIA's implementation and effectiveness.[61] Some flaws are internal to the statute itself – FOIA applies only to federal executive agencies and not to other important government institutions and it does not apply to the private sector at all; there are numerous exemptions that allow agencies to refuse to turn over documents; and requests for information are tightly controlled and often intensely fought. Other critiques focus on institutional or political limitations: the sheer volume of requests makes processing slow, expensive, and unresponsive to priorities; federal courts are highly deferential to agency decisions not to disclose, even when useful information is sought; and non-lawyers reviewing the requests for the agencies may be trained to err on the side of nondisclosure. Moreover, FOIA disclosures do not always directly result in reforms or other consequences (note that the requester does not have to make the acquired documents available to the broader public); document requests frequently result in disclosure of large volumes of information at high cost without corresponding social benefits. This last observation is connected to an early twenty-first-century concern with the increase in secrecy about matters that the government characterizes as related to national security, much of which is unavailable under FOIA. Another related criticism of FOIA has been that the predominant beneficiaries of

---

[58] 5 U.S.C. § 552.

[59] Seth F. Kreimer, *The Freedom of Information Act and the Ecology of Transparency*, 10 U. PA. J. CONST. L. 1011 (2008) (responding to FOIA's critics and suggesting that its operation must be understood within a broader system that he dubs "the ecology of transparency"). The Supreme Court has occasionally embraced FOIA's role in advancing democracy. *See, e.g.*, N.L.R.B. v. Robbins Tire & Rubber Co., 437 U.S. 214 (1978); Nat'l Archives & Recs. Admin. v. Favish, 541 U.S. 157 (2004).

[60] Kreimer, *supra* note 58 (describing some successes by the news media in using FOIA to obtain information from the U.S. government about the global war on terror.).

[61] For a useful compendium of many of these critiques, see David E. Pozen, *Freedom of Information beyond the Freedom of Information Act*, 165 U. PA. L. REV. 1097 (2017). There are also those who have suggested that FOIA is unnecessary because the constitutional system of checks and balances is sufficient to ensure government accountability. *See* Antonin Scalia, *The Freedom of Information Act Has No Clothes*, REGUL., Mar./Apr. 1982.

records requests are not watchdog groups or journalists, but powerful corporate interests[62] and individuals who have specific disputes with the government.[63]

Thus, while FOIA and open records laws are a part of the information-gathering puzzle, they are incomplete, at best, and may in fact lead to a false appearance of transparency that does more harm than good.

### 1.2.2 *Institutional Failures*

There are also information failures at the institutional level. changes in the way that government, particularly at the federal level, operates and the economic hardships suffered by the institutional press have combined to reduce the accountability of both the government and the private sector.

### 1.2.2.1 Increasing Government Secrecy

With respect to the federal government, notwithstanding mandatory disclosure requirements and FOIA, the twenty-first century has emerged as a time during which government leaders in both major political parties tend to make sweeping claims about the need for secrecy to promote national security. Historically, the US government has asserted national security concerns most frequently during times of war, when the courts and the public have been the most deferential to these claims. At the same time, exaggerated security concerns have frequently led to substantial infringements on civil liberties, as with prosecutions of antiwar and labor activists during World War I under the Espionage Act of 1917 and the Sedition Act of 1918, and of suspected Communists under the Smith Act in the mid twentieth century, as well as the detention of persons of Japanese descent in internment camps during World War II.[64]

The contemporary era, with its protracted "war" on terrorism and rapidly changing technology, has brought on both security concern and rights claims quite different from the past contexts of formally declared wars. Whether this is a consequence of living in a post-9/11 world or the long-standing military conflict the United States has been involved in since the World Trade Center towers were toppled, the effects are noticeable. And while government secrecy increases, so do counterpunches from whistleblowers or "leakers" of otherwise secret information, who have taken great personal risks to reveal information of compelling public importance. Predictably, government officials displeased with the leaks have responded severely,

---

[62] Margaret B. Kwoka, *FOIA, Inc.*, 65 Duke L.J. 1361 (2016).
[63] Margaret B. Kwoka, *First-Person FOIA*, 127 Yale L.J. 2204 (2018).
[64] *See generally* Alan K. Chen, *Free Speech and the Confluence of National Security and Internet Exceptionalism*, 86 Fordham L. Rev. 379 (2017).

though evidence is mixed about whether efforts to enforce criminal laws against leakers have changed the situation dramatically.[65]

One of the most visible examples of how leaking works comes from the controversial case of Edward Snowden, an employee of a contractor for the National Security Agency who leaked an extremely large number of classified documents to the press revealing that, despite its public denials, the US government was engaged in massive surveillance of its citizens' private telephone calls, emails, internet browser search histories, and online chats, including both metadata and content.[66] With the cooperation of other governments, this spying reached around the globe. The program had at least two components, one known as PRISM, which allowed the National Security Agency (NSA) to acquire information from existing databases, including data held by tech companies such as Apple, Facebook, Google, and Microsoft, and one known as XKeyScore, which seemed to allow it to monitor data while it was in the process of being transmitted. Both became public knowledge only because of Snowden's leaks. Under federal law, when seeking this data regarding any US "person," the government is supposed to, at a minimum, first seek authorization from a special court under the Foreign Intelligence Surveillance Act.[67] Snowden's revelations documented that the NSA frequently ignored that requirement.

In 2010, prior to Snowden's actions, Chelsea Manning, a private in the US Army, leaked confidential documents to Julian Assange's WikiLeaks organization. The documents Manning released included videos documenting that US air strikes had killed civilians and journalists in Iraq and Afghanistan. Snowden was reportedly concerned about Manning's treatment in the wake of the leaks, and it is believed that this may have factored into his actions, which at first included highly secretive meetings with journalists to whom he leaked the data and plans to evade

---

[65] *Compare* Heidi Kitrosser, *Leak Prosecutions and the First Amendment: New Developments and a Closer Look at the Feasibility of Protecting Leakers*, 56 WM. & MARY L. REV. 1221, 1228 (2015) (describing the Obama administration's "unparalleled numerical record of prosecuting cases" involving leakers) *with* David E. Pozen, *The Leaky Leviathan: Why the Government Condemns and Condones Unlawful Disclosures of Information*, 127 HARV. L. REV. 512, 536 (2013) ("Against a backdrop of 'routine daily' classified information leaks, a suite of eight [Obama administration] prosecutions looks more like a special operation than a war"). *See also* Gabe Rottman, *A Typology of Federal News Media "Leak" Cases*, 93 TUL. L. REV. 1147, 1182–85 tbl.1 (2019) (counting only the prosecutions brought under Section 793).

[66] We draw from the following sources for the Snowden story. Glenn Greenwald, *Xkeyscore: NSA Tool Collects "Nearly Everything a User Does on the Internet,"* THE GUARDIAN (July 31, 2013), www.theguardian.com/world/2013/jul/31/nsa-top-secret-program-online-data; Bryan Burrough, Sarah Ellison, & Suzanna Andrews, *The Snowden Saga: A Shadowland of Secrets and Light*, VANITY FAIR (May 2014), http://fs2.american.edu/dfagel/www/Class%20Readings/Civil%20Disobedienc%20And%20Obligation/Snowden_Vanity%20Fair.pdf; Barton Gellman, *NSA Broke Privacy Rules Thousands of Times per Year, Audit Finds*, WASH. POST (Aug. 15, 2013), www.washingtonpost.com/world/national-security/nsa-broke-privacy-rules-thousands-of-times-per-year-audit-finds/2013/08/15/3310e554-05ca-11e3-a07f-49ddc7417125_story.html.

[67] 50 U.S.C. § 1801 et seq.

detection by US authorities. At this moment, Snowden is living in Russia, where he is free from extradition, while the United States has pending criminal charges against him for alleged violations of the Espionage Act and theft of government property.

The critical role of leakers is underscored by the fact that the federal government's consistent practice has been to deny that it is engaged in surveillance of its citizens, which also means that there are impediments to filing lawsuits to challenge such actions. For example, in *Clapper v. Amnesty International, USA*, the Supreme Court held that the plaintiffs, which included attorneys, human rights organizations, and media organizations that worked with organizations in other nations, did not have legal standing to challenge a program of surveillance of certain foreign persons even though they alleged their work "requires them to engage in sensitive and sometimes privileged telephone and e-mail communications with colleagues, clients, sources, and other individuals located abroad."[68] The Supreme Court held that the plaintiffs' fears of being subject to surveillance were "too speculative" since they could not demonstrate that they were imminently subject to such conduct. Therein lies the problem for citizens seeking to challenge secret surveillance of their activities. They can sue only if they can show that they have or are imminently likely to be spied on, but because the program is secret they will not know about the surveillance until it is too late to stop it from occurring. A leak like Snowden's pertaining to that particular program might have given them such standing. Without whistleblowers, government secrecy and surveillance can be inoculated from legal challenges in court.

The secrecy surrounding federal and state government actions pales in comparison with the privacy demanded by most private businesses. Even publicly traded corporations are required to disclose relatively little information when it comes to specific projects or undertakings that might be unseemly or harmful to the public. When a private company is engaged in its own profit-making endeavors, it may force employees to sign punitive nondisclosure agreements and may also insist on comprehensive non-disparagement agreements. Journalists have detailed the work of lawyers and private investigators who work through harassment and intimidation to enforce nondisclosure agreements and silence would-be whistleblowers.[69] Though there is little empirical evidence available, corporations are reported to engage in the aggressive use of nondisclosure agreements to silence employees who might reveal businesses' deceptive claims about products or research.[70] And nondisclosures in the workplace have recently gained attention in the #MeToo movement, as celebrities and others detail contractual secrecy that kept sex predators safe from prosecution.

---

[68] Clapper v. Amnesty Int'l USA, 568 U.S. 398, 406 (2013).
[69] *See* JOHN CARREYROU, BAD BLOOD: SECRETS AND LIES IN A SILICON VALLEY STARTUP (2018).
[70] *Id.*

Businesses also ensure that when they litigate and settle lawsuits alleging malfeasance, they do so with court-approved secrecy under seal. Indeed, it is common knowledge that a large number of private lawsuits result in settlements that are not open to the public. In addition, companies vigorously assert intellectual property and trade secret protections through lawyers as a means of silencing those who might report on conditions in a factory or otherwise make allegations of corporate misconduct.

Even when private companies are working for or with the government, they enjoy levels of secrecy that insulate them from public rebuke and scrutiny. In 2007, for example, the ACLU filed a federal lawsuit against Jeppesen, a subsidiary of Boeing, alleging that Jeppesen had knowingly facilitated torture programs by the Central Intelligence Agency (CIA). One victim of torture, Binyam Mohamed, did not have to speculate about the government programs at issue, but instead pled specific facts detailing his multi-year extradition to a torture site in Morocco and then Kabul, before eventually being brought to Guantanamo Bay. Yet a federal appellate court dismissed the case, holding that it could not proceed because the litigation against a private company could reveal state secrets.[71]

### 1.2.2.2 A Substantially Diminished Press

At the same time that state and private actors are becoming more powerful and secretive, one of society's most critical monitors is diminishing in power and stature. A central component of a system of free speech is a thriving, independent news media free from state control. The press is designed to be an external check on government. We rely on it to both gather information about public affairs and inform us so that we can hold the state accountable for its actions. In addition, free speech protects not only speakers, but also listeners. The audience for speech enjoys First Amendment protection for the freedom to read and listen to speech they wish to consume. In the United States, the press has long facilitated these interests.[72]

Unfortunately, in recent years, there has been a substantial decline in the availability of institutional news media outlets that have historically served these important functions. This phenomenon has already presented significant challenges

---

[71] Mohamed v. Jeppesen Dataplan, Inc., 614 F.3d 1070, 1083 (9th Cir. 2010)

> (even if the claims and defenses might theoretically be established without relying on privileged evidence, it may be impossible to proceed with the litigation because – privileged evidence being inseparable from nonprivileged information that will be necessary to the claims or defenses – litigating the case to a judgment on the merits would present an unacceptable risk of disclosing state secrets.).

[72] The freedom of the press under the First Amendment has largely been subsumed under the free speech clause because of their close interrelationship, though many scholars have observed the flaws in such an understanding. Sonja R. West, *Press Exceptionalism*, 127 HARV. L. REV. 2434 (2014); Ashutosh Bhagwat, *Producing Speech*, 56 WM. & MARY L. REV. 1029 (2015).

to the continued protection of free speech. First, over the past few decades, and particularly since the expansion of the internet, the news media has declined in large part because of its business model is no longer viable. The media, and in particular newspapers, long relied on a large revenue stream from two sources: classified ads and commercial advertising. The advent of Craigslist and other free online services has nearly caused these revenue streams to vanish. From 2000 to 2012, American newspapers' annual classified ad revenue fell from a high of $19.6 billion to $4.6 billion, a loss of $15 billion per year.[73] An industry once dependent on commercial advertising revenue to subsidize its important journalistic work has lost out to competition for ads on social media platforms and other places on the internet. Indeed, commercial advertising revenue, which peaked around the year 2000, recently fell to levels last seen in the 1950s (although that still leaves $20 billion in revenues nationally, which is not insignificant).[74]

The impact of these losses has been manifest. As a recent *Wall Street Journal* article reported, between 2004 and 2018, nearly 1,800 newspapers have gone out of business.[75] Most of these were local newspapers, which once played an important role in informing Americans. From 1990 to 2016, jobs at American newspapers declined from 465,000 to 183,000. The efforts of some newspapers to move to digital content to reverse this trend have been largely unsuccessful. This is not a problem isolated to the news industry, for as Richard Kluger once noted, "Every time a newspaper dies, even a bad one, the country moves a little closer to authoritarianism."[76]

Major news media that remain have been forced to rely on other revenue streams, so they tend to be controlled by huge corporate interests, which necessarily limits the range of possible different perspectives that their editorial arms can offer. They also emphasize national reporting over local journalism. As the *Wall Street Journal* reported, when large corporations and hedge funds take over newspapers, they follow a familiar "playbook [that] calls for instituting drastic cost reduction and layoffs in hopes of goosing profits in the short term." But the impact is that "Local coverage suffers [and] investigative ambition withers."[77] The disinfecting light that Justice Brandeis promised from transparency has become less common.

---

[73] John Reinan, *How Craigslist Killed the Newspapers' Golden Goose*, MinnPost (Feb. 3, 2014), www.minnpost.com/business/2014/02/how-craigslist-killed-newspapers-golden-goose/.

[74] Derek Thompson, *The Collapse of Print Advertising in 1 Graph*, The Atlantic (Feb. 28, 2012), www.theatlantic.com/business/archive/2012/02/the-collapse-of-print-advertising-in-1-graph/253736/.

[75] Keach Hagey, Lukas I. Alpert, & Yaryna Serkez, *In News Industry, a Stark Divide between Haves and Have-Nots*, Wall St. J. (May 4, 2019), www.wsj.com/graphics/local-newspapers-stark-divide/?shareToken=st4812f966bc45412d9dedb41622863b2f.

[76] Richard Kluger, The Paper: The Life and Death of the New York Herald Tribune (1986).

[77] Michael Posner, *Hedge Funds and Newspapers: A Bad Mix*, Forbes (Jan. 18, 2019), www.forbes.com/sites/michaelposner/2019/01/18/hedge-funds-and-newspapers-a-bad-mix/#53f97c795c53.

A second institutional trend is the increased blurring of the news media's reporting and editorial functions. Looking at a print newspaper, it's easy to distinguish between the news stories and opinion pieces, which are actually located in a separate physical space. When reading an online news magazine or watching a cable news program, however, the programmers do not always neatly distinguish news from opinion. And while Fox News has earned deserved attention in this regard, left-leaning media outlets are also vulnerable to these biases.[78]

Collectively, these changes and others have also led to a sharp decline in the public's trust of the news media. A recent Gallup poll reported that while 51% of Americans had a great deal or a lot of confidence in newspapers in the late 1970s, that figure had dropped to about 27% by 2017 (up from a historic low of 20% in 2016). At the same time, those with little or no confidence in newspapers rose from 13% in the late 1970s to about 36% in 2016.[79]

The reasons for this decline in trust are complex and not easy to explain, but we can certainly speculate. First, in recent years, there has been a downward trend in Americans' trust in most major institutions.[80] Second, there appears to be an unprecedented assault on the media from public office holders. Politicians have complained about and attacked the news media since this country's founding generation, but perhaps no other public office holder has more directly confronted the news media's legitimacy than former President Trump, who has described some parts of the press as the "enemy of the people."[81] It has become commonplace for public officials to denigrate the press.

Simultaneously, as challenges to the press's legitimacy are publicly raised, the news outlets that still exist are threatened by libel suits that can expose them to huge financial liability, even when their reporting is truthful. Despite the Supreme Court's protective standard from *New York Times v. Sullivan*,[82] which held that libel suits by public officials against news media may succeed only if the media publishes a false story with actual malice or reckless disregard for its truth, libel suits continue to cost American media huge amounts in settlements, even when their stories may well be true. In 2017, ABC news paid a settlement of more than $177 million to a South Dakota company that sued it for defamation based on an investigative report

---

[78] Jane Mayer, *The Making of the Fox News White House*, THE NEW YORKER (Mar. 4, 2019), www .newyorker.com/magazine/2019/03/11/the-making-of-the-fox-news-white-house.

[79] Lydia Saad, *Americans' Confidence in Newspapers at New Low*, GALLUP (June 13, 2016), https:// news.gallup.com/poll/192665/americans-confidence-newspapers-new-low.aspx; Art Swift, *In U.S., Confidence in Newspapers Still Low but Rising*, GALLUP (June 28, 2017), https://news .gallup.com/poll/212852/confidence-newspapers-low-rising.aspx.

[80] Frank Newport, *Americans' Confidence in Institutions Edges Up*, GALLUP (June 26, 2017), https://news.gallup.com/poll/212840/americans-confidence-institutions-edges.aspx.

[81] John Wagner, *Trump Renews Attacks on Media as "the True Enemy of the People"* WASH. POST (Oct. 29, 2018), www.washingtonpost.com/politics/trump-renews-attacks-on-media-as-the-true-enemy-of-the-people/2018/10/29/9ebc62ee-db60-11e8-85df-7a6b4d25cfbb_story.html.

[82] N.Y. Times Co. v. Sullivan, 376 U.S. 254, 279–80 (1964).

in which the network featured a US Department of Agriculture biologist who was whistleblowing about what he considered deceptions in the labeling of certain meat product as "ground beef." The scientist, and subsequently ABC, dubbed the product "pink slime," which would seem to either be an entirely accurate factual description or a protected opinion. Nonetheless they were sued. The strength of the First Amendment arguments against such liability were strong, but no media lawyer would risk liability that could bankrupt the client, particularly when the network's fate was in the hands of a local jury. Accordingly, because the local trial judge steadfastly refused to dismiss the case, ABC settled.[83]

One doesn't need to reach far to imagine the consequences of media lawsuits for a less well-heeled news organization. Gawker Media declared bankruptcy after Terry Bollea (aka "Hulk Hogan") successfully sued it for invasion of privacy and won a jury verdict of $140 million for the publication of a story and excerpts from a "sex tape" showing him having sex with a friend's wife.[84] The video posted with the story was one minute and 40 seconds long, but only 9 seconds of that showed sexual conduct. While that may sound like outrageous conduct without more context, as it turns out, Bollea, a widely known celebrity, had openly discussed his sex life and the fact that there was a video of him engaged in an extramarital affair, and this had been previously discussed in the media. Earlier state court rulings had declared that the topic of the story and video regarding Bollea's sex life had become a matter of "public concern" based partly on his own behavior. Another important development that became known after the case was that Bollea's lawsuit was financed by conservative billionaire Peter Thiel, who had specifically hoped to impart substantial financial damage on Gawker in retaliation for the outlet's earlier outing of his sexual orientation. Gawker spent $13 million just in lawyers' fees, while Thiel bankrolled Bollea's case, allowing Bollea's lawyers to aggressively litigate and disincentivizing a pretrial settlement.

And if verdicts and settlements such as these weren't enough of a threat to the press, public officials have called for the expansion of libel laws or to revisit the *New York Times* standard to make it easier to sue news media, as Trump did in public statements and Justice Clarence Thomas did in one of his opinions.[85]

The confluence of these market factors and increasing media vulnerability to private lawsuits at the very least diminishes the role that the press can play in

---

[83] Steven D. Zansberg, *Recent High-Profile Cases Highlight the Need for Greater Procedural Protections for Freedom of the Press*, Comm. L., Nov. 2017, at 7–8.

[84] For a thoughtful discussion of the problems the Gawker litigation might pose for media defendants and a proposal for both substantive and procedural changes that might better protect the media, see Mary-Rose Papandrea, *Media Litigation in a Post-Gawker World*, 93 Tul. L. Rev. 1105 (2019).

[85] McKee v. Cosby, 139 S. Ct. 675, 682 (2019) (Thomas, J., concurring in the denial of certiorari). Former President Trump also argued for changing libel law to make it easier for plaintiffs to prevail. Hadas Gold, *Donald Trump: We're Going to "Open Up" Libel Laws*, Politico (Feb. 26, 2016), www.politico.com/blogs/on-media/2016/02/donald-trump-libel-laws-219866.

informing the public and holding government accountable. Even though we are beginning to see the emergence of some new independent, online news services, often hiring the best journalists from now defunct newspapers, the speech and information ecosystem needs additional actors in the system to help carry out these functions.

It is our claim throughout this book that the totality of current circumstances warrants alternative approaches to accessing information of great interest and reporting it to the public and that undercover investigations, properly understood and executed consistent with a general set of best practices that we provide, are a critical tool for fulfilling this function. We maintain, therefore, that such investigations should be lawful in most circumstances and government attempts to restrict them understood as violations of the freedom of speech under the First Amendment. In the following section, we provide an overview of recent attempts to restrict undercover investigations, which we examine in greater detail in the chapters that follow.

## 1.3 LEGAL AND SOCIAL IMPEDIMENTS TO UNDERCOVER INVESTIGATIONS

While the previously discussed social, political, and institutional conditions underscore the importance of undercover investigations as an alternative source of information that feeds our current system of freedom of expression, there are nonetheless substantial barriers to creating an environment in which such investigations might thrive. These barriers can be broken down into roughly three categories: legal, ethical, and ideological.

### 1.3.1 *Legal Restrictions on Undercover Investigations*

Legal impediments to undercover investigations come in at least three different forms. First, there have been increasing efforts to criminalize the types of affirmative deceptions or omissions that have been used by investigators to gain access to information vital to democratic governance since at least the era of the girl stunt reporters, Upton Sinclair, and the heyday of "muckraking" journalists. On the surface, laws regulating lying or misrepresentation tend to resemble legal constraints on fraud. In truth, although investigative deceptions unequivocally involve overt lying or omissions of the truth, the resulting harms, if any, are a usually a product of the dissemination of the truthful information discovered, which often reveals illegal, unethical, or immoral conduct on the part of the investigation's target.

Instead, those who support such restrictions assert concerns about the target's property and privacy interests. One example of such restrictions is so-called ag-gag laws. These laws, which are the brainchild of the conservative group the American

Legislative Exchange Council,[86] are designed to criminalize conduct that has led to the type of high-profile animal rights investigations discussed earlier. Nearly all such laws make it a crime to use deception to gain access to an animal agricultural facility, either generally or to gain employment.[87] Because most animal agricultural investigations are employment based, these are a substantial impediment to undertaking an investigation. Similarly, Planned Parenthood has successfully lobbied for state laws that prohibit undercover recordings of confidential communications with health care providers or the distribution of such recordings.[88] In addition, laws requiring licenses for private investigators can substantially limit the ability of persons to engage in an undercover investigation. It might violate multiple statutes in some states for a person to engage in the very sort of conduct that was celebrated during the muckraking era.

Gaining access to property to conduct a deception-based investigation is one thing, but documenting what the investigator observes is equally important. Not surprisingly, a second form of government regulation seeks to criminalize the act of surreptitious photography and audiovisual recording without the target's consent. Such recording might be done by an undercover investigator with a hidden camera or cell phone. Other recordings might involve the use of other newer technologies, such as drones. While there have been some successful early legal challenges to laws regulating investigative deceptions and secret recording, the law is still evolving.[89]

A third category of legal impediments to undercover investigations has been invoked by the private sector, whose misconduct is often brought to light by such investigations. Turning to private tort and contract remedies, these businesses can bring private law claims against journalists and activists for invasion of privacy, trespass, violation of the duty of loyalty, or other state torts.[90] The US Court of Appeals for the Ninth Circuit recently upheld a $2.425 million jury verdict against

---

[86] Ag-gag laws appear to be drawn from model legislation drafted by ALEC as "The Animal and Ecological Terrorism Act," which includes a provision that would make the following conduct a crime: "Obstructing or impeding the use of an animal facility or the use of a natural resource without the effective consent of the owner by . . . entering an animal or research facility to take pictures by photograph, video camera, or other means with the intent to commit criminal activities or defame the facility or its owner." *The Animal and Ecological Terrorism Act (AETA)*, AM. LEGIS. EXCH. COUNCIL, www.alec.org/model-policy/the-animal-and-ecological-terrorism-act-aeta/ (last visited Oct. 31, 2022).

[87] *See, e.g.*, Animal Legal Def. Fund v. Wasden, 878 F.3d 1184 (9th Cir. 2018) (invalidating on First Amendment grounds an Idaho statute that prohibited using deception to gain access to animal agricultural facilities, but upholding provision outlawing deception to gain employment at such facilities).

[88] Nick Cahill, *Health Care Sting Videos a Crime in California*, COURTHOUSE NEWS SERV. (Sept. 30, 2016), www.courthousenews.com/health-care-sting-videos-a-crime-in-california/. The law is codified at CAL. PENAL CODE § 632.01 (West 2017).

[89] *See, e.g.*, Animal Legal Def. Fund v. Wasden, 878 F.3d 1184 (9th Cir. 2018); Animal Legal Def. Fund v. Kelly, 9 F.4th 1219 (10th Cir. 2021), *cert. denied*, 142 S.Ct. 2647 (2022).

[90] *See, e.g.*, Food Lion, Inc. v. Cap. Cities/ABC, Inc., 194 F.3d 505, 510 (4th Cir. 1999).

the Center for Medical Progress, the organization that sponsored the undercover investigation of Planned Parenthood and other reproductive choice organizations.[91]

Or, to the extent that engaging in an undercover investigation might violate the terms and conditions of one's employment, employers might bring breach of contract claims, or simply fire those investigators from the jobs they secured with the target. Sometimes these claims might be available under common law, but in some jurisdictions, the legislature has enacted laws that establish new civil claims that can be invoked by private businesses to sue investigators.[92] Because such actions can sometimes result in large financial judgments or at least the potential for such judgments, they further chill participation in undercover investigations in a manner similar to the threat of criminal penalties. Moreover, because of existing procedural doctrines, it may be more difficult for individuals and organizations who conduct investigations to challenge the constitutionality of these claims as applied to investigators.

We discuss these legal issues in greater detail in the forthcoming chapters.

### 1.3.2 *Moral and Ethical Restrictions on Undercover Investigations*

Independent of the law, there may be objections to undercover investigations from an ethical or moral standpoint. To some degree, our arguments in favor of robust undercover investigations might reflect a basic utilitarian suggestion that even if deception is wrong, the greater good that is served by such investigations outweighs that wrong. But moral philosophers from Immanuel Kant to the present day have argued that lying is inherently wrong and suggest that there should be a strong prohibition of lies in most circumstances.

Moral questions about lies sometimes get translated into professional ethics codes. We have already alluded to the idea that professional journalists have conflicting views about investigative deceptions. Sometimes those views may be historically contingent and sometimes they may simply be a function of individual journalists' subjective values.

We take the challenge of these moral and ethical considerations seriously. In Chapter 2, we more fully explore historical evolution of the journalism profession and the ethical debates about undercover investigations. In Chapter 3, we address some of the moral concerns about lying in particular, and suggest some reasons why lies associated with undercover investigations might fall outside even moral objections. Finally, in the book's Conclusion, we offer a set of "best practices" for

---

[91] *See* Planned Parenthood Fed'n of Am., Inc. v. Newman, 51 F.4th 1125 (9th Cir. 2022); Planned Parenthood Fed'n of Am., Inc. v. Newman, No. 20-16068, 2022 WL 13613963 (9th Cir. Oct. 21, 2022).
[92] *See, e.g.,* N.C. Gen. Stat. Ann. § 99A-2 (West 2016); Ark. Code Ann. § 16-118-113 (West 2017). These statutes are currently undergoing legal challenges in federal court.

undercover investigations that promote their use, while delineating safeguards to minimize these objections.[93]

### 1.3.3 *Cultural, Political, and Ideological Impediments*

Even beyond legal, moral, and ethical barriers to engaging in undercover investigations, there are cultural and political/ideological constraints that push back against the idea that such investigations promote the public good. First, there are likely some intuitive negative connotations about such work, which might be viewed (in both journalistic and political contexts) as sensationalistic and unfair. There is something deeply unsettling about the undercover investigator, inherently troubling to many casual observers. The phrase "stunt" journalism, often associated with Nellie Bly, itself implies something outside social or professional norms. Critics have characterized such undercover investigations as a form of spying or trickery and frequently claim that they may infringe on the emotional well-being, privacy interests, and property rights of an investigation's targets. How far can an undercover investigation pry into one's life? If a journalist wants to document an underground activist movement or penetrate a secretive corporate boardroom, can they feign romantic interest and form a relationship with a person who might get them access to information?

And, of course, anyone who has been the target of a sting or undercover investigation is self-interestedly likely to have substantial objections to these techniques. There is also likely a view of such investigations that is ideologically path-dependent – one might look at undercover investigations as healthy, even heroic, when the target is an institution or bad actor on the other end of political or ideological spectrum, but view comparable methods used to investigate one's allies as suspect, an invasion of privacy, an unfair ambush. And precisely because the targets of such investigations span the political and ideological spectrum, there may well be bipartisan, cross-ideological opposition to undercover work. Journalists have targeted Democrats and Republicans, liberals and conservatives, government entities and businesses. Political activists from both the left and right have engaged in these tactics, and both have borne criticism from targets, who argue that the investigations employ duplicitous, unfair practices and that the information gathered is used in misleading ways to misrepresent the truth of what goes on behind closed doors. Thus, in recent years, we have witnessed such arguments from groups as diverse as the animal agriculture industry and Planned Parenthood.[94]

---

[93] Cf. *Undercover and Sensitive Operations Unit, Attorney General's Guidelines on FBI Undercover Operations*, U.S. DEP'T OF JUST. (Nov. 13, 1992), www.justice.gov/archives/ag/ undercover-and-sensitive-operations-unit-attorney-generals-guidelines-fbi-undercover-operations.

[94] Jackie Calmes, *Planned Parenthood Videos Were Altered, Analysis Finds*, N.Y. TIMES (Aug. 27, 2015), www.nytimes.com/2015/08/28/us/abortion-planned-parenthood-videos.html.

This may cause ideological divides within political communities, leading some who would ordinarily favor free speech and robust newsgathering to question the value of undercover investigations, or at least to believe the costs outweigh the benefits. Such complex political and ideological opposition, in addition to the previously mentioned cultural objections, can make the claim for promoting and protecting undercover investigations even more challenging than the legal, moral, and ethical complaints.

## 1.4 THE FIRST AMENDMENT AND UNDERCOVER INVESTIGATIONS

Throughout this book, we examine undercover investigations and the critics of such information-gathering methods against the background of free speech theory and doctrine, ultimately arguing that there are strong reasons to embrace and protect undercover investigations as a critical piece of our speech and information infrastructure. To the extent that there are legal, moral, ethical, or cultural and political constraints on undercover investigations, we maintain there are compelling constitutional arguments for at least a qualified privilege to engage in the conduct necessary to carry them out successfully.

The vast majority of free speech law focuses on *outputs* – it examines what things count as "speech." The protection of expression is the most common explanation for the First Amendment, and thus questions arise as to when, if ever, the state can restrict communications. But an equally important element of our system of freedom of expression is facilitating the protection of *inputs* – the ability to access, acquire, compile, and construct information in ways that will promote the robust outputs that occupy more space in the freedom of expression debate. Without inputs, there can be no outputs; both are necessary to allow us to deliberate about critical political, social, and moral issues of public concern.

Nonetheless, historically, less attention has been paid to the First Amendment's protection of the ability of professional journalists, political activists, and others to gain access to information that both is newsworthy and informs public opinion as well as advances political, moral, and other debates about the course of our republic. Until recently, the structure of free speech doctrine imposed substantial barriers to recognizing a constitutional right to engage in some of the tactics that are key to carrying out undercover investigations. For example, the Supreme Court has never recognized any sort of blanket right of access for journalists or citizens to public proceedings, aside from cases recognizing a First Amendment access right to some types of criminal court proceedings.[95] Furthermore, the Court has never provided

---

[95] *Compare* Houchins v. KQED, Inc., 438 U.S. 1 (1978) (plurality opinion) (rejecting press's claim that it should have First Amendment right to access county jail to examine conditions) *with* Richmond Newspapers, Inc. v. Virginia, 448 U.S. 555 (1980) (upholding press's First Amendment right to gain access to criminal judicial proceedings).

much protection for journalists from legal orders requiring them to disclose their confidential sources.[96] Indeed, despite the existence of an independent freedom of the press located in the First Amendment, journalists do not have special protection from generally applicable laws at all. In addition, there is also typically no right of any person to gain access to another's private property for the purpose of engaging in speech. Taken together, this set of legal rules would suggest that there are important limits to the idea that the First Amendment might protect undercover investigation tactics.

Building on our earlier work, however, this book makes the social and legal case for a qualified constitutional right to engage in undercover investigations. Principles of government neutrality toward speech suggest that investigations, conducted within certain parameters or limits, should be constitutionally protected without regard to the ideological predisposition of the investigator. The neutrality principle is a strong force when it comes to evaluating the constitutionality of restrictions on communication, and should play a comparably strong role in assessing the validity of law governing undercover information-gathering techniques.

Beyond neutrality, there are three doctrinal building blocks on which we rest our assertions. First, we argue for an understanding of free speech that embraces the notion that conduct essential to producing speech is in many instances covered by the First Amendment's guarantees in the same way that the law protects acts of communicating the information that such conduct discovers.[97] Second, we maintain that certain types of lies – what we have called "investigative deceptions" – also constitute "speech" that deserves to fall within the scope and protection of the Free Speech Clause. This contention has found great support in more recent years from the Supreme Court's decision in *United States v. Alvarez*, in which the Court struck down a federal law making it a crime to lie about having been awarded high military honors as a violation of the First Amendment.[98] Third, our analysis also supports the claim that the acts of photography, audio recording, and visual recording are all components of expression that must be protected from government regulation because they are expressive in and of themselves and also are critical precursors to the later publication of such information to the broader public. We therefore argue that there is a First Amendment right to engage in such documentation of events in public (as when a protestor uses their cell phone to record a police officer engaged in the use of excessive force)[99] and, more controversially, even in private, so long as the person doing the recording is lawfully present and the conduct or things that the

[96] Branzburg v. Hayes, 408 U.S. 665 (1972).
[97] *See, e.g.*, Citizens United v. Fed. Election Comm'n, 558 U.S. 310 (2010).
[98] United States v. Alvarez, 567 U.S. 709 (2012) (plurality opinion).
[99] *See, e.g.*, Glik v. Cunniffe, 655 F.3d 78, 82–83 (1st Cir. 2011); Am. C.L. Union of Ill. v. Alvarez, 679 F.3d 583, 595 (7th Cir. 2012); Fields v. City of Philadelphia, 862 F.3d 353, 356 (3d Cir. 2017).

person is photographing or recording is a matter of public concern that advances other values promoted by the freedom of speech.[100]

Through a comprehensive exploration of free speech theory and doctrine, this book will suggest that there is room for a more capacious understanding of the law that would protect a limited privilege to engage in false statements of fact to gain access to private property as well as a right to engage in nonconsensual video recording on the property of others, so long as both activities are directed toward investigating and disclosing matters of broad public concern. It provides a road map for understanding the place of undercover investigations in free speech doctrine as we progress through the twenty-first century.

[100] *Wasden*, 878 F.3d at 1203–05.

2

# Evolving Journalistic Ethical Standards Regarding
# Undercover Investigations

## 2.1 INTRODUCTION

In Chapter 1, we referenced a *Chicago Sun-Times* investigation of local government corruption, one of the most extensive and controversial undercover investigations conducted by American journalists in modern times. In that investigation, spearheaded by reporters Pam Zekman and Zay Smith, the newspaper actually opened and operated a bar called the Mirage Tavern on Chicago's South Side.[1] The elaborate scheme was used to uncover corruption among Chicago's health and safety inspectors, who were revealed to be taking bribes in exchange for not reporting local city code violations. The investigation resulted in an extensive twenty-five-part series in the *Sun-Times* detailing the extent of local corruption.

While there was much praise for the Mirage investigation, there was also substantial criticism of the newspaper's methods. Nowhere was this clearer than in the deliberations over whether the *Sun-Times* should receive the Pulitzer Prize for special local reporting for these stories. The Mirage stories were selected by a nominating jury as a finalist for this prize, but the Pulitzer advisory board voted to give it to another finalist.[2] Board members were divided on the Mirage investigation because a majority of them questioned the methods, and implicitly the ethics, of the elaborate subterfuge at the center of the reporters' investigation. James Reston of the *New York Times* is said to have articulated a distinction between "pretense" and "deception," with the former being permissible but the latter being out of bounds. The difference is that pretense is passive – deception by omission, allowing an investigation's targets to infer something that is not true. Deception involves a journalist's active conduct intending to mislead a subject. With regard to the Mirage stories, the *Washington Post*'s Ben Bradlee has been quoted as saying,

---

[1]  ZAY N. SMITH & PAMELA ZEKMAN, THE MIRAGE (1979).
[2]  The accounts of the Pulitzer advisory board's debate are drawn from Steve Robinson, *Pulitzers: Was the Mirage a Deception?*, 18 COLUM. JOURNALISM REV. 14 (1979).

"It's biblical, man. How can newspapers fight for honesty and integrity when they themselves are less than honest in getting a story? Would you want a *cop* to pose as a *newspaperman?*" Another advisory board member likened the *Sun-Times* investigation to entrapment, implying that the reporters had actively encouraged the misconduct they uncovered.

Other Pulitzer advisory board members were less skeptical about the propriety of the Mirage investigation, and many of them conceded that they had permitted their own journalists to conceal their identities to get a story. Moreover, several members of the nominating jury and the advisory board indicated that they were "impressed by the safeguards the paper took to avoid soliciting illegal behavior." There was also some discomfort about reporters conducting undercover investigations engaging in unlawful conduct themselves. In the Mirage investigation, *Sun-Times* reporters did pay bribes to health and safety inspectors, though they took steps to protect themselves from liability. In their detailed account of the investigation, Smith and Zekman described how they addressed many of these concerns. First, they pre-cleared their investigation with the Illinois Department of Law Enforcement to ensure that they did not run afoul of Illinois law requiring witnesses to a crime to report it to the police.[3] They could not partner with the Chicago Police Department because it was one of the targets of the corruption investigation. To address concerns about entrapment, they studied Illinois law, which did not make it illegal to merely afford a person the opportunity to engage in criminal conduct.[4] Finally, they made sure to avoid violating any other provisions of state law. Because they were recording people in a public place, there was no concern about invasion of privacy. Although Illinois prohibited secret audio recordings of another person, it did not forbid still photography or video recording, so the reporters used soundless video and still photos to document the events they were observing.[5]

Even those who supported the *Sun-Times*'s efforts, however, believed that this type of undercover investigation should be used only as a last resort, where other fact-gathering tactics had failed and there was no other way to obtain the information needed for the story. The critics suggested that the Mirage story could have been investigated without deception. But as Zekman argued, if a Chicago bar owner had spoken with reporters about bribing inspectors, they would soon be out of business.

In contrast, at least two prior Pulitzer Prize recipients had engaged in affirmative deception by posing as employees of the investigative target to gather information for their stories, though they did not go to the lengths of the Mirage investigation. In both 1971 and 1973, Pulitzers were awarded to journalists from the *Sun-Times*'s crosstown rival, the *Chicago Tribune*, for stories done by journalists who concealed

[3]  SMITH & ZEKMAN, *supra* note 1, at 14.
[4]  *Id.* at 12.
[5]  *Id.* at 13.

their identities. The 1971 award went to the *Tribune*'s William Jones, who was hired to work on ambulance crews to expose the misconduct of private ambulance companies, which were rife with "mismanagement, welfare fraud, sadism and payoffs to police" at the expense of their patients.[6] The 1973 prize went to the *Tribune*'s staff for "uncovering flagrant violations of voting procedures in the primary election of March 21, 1972."[7] To gather information for that story, the *Tribune* had seventeen staff members along with eight outside investigators pose as Republican election judges and poll watchers.[8] Without a hint of irony (given the decision about the Mirage investigation), the Pulitzer Prize's official website currently reports on Jones's 1971 story with the subtitle "From Pulitzer's world to the muckraking era and far beyond, reporters often got the goods through guile and guise."[9]

The Mirage investigation and the dispute surrounding its ethical propriety reflects a long-standing and ongoing debate within the journalistic community: When, if ever, is it appropriate for a journalist to lie about their identity to gain access to people, places, and actions that are in the public interest to reveal? And when, if ever, is it permissible for a journalist to use a hidden camera or other recording equipment?

This chapter explores how this professional ethics debate has unfolded in the United States, how we have gone through periods when such investigations are more and less accepted, and the current contours of the discussion. The varying views of journalistic ethical standards over time is not surprising given that such understandings are likely to be historically and socially contingent. As Hazel Dicken-Garcia has written, "notions of right and wrong journalistic conduct at any given time are products of dominant cultural strains."[10] What she means is that changes in culture may lead to changes in how social institutions, such as the press, function. For example, in times where other governmental checks on misconduct are relatively weak, the press's role (and the public's view of whether that role is acceptable) may correspondingly be transformed. Thus, she continues, "Ideas of standards governing the conduct of the tasks of social institutions are related to these perceptions and will likewise change over time."[11]

Although journalism is only one of the several contexts in which undercover investigations take place, it is a field in which there has been the most extensive internal examination of the ethics of the tactics required to carry out such

---

[6]  *Chicago Tribune Goes Undercover for Stunning Exposé*, PULITZER PRIZES, www.pulitzer.org/article/chicago-tribune-goes-undercover-stunning-expose (last visited Nov. 6, 2022).

[7]  *Staff of Chicago Tribune*, PULITZER PRIZES, www.pulitzer.org/winners/staff-9 (last visited Nov. 6, 2022).

[8]  JAMES L. AUCOIN, THE EVOLUTION OF AMERICAN INVESTIGATIVE JOURNALISM 96 (2005).

[9]  THE PULITZER PRIZES, *supra* note 6.

[10]  HAZEL DICKEN-GARCIA, JOURNALISTIC STANDARDS IN NINETEENTH-CENTURY AMERICA 7 (1989).

[11]  *Id.*

investigations. Accordingly, it is a good source to begin any broader consideration of the ethics of undercover investigations.

## 2.2 COMPETING ETHICAL FRAMEWORKS

When discussing professional ethics in journalism, we must start with an overview of different schools of thought about major frameworks for such an inquiry. As in many areas, there is no single ethical model that drives all journalists' decisions in practice about what tactics are ethically permissible. Rather, there are competing models or frameworks against which journalists may choose to measure their own practices. While a complete exploration of these models goes beyond the scope of this book, we offer here a general overview of these frameworks and then offer our own normative argument about the one that most clearly supports undercover investigations. Of course, those who disagree with our framework are likely to also disagree with our ethical assessment of undercover investigations in journalistic practice.

First, as in any discussion of professional ethics, it is important to acknowledge that there are important distinctions between what is "right" or "wrong" from a legal standpoint, an ethical perspective, and a moral view. What is legal may not be ethical or moral; what is ethical or moral may nonetheless not be legal. Legal restraints on a practice are defined by positive law, and violations of those standards may lead to criminal punishment or civil liability. Ethical restrictions typically come from a set of internally established professional norms, such as the Model Rules of Professional Conduct for attorneys. Violation of these norms may lead to professional sanctions where there exists an enforcement body. Journalism is not a profession in the traditional sense, in that there is no formal mechanism for enforcing any ethical standards. That is not to say that journalistic ethical codes are meaningless, because violating them may lead to a reporter being fired by their employer and to public and professional approbation.

For purposes of this material, we define journalistic ethics as a set of governing ethical principles that are widely accepted by the profession, even if they are not each universally held. We concern ourselves in this chapter primarily with journalism ethics, though legal considerations sometimes enter the discussion. Thus, we distinguish between ethics and law in the sense that some may regard a journalist as unethical, even if they would agree that their practices are not unlawful. We think that the law informs morality in this realm, but journalistic ethics should not be equated with pure questions of legality. Moral values define one's own personal sense of what it means to be a "good" person. Sometimes, but not always, whether something is unlawful may shape decisions about whether it is also unethical or immoral in a particular situation.

Professor Stephen J. A. Ward has described journalism ethics as "a species of applied media ethics that investigates the 'micro' problems of what individual journalists should do in particular situations, and the 'macro' problems of what news media should do, given their role in society."[12] These questions should be evaluated "in light of the fundamental public purposes and social responsibilities of journalism."[13]

Professor Ward has observed that there have been four normative theories that have dominated journalism over time and that a fifth "mixed media" model is emerging with the expansion of nonprofessional journalists employing interactive multimedia as their primary vehicle. One normative model is liberal theory, under which journalism is viewed as an independent institution "that informs citizens and acts as a watchdog on government and abuses of power."[14] This theory supports strong views of freedom of the press from censorship and other forms of restraint that deter publication of news.

The second model is grounded in objectivity and social responsibility. This school of thought developed as a response to dissatisfaction with a completely unregulated press and evolved at a time when most news was published by a small number of profit-making news companies owned by a few wealthy individuals whose interests may have been more aligned with profit than with informing the public and serving as a watchdog.[15] The aspiration of journalistic objectivity began to take shape in the early 1900s and was influential through the mid-twentieth century, around the same time journalism associations began to publish their own ethical codes, as discussed below. These codes tended to focus on objectivity, independence from outside governmental or business influences, and a sharp distinction between news reporting and opinion pieces. This model led to under-standings that journalists had an ethical duty to publish the accurate and compre-hensive truth, but also had to do so in a responsible manner that considered possible harms to the subjects of their stories as well as a duty to be accountable to the public for their publication decisions. This objectivity model was closely aligned with social responsibility theory, which also posited that the journalism profession had a duty to inform the public and impose on itself a professional obligation to carry out an important news reporting function that helped promote an exchange of ideas.[16]

A third normative model is one of interpretation and activism – one that stresses that the press should not only inform the public with accurate and truthful facts, but also interpret the news to help explain complex issues and the significance of events.[17] One might see news articles today labeled as "news analysis" to delineate them from pure fact reporting. The theory of an activist press goes a bit further and suggests that part of the duty to inform includes helping the public to challenge the

---

[12]  Stephen J. A. Ward, *Journalism Ethics, in* THE HANDBOOK OF JOURNALISM STUDIES 296 (Karin Wahl-Jorgensen & Thomas Hanitzsch eds., 1st ed. 2008).
[13]  *Id.*
[14]  *Id.* at 298.
[15]  *Id.*
[16]  *Id.* at 299.
[17]  *Id.*

status quo and pursue social causes and reforms.[18] To an important degree, then, the interpretation and activism model eschews complete objectivity, but rather understands that some analysis and persuasion requires presenting the news in a manner to support a particular understanding on the part of the public. But as Professor Ward observes,

> Today, many journalists see themselves as some combination of informer, interpreter and advocate. Traditional values, such as accuracy, are not completely jettisoned. Even the most vocal muckraker or activist journalist insists that their reports are factually accurate, although they reject neutrality.... Rather, they see their facts as embedded in interpretive narratives that draw conclusions. For both interpretive and activist journalism, the main ethical questions are: What are its norms and principles, if objectivity is not the ideal? What ethical theory can restrain the possible abuses or excesses of non-objective journalism?[19]

The fourth ethical model is one of community and care, which may include a perspective from feminist ethics of care. This approach places greater emphasis on journalists minimizing harm to others in the community (subjects, sources, etc.) and shows less concern with the obligation to inform the public at all costs. In contrast with the liberal theory perspective, the community and care approach "stress[es] the impact of journalism on communal values and caring relationships."[20]

At the same time, there are meaningful criticisms of these different approaches. First, there are questions about whether two central tenets of journalism ethics, truth and objectivity, are truly attainable. As Professor Ward summarizes them, there are three main critiques: objectivity is too demanding of a standard, and is therefore a myth; objectivity should not be a central goal because "it forces writers into restricted formats," restraining them from engaging even in analysis and interpretation; and objectivity restricts a free press, which would be better served by allowing the competition of different models of journalism.[21] Particularly relevant to our discussion, early twentieth-century muckrakers rejected neutrality in reporting, which would have impeded their goal of exposing social problems and facilitating reform.

Another criticism of the ethical models in journalism is that they were borne out of Enlightenment norms, making them overly focused on normative preferences by white, male, individualistic thinkers.[22] These critiques tend to come from feminist, postmodern, communitarian, and postcolonial perspectives, and argue for a broader understanding of what is ethical.

---

[18] *Id.*
[19] *Id.* at 299–300.
[20] *Id.* at 300.
[21] *Id.* at 302. Notwithstanding these critiques, Professor Ward contends that "skepticism about journalistic objectivity has not solved any serious ethical problems." *Id.*
[22] *Id.* at 303.

As we discuss the debate over the ethics of undercover investigations throughout the American news media's different eras, we argue from an approach based on utilitarianism – "the view that the morally right action is the action that produces the most good."[23] That is, we regard the greater public good of providing the public with information that promotes public discourse and transparency as outweighing, in most cases, any sort of psychic or autonomy harm to the investigation's target. Sometimes that calculation comes through the interpretation and application of legal standards to journalists who have engaged in such investigations. But since we are primarily concerned with ethics rather than law in this chapter of the book, we use those legal cases only to inform what might count as moral harms to the subjects of undercover investigations in this discussion.

Utilitarianism is not itself a general model of journalism ethics, but we can see how its application to undercover investigations is consistent with at least two of the major ethical frameworks. First, such investigations are certainly consistent with liberal theory's emphasis on the media's role in informing the public and serving as watchdogs on government and abuses of power. Many undercover investigations are focused on large private sector entities with a great deal of economic and political power. Advocating for protection of such investigations therefore addresses a contemporary academic critique of First Amendment doctrine, which is that it does not account for power imbalances among speakers. As Professor Genevieve Lakier has articulated it, "contemporary First Amendment doctrine ... like Lochner-era freedom of contract doctrine ... [has become] a powerful sword for reinforcing the power of the propertied and a shield against government efforts at redistribution."[24]

Next, undercover investigations seem to be consistent with the interpretation and activism framework for journalism ethics. These investigations not only help inform the public, but may also inspire challenges to the status quo and efforts toward social reform. Indeed, that is the goal of many undercover investigators, whether within the journalism field or not.

The utilitarian approach fits less well with the objectivity and social responsibility framework or the community and care model, both of which place greater emphasis on concerns about harms to the subjects and sources of stories and minimizing harms to community. Even here, however, we can find some room for a utilitarian argument. Those models do not necessarily categorically reject undercover investigations, but just require active consideration of relational harms to others (sources, subjected, etc.). In later chapters, we acknowledge that the deceptions and nonconsensual recording often used to conduct undercover investigations may cause

---

[23] *The History of Utilitarianism*, STANFORD ENCYCLOPEDIA OF PHIL. (Mar. 27, 2009), https://plato.stanford.edu/entries/utilitarianism-history/.

[24] Genevieve Lakier, *The First Amendment's Real* Lochner *Problem*, 87 U. CHI. L. REV. 1241, 1245 (2020). *See also* Joseph Blocher, *Free Speech and Justified True Belief*, 133 HARV. L. REV. 439, 452 (2019) (observing that massive resource inequalities distort the First Amendment marketplace of ideas).

some harms; it is not that we reject the notion that harms should be considered, it is that we think those harms are often intangible, overstated, and frequently outweighed by the larger social benefit from the exposure of hidden truths from the public eye.

## 2.3 ETHICAL STANDARDS ACROSS THE DIFFERENT ERAS OF AMERICAN JOURNALISM

The remainder of this chapter describes the different periods of American journalism, the extent to which undercover investigations played any role during these periods, and any corresponding ethical debates about the use of investigative deceptions and secret recordings that arose.

Over these historical periods, there is clear evidence that undercover investigations have led to the disclosure and dissemination of information that was vital to the public interest. That is, the stories produced as a result of such tactics led to the publication of newsworthy material that promoted public discourse and is credited with catalyzing meaningful legal reforms, as well as toppling politicians and bureaucrats. Their instrumental value is underscored by the reality that in most if not all cases, the information would never have come to light but for the undercover investigations. Despite the fact that libel suits were a threat to newspapers and reporters conducting these investigations, in most instances there was no dispute about the truthfulness of the facts that they had uncovered. And finally, these investigations were driven primarily by the intent to engage in the core activity of newsgathering. From a traditional understanding of the role of the press, these are all considered to be valuable and protected functions.

Of course, not all investigations changed public opinion, much less led to meaningful law and policy reforms. Whether the investigations are effective in creating public concern or action is contingent on public attitudes toward and acceptance of the media's credibility, something that has been falling in recent years.[25]

Critics of undercover investigations have long contended that they are ethically questionable, even if they lead to newsworthy information. For some this might be because the use of deceptions is viewed as categorically impermissible and unethical, that it violates principles of objectivity. But even for more consequentialist-minded persons, there are claims that the harm outweighs the benefits because the conduct involved harms subjects, sources, and the community.

It is also important to emphasize from the outset that there are a number of *potential* ethical considerations concerning journalists' use of undercover investigative techniques. By definition, these investigations typically involve (1) deception, either overt or implicit, about the reporters' identity, professional affiliation, and

[25] Jonathan M. Ladd, Why Americans Hate the Media and How it Matters 65–107 (2012).

motives, to gain access to people, places, and things to acquire information whose disclosure is in the public interest and (2) some form of documenting such information that involves video recording, audio recording, or still photography that is made without the consent of those who are recorded or have legal control over the places where the recording takes place. There appears to be a great deal of ambivalence about such tactics within the journalism profession, as illustrated by Peter Benjaminson and David Anderson in their book about investigative reporting:

> One of the most popular ways to do this [investigate government agencies] is for a reporter to get on the receiving end of one of these institutions and write about what it's like. Several reporters who could pass for eighteen-year-olds have enrolled themselves in high schools and written stories that had school administrators and bureaucrats explaining themselves for months afterward. Others have had themselves committed to mental institutions and have written revealing stories about conditions inside. Reporters have taken jobs in automobile factories, as ambulance drivers, in garment-district sweatshops, and as helpers to drug dealers preparing dope for distribution, to name but a few. But such participatory journalism is not always necessary or desirable.[26]

For critics of these investigative techniques, there appear to be a handful of recurring concerns. These concerns are framed as legal interests and are often also used by governments to justify their attempts to legally prohibit such investigations, but to the extent that they also impose harm on the investigation's targets, they can also be understood as ethical harms. That is, these investigations may not sufficiently account for the impact on the investigation's subjects, may impair communal relationships, and may ignore the importance of caring for others. This relational approach suggests that although journalists have a duty to their audience, they should consider the impact of their reporting on others in the community as well.

First, there is a claim that undercover investigations are, or could lead to, an invasion of *privacy* for those who are under investigation (or their employees). Intrusions of this sort are viewed as indefensible, even if matters of considerable public concern are exposed. Second and closely related, some critics argue that such investigations involve accessing the property of another in a manner that is tantamount to a *trespass*, at least where journalists gain access to private property not otherwise open to the public to conduct their investigations. Third, some opponents claim that undercover investigations premised on deception are a type of *fraud*, though it is questionable whether the publication of truthful information causes legally recoverable money damages under the law of fraud. Fourth, there is a professional criticism of investigative deceptions and secret recordings that suggests that such conduct *undermines the integrity of journalism* because, as a profession that seeks truth, journalists should never lie. That is, they claim that journalists who

---

[26] Peter Benjaminson & David Anderson, Investigative Reporting 19 (2d ed. 1990).

engage in these tactics are tainted by using deception, even if the facts they uncover and the stories they report are true. Lies, it is argued, can never be justified by their results. As we discuss below, this position is consistent with the views of some philosophers, such as Immanuel Kant, who argue that lying violates basic duties to others without regard to the benefits they may produce.

A related critique suggests that when journalists go undercover, they become part of the story instead of being a detached outside observer. Finally, at least since the Progressive Era, those who oppose undercover investigations have contended that the resulting exposés harm journalistic reputations and are driven not by purely altruistic journalistic intent but by the profit motive to sell more newspapers.

It should be noted, however, that within this broader discussion, there is also a definitional dispute about what it means for a journalist to lie or deceive their investigative target. Recall James Reston's distinction between pretense and deception, for example.

Throughout the historical periods from the Progressive Era forward, there has been a consistent debate over the journalistic ethics of undercover investigations. Even today this ethical debate remains unresolved. In part, this is because there is no ethical standard that is binding on all American journalists. Individual publications have written standards, but those apply only internally to their employees. Professional journalism organizations also have articulated standards, but they are not enforceable in the same way as, for example, the ethics rules in the legal and medical professions.

### 2.3.1 *American Newspapers at the Beginning of the Republic*

Although the framers of the Constitution embedded press rights in the text of the First Amendment, their views on the value of the press varied. It's interesting to compare, for example, how Thomas Jefferson's impressions of the press changed from the period before the Constitution was ratified with after he became the President.[27] His pre-Constitution views were quite supportive of the press and reflected an understanding of its institutional role in informing the public. As he wrote then, "were it left to me to decide whether we should have a government without newspapers, or newspapers without a government, I would not hesitate a moment to prefer the latter."[28] But after he became President, he demonstrated antipathy toward the press. He once suggested that "the man who never looks into a

---

[27] Much of the historical material in this chapter is drawn mostly from five sources: DICKEN-GARCIA, *supra* note 10; AUCOIN, *supra* note 8; THE ROUTLEDGE COMPANION TO NEWS AND JOURNALISM (Stuart Allan ed., 2010); BROOKE KROEGER, UNDERCOVER REPORTING: THE TRUTH ABOUT DECEPTION (2012); and LADD, *supra* note 25.

[28] Letter from Thomas Jefferson to Edward Carrington, Delegate to the Continental Congress (Jan. 16, 1787), *in* THOMAS JEFFERSON: WRITINGS 879, 880 (Merrill Peterson ed., 1984).

newspaper is better informed than he who reads them[,] inasmuch as he who knows nothing is nearer to truth than he whose mind is filled with falsehoods and errors. He who reads nothing will still learn the great facts, and the details are all false."[29] Other political leaders, including George Washington, similarly became disillusioned about the press, complaining about its lack of truth and fairness.[30] Outside observers also had low opinions of the press. Alexis de Tocqueville, for example, once said that "American journalists have a low social status, their education is only sketchy, and their thoughts are often vulgarly expressed."[31]

In modern times, one might chalk up these criticisms of the press to a typical politician's complaint whenever the press plays its important institutional role as a check on the government. But the state of newspapers in the early years of the republic was far different from what would exist by the twentieth century. Indeed, for the most part, the average person today would not even recognize newspapers from the founding era of the United States. The "press" had not yet developed an independent institutional identity. Newspapers during this era were largely partisan, serving as mouthpieces for the political parties rather than an independent source of information and news analysis. In fact, the newspapers in this era received much of their financial backing from the political parties. Some commentators have labeled this the era of the "party press." Professional, independent journalism had not yet emerged.

It might at first seem puzzling that the framers of our Constitution had such a dim view of the press yet embedded an explicit textual provision in the First Amendment guaranteeing its freedom. This is most likely because they viewed the press as an important propaganda tool for their respective parties. As Jonathan Ladd has suggested, "their support occurred in the context of not only Enlightenment political thought but also a recent history when newspapers either eschewed politics or were useful subordinate tools of the framers' own political movement."[32] Accordingly, it is probably the case that the parties were concerned that when their political opponents were in power, they might try to restrict the other party's newspapers.

Both because newspapers played such a partisan role and since reporters were not engaged in any real forms of newsgathering and reporting during this generation, there was not yet any such thing as an undercover investigation. Accordingly, there was no sense of any ethical quandaries about such investigations during this era.

---

[29]  Letter from Thomas Jefferson, President, to John Norvell (June 11, 1807), *in* 11 THE WRITINGS OF THOMAS JEFFERSON 222, 225 (Andrew A. Lipscomb & Albert Ellery Bergh eds., Definitive ed. 1905).
[30]  LADD, *supra* note 25, at 27–28.
[31]  *Id.* at 27.
[32]  *Id.* at 21–22.

### 2.3.2 *American Newspapers from the Early 1800s through the Civil War*

Researchers differ in their opinions about when journalism began to develop into a professional undertaking independent of the political parties and the government. Most indications are that it was a gradual process that occurred over many decades. By the mid-nineteenth century, newspapers began to transform into vehicles of newsgathering and reporting – their focus was more on informing the people than on spreading partisan ideas. This resulted from changes in the financing and structure of the industry as well as a rethinking of the public function served by newspapers. The press moved away from parties as a primary funding source to other sources of revenue, including advertising. Courting a large audience by promising truth-seeking, objective coverage was, at least in part, a financial decision; the more papers sold, the more advertising revenue generated. During this era, the "penny press" emerged, broadening access to newspapers from the political and social elite to the average citizen. An orientation toward reform began to take root and more news institutions began to view themselves as a vehicle for promoting democracy and the common good of the people.[33] In a related development, by the second half of the century, the press was viewed as an institution that had the power and ability to both create and shape public opinion.[34]

These evolving conceptions of newspapers' roles also led to changes in how reporters worked. It is during this period that newspaper reporting first became a full-time job. The work also began to more closely resemble what we would now view as what journalists do; because informing the public was now a primary function, reporters had to engage in newsgathering to support their stories. This meant that seeking information from primary sources, such as eyewitnesses to newsworthy events, became more important. This led reporters to engage in more interviewing of sources and digging for other firsthand information for their stories.

Those newsgathering techniques also involved the incorporation of new technologies. As reporting news to the public was viewed as a central function of newspapers, the speed with which news was conveyed became more urgent. Thus, the telegraph became an important device for transmitting news quickly, and the first news wire services, such as the Associated Press, were established. Illustrations did not initially appear regularly in journalism due to the cost and scarcity of cameras in the early and middle nineteenth century.[35] However, this changed after the Civil War – as the appearance of photographs and technology began to improve, so too did the demand for images in the media.[36] Photojournalism began to grow and expand, and by 1900, illustrations were expected

---

[33] DICKEN-GARCIA, *supra* note 10, at 44.
[34] *Id.* at 48.
[35] Grant Piper, *The First Photograph Ever Used in News*, EXPLORING HIST. (July 2, 2021), https://medium.com/exploring-history/the-first-photograph-ever-used-in-news-e87fa3f9eebf.
[36] *Id.*

rather than a cherished novelty.[37] And though it would be some time before institutions would begin to develop anything resembling professional standards for journalists, reporters developed a norm of relying on multiple sources for their stories.[38]

None of this is to say that party-controlled newspapers disappeared, and indeed even by the onset of the Civil War, 80% of newspapers were still partisan.[39] But the Civil War was another transformational event in the evolution of the American newspaper. Because of the war's salience to the average citizen and because its events were unfolding in distant locations, newspaper reporting on the war served the function of informing the public in a manner that no other institution could. To carry out this role, reporters had to find new ways of gathering information, beginning in the period leading up to the war. Some reporters traveled with the troops so they could not only witness events personally but have access to multiple sources.[40] Today we might view this practice as "embedding."

One noteworthy form of newsgathering that arose during the Civil War era was undercover reporting.[41] As described in Chapter 1, some journalists and political activists hid their true identities in order to gather and disseminate information about the abominable conditions of American people who were enslaved, and their reports most likely strongly influenced the abolition debate. Also, as the Civil War drew closer, reporters from Northern newspapers wanted to gain direct access to the activities in the South. While reporters from Southern newspapers did not try to conceal the identity of their reporters, Northern reporters had much to fear if they ventured into the South. In the South, there were suspicions that Northern journalists in their midst were "Lincoln spies" who were secretly gathering information that might have threatened the Confederacy's security. Thus, there was legitimate concern on the part of Northern newspaper editors about sending their correspondents to the South, with one Southern newspaper editor implying that those Northern reporters would be hanged. Thus, "Even before the election of 1860, some of the New York papers instituted the practice of concealing the identities of their Southern correspondents."[42]

For example, the *New York Times* sent reporter George Forrester Williams into the South disguised as a young English tourist who was curious about American politics and learning about the Southern states. The *Times* went so far as to acquire clothing from London to help establish the legitimacy of Williams's cover. Some

---

[37] *Id.*

[38] DICKEN-GARCIA, *supra* note 10, at 54–55. Though there were no such standards, some in the industry began calling for them as early as 1856. *Id.* at 183.

[39] *Id.* at 40.

[40] *Id.* at 55.

[41] The material about Northern journalists reporting in the South is drawn from J. CUTLER ANDREWS, THE NORTH REPORTS THE CIVIL WAR 6–34 (1985).

[42] *Id.* at 15.

reporters escaped the South in disguise as suspicion that they were Northern journalists grew. Journalists from the North were also provided with "campaign outfits" when they were assigned to military units, though it is unclear whether they disguised themselves as Southern soldiers as well.[43] As far as we can tell, the reporters who investigated the conditions of slavery in the antebellum South, and those who reported from the South during the war, are the first documented instances of American journalists obscuring their identities and using subterfuge to facilitate their newsgathering. These may have served as models for future journalists' investigations.

Not only were Northern reporters in danger of being identified by their presence, but also they had to take care that the news they reported was not intercepted by Southern officials, who would then be able to determine their true identities. Accordingly, they disguised their correspondence as well. The *Times*'s Williams sent different parts of stories to his friends, who would then pass them on to the newspaper. Even those reports included mixed-up dates and fictitious names to minimize the chance of detection. Albert D. Richardson of the *New York Tribune* sent his reports disguised as business letters to New York financial and commercial companies, who would similarly forward them to his paper. He also had to incorporate fictitious names and places and develop different types of codes, including one in which his editors understood that when words appeared in brackets they were meant to convey the exact opposite. The main point of discussing these episodes in American journalism both before and during the Civil War is that use of deception and subterfuge was necessary to gather information of public concern. Thus, undercover investigations have a longer heritage than might currently be recognized by most observers.

In many ways, the press's role in reporting the Civil War solidified its institutional role as a gatherer and disseminator of information. After the war, the newspaper industry again began to change with the ascension of Joseph Pulitzer and William Randolph Hearst as highly visible rival newspaper editors. But there were both important improvements to and valid critiques of the press during this era. On the positive side, more attention was paid to professionalizing newsgathering and reporting. Pulitzer viewed professionalism in journalism to be an important step. He urged his editors to pay attention to accuracy and fairness in their stories. After his death, and because of his financial support, the Columbia School of Journalism opened its doors in 1912.

On the negative side, newspapers during this era were often accused of engaging in "yellow" journalism, sensationalistic reporting designed to sell newspapers rather than emphasizing journalistic integrity. This was reflected in the fact that papers began to pay increasing attention to celebrity news and gossip, stories about everyday crime, and other matters that were not viewed as central to hard news. At the same

---

[43] *Compare* DICKEN-GARCIA, *supra* note 10, at 55 *with* ANDREWS, *supra* note 41, at 20.

time, in order to gain information for those stories, reporters sometimes engaged in intrusive newsgathering tactics that some viewed as invasions of privacy. And while Hearst may be more closely associated with sensationalism, Pulitzer's publications also engaged in the same type of reporting as the two rivals engaged in stiff competition for readers.

There do not appear to be any specific ethical concerns raised about the types of undercover investigations conducted by Northern reporters during and around the time of the Civil War. Perhaps this is because the nation's focus was on the war or because awareness of these investigations was not widespread. Furthermore, the types of privacy concerns mentioned above seem to have been directed at the practice of snooping into ordinary people's private lives and publishing stories about them and not toward the tactic of investigative deceptions to gain access to information for news articles.

### 2.3.3 *American Newspapers around the Time of the Progressive Era*

After the Civil War and into the early twentieth century, the nation was transformed in multiple ways that affected journalism. There were technological innovations, most notably the development and expansion of a national railway system, which led to increased mobility, allowing publishers to circulate their newspapers more widely and reporters to travel to their stories' locations. These innovations also spurred the industrialization of the American economy, which led to an expanding national market, but also created new and challenging social problems. During this period, there was increasing concern about workplace safety, environmental hazards resulting from industrialization, and concerns associated with a rapidly growing immigrant population, among other issues.

At the same time, newspapers' roles continued to evolve in material ways, while criticisms from the end of the previous era were amplified. On what many, though not all, would regard as a positive side, this is the period in American journalism when more reporters began to engage in investigative journalism through undercover investigations that involved deception. All sorts of pejorative labels were placed on such investigations by critics hoping to undermine their legitimacy. The most commonly invoked term was "muckrakers," a term first attributed to President Theodore Roosevelt.[44] Although the term is now frequently associated with transparency and accountability, Roosevelt did not initially mean the term to have such connotations. But Roosevelt's relationship with the muckrakers was complicated and he was not always critical of undercover work.[45] Indeed, at times Roosevelt

---

[44] Mark Feldstein, *Muckrakers, in* 3 Encyclopedia of Journalism 919 (Christopher H. Sterling ed., 2009).

[45] *Muckraker*, Theodore Roosevelt Ctr. at Dickinson State Univ., www .theodorerooseveltcenter.org/Learn-About-TR/TR-Encyclopedia/Culture%20and%20Society/ Muckraker (last visited Nov. 6, 2022).

publicly recognized the achievements of investigative journalists, praising them as a critical component to social reform and noting that "men with the muckrakes are often indispensable to the well-being of society."[46] These muckrakers, like Upton Sinclair, are often credited in part with Roosevelt's political rise. But as is the case with many examples over history, undercover investigations seem like a great journalistic approach unless you happen to be the one targeted and exposed by an investigation.

It should be noted that muckraking is a term that was applied to a wide range of investigative reporting, not just to undercover investigations. For instance, writers such as Lincoln Steffens and Ida Tarbell were also dogged investigative journalists, but did not use deceptive tactics to gain access to the sources for their stories. Perhaps the leading forum for muckraking journalism during this era was *McClure's* magazine, which pioneered investigative journalism and was a strong influence on the profession.[47] The photographer Jacob Riis used photojournalism to document the plight of the poor in New York City, resulting in an exposé of the city's slums published by Scribner's and later, in an expanded version, in his famous book *How the Other Half Lives: Studies among the Tenements of New York* in 1890.[48] Photography played an essential role in memorializing social ills and complementing the newspaper stories' narratives exposing such difficult truths.[49]

Muckraking journalism is also often linked to the politics of the Progressive Era. Much of the reporting was consistent with reform movements in that it exposed the excesses of capitalism, the conditions of sweatshop labor and life in the inner city, and other prevailing social problems. This may have spawned additional attacks on muckrakers based on powerful antisocialist sentiments. Increasing literacy rates, along with the technological innovations discussed above, helped expand the audience for these stories and also, presumably, their influence on public opinion.

Though the muckraking label was often intended to denigrate reporters who engaged in such investigations, these journalists came to embrace the name. But critics tried to diminish the legitimacy of undercover investigations by labeling the practice "stunt" journalism or "detective" journalism. These names were meant to attack the reporters' credibility by suggesting both that they were driven by their newspapers' profit motives and that their sensationalistic nature was distinguishable from legitimate forms of journalistic reporting. This may have led some to be more dismissive about the fact that some of these investigations revealed serious information that would otherwise have been hidden from public view.[50] In addition, because many of these journalists were women emerging in a field previously

---

[46] *"Muchraker": 2 Meanings*, N.Y. TIMES (Apr. 10, 1985), www.nytimes.com/1985/04/10/us/muchraker-2-meanings.html.
[47] *See generally* HAROLD S. WILSON, MCCLURE'S MAGAZINE AND THE MUCKRAKERS (1970).
[48] LAURIE C. HILLSTROM, THE MUCKRAKERS AND THE PROGRESSIVE ERA 128–31 (2009).
[49] AUCOIN, *supra* note 8, at 30.
[50] *Id.* at 3.

dominated by men, there may be a significant gendered component to these disparagements.

For those who did engage in overt or implicit forms of deceit to engage in newsgathering, it is difficult to dispute their effectiveness despite critiques about their tactics. Most accounts suggest that this period was the heyday for muckraking journalism. We have already recounted the efforts of Nellie Bly and Upton Sinclair in Chapter 1. But there are numerous examples from this era that are less well known. For example, Rheta Childe Dorr, who would later become a strong supporter of women's right to vote, conducted undercover investigations to gather information about working conditions for women in both the industrial and retail sectors.[51] Unfortunately, her work was then published in *Everybody's Magazine* under the byline of a male reporter. Ida M. Tarbell redefined investigative journalism through a nineteen-part series in *McClure's* magazine, a relentless indictment that brought down John D. Rockefeller, Sr., and in effect broke up his Standard Oil Company's monopoly.[52] And Lincoln Steffens, who uncovered evidence of political corruption by businessmen pursuing special privileges, published articles later collected as *The Shame of the Cities*, a piece more like a sociological case study than an extraordinary journalistic exposé.[53]

### 2.3.3.1 Ethical Concerns during the Progressive Era

As already explained, newspapers were not primarily in the business of newsgathering until the mid-1800s. In one sense, printed newspapers were really just a profit-seeking project of printing press operations; early newspapers did not gather news so much as they simply set into type and printed the "news" that persons would bring into their shop.

Thus, it is probably unsurprising that ethical standards had not emerged in the early periods of US journalism. In fact, the first call for professional standards does not appear to have been made until the editor George Lunt did so in 1856, and the first actual code of conduct was not published until the late 1890s.[54] These early efforts tended to be relatively broad and aspirational, rather than addressing specific newsgathering tactics.

Thus, when undercover investigations began to gain traction and produce major exposés in the late 1800s, there was no widely accepted set of standards that journalists might consult.[55] The lack of standards did not just pertain to undercover

---

[51] *Id.* at 45.

[52] Gilbert King, *The Woman Who Took on the Tycoon*, SMITHSONIAN MAG. (July 5, 2012), www .smithsonianmag.com/history/the-woman-who-took-on-the-tycoon-651396/.

[53] The Editors of Encyclopaedia Britannica, *Lincoln Steffens: American Journalist*, ENCYCLOPAEDIA BRITANNICA (Aug. 5, 2022), www.britannica.com/biography/Lincoln-Steffens.

[54] DICKEN-GARCIA, *supra* note 10, at 8 & n.11, 183.

[55] *Id.* at 20.

investigations. It was not then even a common practice for reporters to specify in their work how they obtained their information, much less to openly debate the ethics of newsgathering methods.

Not surprisingly, it is right around this time that more journalistic ethics codes began to appear. Though there were several attempts to articulate a set of principles, the first formal code appears to have been written by Will Irwin and published in a series of articles called "The American Newspaper" in *Collier's Magazine* in 1911.[56] Presumably, Irwin was addressing concerns about journalistic practices he had observed in his time. For example, he tried to draw a sharp line between information obtained in a professional capacity, which was fair game, and information obtained through social interactions.[57] He also admonished reporters not to publish anything "without full permission of your informant," unless the informant was a criminal.[58] Most relevant to the current discussion is Irwin's third provision, titled the "'Keyhole Reporting' Taboo." In that provision he warned:

> Never sail under false colors. State who you are, what newspaper you represent, and whether or no [sic] your informant is talking for publication. If there is keyhole work to be done, leave that to the detectives, who work inside the law.[59]

As far as we can tell, this is the first source to express ethical objections to investigative deception. No undercover work can occur, of course, if journalists must identify themselves and disclose the newspapers they represent. And perhaps this was the point. Maybe Irwin meant to admonish those pioneers like Nellie Bly who had become remarkably successful by doing undercover investigations and publishing stories based on the information obtained. It is also interesting that Irwin placed failure to disclose one's identity into the same category as "keyhole" work, which conjures up images of peeping through another's keyhole. The latter seems to be a type of invasion of privacy in which the subject of the investigation is unaware that they are being spied on. When undercover journalists assume another identity to get a story, the investigative target is aware that *someone* is observing their conduct even if they are under the misimpression that the observer is an ally. Likewise, Irwin's deference to law enforcement detectives as the only ones who should be engaging in such tactics, and his assumption that their claim to ethical or legal compliance was stronger than that of journalists, is difficult to understand. Irwin seems to assume that the journalistic act of undercover investigating or keyholing is outside "the law," and equates this with journalistic impropriety.

---

[56] *Id.* at 257–58 n.11. The complete series is set out in WILL IRWIN, THE AMERICAN NEWSPAPER (1969), which was compiled with commentary by Clifford F. Weigle and David G. Clark.

[57] IRWIN, *supra* note 56, at 47 (original Collier's pagination, at 19). This article was part eight of the fifteen-part series.

[58] *Id.*

[59] *Id.* at 48 (original Collier's pagination, at 30).

Another early code was produced by the American Newspaper Publishers Association (ANPA) in 1923, borrowed shortly thereafter by Sigma Delta Chi, which would later become known as the Society of Professional Journalists (SPJ). The original ANPA code discussed the need for independence, avoidance of conflicts of interest, impartiality, accuracy, and fairness, but unlike Irwin's code, it mentioned nothing about using deceptive tactics in newsgathering.[60] These standards remained unchanged through 2001, their last published revision. The ANPA, which has since changed its name to the News/Media Alliance, does not appear to have since updated the ANPA code or published a new set of standards.[61]

### 2.3.4 A Midcentury Lull

For a variety of reasons, despite its popularity during the Progressive Era, investigative journalism, and along with it, undercover investigations, substantially diminished from roughly 1917 to 1960.[62] One factor may have been the major distraction of the two World Wars that drew public and journalistic attention more strongly to global affairs. In addition, some have attributed the rise of libel suits by the targets of such journalism as deterring muckraking investigative reporting.[63] Although some measure of the journalistic community continued to pursue investigative journalism, there was also a movement toward the objective ethical framework for journalistic practices. As discussed below, professional journalism standards began to take hold during this period. To the extent that there were concerns about the professionalism critiques of undercover reporting, these standards may have also pushed back against the tide of investigations.

### 2.3.5 Watergate and Its Aftermath

By most accounts, the resurgence in investigative journalism began in the early 1970s, when Carl Bernstein and Bob Woodward of the *Washington Post* engaged in an extensive newsgathering effort to uncover the truth about the Watergate scandal.[64] The scandal originated with reports about a burglary of the Democratic National Committee's headquarters in the Watergate Office Building a few months before the 1972 presidential election. Early on in the investigation, the burglars were

---

[60] American Society of Newspaper Editors, *Code of Ethics or Canons of Journalism*, CTR. FOR THE STUDY OF ETHICS IN THE PROS. (1923), http://ethicscodescollection.org/detail/b3120d51-fa20-4dfb-b8b4-8cb4a9222635.

[61] *See* NEWS/MEDIA ALLIANCE, www.newsmediaalliance.org/ (last visited Nov. 7, 2022).

[62] MICHAEL SCHUDSON, THE POWER OF NEWS (1996) (noting that around this period muckraking had "no culturally resonant, heroic exemplars").

[63] AUCOIN, *supra* note 8, at 33.

[64] That is not to say that undercover investigations were dormant until the early 1970s. As Brooke Kroeger recounts in her extensive coverage of such tactics, several important undercover investigations took place in the late 1950s and early 1960s. KROEGER, *supra* note 27, at 233–40.

connected to the committee to reelect President Nixon. There was speculation that the President and his highest-level aides might have been involved, if not in the burglary, then in the attempt to cover up the connections to the reelection campaign. The scandal was extensively investigated by congressional committees and an appointed Special Prosecutor. Over the course of the next two years, additional information leaked out, and it was eventually discovered that President Nixon secretly taped all conversations that occurred in the Oval Office. When those tapes were subpoenaed by the Special Prosecutor in charge of the investigation, Nixon asserted executive privilege, but a unanimous Supreme Court rejected that claim.[65] Once the tapes were produced, they revealed that Nixon was involved in a conspiracy to cover up the burglars' connection to his campaign. After it was clear that he was going to be impeached by the House of Representatives, Nixon resigned from office.

Throughout this period, the Watergate story was covered by national journalists, including Woodward and Bernstein. Their reporting uncovered a great deal of information critical to exposing the scandal and was chronicled in their book *All the President's Men*, which was later made into a successful movie. Woodward and Bernstein carried out their investigation by doggedly pursuing sources, including an anonymous source known at the time only as "Deep Throat." There were some criticisms about their investigative methods, and it is unclear whether they ever used deception to gain access to sources or information. In one account in their book, they concede that in one situation, Bernstein left his name and phone number with a source without identifying himself as a reporter, presumably because he did not think the source would return the call if he did.[66] In another situation, they may have been less than candid in trying to interview grand jurors investigating the Watergate scandal, perhaps even leading sources to believe that one of them was an FBI agent. As they write (the book is written in the third person): "They had chosen expediency over principle and, caught in the act, their role had been covered up. They had dodged, evaded, misrepresented, suggested and intimidated, but they had not lied outright."[67] It's unclear what they mean by "misrepresented" or "suggested," but as discussed below, one ethical line that has been drawn by some journalists is the one between affirmative lies and omissions that lead to mistaken impressions about their identities, with the latter being, according to some, less objectionable.

Perhaps in part because of Woodward and Bernstein, there seems to have been a resurgence in undercover investigations during the 1970s. Examples of other undercover work in this period include the Mirage investigation by the *Chicago Sun-Times* and the *Chicago Tribune's* investigations described earlier in this chapter.

---

[65] United States v. Nixon, 418 U.S. 683, 706 (1974).

[66] CARL BERNSTEIN & BOB WOODWARD, ALL THE PRESIDENT'S MEN 125 (1974).

[67] *Id.* at 250. Cf. BENJAMINSON & ANDERSON, *supra* note 26, at 9 (noting that Woodward and Bernstein lied to employees of the President's reelection campaign committee by telling them that other employees said they might be willing to talk to the press).

The *Tribune*'s reporter William Gaines went undercover as a janitor at a local private hospital to gather information about a range of medically and ethically questionable practices, taking notes on paper towels that he hid until he could turn them over to other reporters.[68] The stories produced from the investigation led to the hospital being closed and the *Tribune* winning the 1976 Pulitzer Prize for Local Investigative Specialized Reporting. It's also worth noting that during this era – the *Sun-Times*'s Pulitzer Prize snub notwithstanding – there seemed to have been less concern about the ethics of undercover investigations of newsworthy matters. Indeed, a public opinion poll in the wake of the Mirage investigation revealed that 85% of respondents believed the newspaper's stories to be true, notwithstanding the tactics used to gather information for them.[69]

Other factors also may have contributed to the resurgence in undercover investigative journalism during this time. First, as during the Progressive Era, the 1960s and 1970s were a time of social upheaval and the emergence of many different movements on the left. Nationally controversial issues such as American involvement in the Vietnam War and the civil rights movement may have inspired the press to take a stronger role in pushing for accountability and transparency for our democratic institutions. There were also technological developments, making available to reporters more affordable tape recorders, cameras, and other devices that could be easily concealed.[70]

### 2.3.5.1 Ethical Concerns during the Watergate Era

The Watergate era seems to have generated much greater public and professional attention to articulating ethical standards for journalists. The SPJ published its own first code in 1973, while the Watergate investigation was underway.[71] Like other prior codes, the SPJ code discussed conflicts of interest, accuracy and objectivity, and fairness. In addition, it expressly noted that it is "sound practice" to make clear to readers the distinction between the news and editorial functions of the press, and it also set forth the importance of protecting the confidentiality of sources. While there is no specific provision addressing undercover investigations, there are two aspects of the 1973 SPJ code that suggest the beginnings of some discomfort with such tactics. First, there is a provision admonishing the news media to "guard against invading a person's right of privacy," although that could refer to a range of newsgathering and publication decisions besides undercover work. Second, another provision advises journalists to avoid "[s]econdary employment" "if it compromises the integrity of

---

[68] KROEGER, *supra* note 27, at 172–76.

[69] *Id.* at 398 n.75.

[70] AUCOIN, *supra* note 8, at 78.

[71] Society of Professional Journalists, *Code of Ethics Sigma Delta Chi*, CTR. FOR THE STUDY OF ETHICS IN THE PROS. (1973), http://ethicscodescollection.org/detail/30ff3ab1-53c6-44aa-9350-ddaa074504e1.

journalists and their employers." To the extent journalists might seek out stories by getting hired by the targets of their investigations, the secondary employment provision seems geared more toward avoiding conflicts of interest, as when a reporter works for both a newspaper and a politician whom they are covering.[72] That is, it seems directed more at moonlighting than at undercover tactics. Thus, at least at this point, there does not seem to be an explicit disapproval of investigative deceptions. The SPJ revised its code twice in the 1980s, though it still resembled the 1973 code in most ways. It did, however, add an overt requirement for journalists to give due regard not only to privacy but also to the "dignity" and "rights" of people they encounter during their newsgathering.[73] These changes reflect a move toward the social responsibility and the community and care frameworks for journalism ethics. They could also be interpreted to apply to undercover investigations to the extent that, as some philosophers argue, to lie to another person for *any* reason is to deprive that person of their autonomy.[74] But it would be quite a stretch to suggest that these provisions directly, or intentionally, sought to target undercover investigations.

Another development during this era was the 1975 founding of Investigative Reporters and Editors (IRE), a nonprofit organization dedicated to supporting the work of investigative journalists. IRE, which is based at the University of Missouri School of Journalism, was formed shortly after President Nixon's resignation. The idea was to create an organization that would provide mutual support across the country to share ideas about stories, newsgathering techniques, and news sources.[75] IRE formed an ethics committee to address questions about investigative methods.[76]

It was only a few years after the founding of IRE that the *Chicago Sun-Times* conducted its Mirage investigation and was short-listed for, but denied, a Pulitzer Prize because of concerns about the ethics of their investigative methods. Admittedly, the breadth and depth of that investigation far exceeded the average undercover investigation, which was probably one reason it received so much negative attention. Moreover, it took enormous resources for the newspaper to set up and operate a fake tavern for the course of the investigation, so such elaborate schemes are unlikely to be common.

No agreement on a uniform ethics standard for journalists was reached during the aftermath of Watergate (nor, indeed, since then), but the debate occupied the

---

[72] The potential legal concern about "serving two masters" would later arise in the *Food Lion* case, discussed below.

[73] Society of Professional Journalists, *Society of Professional Journalists – Code of Ethics*, CTR. FOR THE STUDY OF ETHICS IN THE PROS. (1986), http://ethicscodescollection.org/detail/fea9288f-b399-4a86-a95d-26f501aee740.

[74] *See The Morality of Lying*, ENCYCLOPAEDIA BRITANNICA, www.britannica.com/topic/lying/The-morality-of-lying (last visited Nov. 7, 2022).

[75] Investigative Reporters & Editors, *About IRE*, MO. SCH. OF JOURNALISM, www.ire.org/about-ire/ (last visited Nov. 7, 2022).

[76] AUCOIN, *supra* note 8, at 84.

attention of news institutions, working reporters, and media and communications scholars throughout the era. Across different periods of American journalism, the historical materials reflect substantial ambivalence about undercover investigations. On one hand, the value of such investigations is widely accepted; on the other hand, there has always been some level of discomfort with the tactics necessary to carry out those investigations. This would not change with the onset of the next era, which featured an increase in undercover investigations through a new form of journalism.

### 2.3.6 *The Rise of Television Newsmagazines*

The next stage of advancement in undercover investigations was the advent of television newsmagazine shows, which allowed television journalists to go beyond reporting on discrete stories of the day to taking on broader, more time-consuming, and more expensive investigations. These produced television investigations were equivalent to long-form journalism. Popular shows such as CBS's *60 Minutes*, NBC's *Dateline*, ABC's *20/20*, and PBS's *Frontline* capitalized on the ability to carry out longer, more involved investigations to produce widely viewed programming exposing a range of scandals. If hidden tape recorders were essential to the newspaper reporter, hidden cameras were the next level of documenting stories for television journalists.

In the late 1990s, *20/20*'s Diane Sawyer investigated and broadcast a story about the neglect and abuse of thousands of children with disabilities living in Russian orphanages.[77] As part of her investigation, she placed a hidden camera in her purse to document the children's treatment and living conditions. The resulting story earned Sawyer and ABC News the 2000 Alfred I. duPont-Columbia University Award. Much more controversial was Dateline NBC's *To Catch a Predator* series, which debuted in 2004 and televised undercover investigations of potential child sexual predators.[78] Though the series was extremely popular, there were questions about the network's independence since it produced the series in conjunction with a nonprofit advocacy group. Others claimed that the show was more like entrapment than journalism. However, a *Frontline* documentary on sex trafficking between Ukraine and Turkey, which also involved the use of hidden cameras to reveal the manner in which the sex slave trade operated, did not generate the same extent of negative publicity.

One of the more widely discussed undercover television investigations involved a Prime Time Live broadcast of a story about the retail food chain Food Lion, a broadcast also anchored by Sawyer, which we briefly described in Chapter 1. Two ABC reporters obtained jobs with two different Food Lion stores and used hidden video cameras to document and confirm what sources had initially reported – that

[77] KROEGER, *supra* note 27, at 186–87.
[78] *Id.* at 54–55.

Food Lion's food-handling practices were highly unsanitary and probably illegal. In a court case about the investigation, a federal appeals court described the resulting story as follows:

> The broadcast included, for example, videotape that appeared to show Food Lion employees repackaging and redating fish that had passed the expiration date, grinding expired beef with fresh beef, and applying barbeque sauce to chicken past its expiration date in order to mask the smell and sell it as fresh in the gourmet food section. The program included statements by former Food Lion employees alleging even more serious mishandling of meat at Food Lion stores across several states.[79]

The Food Lion investigation resulted in a major lawsuit against ABC News for fraud, breach of the duty of loyalty, trespass, and other claims. Despite the fact that the story revealed disgusting food handling practices, the jury awarded Food Lion $1,402 in compensatory damages and $5.5 million in punitive damages (though after appeal the ultimate financial judgment was nominal). To the extent that a sample of public opinion is relevant to our inquiry into journalistic ethics, it is notable that interviews with the jurors after the trial revealed a strong antipathy toward the press's tactics in the Food Lion investigation and a mistrust of the media in general. After the trial, the jury foreperson was quoted as saying, "The news media has the right to bring the news.... But they have to have guidelines, too. How far can they go before they can bring up something like this?"[80] He added that ABC's "misrepresentation was an act of fraud."[81] Another juror stated, "The news media is going to have to come around with a better way of collecting news without misrepresenting themselves."[82] And yet another juror said, "I don't have anything against undercover investigations.... But if you are going to do them, just do them legal,"[83] which of course begs the question. These sentiments resonate with some of the critics of undercover investigations who worry that they will undermine the overall credibility of journalists.

Although the federal appeals court overturned the substantial damages award and most of the theories of liability, it rejected ABC's claim that the First Amendment protected them categorically from fraud or breach of the duty of loyalty. The court of appeals held that the claims for trespass based on the deceptive employment were actionable, though it permitted only nominal damages.

The Food Lion decision, which did not go up to the Supreme Court, seems to have raised sufficient doubts about undercover investigations to at least deter some organizations from continuing to sponsor them. Of course, the examples cited above

[79] Food Lion, Inc. v. Cap. Cities/ABC, Inc., 194 F.3d 505, 511 (4th Cir. 1999).
[80] Cornelius B. Pratt, *Food Lion Inc. v. ABC News Inc.: Invasive Deception for the Public Interest?*, 42 PUB. REL. Q. 18, 19 (1997).
[81] *Id.*
[82] *Id.*
[83] Barry Meier, *Jury Says ABC Owes Damages of $5.5 Million*, N.Y. TIMES (Jan. 23, 1997), www.nytimes.com/1997/01/23/us/jury-says-abc-owes-damages-of-5.5-million.html.

show that the investigations did not come to a halt, but the Food Lion decision seems to have dampened the enthusiasm for television newsmagazines to devote a lot of money and time to stories based on undercover work. Among the concerns spawned by the case were questions about whether, regardless of the law, undercover investigations involving deception and secret video recordings violated the principles of journalistic ethics.

### 2.3.6.1 Ethical Concerns from the 1990s to the Present

Perhaps because of the increase in television newsmagazines conducting hidden camera investigations, by 1996 the SPJ revised its code to expressly address the topic of undercover investigations. That version of the SPJ code directs journalists to "Avoid undercover or other surreptitious methods of gathering information except when traditional open methods will not yield information vital to the public" and further advises that "Use of such methods should be explained as part of the story."[84] Even here, it is worth noting that the prohibition is not absolute. There is an exception for investigations seeking information that could not be obtained by "traditional open methods."

Finally, there were also several other references to journalistic behavior that could be viewed as governing undercover investigations, even if only implicitly. These parts of the code embrace principles drawn from the social responsibility and community and care ethical frameworks. For example, it contains general references to journalistic integrity, setting out that "[c]onscientious journalists" should "serve the public with thoroughness and honesty" and asking journalists to "be honest, fair, and courageous" not only in reporting information but in gathering it. The 1996 SPJ code also clarified that "[e]thical journalists treat sources, subjects and colleagues as human beings deserving of respect" and warned that "gathering and reporting information may cause harm or discomfort." It also embellishes prior versions' comments about privacy and draws a distinction between public and private citizens as subjects of stories, recognizing that "private people have a greater right to control information about themselves than do public officials and others who seek power, influence or attention. Only an overriding public need can justify intrusion into anyone's privacy." The SPJ code was updated again in 2014, though the provisions that might apply to undercover investigations are virtually identical.[85]

---

[84] Society of Professional Journalists, *Society of Professional Journalists – Code of Ethics*, Ctr. for the Study of Ethics in the Pros. (1995), http://ethicscodescollection.org/detail/431146b3-9c90-495d-b530-0f5d31b05cda.

[85] Society of Professional Journalists, *Society of Professional Journalists Code of Ethics (2014)*, Ctr. for the Study of Ethics in the Pros. (2014), http://ethicscodescollection.org/detail/d7d99b2f-973d-4117-a182-c643132bb0eb. The one exception is that the 2014 code omitted the earlier requirement that journalists should explain their methods in their stories if they used undercover investigations.

Like earlier standards, even the later versions of the recent SPJ codes are not absolute. Though they warn more strongly against undercover investigations, they do not categorically prohibit them, but rather advise journalists to avoid them and provide an exception in which traditional methods will not lead to information "vital" to the public.

Thus, even here we see a standard that can be departed from based on the importance of the information targeted by the investigation, which at least recognizes a utilitarian approach that considers the value of the newsgathering and suggests that it can sometimes outweigh the negative impacts on its subjects. But it doesn't provide very helpful guidance in that respect. For in the vast majority of undercover investigations by journalists, the methods are employed specifically to reveal information that is vital to the public. The targets of serious investigations are seldom or never going to be forthcoming about the information being sought because it will be harmful to them in some way. It might be illegal, hypocritical, or unethical, or may cause them to lose respect or suffer more tangibly, such as when a company loses business. That leaves it to journalists to sort out what is "vital" to the public interest in their stories. It also requires them to be clairvoyant. This is problematic as a source of guidance, though, because no journalist can know in advance exactly what information an undercover investigation might uncover, and whether that information will turn out to be vital.

In their book on investigative journalism, Benjaminson and Anderson reflect the type of ambivalence about undercover investigations that frequently plays out in debates about such tactics.[86] In terms of the value of such investigations, they fully acknowledge that one of the primary challenges to investigative journalists is that much of the information they need to produce a story is not publicly available. Because such information is not easily obtained, they describe being dishonest or fraudulent as one of the "fundamental techniques" of investigative reporting.[87] At the same time, they argue that the ethics of such tactics depends on a weighing of the value of such information against the harm that may result from the deception:

> Most reporters use deceptive methods to gather information – on the theory that in a democracy the public's right to information outweighs a public official's right to expect complete candor from journalists. *Deceptive methods are justified, however, only when greater harm will be done to the public if the information remains concealed than the harm done to individuals by its publication.* A reporter should never resort to questionable methods if the information can be obtained in another way.[88]

Thus, they take a utilitarian approach to the ethical analysis, one that is sometimes reflected in formal ethical standards that address this subject. But while they express

[86] BENJAMINSON & ANDERSON, *supra* note 26.
[87] *Id.* at 6.
[88] *Id.* at 6–7 (emphasis added).

discomfort with the deception associated with traditional undercover work, they embrace other types of dishonesty or misleading behavior, such as when a reporter falsely pretends to believe or be sympathetic to a source's personal story in order to encourage them to be more forthcoming.[89]

Because of the absence of any uniform, enforceable code of journalistic ethics, the debates about undercover investigations tend to be played out in the context of specific stories. Though television stories built around investigative deceptions and hidden cameras continued to be broadcast, there was an increasing backlash against them during this era. This may be due in part not to changes in ethical standards but to the seeming proliferation of legal actions brought against television networks who sponsored undercover work as in the *Food Lion* case. Until the 1990s, legal actions challenging the legality of newsgathering techniques were uncommon.[90] The executive director of the Libel Defense Resource Center warned that these actions would likely lead to journalists acting more cautiously, perhaps unduly so.[91]

Another example of a major suit brought during this time was a claim against ABC for a different story on *Primetime Live*, the same program that led to the Food Lion litigation. In 1994, a jury awarded $1 million to plaintiffs who had been the subject of a hidden camera investigation of their business providing psychic information to telephone callers. The plaintiffs there claimed the investigation violated their privacy.[92] Although most suits against news media were not brought as libel actions because the truth of the reporting served as an affirmative defense against such claims, a federal jury found for the owner of an electronics repair store who had been the target of a 1992 *Primetime Live* investigation that accused him of overcharging customers and making unnecessary repairs. Though the jury in that case awarded only $1 in damages, it sent a note back to the courtroom admonishing the network to reexamine its newsgathering practices.[93]

While television news programs might have become more reluctant to carry out undercover investigations for their reporting after the *Food Lion* case, they have not been shut down completely and have continued to generate controversy. For example, in 2014 a dispute arose over reports by the NBC *Today Show* and two local television stations, all of whom sent journalists into public schools to

---

[89] *Id.* at 130.

[90] Barry Meier & Bill Carter, *Undercover Tactics by TV Magazines Fall under Attack*, N.Y. TIMES (Dec. 23, 1996), www.nytimes.com/1996/12/23/business/undercover-tactics-by-tv-magazines-fall-under-attack.html.

[91] *Id.*

[92] *See Network Pays Out $900,000 in Hidden Camera Claim*, REPS. COMM. FOR FREEDOM OF THE PRESS (Feb. 23, 2000), www.rcfp.org/network-pays-out-900000-hidden-camera-claim/.

[93] Peter Y. Hong, *For Store Owner, $1 Is Priceless*, WASH. POST (Nov. 25, 1993), www.washingtonpost.com/archive/local/1993/11/25/for-store-owner-1-is-priceless/6a41c95b-8e4b-4fdd-8914-5e7909a32eba/.

investigate lax security measures in the wake of a number of school shootings.[94] The reporters in each case entered schools without permission and wore hidden cameras, presumably so they would not give away their identity as television journalists. All of them broadcast stories showing that schools allowed them to enter and wander around the school buildings for several minutes before being detected or confronted in any way by school officials. One local television reporter entered a St. Louis area public high school and was able to move about the building for more than three minutes. He entered the school office and asked to speak with someone about security, and left his name and phone number with the office staff while purporting to go to the bathroom, but then headed off in a different direction. At no point was he stopped by security. One account pointed out that these types of undercover investigations were commonly used to evaluate security measures after the 9/11 terrorist attacks.

There were harsh criticisms of these investigations, which in some cases led to the schools being locked down. School officials complained that the reporters' stories did not accurately depict the actual effectiveness of the schools' security measures. One journalism critic argued that the investigations could have gone badly awry if they led to a school security guard pulling a gun on a reporter.

For their part, the television network and stations defended their practices as revealing information critical to public safety and argued that the value of such news was greater than the potential costs. This type of utilitarian analysis is frequently invoked in ethical debates about undercover investigations. In addition, they contended that undercover investigations provide access to information that would not otherwise be discoverable. Defending the *Today Show*'s story, Alexandra Wallace, a senior vice president at NBC News, said, "'I don't know how you see what the truth is if you don't go in that way,' [...] referring to the hidden camera technique. 'The moment you show up with a big camera, things look a lot better.'"[95]

A similar debate ensued about a high-profile undercover story by the investigative unit of Al Jazeera, the international news network based in Qatar. In 2015, journalists at the network planned and executed an extensive undercover investigation in which a reporter lied by identifying himself as an Australian gun lobbyist. Under this guise, he carried a hidden camera and gained access to meetings at the National Rifle Association (NRA) and One Nation, a far-right Australian political party.[96]

---

[94] John Eligon, *Undercover TV Reports on School Security Raise Ethical Questions*, N.Y. TIMES (Mar. 16, 2014), www.nytimes.com/2014/03/17/business/media/undercover-tv-reports-on-school-security-raise-ethical-questions.html?searchResultPosition=1.

[95] *Id.*

[96] Isabella Kwai, *Deception for Investigative Journalism: Right or Wrong?*, N.Y. TIMES (Mar. 28, 2019), www.nytimes.com/2019/03/28/world/australia/al-jazeera-one-nation-nra.html. Not all efforts to show up without a camera are greeted by a warm reception from the media. Project Veritas, a right-wing group that engages in investigations, has been vilified by the media, at times for investigations that look analogous to those that would otherwise be celebrated but for the politics of the investigated target. *See* Adam Goldman & Mark

The investigation resulted in a two-part documentary shown by the Australian Broadcasting Corporation that revealed private conversations within the two organizations. One party official was shown talking about how donations from an American gun lobbyist could help gain access to members of the Australian Parliament. NRA officials discussed with the reporter its public relations strategies for responding to mass shootings and influencing public opinion more favorably toward gun ownership. These were particularly controversial statements for the general public to hear given the strong gun regulation laws in place in Australia.

The documentary was criticized by One Nation's party leader and some media ethicists, who argued that the undercover tactics of the network might be unethical. As discussed below, the *New York Times*, like many other major newspapers, has a blanket policy against misrepresentation of a reporter's identity. Phil Corbett, the *Times*'s standards editor, focused on that policy in commenting on the Al Jazeera investigation, but also noted, "Exceptions involving sustained deception have been extremely rare.... Overall, we think, this is the best way to insure both fairness to our subjects and credibility with our readers."[97] Other critics also expressed discomfort with Al Jazeera's tactics. Andrew Dodd, director of the Centre for Advancing Journalism at the University of Melbourne, and Peter Greste, a University of Queensland professor and former professional journalist, were both wary of the use of a hidden camera. While they did not comment specifically about the deception involving the reporter's true identity, they raised a separate critique that the undercover journalist should not become part of the story itself.

At the same time, Corbett, Dodd, and Greste fully acknowledged the value to the public interest of the information produced from the story. And Corbett recognized that other news outlets had different ethical standards and that there is a long history of valuable undercover investigations in journalism. Dodd also noted that the fact that Al Jazeera explained how they undertook the investigation to the audience was a positive factor because it allowed the viewers to make their own decisions about the story's credibility. And he added that the report's insights about the NRA were valuable, observing, "You see a glimpse of the truth in that moment that you couldn't get in a two hour debate."[98] But Greste also commented that while the information revealed by the investigation was valuable, neither the NRA nor One Nation was engaged in anything illegal, implying that if the latter were true, the ethical balance might be recalculated. He also criticized the response to the story, which was that One Nation referred Al Jazeera to Australia's national security agency. Government backlash against such investigations could seriously compromise the freedom of the press.

Mazzetti, *Project Veritas and the Line between Journalism and Political Spying*, N.Y. TIMES (Nov. 12, 2021), www.nytimes.com/2021/11/11/us/politics/project-veritas-journalism-political-spying.html.

[97] Kwai, *supra* note 96.
[98] *Id.*

Not all ethical debates during this latest era arose in the context of television journalism. As we recounted in Chapter 1, Ken Silverstein's undercover investigation to expose the operation of powerful Washington lobbying firms in representing the interests of foreign governments was criticized by then-*Washington Post* reporter Howard Kurtz, who argued against utilitarian reasoning to justify such investigations.[99] As many undercover journalists do, Silverstein defended his tactics based on their utility and importance and by comparing his ethics with those of his targets. "If you want to weigh my ethics in making up a firm against the ethics of agreeing to represent and whitewash the record of a Stalinist dictatorship," he said, "I'm pretty comfortable with that comparison."[100] For his part, Kurtz responded that the practice of undercover investigations was decreasing. He claimed that by 2007,

> No newspaper today would do what the Chicago Sun-Times did in the 1970s, setting up a bar to entrap crooked politicians. Fewer television programs are doing what ABC did in the 1990s, having producers lie to get jobs at a supermarket chain to expose unsanitary practices. NBC's "Dateline" joins in stings against child predators, but by tagging along with law enforcement officials.[101]

The recent case of *Democracy Partners v. Project Veritas* has generated more public discourse about undercover investigations. In 2016, in the midst of the presidential campaign, Project Veritas set up an undercover investigation of Democracy Partners, an umbrella group of left-leaning political consulting firms.[102] Democracy Partners sued Project Veritas for an undercover operation in which a Veritas representative, using a false name, made a $20,000 donation to one of the firms, helping to secure an internship for another Veritas representative posing as his niece. The "niece" then recorded two consultants who worked with Democracy Partners making ill-advised statements about unethical campaign tactics, such as pursuing strategies to provoke violence at Republican rallies. Project Veritas published a series of video stories revealing these conversations, and Democracy Partners lost some major contracts as a result. Democracy Partners sued Project Veritas for unlawful interception of oral communications and fraudulent misrepresentation, and civil conspiracy. The trial judge dismissed their claims of trespass and breach of fiduciary duty, including the duty of loyalty.[103] However, the case proceeded on Democracy Partners' claims of unlawful wiretapping and fraudulent

---

[99] Howard Kurtz, *Undercover Journalism*, WASH. POST (June 25, 2007, 7:24 AM), www .washingtonpost.com/wp-dyn/content/blog/2007/06/25/BL2007062500353.html; Ken Silverstein, *Their Men in Washington: Undercover with D.C.'s Lobbyists for Hire*, HARPER'S BAZAAR, July 1, 2007, at 53.

[100] Kurtz, *supra* note 99.

[101] *Id.*

[102] Democracy Partners v. Project Veritas Action Fund, 453 F. Supp. 3d 261, 267–72 (D.D.C. 2020), *reconsideration denied*, No. CV 17-1047 (ESH), 2020 WL 5095484 (D.D.C. Aug. 27, 2020).

[103] *Id.* at 278, 283.

misrepresentation. In September 2022, the case went to trial and the jury found for Democracy Partners, awarding it $120,000 in damages.

As it has continually maintained, Project Veritas asserted in the litigation that it is a journalistic enterprise rather than a political activist organization and that its investigation was protected by the First Amendment. But it did not prevail on this theory. And even if it had, one commentator has argued that contemporary journalism has moved away from the belief that undercover investigations are a legitimate practice. In an opinion piece by *Washington Post* media critic Erik Wemple, he argues that the verdict "upends" the claim that undercover investigations are "old fashioned journalism."[104] Wemple opines that the news media is "falling out of love with undercover tactics" and suggests that undercover investigations are disfavored and out of fashion.

As our review of this debate suggests, Wemple is far from alone in this opinion, but neither is his position universally held. Even if the enthusiasm for such investigations has waned, however, the debate about these tactics has not.

## 2.4  ETHICAL STANDARDS IN PRACTICE AND IN SCHOLARSHIP

This chapter concludes with a discussion of how news institutions adopt and implement ethical standards in practice and about scholarly commentary concerning undercover investigations by journalists. These standards and opinions may then help inform us about how the law and the US Constitution might apply to such investigations by not only journalists, but also political activists and others who might employ these tactics.

### 2.4.1  *News Organizations' Internal Ethical Standards*

Today, it is not uncommon for individual news media outlets to maintain their own internal standards for ethical journalistic practices and to publicly disclose those standards. These standards, too, seem slightly ambivalent toward the subject of undercover investigations. Many major national newspapers have express provisions warning their staff not to affirmatively misrepresent their identities, though they provide exceptions as well. For example, the *New York Times* standards for ethical journalism require their reporters to disclose their identities to "people they cover," but also state that reporters

> need not always announce their status as journalists when seeking information normally available to the public. Staff members may not pose as police officers, lawyers, business people or anyone else when they are working as journalists.

[104] Erik Wemple, *Journalism or Political Activism? Project Veritas Is on Trial over 2016 Sting*, Wash. Post (Sept. 13, 2022), www.washingtonpost.com/opinions/2022/09/13/project-veritas-trial-lawsuit-sting/.

(As happens on rare occasions, when seeking to enter countries that bar journalists, correspondents may take cover from vagueness and identify themselves as traveling on business or as tourists.)[105]

Thus, there is an exception for protecting or even obscuring a reporter's identity when they might be endangered or unable to access a country they are visiting, though those are supposed to be "rare occasions." The *Times* also makes some allowances for its critics:

> Theater, music and art critics and other writers who review goods or services offered to the public may conceal their Times connection but may not normally assert a false identity or affiliation. As an exception, *restaurant critics may make reservations in false names to protect their identity*. Restaurant critics and travel writers must conceal their Times affiliation to eliminate the possibility of special treatment.[106]

Moreover, the *Times* also prohibits its staff from any type of secret recording, even when it is permissible under the local jurisdiction's laws, noting that such conduct "is a deception." Here, too, the paper's rule is not absolute, as the provision goes on to say, "Masthead editors may make rare exceptions to this prohibition in places where recordings made secretly are legal."[107]

Other major media entities have comparable prohibitions on lying and deception. The *Washington Post* also forbids its reporter to engage in deception, stating that "journalists will not misrepresent their identity or their occupation. They will not portray themselves as police officers, physicians or anything other than journalists."[108] This provision was in place when Woodward and Bernstein were reporting on the Watergate scandal. The *Post* does not appear to prohibit secret recordings, though it notes that its policies are "not meant to be comprehensive."

There is at least a perception that television journalists are more likely to engage in, and perhaps are more ethically comfortable with, investigative deceptions and secret recordings, perhaps because of the success of television newsmagazines.[109] It is less easy to access the ethical codes for the major television networks, though, much less their flagship newsmagazine shows. In fact, none of the three major television broadcasting networks make their journalistic standards publicly available. CNN News similarly does not make its standards available, and in fact has fought

---

[105] *Ethical Journalism: A Handbook of Values and Practices for the News and Editorial Departments – Pursuing the News*, N.Y. TIMES, www.nytimes.com/editorial-standards/ethical-journalism.html# (last visited Nov. 7, 2022).

[106] *Id.* (emphasis added).

[107] *Id.*

[108] *Policies and Standards – A Journalist's Role*, WASH. POST, www.washingtonpost.com/discussions/2021/01/01/policies-and-standards/ (last visited Nov. 7, 2022).

[109] Seow Ting Lee, *Lying to Tell the Truth: Journalists and the Social Context of Deception*, 7 MASS COMMC'N & SOC'Y 97, 100 (2004).

the public disclosure of their guidelines in litigation.[110] Fox News's parent, Fox Broadcasting Company, publishes its *Standards of Business Conduct*.[111] These standards do not directly address the issue of undercover investigations or deception, though they do state that "[a]s a company, we are at all times truthful and accurate when dealing with government entities or officials."[112] Finally, most of the major companies that own and operate large numbers of local news television stations, such as TEGNA, Sinclair Broadcasting Group, and E. W. Scripps Company, do not have a code of conduct that specifically addresses undercover reporting.

The Public Broadcasting System's award-winning documentary show *Frontline* does have publicly accessible standards. Television news stories are typically driven by a producer as well as affiliated reporters, so *Frontline*'s standards focus on the producer's conduct. With regard to investigative deceptions, *Frontline* has three relevant provisions:

> 28. In general, a person whose participation or cooperation in a documentary or news production is sought should know the identity of the producers and why the producer is seeking the person's involvement.
>
> 29. Material gathered under false pretenses may not carry the same implication of consent that otherwise applies to information freely given to a journalist. If a case arises that calls for a producer to hide her/his identity, it must be approved by the Executive Producer in advance of shooting unless producing under dangerous conditions does not permit.
>
> 30. In some cases it may be necessary for a producer to withhold her/his identity. Such cases are still exceptional and should be discussed in advance with the Executive Producer unless producing under dangerous conditions does not permit.[113]

Though discouraging the practice of obscuring one's identity, *Frontline*'s standards are more flexible than some of the major newspapers' standards, hedging a bit with qualifying phrases like "In general" and building in the possibility of necessity as an exception. Many of *Frontline*'s standards, like other journalistic outlets, also require consultation with higher-ups to seek approval of undercover work. Thus, to invert an old adage, *Frontline*'s approach is that it's better to ask permission than ask for forgiveness.

*Frontline* also appears to be a bit more flexible about the practice of secret recordings. For example, the following standard implies that even in places where

---

[110] Erik Wemple, CNN *Fights to Keep Internal Editorial Guidelines under Wraps. Why?*, WASH. POST (May 7, 2018, 4:39 PM), www.washingtonpost.com/blogs/erik-wemple/wp/2018/05/07/cnn-fights-to-keep-internal-editorial-guidelines-under-wraps-why/.

[111] *Standards of Business Conduct*, FOX BROAD. CORP. (June 2022), https://media.foxcorporation.com/wp-content/uploads/prod/2022/06/17135056/Fox-6.15.22-SOBC.pdf.

[112] *Id.* at 12.

[113] *Journalistic Guidelines – Avoid Misrepresentation*, FRONTLINE, www.pbs.org/wgbh/frontline/about-us/journalistic-guidelines/ (last visited Nov. 7, 2022).

two-party consent is required by law for audio recordings, producers may seek and obtain prior approval to make such recordings. Perhaps that means only that such approval will be granted in one-party consent jurisdictions, but the standard is not clear what circumstances might lead to approval. The standard also states that it doesn't apply to producers and reporters who wish to record telephone conversations, though it seems to still require compliance with the jurisdiction's consent laws:

> 27. Depending on the circumstances, electronic listening and the use of hidden cameras and recording devices are illegal in a number of jurisdictions, and therefore should not be undertaken without the Executive Producer's approval and consultation with the WGBH Legal Department, as well as the VP for National Programs and/or the GM for Local Radio and TV when appropriate. This guideline does not apply to situations in which a telephone conversation is recorded with the consent of both parties (one is sufficient in some jurisdictions) for purposes of accuracy. Producers should be aware that the broadcast of a telephone conversation that was recorded without the consent of all parties may violate FCC regulations.

We have not discussed radio journalism to this point, but National Public Radio does have a policy that expressly forbids their journalists to engage in undercover investigations. The policy states that "[w]e do not conceal our identities, pose as someone or something we are not, use hidden microphones or cameras to collect information, or record phone calls without the permission of all parties on the line, except in the very rarest of circumstances, outlined below."[114] However, NPR's policy does allow for two exceptions. First, the policy against undercover investigations does not apply where they are foreign journalists trying to protect their safety in a war zone or in a country with a repressive regime.[115] Second, NPR permits undercover work when a story is "so important we might consider the use of a hidden microphone because we exhausted all other ways to get the information. But only the rarest of circumstances might merit that decision."[116]

### 2.4.2 *Scholarly Commentary on the Ethics of Undercover Investigations by Journalists*

The ethics of undercover investigations has also been debated in academic discourse. Recall Professor Ward's outlining of four major ethical frameworks that have frequently framed the debates over journalism ethics: liberal theory, objectivity and social responsibility, interpretation and activism, and community and care. As we have already alluded to, undercover investigations seem more justifiable under the liberal theory and interpretation and activism models. Liberal theory would seem to

---

[114] *NPR Ethics Handbook*, Nat'l Pub. Radio, www.npr.org/about-npr/688367308/honesty#hones tyinreportingandinterviewing (last visited Sept. 29, 2022).
[115] *Id.*
[116] *Id.*

support the idea of using undercover investigations as the work of independent press institutions whose role is to serve as a watchdog on government and abuses of power, which would include private power. The interpretation and activism approaches to journalism ethics embrace a more active role for the press and less of a concern with objectivity, which might be either unattainable or overvalued.

In contrast, undercover investigations might be viewed as a violation of the social responsibility model because they may cause some harm to the subjects or targets of the investigation. Similarly, to the extent the community and care models stress the importance of care for others and the importance of relational issues, they could be seen as a basis for arguing that undercover investigations are unethical. But even under these models, we might see room for arguments justifying undercover investigations. Undercover investigations might not necessarily be categorically rejected under these models. Rather, one could argue that these frameworks require journalists to engage in active consideration of relational harms to others (sources, subjects, etc.) before conducting an undercover investigation. In this way, even these models are arguably more flexible than Kant's seemingly inflexible objection to lies.

Not surprisingly, scholars disagree in their treatment of the ethics of undercover investigations. In James Aucoin's examination of investigative journalism, he suggests that undercover work by reporters is ethically troubling. Drawing on the work of moral philosophers and other media ethicists, Aucoin contends that undercover journalism undermines the credibility of "serious" investigative journalism because journalists must practice virtue as an aspect of professionalism.[117] Thus, he seems to rely on a perspective drawn from Kant. Furthermore, he takes a dim view of the journalistic value of undercover work. "'Investigations' that use undercover cameras and other investigative techniques to examine issues of limited or negligible impact on most people are not considered by serious investigative journalists to be investigative journalism. This latter type of reporting is driven by entertainment values, not journalism values."[118] He also suggests that exposure to litigation, especially libel suits, during the 1980s led television reporters to rethink many of their tactics, including hidden cameras and undercover reporting.[119]

But like many others, Aucoin is not without some ambivalence. First, his statement conflates the use of undercover investigations with the reporting of stories that are not of great public interest because they have little impact on most people. But what about undercover investigations that lead to stories that reveal information of great public interest? At another point, he seems to embrace undercover tactics when he describes the work of Nellie Bly admirably, noting that "undercover investigations have become an established method for rooting out misdeeds and

[117] AUCOIN, *supra* note 8, at 98–99.
[118] *Id.* at 2.
[119] *Id.* at 202.

malfeasance" and that her groundbreaking work "contributed to a form of reporting referred to in the profession of the time as 'detective' journalism, and which we call 'investigative reporting' today."[120]

In contrast, noted legal ethics scholar Stephen Gillers has articulated a stronger defense of undercover investigations by journalists, underscoring that such investigations may even be constitutionally protected by the First Amendment's Press Clause.[121] While recognizing that many national news entities forbid their reporters to engage in deception and that such standards make "good business sense," Gillers argues nonetheless that the Constitution should protect some newsgathering that involves investigative deception.[122] Although he cautions against granting unfettered access to all places for newsgathering, he contends that freedom of the press should include "access to places closed to the public, like prison and jails, unless good reasons justify exclusion."[123]

Gillers devotes an entire chapter of his book to the idea that the press should have a constitutional privilege to engage in undercover work, a "right that no one outside of law enforcement has. It subordinates some property and privacy rights to the press's (and therefore the public's) interest in newsgathering."[124] He acknowledges that a number of state laws may prohibit activity that is necessary to engage in such types of undercover work, including laws forbidding trespass, disloyalty, invasion of privacy, deception, and unlawful recording. Nonetheless, he argues that in some situations, such generally applicable laws must give way to the work of undercover journalists. Those situations first must involve newsgathering about information of a "public concern," a standard sometimes used by the Supreme Court in other First Amendment contexts. Generally, this refers to reporting about "'any matter of political, social, or other concern to the community,' or when it 'is a subject of legitimate news interest; that is, a subject of general interest and of value and concern to the public.'"[125]

Gillers then argues that the resolution of whether the press's newsgathering rights outweigh the potential harm to the subject of an undercover investigation would have to be resolved under an open-ended balancing approach, citing opinions by Justices Breyer and Souter as examples of how such an approach might look in practice.[126] Interestingly, for purposes of the broader discussion in this book, he points to the way that courts have handled First Amendment challenges to state

---

[120] *Id.* at 30.
[121] STEPHEN GILLERS, JOURNALISM UNDER FIRE: PROTECTING THE FUTURE OF INVESTIGATIVE REPORTING (2018).
[122] *Id.* at 90–91.
[123] *Id.* at 115.
[124] *Id.* at 116.
[125] Snyder v. Phelps, 562 U.S. 443, 453 (2011) (citations omitted).
[126] Cohen v. Cowles Media Co., 501 U.S. 663, 676 (1991) (Souter, J., dissenting); GILLERS, *supra* note 121, at 132–36 (citing Bartnicki v. Vopper, 532 U.S. 514, 535 (2001) (Breyer, J., concurring)).

ag-gag laws as a "good example of how judicial balancing might inform the Press Clause."[127]

To be sure, Gillers's work focuses on a legal and constitutional question, rather than an ethical one, but much of his reasoning mirrors the utilitarian model that we believe frequently justifies undercover investigations. Other ethics scholars and many journalists do not agree with utilitarian reasoning to justify such investigations. As Professor Seow Ting Lee asserts,

> The main weakness of utilitarianism is its simplistic calculation of risk and benefit, which is vulnerable to uncertainty and imprecision. Utilitarianism implies that a lie and a truthful statement that achieve the same utility are equal, but we know a lie is negatively weighted to begin with. Often, it is difficult for a person to remain objective when evaluating the consequences of his or her decision to deceive or not deceive.[128]

In other words, a concern exists that journalists will simply use utilitarian reasoning to justify getting a story, and will tend to undervalue the harms to those they deceive. We recognize this as a legitimate concern, but at the same time, as some of the legal cases on this issue reflect, it is also quite common for those opposed to investigative deceptions to overstate the government's interest in preventing legal harms. That is, there is an equal danger, we submit, that opponents of undercover investigations will overstate their own harms. And often they would have great incentive to do so if the resulting story exposes their conduct as unlawful, unethical, or immoral. Outside the litigation context, of course, there is no independent body to evaluate the benefits and harms of an undercover investigation. So, the judgment must take place on the journalist's and editor's part before an investigation is carried out.[129]

Professor Lee also observes that many journalists and media scholars consider deception to be a "necessary evil," in that it is sometimes required in order to gain access to the truth.[130] At the same time, survey research has shown that journalists in the field struggle with this calculation. Journalists responding to a survey indicated that they were more comfortable with deception involving omission, such as with-holding or not being forthcoming with information, than with commission, includ-ing lying about one's identity.[131] Interestingly, that same research shows that while journalists are very uncomfortable with impersonation, they are less concerned with the use of hidden cameras, which many "would consider to be a guileless, objective tool of information gathering."[132]

---

[127] GILLERS, *supra* note 121, at 142.

[128] Seow Ting Lee, *The Ethics of Journalistic Deception, in* THE MORAL MEDIA: HOW JOURNALISTS REASON ABOUT ETHICS 93–94 (Lee Wilkins & Renita Coleman eds., 2004).

[129] Interestingly, this process bears some similarity to Sissela Bok's Scheme of Applied Publicity, which we discuss in Chapter 3.

[130] Lee, *supra* note 128, at 92.

[131] *Id.* at 100.

[132] *Id.* at 101–02.

At the same time, journalist tend to make complex moral calculations when considering whether to conduct an undercover investigation. They valued using deception where it helped them fulfill their responsibility to their audiences. And they appeared to be more tolerant of lying when the target of the investigation was a wrongdoer. Similarly, some journalists viewed deception as a "part of a strategy to level a perceived power imbalance."[133]

The work of scholars in assessing the ethics of undercover investigations by journalists represents several different ways to approach the issue. It is noteworthy that, like many of the ethical standards that are publicly available, many of the scholars writing in this area reject an absolutist approach in either direction, though they differ on where the presumptions about the validity of investigative deception should lie.

* * *

Needless to say, it is highly contested among professional journalists, news organizations, and scholars whether undercover investigations by journalists are ethical. Moreover, it is likely that those ethics are at least partly context dependent. The development of a uniform set of journalism ethics standards can never be more than aspirational. Because journalism is not a profession in the sense that there are no governing bodies to regulate behavior, no ethical standard is enforceable beyond the institution that adopts it. Those entities can punish or fire journalists who don't adhere to their code. But across the field of journalism, publications and other news outlets may disagree about which standards are important.

Furthermore, ethical standards are historically and culturally contingent. As we have described, undercover investigations by journalists have come into favor during some periods and have been disfavored during others. This may be related to the structure and strength of other institutions; the degree to which the public trusts the news media vis-à-vis the government; how such investigations are viewed in other contexts, such as law enforcement and civil rights testing; and whether there are laws in place that prohibit or impede such undercover tactics. There may also be important questions about moral relativism that affect debates about ethical codes. Are there certain historical, social, or cultural circumstances in which even journalists who ordinarily shun investigative deception might change their views about the ethics of undercover investigations depending on the value of the information that is discovered through their work? Or during times of low public trust in government, as in the Watergate era, are undercover investigations more tolerable? In the end, it may be, as Dicken-Garcia has suggested, that "beyond certain preliminary, basic tenets of practice, there is

---

[133] *Id.* at 104.

little consensus among journalists about what is right or wrong about methods of gathering, presenting, and distributing news."[134]

In the next chapter, we examine whether there are constitutional protections for the lies told as part of undercover investigations and whether, if so, they extend to political activists and other investigators who are not formally affiliated with the professional news media.

---

[134] DICKEN-GARCIA, *supra* note 10, at 242.

# 3

# Investigative Deception and the First Amendment

## 3.1 INTRODUCTION

Merle Linda Wolin was a reporter with the *Los Angeles Herald Examiner* in 1980, when she began an eight-month-long undercover investigation of the Los Angeles garment worker industry. To gain access to the day-to-day working conditions of garment workers, Wolin first had to create a false identity and background to blend in with the largely immigrant workforce. As she described it, "Transforming a fair-skinned, green-eyed Jewish reporter into Merlina De Novais, a poor, illegal Brazilian worker required study."[1] Thus, she misrepresented her name, her ethnic identity, her primary language, and her immigration status. She chose to pretend she was from Brazil because there would likely be fewer garment workers from that country, where the primary language is Portuguese rather than Spanish, and she could get by with a "rather strange Spanish accent." "If I were asked to speak Portuguese," she reported, "I would make up words or smile evasively."

Wolin's creation of a fake identity was successful, and she ended up working for several different Los Angeles sewing factories, where she was paid far less than minimum wage, observed obvious violations of health codes, and experienced the oppressive working conditions garment workers typically had to bear. During her undercover investigation, she interviewed more than 150 people and gathered

---

[1] This narrative is drawn from Merle Linda Wolin, *Sweatshop: Undercover in the Garment Industry*, L.A. HERALD-EXAMINER (Jan. 14, 1981), https://undercover.hosting.nyu.edu/files/original/ d4b853967f695bfddoced22a69e1943f8ob61082.pdf; Merle Linda Wolin, *Merlina Faces the Labor Commissioner – And Wins*, L.A. HERALD-EXAMINER (Jan. 20, 1981), https://undercover .hosting.nyu.edu/files/original/e6f76571757ee2bdf2a67a393boaoa2fa6e5fe23.pdf; Merle Linda Wolin, *Bradley: "I Wouldn't Want to Speculate . . .."* L.A. HERALD-EXAMINER (Jan. 29, 1981), https://undercover.hosting.nyu.edu/files/original/9c85aa9bo8cf89o1c929b5bf10262302889e765a .pdf; Merle Linda Wolin, *Brown: It's Wrong for a Civilized Society . . .* , L.A. HERALD-EXAMINER (Jan. 30, 1981), https://undercover.hosting.nyu.edu/files/original/66bo6a5c673 ccfaeo55405bbca8ocfa3e4256546.pdf.

firsthand information from her observations, which she was able to access only because she posed as a worker. The resulting sixteen-part series published in the *Herald Examiner* brought these untenable conditions to the surface and caught the attention of elected officials. Wolin testified before a congressional committee on labor about her experiences after her stories were published.

Her investigation was far reaching, seeking to expose not only the garment industry itself, but also clothing manufacturers and retail clothing stores that enabled the sweatshops to thrive by buying their products (not to mention wealthy consumers who purchased the clothing from those stores) and government officials who failed to take meaningful steps to enforce existing laws or envision new ones. With respect to government officials, in a move that went beyond most other journalistic investigations, Wolin, identifying herself *as* her alter ego, Merlina De Novais, filed and won a complaint for unpaid wages against one of her employers before the State Labor Commission. She even had to produce a fake social security card so that the Commission would forward her a check from her employer for the unpaid wages. Her entreaties to other government officials were less successful. As part of the series, she interviewed California Governor Jerry Brown, Los Angeles Mayor Tom Bradley, and several city officials responsible for enforcement of fire and safety codes. Brown and Bradley seemed underinformed about the issues and, while claiming to be sympathetic to the plight of workers, had few ideas about how to push forward meaningful reforms.

For her investigative work, Wolin was nominated for the Public Service award for the 1982 Pulitzer Prize and was voted unanimously to receive the award, but that decision was overturned by the Pulitzer Board. It is probable that this decision, like the Board's rejection of the *Chicago Sun-Times's* award for its Mirage investigation, was due to the Board's discomfort with investigative deception. After all, as with all other undercover investigations, Wolin intentionally lied to get the access necessary to produce her stories. Wolin would go on to become one of the founders of *Mother Jones* magazine, which heralded its own pathbreaking undercover journalism investigations.[2]

As we have seen already, investigative deception plays a key role in carrying out undercover investigations in at least five major contexts: civil rights testing, union salting, law enforcement operations, journalism, and political advocacy.[3] In each of these contexts, deceptions have led investigators to infiltrate groups across the political spectrum as well as groups with no particular political or ideological affiliation. Persons have gained access to and spied on prisons, mental health

[2]  Joseph Farah, *The Bravest Reporter I Know*, WND (Oct. 3, 2007), www.wnd.com/2007/10/43817/.

[3]  For a discussion of how the law views undercover investigations across these different contexts in a starkly different manner, see Alan K. Chen, *Investigative Deception across Social Contexts*, KNIGHT FIRST AMEND. INST. (Dec. 16, 2022), https://knightcolumbia.org/content/investigative-deception-across-social-contexts [https://perma.cc/Y3LN-7CKZ].

facilities, gangs, white supremacist organizations like the KKK or the Proud Boys, reproductive freedom organizations, factory farms, and sex trafficking rings.[4] These deception-based investigations appear to have catalyzed efforts in support of law reform, led to civil and criminal enforcement actions, and prompted national conversations that were impossible, even unimaginable, without the deception-based investigation.[5]

But there has been a backlash against investigative deceptions from state governments as well as the targets of these investigations, who have argued that these lies violate their legal rights. Critics of undercover investigations contend that lies to gain access to private property constitute a trespass under applicable state law. Others claim that undercover investigations based on deception violate the privacy and autonomy rights of the investigation's targets. When an investigator secures employment with the investigation's target to gain access to the employer's place of business, it has been claimed that this conduct violates the common law duty of loyalty because the investigator is simultaneously serving the interests of the investigating entity and the target. There is palpable legal tension between these common law state interests and the value of investigative deception as a category of protected speech. In conducting her investigation, did Wolin violate any of these legal interests? If so, did the First Amendment nonetheless shield her from liability under those laws?

In this chapter, we examine how the law applies to investigative deception and to what degree, if any, the First Amendment to the US Constitution might protect such lies from the State's imposition of civil and criminal legal sanctions.

## 3.2 CONSTITUTIONAL OVERVIEW: HISTORICAL SCOPE OF PROTECTION FOR LIES AS EXPRESSION

Lying has a complicated relationship with the First Amendment.[6] It is beyond question that some lies – such as perjury and fraud – are simply not covered by the Constitution's free speech clause. But it is equally clear that some lies are entitled to First Amendment protection. Historically, most constitutional protection for lies was purely prophylactic – it provided protection to the truth-speaker by also incidentally protecting the liar. We agree that protecting lies is important in order to

---

[4] One memoir about child sex trafficking investigations is DANIEL WALKER, GOD IN A BROTHEL: AN UNDERCOVER JOURNEY INTO SEX TRAFFICKING AND RESCUE (2011).

[5] As we highlight in Chapter 6, however, some studies have concluded that investigative reporting may not have had as substantial an impact on law reform efforts as might have been assumed.

[6] In this chapter we are specifically interested in intentional lies, not merely mistaken factual claims, made as part of an undercover investigation. To date, many scholars have assumed that "false statements" are entitled to greater protection than deliberate "lies." *See* CASS SUNSTEIN, LIARS: FALSEHOODS AND FREE SPEECH IN AN AGE OF DECEPTION, 131 (2021); *id.* at 47 ("the speaker's state of mind matters").

avoid chilling the speech of truthful speakers, but in this chapter we make the case for affirmatively recognizing that other lies need constitutional protection because they actually serve the underlying goals animating free speech protection. We contend that what we have called "high value lies" have played an important role in American history, and affirmatively further the three most commonly invoked theoretical goals of free speech: enhancing political discourse, revealing truth, and promoting individual autonomy.[7] To the extent that such lies might cause harms, we submit that the speech value of investigative deception usually outweighs those harms.

Specifically, our focus here is on the relationship between law and the lies used for investigations. We start by providing a historical overview of the law's protection for lies, focusing in particular on the Supreme Court's seminal decisions in this area. Next, we offer a taxonomy of lies that suggests that lies that facilitate the discovery of truth (e.g., a lie during a Socratic dialogue) or that facilitate discourse and debate on matters of public concern (perhaps an investigation of a politician) should be recognized as uniquely valuable for free speech, and jealously guarded against legal restrictions. We consider how investigative deceptions fit into the traditional rationales for protecting free speech, and offer guidance on where the law is likely to evolve on these questions.

### 3.2.1 *A Taxonomy of Lies*

For decades, it was taken for granted that false factual statements are of no value to public discourse and thus fall entirely outside the First Amendment's protections.[8] Consider an example familiar to most laypeople. One may not falsely shout "Fire!"

---

[7]  These are the most widely articulated justifications for the constitutional protection of expression under contemporary free speech theory. *See, e.g.*, KATHLEEN M. SULLIVAN & GERALD GUNTHER, CONSTITUTIONAL LAW 744 (16th ed. 2007). For earlier scholarly treatments of the First Amendment coverage of the types of lies we discuss here, see Jonathan D. Varat, *Deception and the First Amendment: A Central, Complex, and Somewhat Curious Relationship*, 53 UCLA L. REV. 1107 (2006); Helen Norton, *Lies and the Constitution*, 2012 SUP. CT. REV. 161 (2012). Not surprisingly, legal scholars have paid increasing attention to lies in recent years. *See, e.g.*, SUNSTEIN, *supra* note 6; CATHERINE J. ROSS, A RIGHT TO LIE?: PRESIDENTS, OTHER LIARS, AND THE FIRST AMENDMENT (2021); Rebecca Aviel & Alan K. Chen, *Lawyer Speech, Investigative Deception, and the First Amendment*, 2021 U. ILL. L. REV. 1267 (2021); Alan K. Chen, *Free Speech, Rational Deliberation, and Some Truths about Lies*, 62 WM. & MARY L. REV. 357 (2020); Courtney M. Cox, *Legitimizing Lies*, 90 GEO. WASH. L. REV. 297 (2022); Bruce A. Green & Rebecca Roiphe, *Lawyers and the Lies They Tell*, 69 WASH. U. J.L. & POL'Y 37 (2022); Richard L. Hasen, *Deep Fakes, Bots, and Siloed Justices: American Election Law in a "Post-Truth" World*, 64 ST. LOUIS U. L.J. 535 (2020); Renee Knake Jefferson, *Lawyer Lies and Political Speech*, 131 YALE L.J. F. 114 (2021).
[8]  There were, however, some free speech concerns about the regulation of libel during the earlier years of the Republic. *See* Genevieve Lakier, *The Invention of Low-Value Speech*, 128 HARV. L. REV. 2166, 2184–86 (2015).

in a crowded theater.[9] This lie is not deserving of speech protection, because (1) *it has no value* and (2) *it can cause tangible social harm* (unnecessarily alarming people might cause panic, leading to physical injuries). But lies have been painted with too broad a brush. Many bear no resemblance to the fire-yelling falsehood. In law, as in life, not all lies are alike. Accordingly, in examining whether some lies ought to receive First Amendment protection, it is important to understand that lies fall into distinct categories. The remainder of this section takes up this task of creating a taxonomy of lies, and explores whether differences among lies ought to lead to a distinction in the degree of constitutional protection that they are afforded. Our basic point here is that not all lies should be treated the same, and that lies that facilitate the revelation of truthful facts of urgent public concern ought to be entitled to some of the greatest speech protections.

### 3.2.1.1 Category One: Lies as No-Value Speech

Lies that have no speech value do not warrant any free speech protection. Free speech doctrine under the First Amendment has long been understood to follow the so-called two-level speech theory.[10] There is a universe of expressive actions that count as speech, and then there is a small set of speech activities that are said to fall entirely outside the First Amendment's coverage.[11] The longest standing expression of this dichotomy comes from the often quoted dictum in the Court's fighting words case, *Chaplinsky v. New Hampshire*.[12] There, in declaring that speech rights under the First Amendment are not absolute, the Court listed several categories of speech that fall beyond its coverage. "There are certain well-defined and narrowly limited classes of speech, the prevention and punishment of which has never been thought to raise any Constitutional problem. *These include the lewd and obscene, the profane, the libelous, and the insulting or 'fighting' words*."[13] In addition to the

---

[9]  Schenck v. United States, 249 U.S. 47, 52 (1919).
[10]  *See* Geoffrey R. Stone, *Kenneth Karst's Equality as a Central Principle in the First Amendment*, 75 U. CHI. L. REV. 37, 43 (2008) (discussing the application of the "two-level" theory); Virginia v. Black, 538 U.S. 343, 358–59 (2003) (describing the permissibility of government regulation of "certain categories of expression").
[11]  *See* United States v. Stevens, 559 U.S. 460, 468 (2010) (describing the categories of unprotected speech). Where we refer to the idea that a particular category of speech is "covered" by the First Amendment, we mean that its regulation will be subject to some form of judicial scrutiny under free speech doctrine. Speech that is not covered does not even trigger First Amendment concerns, and therefore may be regulated without meaningful judicial oversight. For categories of speech that *are* covered by the First Amendment, there are different levels of *protection*, depending on the nature of the speech, the context, and the type of regulation involved. Speech that is not covered by the First Amendment is, ipso facto, not protected. But not all speech that is covered is necessarily protected identically. On the coverage/protection distinction generally, see Frederick Schauer, *The Boundaries of the First Amendment: A Preliminary Exploration of Constitutional Salience*, 117 HARV. L. REV. 1765 (2004).
[12]  315 U.S. 568 (1942).
[13]  *Id.* at 571–72 (emphasis added).

implied historical pedigree[14] of these categories of unprotected speech, the Court articulated a functional rationale for their exclusion from the First Amendment. "[S]uch utterances are no essential part of any exposition of ideas, and are of *such slight social value* as a step to truth that any benefit that may be derived from them is clearly outweighed by the social interest in order and morality."[15] Simply put, under the two-level theory, some types of speech have little or no value, and therefore receive no protection.[16]

Several different categories of lies have historically been held, or are assumed, to fall outside the First Amendment's protection because they lack any social value and cause tangible harms to third parties or to society at large. Laws banning fraud, which regulate speech designed to induce listeners to give money to the speaker under false pretenses, are well-accepted examples of speech regulations the government may enforce without much constitutional limitation.[17] In *Illinois ex rel. Madigan v. Telemarketing Associates, Inc.*,[18] the Court rejected a First Amendment challenge by a professional charitable fundraising organization that was sued by the state for making false and misleading misrepresentations to donors.[19] In doing so, it made it clear that "the First Amendment does not shield fraud."[20]

---

[14]  Genevieve Lakier discredits this historical narrative and demonstrates that neither the Supreme Court nor other federal or state courts in the period prior to the New Deal routinely recognized categories of low-value speech. *See* Lakier, *supra* note 8, at 2177–79. Indeed, there was both more and less First Amendment protection for categories of speech that the modern Court deems as having no or little value. On one hand, prior restraints were presumptively invalid for all categories of speech. *Id.* at 2179–81. On the other hand, criminal penalties on both high- and low-value speech were tolerated much more than they are today. *Id.*

[15]  *Chaplinsky*, 315 U.S. at 572 (emphasis added).

[16]  Although two-level speech theory focuses primarily on the *value* of expression, the Court also tends to examine the *social harms* associated with a category of speech when determining whether it is covered by the First Amendment. For categories of expression deemed unprotected, the Court's normal mistrust of government justifications is set aside, not only because these types of speech have no or little value, but also because the states' interests are not speculative, but tangible and easily understood. Thus, fighting words may have no value, but they also arguably may provoke immediate physical violence. Obscenity is said not to facilitate any traditional speech value, but some people argue that it also may undermine societal morals and cause harm to women. And so forth.

[17]  Other types of fraudulent inducement unrelated to financial gain may also fall outside the free speech clause. For example, in Gilbert v. Minnesota, 254 U.S. 325, 333 (1920), the Court rejected a First Amendment claim by a person charged with discouraging military enlistment in part because his statements were deliberate misrepresentations.

[18]  538 U.S. 600 (2003).

[19]  *Id.* at 624.

[20]  *Id.* at 612. Although fraud is generally not covered by the First Amendment, government regulations directed at fraud are not entirely immune from scrutiny. *See, e.g.,* Schneider v. New Jersey, 308 U.S. 147, 164–65 (1939); Riley v. Nat'l Fed'n of the Blind of N.C., 487 U.S. 781, 800 (1988); Sec'y of State of Md. v. Joseph H. Munson Co., Inc., 467 U.S. 947, 967–68 (1984); Schaumburg v. Citizens for a Better Env't, 444 U.S. 620, 636 (1980).

Fraudulent speech has no First Amendment value and also causes harm to its targets.[21]

Similarly, the government has unquestioned power to regulate false statements of fact in the context of perjury. It would border on the absurd to argue that a person's lies under oath would advance any First Amendment values, since such speech obscures, rather than leads to, truth finding. Indeed, judicial proceedings are designed to smoke out the truth and resolve disputes; lies that distort or impair the judicial process directly impede these goals.[22] Perjured testimony can lead to harm to third parties (say, a wrongfully convicted criminal defendant), to the justice system itself (by undermining its ability to accurately resolve disputes), and in some cases may materially benefit the speaker (by enabling them to evade liability or conviction).[23] Not surprisingly, then, the Court has repeatedly classified perjury as speech beyond the First Amendment's protection.[24] The same could be said for laws that prohibit or criminalize making false statements to government officials in the course of their official duties.[25]

Other lies that compromise the integrity of government processes also fall outside the First Amendment, even when the misrepresentation is not made under oath. For instance, when a private citizen falsely represents that they are a police officer or other government official, that statement is not protected speech.[26] Like the preceding examples, this type of speech has the effect not of advancing democracy or facilitating the search for truth, but of interfering with these goals. Speakers who engage in this conduct risk undermining the integrity of government processes and potentially misrepresenting or misappropriating the position and power of the state.[27] As the Court has explained, statutes criminalizing the impersonation of public officials serve to avoid tangible harm to "the general good repute and dignity

[21] In other areas in which the government regulates fraud, there is frequently not even a discussion or consideration of First Amendment limitations because the issue is treated as self-evident. *See, e.g.*, Michael R. Siebecker, *Corporate Speech, Securities Regulation, and an Institutional Approach to the First Amendment*, 48 WM. & MARY L. REV. 613, 641–42 (2006) (observing the many ways in which securities regulations affect speech yet are assumed to fall outside First Amendment scrutiny).
[22] United States v. Alvarez, 567 U.S. 709, 720–21 (2012) ("Perjured testimony 'is at war with justice' because it can cause a court to render a 'judgment not resting on truth'") (citation omitted).
[23] *See id.*
[24] *See, e.g.*, Konigsberg v. State Bar of Cal., 366 U.S. 36, 49 n.10 (1961).
[25] The Federal False Statements Act is one example of such a law. *See* 18 U.S.C. § 1001 (2012); *see also Alvarez*, 567 U.S. at 720.
[26] *See, e.g.*, United States v. Swisher, 771 F.3d 514, 522–23 (9th Cir. 2014) (discussing the dangers created by the impersonation of government officials).
[27] *Alvarez*, 567 U.S. at 721. *See also* Norton, *supra* note 7, at 198 (observing that lying about being a law enforcement officer harms "the public's trust in, and thus the effectiveness of, law enforcement"). Of course, it is possible that in some narrow instances impersonating a government employee could serve the interests of truth and, on balance, benefit the goals of free speech.

of the (government) service itself."[28] These lies almost always present a risk of injury to the public reputation of the office or institution in question.[29] In addition, because government actors have the imprimatur of official authority, misrepresenting oneself as having such authority presents special dangers to third parties, who believe they are dealing with, and may yield to, one who has the apparent backing and authority of the state.[30] Consistent with the current law, we believe that impersonating a public official is a unique category[31] of lying that, even when done in an investigative context, falls outside the First Amendment's scope.

Still another category of deception that is generally exempted from First Amendment protection is commercial speech.[32] At one time, the Court categorically excluded commercial speech from First Amendment coverage.[33] More recently, the Court has recognized that commercial speech may have substantial value because it advances the economic interests of the speaker and provides important information to consumers and society at large.[34] But the Court has made it clear that the government has wide latitude to regulate false or misleading commercial speech. As the Court has explained, "there can be no constitutional objection to the suppression of commercial messages that do not accurately inform the public about lawful activity. The government may ban forms of communication more

---

[28] United States v. Lepowitch, 318 U.S. 702, 704 (1943).

[29] *Id.* We say *almost* always because perhaps it is conceivable that someone's drunken braggadocio over a few beers does not cause harm. *See* Helen Norton, *Lies to Manipulate, Misappropriate, and Acquire Governmental Power, in* LAW AND LIES 167–68 (Austin D. Sarat ed., 2015) ("Lies about being the government that constitute mere bragging or puffery, for example, may be relatively harmless and thus undeserving of punishment"). For our part, we think that even this sort of deception about being employed by the government may create risks of harm, but we don't take up that question here.

[30] Norton, *supra* note 7, at 198.

[31] By describing this as unique, we don't mean to suggest that we have created an exhaustive account of the types of lies that warrant no speech protection. We also think that certain lies, even if they would otherwise be what we later define as high-value lies, raise interesting questions that warrant more attention. For example, what about lies told about one's race, gender, or religion in order to gain entry to a private space to conduct an investigation? Should an employment application by someone claiming to be Black be treated similarly for speech purposes as one that denies an association with any private investigation firms? And if states may proscribe lies about one's race, could they also prohibit lies about political party? Our inclinations are strongly in the direction of recognizing First Amendment coverage here, but this topic warrants a fuller treatment elsewhere.

[32] Commercial speech is "expression [that is] related solely to the economic interests of the speaker and its audience." Cent. Hudson Gas & Elec. Corp. v. Pub. Serv. Comm'n of N.Y., 447 U.S. 557, 561 (1980); *see also* Va. State Bd. of Pharmacy v. Va. Citizens Consumer Council, Inc., 425 U.S. 748, 771 (1976) (distinguishing between truthful and deceptive commercial speech).

[33] Valentine v. Chrestensen, 316 U.S. 52, 54 (1942), *overruling recognized by* Bose Corp. v. Consumers Union of U.S., Inc., 466 U.S. 485, 504 n.22 (1984).

[34] *Cent. Hudson*, 447 U.S. at 562–64 (recognizing intermediate scrutiny as the proper standard of review for content-based restrictions on commercial speech); *Bose Corp.*, 466 U.S. at 504 n.22 (discussing the history of the Court's treatment of commercial speech).

likely to deceive the public than to inform it."[35] As with the preceding categories of lies that are beyond the scope of constitutional protection, false or misleading commercial speech is not valuable to the ends served by the First Amendment and also has the potential to cause harm to those who are misled by it.[36]

When it comes to no value, Category One lies, we are comfortable saying that they fall entirely outside the scope of the First Amendment and may be regulated or banned by state actors.

### 3.2.1.2 Category Two: Lies That Are Protected to Avoid Chilling Truthful Speech

As discussed previously, most constitutional protection for lies prior to the twenty-first century was established not to protect those lies from regulation per se but to protect the truthful speech that might be swept into such regulations. *New York Times v. Sullivan* is illustrative of this reasoning. In that case, the Court reviewed a $500,000 judgment on a defamation claim brought by a Montgomery, Alabama, county commissioner against several civil rights activists and a major newspaper.[37] The newspaper had published the activists' advertisement criticizing the local Montgomery police, who were ostensibly under the commissioner's direction, for engaging in antagonistic conduct toward civil rights demonstrators. It was undisputed that some of the factual statements contained in the ad were inaccurate. The trial judge had instructed the jury that these types of statements constituted libel per se, meaning that the plaintiff need not prove actual harm or malicious intent on the speaker's part in order to recover damages.

On appeal, the Supreme Court overturned the Alabama courts' rulings upholding the defamation verdict against the defendants. Rejecting the claim that defamatory statements are categorically unprotected by the First Amendment, the Court distinguished prior cases addressing free speech and defamation because they did not involve statements critical of public officials, observing that this dispute must be evaluated "against the background of a profound national commitment to the principle that debate on public issues should be uninhibited, robust, and wide-open, and that it may well include vehement, caustic, and sometimes unpleasantly sharp attacks on government and public officials." The Court took for granted that in the context of criticism of government officials or heated debate on important public issues, speech would sometimes be exaggerated or even contain false

---

[35] *Cent. Hudson*, 447 U.S. at 563.
[36] For further elaboration of categories of false factual statements that are not covered by the First Amendment, see Brief of Professors Eugene Volokh and James Weinstein as Amici Curiae in Support of Petitioner at 3–11, United States v. Alvarez, 567 U.S. 709 (2012) (No. 11-210), 2011 WL 6179424, at *3–11.
[37] The facts and descriptions of the Court's legal analysis in this section are drawn from the Court's opinion. *See* N.Y. Times Co. v. Sullivan, 376 U.S. 254 (1964).

statements. It went on to observe that "erroneous statement is inevitable in free debate, and that it must be protected if the freedoms of expression are to have the 'breathing space' that they 'need to survive.'" The need to allow broad latitude for public discourse, the Court reasoned, required the protection of even false state-ments of fact.

In order to protect these interests, the Court held that where defamation claims are brought by public officials against speakers who criticize their conduct, those claims may not be upheld unless the plaintiff can show that the speaker's statement was made with "actual malice," meaning that the speaker made the defamatory statement with knowledge that it was false or with reckless disregard for its falsity.[38] In addition, the Court held that in order to ensure that speech is not chilled, states must require plaintiffs to prove the defendants' state of mind by clear and convin-cing evidence.[39] The point of imposing a high burden on public official defamation plaintiffs was not that the false statements themselves had intrinsic value, but that if critics of the government were exposed to substantial tort liability, they might rein in their rhetoric in ways that would result in self-censorship of even truthful criticisms. Later, in *Curtis Publishing Co. v. Butts*, the Court applied these same heightened protections to defendants accused of defamation against *any* "public figures," "non-public persons who 'are nevertheless intimately involved in the resolution of import-ant public questions or, by reason of their fame, shape events in areas of concern to society at large.'"[40]

The Supreme Court has also extended the *New York Times* standard to so-called false light invasion of privacy claims under state tort law. In *Time, Inc. v. Hill*, the Court reviewed a tort judgment against a newsmagazine that had published an article and photo spread connected to the opening of a fictional play loosely based on an actual crime involving individuals who held a Pennsylvania family hostage in their home.[41] The family complained that the magazine story represented the play as accurately depicting the actual crime, when in fact the play had embellished and altered the story in significant ways. The Supreme Court invalidated the jury's verdict for the family on the ground that the First Amendment protects the freedom of speech and press in the publication of material about matters of public concern.

As in the context of defamation, the Court's limitation of state privacy torts was based not on the value of the false or inaccurate statements (even intentionally false statements) in the article but on the fear that zealous enforcement of state law to police untrue statements would likely suppress a wide range of speech, including truthful speech about matters of public concern. Such tort liability could create a chilling effect and "saddle the press with the impossible burden of verifying to a

---

[38]  *Id.* at 279–80.
[39]  *Id.* at 285–86.
[40]  388 U.S. 130, 164 (1967) (Warren, C.J., concurring in result).
[41]  385 U.S. 374, 377 (1967).

certainty the facts associated in news articles with a person's name, picture or portrait, particularly as related to nondefamatory matter."[42]

Another context in which the Court has deemed false speech to be constitutionally protected is in its assessment of the First Amendment implications of the tort of intentional infliction of emotional distress. If all lies are not protected by the First Amendment, we might imagine the quick death of satire or mockery. In *Hustler Magazine, Inc. v. Falwell*, the Court reviewed a tort judgment against a magazine that published a parody in the form of a fake liquor advertisement implying that a nationally known, politically active minister had lost his virginity to his mother in an outhouse.[43] The Court overturned a state court judgment that imposed substantial civil liability on the magazine, holding that this type of penalty for even an "outrageous" parody of a public figure cannot withstand First Amendment scrutiny unless the plaintiff demonstrates that there was a false statement of fact made with knowledge of its falsity or reckless disregard for the truth of the matter, essentially the same as the *Sullivan* standard.[44] Recognizing a long history of parodies of public figures in political and other public discourse, the Court concluded that the threat of tort liability could create a chilling effect in the absence of a more restrictive standard. Similarly, in *Snyder v. Phelps*, a case involving a protest with highly offensive signs outside a military veteran's funeral, the Supreme Court reversed a tort judgment in favor of plaintiffs, not because the speech on the signs in question was true – no one takes seriously the Westboro Baptists' claims that persons who are gay "Doom Nations."[45] Instead, the Court reiterated the reasoning from *Sullivan* that courts must be careful to avoid rules that would chill truthful speech, because of "the principle that debate on public issues should be uninhibited, robust, and wide-open." Parodies and protests may be nasty, hurtful, and condemnable, but failing to provide clear and robust speech protection might threaten this form of political expression altogether. In short, sometimes many lies are protected not because we value or like the speech at issue, but because doing so is instrumental to protecting *truthful* speech.

Finally, there is a broad swath of what we call "socially routine lies," intentionally false statements of fact that have some social utility, but do not promote political or social discourse. We think that most lies are probably of this innocuous type. As Justice Stephen Breyer observed,

> False factual statements can serve useful human objectives, for example: in social contexts, where they may prevent embarrassment, protect privacy, shield a person from prejudice, provide the sick with comfort, or preserve a child's innocence; in

---

[42] *Id.* at 389.
[43] 485 U.S. 46, 47–48 (1988).
[44] The Court failed to acknowledge that most parodies do, in fact, involve knowingly false statements or depictions.
[45] 562 U.S. 443, 454 (2011).

public contexts, where they may stop a panic or otherwise preserve calm in the face of danger; and even in technical, philosophical, and scientific contexts, where (as Socrates' methods suggest) examination of a false statement (even if made deliberately to mislead) can promote a form of thought that ultimately helps realize the truth.[46]

Thus, on the continuum of social value, these types of lies are less valuable than high-value lies, but potentially have greater value than lies that have historically been subject to strong regulation, such as fraud or perjury.

Moreover, while there is not as great a danger that laws regulating socially routine lies would deter people from engaging in political discourse or dissent, they could nonetheless chill socially valuable speech. In this way, regulation of such lies would implicate free speech concerns similar to those involved in the imposition of tort liability on those who engage in libel or parodies of public officials and figures. Suppose, for example, a legislature enacted, in good faith, a law making it a crime for any person to tell a lie during a public safety emergency. The underlying legitimate purpose of the law might have been to ensure that no person is misled during a fire or at an accident scene in ways that might be potentially harmful, such as an ambulance-chasing lawyer who tells an accident victim, "If you don't imme- diately retain me to represent you, your chances of a large recovery will be severely affected." But suppose an emergency relief worker tells a lie to an injured victim to minimize the chance that he will panic, go into shock, or give up hope ("We're definitely going to get you out of here safely"). That emergency worker may forgo the calming statement for fear of being subject to criminal penalties. Or consider a law prohibiting telling lies to family members, enacted by a state legislature to "facilitate family harmony and stability." Such a law might deter a wide range of lies that family members employ for socially beneficial purposes, as in the case of parents telling a frightened child that "no one ever dies in plane accidents."

Though this category of innocuous lies materially differs in kind from libel, parodies, and protests, their regulation could well lead to similarly undesirable chilling effects.

### 3.2.1.3 *A Watershed Moment*: United States v. Alvarez

The legal landscape of the constitutional protection for lies dramatically shifted when the Supreme Court decided *United States v. Alvarez*.[47] In one of the more memorable opening lines, the *Alvarez* opinion begins with the simple phrase, "Lying was his habit." The plurality opinion goes on to describe Xavier Alvarez's pattern of lying, noting that the record reflected that he "lied when he said that he

---

[46] *Alvarez*, 567 U.S. at 733 (Breyer, J., concurring).
[47] The facts and descriptions of the Court's legal analysis in this section are drawn from the Court's opinion. *Alvarez*, 567 U.S. at 709 (plurality opinion).

played hockey for the Detroit Red Wings and that he once married a starlet from Mexico."[48] The lie that got Alvarez into *legal* trouble, however, was his false claim that he had been awarded the military's highest honor, although federal prosecutors took the apparent position that any of his lies could subject him to criminal punishment.[49] Alvarez was prosecuted and convicted of violating the federal Stolen Valor Act, which made it a crime for persons to falsely represent themselves to have been awarded a US military decoration or medal.

In the view of the United States in *Alvarez*, "the general rule is that false statements of fact are not protected by the First Amendment."[50] That position suggests that government regulation of lies is subject to no judicial scrutiny. Rejecting that position, the Court instead for the first time recognized some constitutional protection for even thoroughly valueless and reprehensible intentional lies. Xavier Alvarez was charged not with merely stating a "falsehood" but with an intentional "lie"; nor was he joking or engaging in satire about military honors. He was not simply engaging in puffery or exaggeration while on a date or out drinking with friends. Instead, Alvarez was a local water board official making a speech to the public when he brazenly boasted to his constituents that he had been awarded a Congressional Medal of Honor for his military service. The Court invalidated Alvarez's conviction, holding that the act violated the First Amendment, and in so doing articulated a number of important rationales for limiting government power to punish lies. This clear statement by the Court that lies, even lies like those told by Alvarez, are constitutionally protected was a jolt to many legal scholars. One preeminent scholar, Cass Sunstein, went so far as to say that the "ultimate ruling was wrong, even preposterous."[51]

The decision refused to distinguish lies from falsehoods, and concluded that valueless, narcissistic lies of the sort at issue in *Alvarez* are "speech" within the First Amendment's meaning. It is worth pausing to acknowledge *Alvarez*'s sharp break from earlier case law and to carefully parse the Court's reasoning in order to

---

[48] *Id.*

[49] Brief for Petitioner, United States at 18–20, United States v. Alvarez, 567 U.S. 709 (2012) (No. 11-210), 2011 WL 6019906, at *18–20.

[50] Brief of United States at 10, 19, United States v. Alvarez, 567 U.S. 709 (2012) (No. 11-210), 2011 WL 6019906, at *10, *19 (arguing that "this Court's First Amendment decisions have long recognized that false factual statements 'are not protected by the First Amendment in the same manner as truthful statements'" (quoting Brown v. Hartlage, 456 U.S. 45, 60–61 (1982)); *see also* *Alvarez*, 567 U.S. at 750 (Alito, J., dissenting) (quoting Gertz v. Robert Welch, Inc., 418 U.S. 323, 342 (1974)) (stating false statements are entitled, at most, only to a limited "measure of strategic protection" that derives from the need to ensure that any false speech restriction does not chill truthful and other fully protected speech). In contrast, mocking the notion that lies are almost "always" unprotected, Chief Judge Kozinski, in one of the lower court decisions in the case, exclaimed, "'Always' is a deliciously dangerous word, often eaten with a side of crow." United States v. Alvarez, 638 F.3d 666, 673 (9th Cir. 2011) (Kozinski, C.J., concurring in denial of rehearing en banc).

[51] SUNSTEIN, *supra* note 6, at 42.

understand its likely application to lies used to gain access for investigative purposes. The government's claim was not entirely without support in the Court's prior case law. In *Gertz v. Robert Welch, Inc.*, the Court said false statements of fact "belong to that category of utterances which 'are no essential part of any exposition of ideas, and are of such slight social value as a step to truth that any benefit that may be derived from them is clearly outweighed by the social interest in order and morality.'"[52] Even stronger, in *Hustler Magazine, Inc. v. Falwell*, the Court explained that "[f]alse statements of fact are particularly *valueless*; they interfere with the truth-seeking function of the marketplace of ideas, and they cause damage."[53] And these sentiments were echoed and amplified in an amicus brief submitted by two respected free speech scholars, who asserted: "[T]he Stolen Valor Act, if read to apply only to knowingly false representations, should be seen as constitutional, on the grounds that the First Amendment generally does not protect knowingly false statements of fact."[54]

The most significant feature of the *Alvarez* decision is its clear break from this line of thinking. By a six to three margin, the Court renounced any notion that there is a "general exception to the First Amendment for false statements" and disavowed the suggestion that its prior cases regarded "false statements, as a general rule, [as] beyond constitutional protection."[55] Instead of a general rule against speech protection for lies, *Alvarez* suggests a presumption that lies *are* covered by the First Amendment. After *Alvarez*, even worthless lies that serve no obvious function in the marketplace of ideas and, worse still, might impede the search for truth, are thus deemed fundamental to the First Amendment's protections. As Professor Sunstein also observed, "[u]nder *Alvarez*, it is not easy [for a government] to defend any ban on lies."[56]

3.2.1.3.1 UNDERSTANDING *ALVAREZ:* NOT EVERY LIE IS A PROTECTED FORM OF SPEECH Although the earlier scholarly and judicial analysis of lies tended to diminish the importance of lies and the speech protections owed to them, *Alvarez* fundamentally altered the landscape by acknowledging that governmental efforts toward limiting lies, even valueless lies about winning military honors, "illustrates, in a *fundamental way*, the reasons for the law's distrust of content-based speech prohibitions."[57] Even so, not all lies are protected.

**Lies That Cause Legally Cognizable Harms**   After *Alvarez*, harm is a relevant limiting principle. In rejecting the government's claim that all lies are no-value

---

[52]  418 U.S. at 340 (quoting *Chaplinsky*, 315 U.S. at 572).
[53]  485 U.S. 46, 52 (1988) (emphasis added).
[54]  Volokh & Weinstein Amicus Brief, *supra* note 36, at 34.
[55]  *Alvarez*, 567 U.S. at 718.
[56]  SUNSTEIN, *supra* note 6, at 46.
[57]  *Alvarez*, 567 U.S. at 722 (emphasis added).

speech under the First Amendment, Justice Kennedy's plurality opinion noted that the prior case law was confined to categories of regulation targeting lies that caused a "legally cognizable harm."[58] Some categories of lies, such as fraudulent misrepresentations, cause material financial harm to specific victims. As we have already discussed, other types of lies prohibited by these laws undermine both the truth-finding function and the integrity of government processes in ways that tangibly and fundamentally interfere with those matters.[59]

Justice Breyer's concurrence elaborates on harm as a relevant limiting principle. He wrote that lies that cause "specific harm to identifiable victims," whether the victim be the government, a business, or an individual, fall beyond the reach of the First Amendment.[60] The category of lies that are unprotected, then, must be discrete and identifiable based on "requirements of proof of injury,"[61] or instances where "tangible harm to others is especially likely to occur."[62] Justice Breyer explained that such "limitations help to make certain that ... [the law does not] discourage[e] or forbid[] the telling of [a] lie in contexts where harm is unlikely or the need for the prohibition is small."[63]

Justice Breyer's emphasis on actual harm or likelihood of harm led him to conclude that the law in question criminalizing lies was too broadly drafted. In contrast, he noted, "a more finely tailored statute might, as other kinds of statutes

---

[58] *Id.* at 718.

[59] Impersonating a government official is a unique type of lie. Typically, pretending to be someone other than yourself is not a material harm that eliminates First Amendment protection. *See id.* at 720. But pretending to be a representative of the government is different. Statutes covering such behavior serve the goals of protecting the democracy by "maintain[ing] the general good repute and dignity of ... government ... service itself." *Id.* at 721 (alterations in original) (quoting United States v. Lepowitch, 318 U.S. 702, 704 (1943)); Norton, *supra* note 7, at 198.

[60] *Alvarez*, 567 U.S. at 734 (Breyer, J., concurring). As Mark Tushnet has written,

> Justice Breyer's overbreadth analysis focuses not only on "specific harm," mostly to "identifiable victims" but also, with reference to the federal "false statements" statute, "where a lie is likely to work particular and specific harm by interfering with the functioning of a government department." Perhaps the harm associated with Stolen Valor Act lies is not visited on identifiable individuals, though we can identify the class that is harmed – those who have actually received the medals and now find the recognition the medals represent worth less.

Mark Tushnet, *Justice Breyer and the Partial De-Doctrinalization of Free Speech Law*, 128 HARV. L. REV. 508, 513 (2014) (quoting *Alvarez*, 567 U.S. at 734–35 (Breyer, J., concurring)); *see also* United States v. Swisher, 811 F.3d 299, 308 (9th Cir. 2016) ("[L]aws punishing fraud, defamation, or intentional infliction of emotional distress generally 'requir[e] proof of specific harm to identifiable victims,' and statutes prohibiting the impersonation of a public official 'may require a showing that, for example, someone was deceived into following a "course [of action] he would not have pursued but for the deceitful conduct"'") (second and third alteration in original) (quoting *Lepowitch*, 318 U.S. at 704).

[61] *Alvarez*, 567 U.S. at 737 (Breyer, J., concurring).

[62] *Id.* at 734.

[63] *Id.* at 736.

prohibiting false factual statements have done, insist upon a showing that the false statement caused specific harm or at least was material, or focus its coverage on lies most likely to be harmful or on contexts where such lies are most likely to cause harm."[64]

The dissenters, too, acknowledged the relevance of harm in analyzing the constitutionality of government regulation of false factual statements. Justice Alito emphasized that there are instances in which lying about military honors can lead to tangible harms.[65] For example, he pointed out that some individuals who lied about military honors were found to have defrauded the US Department of Veterans Affairs of $1.4 million in undeserved benefits.[66] But more significantly, the dissent believed that the range of potential harms that would suffice to remove constitutional protection for a lie was much broader than that adopted by the majority.[67] In the dissent's view, intangible, unquantifiable harms such as the emotional insult suffered by a truly decorated veteran were sufficient to justify stripping First Amendment protection from a lie.[68] The key difference between the six justices in the majority and the three in dissent, then, was the extent to which they were willing to defer to the government's conclusions that emotional or intangible harms were caused by lies about military honors. But even the dissent expressed concern about the possibility that criminalizing lies in some contexts might open "the door for the state to use its power for political ends."[69]

Lies that cause specific, articulable harm rather than abstract injury fall outside the coverage of free speech protections. This means that all manner of traditional fraud and similar conduct continues to be fairly viewed as an unprotected lie.

**Lies That Produce Undeserved Material Gains**   The opinions in *Alvarez* also suggest another valid reason for government regulation of lies. Even in the absence of (or in addition to) harm, the state may prohibit lying to stop the liar from obtaining an undeserved personal benefit. Thus, lies that produce "material gain" for the speaker are also not covered by the free speech clause.[70] Justice Kennedy noted in his plurality opinion that one of the flaws of the Stolen Valor Act was that it

---

[64] *Id.* at 738. At least one lower court views Justice Breyer's concurrence in precisely this analytical frame. *See Swisher,* 811 F.3d at 308–09 (describing Breyer's view as limiting the types of lies that may be prohibited by the state to those that cause or are likely to cause tangible harm).

[65] *Id.* at 741–43 (Alito, J., dissenting).

[66] *Id.* at 743.

[67] *Id.* at 742–43.

[68] *Id.* at 743.

[69] *Id.* at 751–52 (identifying "philosophy, religion, history, the social sciences, the arts, and *other matters of public concern*" as categories of lies that would be uniquely dangerous to criminalize because of the risk that truthful or debate-enhancing speech could be chilled, but failing to consider that some lies – lies told by investigators or whistleblowers to gain access, for example – may actually serve the goal of producing truth) (emphasis added).

[70] *Id.* at 723 (plurality opinion).

did not limit criminal liability to those who lied about military honors to produce a "material gain" or "material advantage."[71] As he wrote, "Where false claims are made to effect a fraud or secure moneys or other valuable considerations, say offers of employment, it is well established that the Government may restrict speech without affronting the First Amendment."[72] Enforcement of the Stolen Valor Act did not fall within this category because Alvarez's lies "do not seem to have been made to secure employment or financial benefits or admission to privileges reserved for those who had earned the Medal [of Honor]."[73]

But these passages prove enigmatic on careful study. It is not entirely clear whether material gain is an independent factor that permits the government regulation of lies or if it is simply the flip side of the harm limitation. Most lies that cause third-party harm also produce material gains for the speaker, and vice versa. Fraud, for example, causes financial harm to the victim and undeserved financial benefits to the speaker. Similarly, misappropriated trademarks can cause harm to the trademark holder and to consumers, who may be misled into purchasing the wrong product, but also produce unjust commercial gains for the infringer.[74]

As a practical matter, it is difficult to conceive of a benefit that one could obtain that would be improper in the absence of a corresponding cognizable harm to another. There do not appear to be any existing laws, including those authorizing recovery for unjust enrichment, that would allow one to recover for one's material gain that did not also cause harm to the complaining party. Indeed, Congress's amendment of the Stolen Valor Act after *Alvarez*, while referring only to a material gain, implies a defrauded or injured victim. The new statute makes it a federal offense to fraudulently hold oneself out as a recipient of the military honors covered by the original Stolen Valor Act "with [the] intent to obtain money, property, or any other tangible benefit."[75] By definition, the material gain must be at the expense of a private or public entity who is providing an undeserved benefit. Harm and benefit are likely inextricably linked in the context of misrepresentations.

### 3.2.1.4 A New Category: High-Value Lies

Lies can be valuable. As Justice Breyer's opinion in *Alvarez* expounding on the need to protect lies notes, they may serve "useful human objectives."[76] One useful human objective is the use of mistruths to facilitate investigations on matters of public

---

[71] *Id.*
[72] *Id.*
[73] *Id.* at 713.
[74] *Id.* at 743 (Alito, J., dissenting).
[75] 18 U.S.C. § 704(b) (Supp. I 2013).
[76] *Alvarez*, 567 U.S. at 733 (Breyer, J., concurring); *see also* Norton, *supra* note 7, at 164 ("Some lies have instrumental or even moral value").

concern. As we have already seen, the tactical deployment of such lies in this context has been an important ingredient in our democracy.

There is a long tradition of using deception as a means of gaining access to knowledge that would otherwise be obscured from public view. Without investigative deceptions (and their respective legal protection), much information critical to public discourse would have remained secret. We have thoroughly recounted these efforts in Chapters 1 and 2 of this book, describing the extensive use of investigative deceptions by undercover journalists, civil rights testers, union "salts," law enforcement officers, and political activists. While the context and goals of these investigations are substantially different, what connects them all is the use of intentional lies, including but not limited to falsehoods about the investigator's name, identity, and background; institutional or political affiliation or employer; actual objectives; and genuine motivation. Moreover, these lies are used to obtain access to private property where the investigators would not be permitted to go if the investigation's target knew the truth, potentially impose on the target's privacy, and perhaps transgress other potential common law legal rights. One might disagree with the tactics employed by these investigators, but it is difficult to dispute the import of what these investigations frequently reveal to the public eye. That is, while there is deception at the front end, in order to gain access to information, there is not deception at the back end, when investigators reveal their findings to the public. As the court in the *Food Lion* case clearly stated, "The truth of the *PrimeTime Live* broadcast was not an issue in the litigation."[77]

In addition to the breadth of contexts in which investigative deceptions are used, it also seems that they are used by organizations and individuals from across the political spectrum. There has recently been negative attention, as well as meaningful legal action, against anti-abortion groups such as the Center for Medical Progress (CMP) that have sent investigators with fabricated identities to conferences and meetings of reproductive freedoms groups such as Planned Parenthood. They claimed that abortion rights groups were violating the law by selling fetal tissue.[78] Critics of CMP and other groups have argued that these actions constitute fraud, invasions of privacy, extreme examples of trespass, and violations of the Racketeer Influenced and Corrupt Organizations Act, and that to the extent they involve people identifying themselves as journalists, are professionally unethical. As legal scholars, we do not purport to speak directly to the question of journalistic/investigative ethics. However, we doubt very much that courts applying the First

---

[77] Food Lion, Inc. v. Capital Cities/ABC, Inc., 194 F.3d 505, 511 (4th Cir. 1999).
[78] Federal law prohibits such sales for profit. *See* 42 U.S.C. § 289g-2(a) (making it a crime "for any person to knowingly acquire, receive, or otherwise transfer any human fetal tissue for valuable consideration if the transfer affects interstate commerce") and 42 U.S.C. § 289g-2(e)(3) (defining term "valuable consideration" as not including "reasonable payments associated with the transportation, implantation, processing, preservation, quality control, or storage of human fetal tissue").

Amendment are capable of refereeing the differences of degree between the investigations of Upton Sinclair, civil rights testers, undercover cops, animal rights activists, union salts, and groups like CMP. For persons on either side of the political aisle, if transparency and investigation are important goals, then the political motivation underlying the investigation should not matter from a free speech perspective. And we don't think there is an obvious reason to separate the investigative tactics of persons whose lies include not just oral communications but more elaborate deceptions such as fabricated websites, business cards, or resumes.[79]

In sum, lies have emerged as a central element if not a staple of investigative journalism, civil rights testing, union salting, law enforcement, and political activism. Particularly in a time when the traditional print media is suffering huge economic losses and, as we have discussed earlier, there are substantial internal professional critiques of journalists engaging in investigative deception, undercover investigations by other entities have filled a necessary role in helping expose truthful information about matters of public concern. Moreover, it is hard to doubt that if placed on a continuum of social value, investigative deceptions would be viewed as promoting greater good than Mr. Alvarez's gratuitous, self-serving lies about winning the Medal of Honor. Investigative deceptions used to gain entry typically produce much more benefit than they cause harm. As we elaborate on below, any harms they cause are likely to be relatively minor in relation to the values of the resulting disclosures, which produce benefits not only to individuals but frequently to the public at large. This is particularly so when the private property accessed is commercial property in a highly regulated industry, as opposed to a private individual's personal residence or the confines of a private space such as a restroom or locker room, where privacy interests are significantly higher.

Unlike lies that cause intangible personal benefits or cognizable harm to another, investigative deceptions are affirmatively valuable. They are high-value lies. As a federal district court in one of the ag-gag cases explained, "undercover investigators tell such lies in order to find evidence of animal abuse and expose any abuse or other

---

[79] This is not to suggest that all deception-based investigations will be protected by the First Amendment. One might portray what the investigation reveals in a misleading or false way that could constitute defamation. Or one might even use the investigation as a call for violence. And it would be ahistorical to ignore the violence that has been inflicted by activists on persons who have worked in the abortion field, thus making the context for those investigations unique. Many undercover investigations that expose wrongdoing could potentially result in some number of disgusting threats, even death threats. But so far as we know, it is only in the context of extreme anti-abortion activists that physical violence has resulted. Mireille Jacobson & Heather Royer, *Aftershocks: The Impact of Clinical Violence on Abortion Services*, 3:1 AM. ECON. J: APPLIED ECON. (Jan. 2011) (noting that between 1973 and 2003, anti-abortion activists committed over 300 violent acts at abortion facilities and on abortion providers, including arsons, bombings, butyric acid attacks, and murders). However, it should be noted that those were *not* in the contexts of undercover investigations, which can be considered to be a more mainstream and legitimate exercise of political advocacy.

bad practices the investigator discovers."[80] Beyond instrumental value, as the next section explains, the vigorous protection of this type of lie also comports with traditional free speech theory.

### 3.3 SPEECH THEORY AND THE FIRST AMENDMENT VALUE OF INVESTIGATIVE DECEPTIONS

This section examines the intersection of the First Amendment and lying. We contend that, contrary to conventional wisdom, lies by journalists, law enforcement officers, civil rights testers, union salts, and political activists told for the purpose of exposing illegality or other private misconduct that involves matters of important public concern fundamentally advance the First Amendment's values, and therefore have particularly strong *instrumental* value.[81] Most contemporary free speech theory is grounded in instrumental justifications for constitutional protection of expression,[82] and investigative deceptions serve the values underlying the First Amendment. High-value lies promote the three primary theoretical purposes of the First Amendment: democracy, truth facilitation, and self-realization.

#### 3.3.1 *Investigative Deceptions Promote Democratic Self-Governance*

One of the dominant speech theories argues that expression must be protected to ensure the advancement of democratic self-government. As one of its most prominent proponents has written, "The primary purpose of the First Amendment is . . . that all the citizens shall, so far as possible, understand the issues which bear upon our common life."[83] Meaningful deliberation about such issues can take place only with free and open discourse. More recently, Robert Post has observed that the democracy-based theory of speech requires protection of the process of forming public opinion.[84] On this view, the First Amendment ought to protect "those speech

---

[80]  Animal Legal Def. Fund v. Otter, 118 F. Supp. 3d 1195, 1204 (D. Idaho 2015), *aff'd in part, rev'd in part sub nom*, Animal Legal Def. Fund v. Wasden, 878 F.3d 1184 (9th Cir. 2018).

[81]  *See* Norton, *supra* note 7, at 164 ("Some lies have instrumental or even moral value").

[82]  Some scholars reject instrumentalist theories of speech and argue instead that the freedom of expression can best be understood by focusing on the government's reasons for regulation. Professor Larry Alexander argues that "[f]reedom of expression is implicated whenever an activity is suppressed or penalized for the purpose of preventing a message from being received." LARRY ALEXANDER, IS THERE A RIGHT OF FREEDOM OF EXPRESSION? 9 (2005). *See also* Andrew Koppelman, *Veil of Ignorance: Tunnel Constructivism in Free Speech Theory*, 107 Nw. U. L. REV. 647, 690–91 (2013) (rejecting free speech scholars' focus on self-realization and democracy as too narrowly drawn).

[83]  ALEXANDER MEIKLEJOHN, FREE SPEECH AND ITS RELATION TO SELF-GOVERNMENT 88–89 (1948); Robert H. Bork, *Neutral Principles and Some First Amendment Problems*, 47 IND. L.J. 1, 26 (1971) (arguing that democratic principles and First Amendment are inextricably intertwined, regardless of whether that was the specific intent of the Framers).

[84]  Robert Post, *Participatory Democracy and Free Speech*, 97 VA. L. REV. 477, 483 (2011).

acts and media of communication that are socially regarded as necessary and proper means of participating in the formation of public opinion," which he calls "public discourse."[85] "The function of public discourse," he writes, "is to enable persons to experience the value of self-government."[86]

Both its strength and weakness as a First Amendment theory is the fact that self-governance is a justification for protecting only speech that is at least somewhat related to public affairs, in the context of either electoral politics or public policy debates. While some types of expression are more difficult to defend on democracy grounds,[87] investigative deceptions are directly connected to the advancement of self-governance. After all, as we have described, some of the most famous and award-winning journalism is predicated on an investigative deception that led to access to a commercial, governmental, or other non-intimate enterprise. Deception and lies can effectively uncover criminal conduct, enhance transparency in government, expose race discrimination, and reveal animal abuse, among many other types of illegal or unethical conduct.[88] These are all matters of public concern, and enhancing citizen scrutiny of them advances public discourse and democracy in meaningful ways. Thus, investigative deceptions seem well anchored in the promotion of self-governance.

Exposing unsavory behavior by private Washington lobbyists, providing an inside look at the ways factory farms operate, and uncovering racial steering in the housing market all unquestionably contribute to citizen self-governance in meaningful ways. Investigative deceptions seem to contribute to political debate and self-governance.

### 3.3.2 *Investigative Deceptions Promote the Broader Search for Truth*

Under another understanding, protection of speech from state interference is necessary to advance the search for "truth," which is defined as broader than political truth and extending to a more general theory of social enlightenment.[89] The notion of truth under this theory emphasizes the truth of ideas, rather than factual truths. A key notion here, and one that is often drawn on in judicial decisions about speech,

---

[85] *Id.*

[86] *Id.*

[87] *See, e.g.,* Alan K. Chen, *Instrumental Music and the First Amendment*, 66 HASTINGS L.J. 381, 385 (2015).

[88] *See generally* BROOKE KROEGER, UNDERCOVER REPORTING: THE TRUTH ABOUT DECEPTION (2012) (analyzing ethical debates surrounding journalists' use of deception and asserting the public service provided by such reporting should be celebrated).

[89] JOHN STUART MILL, ON LIBERTY 91–92 (1859); JOHN MILTON, AREOPAGITICA 4–5 (1644); *see also* Eugene Volokh, *In Defense of the Marketplace of Ideas/Search for Truth as a Theory of Free Speech Protection*, 97 VA. L. REV. 595, 596–98 (2011) (arguing that government regulation of ideas in the marketplace would lessen the public's belief in the idea because contrary ideas challenging thoughts is how we decide what is truthful or not).

is that there is no such thing as a false idea and that truth can ultimately emerge only through robust, open discourse in the so-called marketplace of ideas.[90]

Even beyond the legal and public policy questions that are placed into issue when exposés of wrongdoers are conducted, undercover investigations on matters of public concern inform significant moral and philosophical questions relevant to the broader search for truth protected by the First Amendment. For example, while some might believe that agricultural animals are merely unfeeling, unthinking forms of property, like tractors or barns, others believe that any use or exploitation of animals for human gain is immoral. Investigations by CMP and other anti-abortion organizations may be similarly motivated in part by the goal of persuading the public that abortion is an immoral act. In some ways, the investigations become a key piece of the moral as well as the legal debate on a topic.

While there is certainly an overlap between this moral discourse and the public policy debates on related issues, the search for truth in the sense of social enlighten-ment is also advanced by the information produced by investigative deceptions. Again, to take agricultural investigations as an example, such lies serve to expose the hidden conduct of commercial agricultural operations. These revelations may affect the public's thinking about the morality of modern agricultural practices. While an investigator cannot control the manner in which their videos are received, one can be sure that the investigator is prompting the kind of reflection that shapes public opinion. The same could be said about investigations in other fields, ranging from prisons to abortion providers to schools and police departments. One may not appreciate the investigation or the content – depending, perhaps on one's political priors – but the investigation facilitated by a lie informs and shapes public debate. Thus, under the truth-serving theories of the First Amendment, investigative decep-tions may be powerfully justified.[91]

### 3.3.3 *Investigative Deceptions Promote Individual Autonomy*

The third widely accepted justification for free speech argues that the function of free speech is to promote individual autonomy or self-realization. The autonomy theory focuses not on the value of speech to the broader society but on its enhance-ment of the speaker's and listener's personal liberty. Professor Thomas Scanlon

---

[90]  *See* Abrams v. United States, 250 U.S. 616, 630 (1919) (Holmes, J., dissenting) ("[T]he best test of truth is the power of the thought to get itself accepted in the competition of the market").

[91]  Our point is not that all lies are valuable in society's search for truth. Intentional falsehoods will often impede this effort, and based on social science research there is reason to worry that the spread and acceptance of false claims is faster and deeper than that of truthful claims. SUNSTEIN, *supra* note 6, at 73–89. But even a strong skeptic about the value of lies concedes that in appropriate circumstances, "liars can prompt people to think more and better." *Id.* at 67. We assert that investigative deceptions are one of those circumstances.

defined autonomy as necessitating the protection of an individual's freedom to engage in self-determination in forming the individual's own opinions and beliefs.[92]

The case can be made that laws barring investigative deceptions interfere with the autonomous choices of journalists, government agents, and activists to choose how to identify themselves in the context of an undercover investigation. For many who engage in undercover investigations, it is the single most important or defining aspect of their identity. It is a form of expression that strikes at the core of one's identity and self-definition.

To be sure, autonomy arguments for speech have generally tended to focus on the freedom of the speaker to determine their own feelings, beliefs, and thoughts without government interference rather than on the liberty to frame (truthfully or falsely) one's identity. Still, there are arguments that might focus more on the way that lies may promote the autonomy of self-identity, whether it be for the purpose of individual self-esteem ("I am the *best* law professor in the world"), to gain respect from others ("I volunteer at the soup kitchen *every* week"), or to gain access to an area where one believes illegal conduct may be occurring ("I am not affiliated with any group antagonistic to your industry").

Professor David Han has suggested that what he calls individual "self-definition" is an important aspect of autonomy that ought to be recognized under First Amendment doctrine.[93] Thus, sometimes, autobiographical lies may be a form of speech protected as a means of promoting individual autonomy. As he observes, "Under any basic conception of autonomy... a fundamental component of being an autonomous individual is exercising control over who you are – and who you are is, to a significant extent, a function of who you *define yourself to be* to others."[94] Han's theory could offer an alternative basis for understanding the Court's decision in *Alvarez*. Alvarez provided a biographical summary of his career after being elected to a local political position, and he claimed to have served in the military and to have won the Congressional Medal of Honor. None of this was true, but the Court held that such lies were protected speech even though they had seemingly minimal truth or governance value.

Consistent with this view, Professor R. George Wright has suggested that lying might be better examined as part of a broader moral context, in which lies might

---

[92]  Thomas Scanlon, *A Theory of Freedom of Expression*, 1 PHIL. & PUB. AFF. 204, 215 (1972). In later work, Scanlon modified his views about speech and autonomy. T. M. Scanlon, Jr., *Freedom of Expression and Categories of Expression*, 40 U. PITT. L. REV. 519, 531–35 (1979). Other autonomy theorists take a slightly broader view that includes the protection of the individual's ability to develop their powers and abilities and to control their own destiny through the autonomy of decision making. Martin H. Redish, *The Value of Free Speech*, 130 U. PA. L. REV. 591, 593 (1982).

[93]  David S. Han, *Autobiographical Lies and the First Amendment's Protection of Self-Defining Speech*, 87 N.Y.U. L. REV. 70, 92 (2012).

[94]  *Id.* at 99.

advance personal autonomy and liberty in ways that supersede their moral costs.[95] Analyzing lies in the historical context of an imagined lie to a fugitive slave hunter or Nazi officer seeking to find Jews during the Holocaust, Wright argues that lies might have moral value in advancing the autonomy of the liar as well as of those the liar seeks to protect from harm.[96] "The lie may be instead motivated by a sense of the equal or irreplaceable value and infinite dignity of persons, or even by genuine concern for the questioner's moral or spiritual well-being."[97] For Wright, then, there are complex moral dimensions to lying that are highly contextual. In the context of many investigations, similar moral claims are advanced by investigators. Certainly, those seeking to expose child trafficking through undercover investigations have talked about these acts in spiritual and religious terms.[98] Animal rights investigators, likewise, seek to promote the dignity and autonomy of nonhuman animals, which is a moral calling for these individuals.[99]

One might argue that the autonomy benefits of lying must be balanced against the countervailing loss of autonomy potentially experienced by the listener. This argument is often used to explain why lies ought not be protected under the First Amendment.[100] Derived from the writings of Immanuel Kant and other moral philosophers, this claim suggests that lies are morally problematic because they deprive the listener of the very same autonomy that free speech is designed to promote.[101] Kant was something of a truth "absolutist" in that he rejected an instrumental theory under which lies could ever be understood in context as socially

---

[95] For an argument that lying may sometimes be protected speech on moral grounds, see R. George Wright, *Lying and Freedom of Speech*, 2011 UTAH L. REV. 1131, 1142 (2011) ("The obvious and quite substantial moral benefits of 'benevolent' lies should also be taken into account").

[96] *See id.* at 1145–46.

[97] *Id.* at 1146.

[98] WALKER, *supra* note 4, at 17 (Walker explains in his memoir describing his work uncovering human sex trafficking that "[a]s a follower of Christ, serving Jesus is central to [his] motivation and passion for this work"); *see also id.* at 28, 50.

[99] *See, e.g.*, PETER SINGER, ANIMAL LIBERATION: THE DEFINITIVE CLASSIC OF THE ANIMAL MOVEMENT 239–40 (First Harper Perennial ed. 2009) (arguing that attempts to distinguish humans from animals based on the "intrinsic dignity of human beings" disregard a lack of actually relevant distinguishing characteristics).

[100] *See* Varat, *supra* note 7, at 1114 ("[T]he First Amendment's protection against government efforts to prevent persuasion rests on respect for people's autonomy. Lies disrespect autonomy so fundamentally that they can lay no claim to that protection"); Wright, *supra* note 95, at 1143 (explaining the Kantian principle that "lying whenever a lie is advantageous . . . would sabotage the credibility of assertions . . . and appeal of the cultural institution of making and paying attention to verbal assertions"). *See also* SEANA VALENTINE SHIFFRIN, SPEECH MATTERS: ON LYING, MORALITY, AND THE LAW (2014) (arguing that government regulation of lies advances social interests in protecting moral agency in human communication and is not incompatible with freedom of speech).

[101] Wright, *supra* note 95, at 1145 ("The first inherent disvalue is the immediate restriction of the deceived's freedom") (quoting Joseph Kupfer, *The Moral Presumption against Lying*, 36 REV. METAPHYSICS 103, 103 (1982)).

valuable.[102] He believed that lies were problematic even if the liar's goals are unselfish and altruistic.[103]

As Professor David Strauss has written,

> [The] Kantian account gives relatively clear content to the notion that lying is wrong because it violates human autonomy. Lying forces the victim to pursue the speaker's objectives instead of the victim's own objectives. If the capacity to decide upon a plan of life and to determine one's own objectives is integral to human nature, lies that are designed to manipulate people are a uniquely severe offense against human autonomy.[104]

Modern philosophers Sissela Bok and Seana Valentine Shiffrin have made similar arguments.[105] In addition to claims about listener autonomy, they each make distinct claims about the harms of lies. Bok asserts that there should be a strong moral presumption against lying. She suggests that a world with lies generates a fundamental epistemological problem because if no one can rely on the statements of others, each person must discover all knowledge independently. However, Bok does allow for the idea that sometimes lies may be justified. She develops a procedure for thinking about lies called the "Scheme of Applied Publicity," which has both introspective and active components. The introspective part asks the prospective liar to consider, among other things, whether there are "truthful alternatives" to lying and a sort of cost-benefit analysis comparing the good and bad things the lie will produce, and also asks for consideration of how a reasonable person would react to these justifications. The active part of her scheme directs the liar to consult peers, associates, and friends as well as persons who might have a different perspective on the issue.

Interestingly for our purposes, both Bok and Shiffrin maintain that lies are especially harmful when invoked by government officials because they have a special duty of trust.[106] Shiffrin makes an additional claim, which is that the liar

---

[102] *Id.* at 1143.

[103] Immanuel Kant, *Kant's Critique of Practical Reason and Other Works on the Theory of Ethics*, 363–64 (London: Longmans, Green & Co. eds., 4th ed. 1889) ("Whoever then tells a lie, however good his intentions may be, must answer for the consequences of it"); *see also* David A. Strauss, *Persuasion, Autonomy, and Freedom of Expression*, 91 COLUM. L. REV. 334, 355 (1991).

[104] Strauss, *supra* note 103, at 355; *see also* C. Edwin Baker, *First Amendment Limits on Copyright*, 55 VAND. L. REV. 891, 910 (2002) ("With lies, the speech operates by tricking the other, purposefully undermining the other's capacity for successfully autonomous acts"). Other leading scholars have rejected the view that lying harms the autonomy of listeners in all contexts. Wright, for example, suggests that a lie might paradoxically enhance rather than diminish the *listener's* autonomy. Wright, *supra* note 95, at 1145–46. As he observes, "[c]ould not a lie to a murderous SS officer also promote the rationality, personhood, or dignity of that SS officer over the longer term?" *Id.* at 1143.

[105] SHIFFRIN, *supra* note 100; SISSELA BOK, LYING: MORAL CHOICE IN PUBLIC AND PRIVATE LIFE (1999).

[106] BOK, *supra* note 105, at 180; SHIFFRIN, *supra* note 100, at 198.

causes a moral harm to the listener by failing to treat the listener as "an equal moral partner and as a rational agent who deserves to receive warrants that she may accept as representing the listener's beliefs." She also argues that such behavior undermines social relationships.[107]

A couple of other factors might mitigate the concern over listener autonomy, at least in the context of investigative deceptions used to gain access to private, commercial, business operations. First, the employer or fellow employee who is lied to and allows access to a commercial facility is unlikely to be directly harmed by the lie in any material way. That is, to the extent that their autonomy is lost by being persuaded to permit an undercover investigator to enter the facility, it is not a personal loss, as it would be if their individual privacy were somehow compromised by the exchange. Lies that facilitate access to intimate, personal details may very well produce too much harm to the listener's autonomy to be tolerated by the autonomy theory.[108] One could argue that the business's autonomy is harmed by the lie insofar as it has lost complete control over its property. But it is not clear that a conception of autonomy grounded in an indiscriminate right to be free from whistleblowers and exposés ought to be taken seriously. As long as there are limits on collecting obviously protected information such as trade secrets, tax records, or employees' medical records, we would argue the harm of that autonomy loss is minimal or nonexistent. Moreover, there may even be an "unclean hands" argument that where unsavory or illegal conduct is occurring and the business's employees are arguably complicit (or vicariously responsible), the loss of listener autonomy that occurs when an investigator lies to gain access to the property is at least less of a concern than it would be in other contexts.[109]

## 3.4 SOME TRICKY ISSUES AROUND INVESTIGATIVE LIES: THE POST-*ALVAREZ* CASE LAW

Having explained that lies are presumptively covered by the First Amendment, and recognizing the conceptual and functional value of investigative lies, this section considers the remaining gray areas of legal concern.

---

[107] SHIFFRIN, *supra* note 100, at 24. For an extensive discussion of a specific subcategory of lies, see JILL ELAINE HASDAY, INTIMATE LIES AND THE LAW (2019).

[108] In addition, there may be circumstances in which the listener's individual autonomy is compromised by an investigative lie because it is tantamount to coercion over their personal will. In those situations, we would not argue that the lie should be constitutionally protected.

[109] Critics might argue that the unclean hands response offers a justification for lying that is entirely ex post. That is, an investigator does not know at the time they enter a facility whether they will necessarily find unlawful or unethical behavior on the premises, yet will have already compromised the listener's autonomy. While we acknowledge this concern, we maintain that the notion that the listener is affected entirely in a business or professional context still mitigates the autonomy concerns even if it does not eliminate them altogether.

### 3.4.1 *The Illusiveness of the* Alvarez *Harm/Benefit Standard*

*Alvarez* held that lies that do not cause legally cognizable harm to the listener or yield benefits to the speaker are presumptively protected from government regulation by the First Amendment. Unfortunately, *Alvarez* utterly fails to elaborate on the harm/benefit limiting principle, and thus there remains a great deal of confusion over just what type of lies the government may ban. What are the lies that cause benefits or harm that warrant prohibiting them? And what type or degree of harm counts sufficiently to override the speaker's rights?

Many lies are assumed to "cause serious danger" and harm.[110] And this can even be said of Alvarez's lie about winning the Medal of Honor. As a starting point, it warrants emphasizing that the Court recognized that Alvarez's lie about having been awarded high military honors was deemed worthy of free speech protection. Nonetheless, it cannot really be said that Alvarez's lie was harmless or that it did not benefit him. After all, it is certainly plausible that, as the government claimed, veterans who actually received military honors are harmed by the dilution of the value of their medals by those who falsely claimed to have earned them. As the dissenters observed, by analogy to trademark protections, "[s]urely it was reasonable for Congress to conclude that the goal of preserving the integrity of our country's top military honors is at least as worthy as that of protecting the prestige associated with fancy watches and designer handbags."[111] Similarly, if Alvarez's lie helped him "gain respect" with any listener that he otherwise would not have enjoyed, that could be understood as an undeserved gain.[112]

If the lie at issue in *Alvarez* arguably produces some benefits and harms, then how could the Court decide that Alvarez's lies were covered by the First Amendment, and that the Stolen Valor Act was unconstitutional? The answer is simple: the plurality opinion greatly overstated the harm and benefit limitation. *Every lie* causes some harm and/or produces some degree of benefit – but lies may greatly vary in the degree of those impacts. This is a sufficiently important point that it warrants pausing to develop it before moving on.

On its face, a constitutional protection for nonharmful lies seems reasonable enough. But this intuitively sensible limit creates a paradox, if we are correct that in the realm of intentional lies, it is fair to say that all lies produce benefits and/or cause harm. One tells an intentional lie only in order to obtain some benefit or affect some outcome. The benefit could be as benign as protecting a child's innocence ("No one was hurt in the accident") or persuading a police officer not to issue a citation ("I have been a lifelong donor to the Police Benevolent Association!"). The harm may be as innocent as shielding a child from knowledge

---

[110] SUNSTEIN, *supra* note 6, at 107.
[111] *Alvarez*, 567 U.S. at 744 (Alito, J., dissenting).
[112] *Id.* at 713.

about the metaphorical birds and bees, or as malevolent as a fraudulent scheme resulting in the appropriation of an elderly person's retirement savings. But the deliberately told lie almost always has an impact on the listener, often on the speaker, and sometimes on society or its institutions more generally.

Some who are skeptical of the need to provide constitutional protection for lying have posited that a wide range of the most common lies need not even be classified as lies. It has been suggested that innocuous lies and exaggerations, for example, are qualitatively different from other lies; they are so petty that they do not cause real injury.[113] But this argument proves either too much or too little. If it is the case that courts are going to have to engage in a case-by-case analysis of whether a lie on a particular topic in a given context is or is not sufficiently harmful to justify its regulation, then we have entrusted to the government a "broad censorial power unprecedented in this Court's cases or in our constitutional tradition."[114] If some lies are to be redefined for constitutional purposes as non-lies, all that is accomplished is a bit of judicial obfuscation, and the debate about harm has simply been pushed further upstream so as to become part of the definition of the term "lie," as opposed to the inquiry being focused on whether a particular category of lie causes harm.

Or, more likely, this characterization of certain lies as entirely "harm-free" is just "patently not true."[115] And unfortunately, the concept of materiality – understood as a lie about a fact that is relevant to one's actions or decisions – does not provide much assistance. An applicant's lie to a potential employer by telling them that they have "beautiful kids" or that the applicant's only weakness is that "I work too hard" could very well be *material* insofar as the answers shape the employer's impression of the candidate and ultimately affect the hiring decision. Innocuous lies, exaggerations, and puffery are easy to dismiss as not "real" lies, but if the falsehood is stated deliberately and alters the listener's course of behavior in any way, there is no analytical distinction that separates them from other lies. Likewise, there would be no reason for such lies to be so common if they were not believed to be beneficial. Simply put, there is no obvious dividing line between puffery and socially routine lies, on the one hand, and fraud or injurious deception, on the other.

A useful example in this regard is the class of lie at issue in *Alvarez* – a lie to "puff up oneself." Such a lie does not inform, inspire, or provoke thinking about matters of public significance. It almost never contributes in a meaningful way to discourse or the discovery of truth, and its prohibition does not chill truthful, valuable speech.

---

[113] *Alvarez*, 638 F.3d at 686 (O'Scannlain, J., dissenting from denial of rehearing en banc) (explaining that such lies "would hardly be falsifiable"); *see also Alvarez*, 567 U.S. at 749 (Alito, J., dissenting) ("[M]any in our society either approve or condone certain discrete categories of false statements, including false statements made to prevent harm to innocent victims and so-called 'white lies'").

[114] *Alvarez*, 567 U.S. at 723. This concern led Justice Breyer to also worry about the problem of selective enforcement of laws prohibiting lying. *Id.* at 734 (Breyer, J., concurring).

[115] *Alvarez*, 638 F.3d at 675 (Kozinski, C.J., concurring in denial of rehearing en banc).

But quite often such a lie will create a web of benefits and burdens. For example, the fact that people might take someone more seriously because they believe he is a decorated war veteran could suffice to render the lie in *Alvarez* unprotected based on the harm principle. A person falsely claiming military honors might as a result be elected as a public official, thereby providing them material gain. A journalist or blogger who writes opinion pieces might have their opinion sought after, at least in part, because they falsely represent themself to be a Medal of Honor recipient and thereby produce a newsworthy story. In yet another scenario, perhaps someone who operates a "fake news" website may attract more readers (and earn money through advertising for each click on their website) by claiming to be a decorated military veteran. Or more mundanely, one who falsely claims to be a veteran might attract more customers to their newly opened commercial gym. These are just some scenarios that suggest the range of benefits and harms that could directly result from a lie about military honors. Indeed, a similarly and staggeringly broad range of harms and benefits might flow from the universe of other types of lies that might be subject to government regulation.

More importantly, any such categorization misses the point. Designating certain small or common lies as less harmful and therefore protected is a merely semantic exercise. To say that *any* benefit or harm removes the mistruth from the protections of the First Amendment altogether would be to render *Alvarez* a dead letter. As with the Court's general guidance for finding expression outside of the coverage of the First Amendment, history is a key factor.

Only when a lie closely resembles the sort of tangibly or legally cognizable harmful lie that has been historically unprotected do the First Amendment protections fall away.[116] Stated differently, most of the harm incidental to a lie is not of such a form or degree as to warrant stripping the lie – as an act of pure speech – of First Amendment coverage. But the closer a lie gets to true fraud, or one of the other historically unprotected categories, the more likely it is that the lie will be treated as outside the reach of the First Amendment. Without such a mooring, *Alvarez*'s promise that the First Amendment protects lies will be rendered meaningless.

### 3.4.2 *The Emptiness of the "Falsity Alone" Limiting Principle*

Another limitation that might be drawn from the Court's opinion in *Alvarez* is that the government may never punish or regulate statements for their criminalized "falsity alone" or falsity and "nothing more."[117] But for reasons similar to the point

---

[116] SUNSTEIN, *supra* note 6, at 113 (noting that *Alvarez*'s reasoning adheres to the view that "longevity creates a kind of legitimacy," and the Court was "reluctant to add new categories of regulable falsehoods").

[117] *Alvarez*, 567 U.S. at 719. At the time, the Stolen Valor Act stated: "Whoever falsely represents himself or herself, verbally or in writing, to have been awarded any decoration or medal authorized by Congress for the Armed Forces of the United States … shall be fined under

we make in the previous section, this cannot be a meaningful limiting principle for the constitutional protection of lies either, because it is really just another way of saying that the lie has to cause a harm or yield a benefit – that is, to have some effect other than its untruth in order for the government to have the power to regulate it.

In the foreseeable future it is unlikely that there will be any broad legislative efforts to criminalize any or all lies. It is simply not politically palatable, much less practicable, to criminalize all lies, or even a large swath of them. But there have been a number of laws seeking to prevent undercover investigations generally, or investigations in a particular industry. Those laws might be defended on the ground that an investigative deception is not a regulation of "falsity alone" because such lies may cause actions or changes in behavior that governments can argue go beyond regulating the statements' falsity.

A notable example of a bold approach to the falsity alone argument is the defense of ag-gag laws by several states.[118] The Idaho ag-gag law, for example, criminalized all misrepresentations told in order to gain access to an agricultural facility. Thus, lies about the need to use the restroom, a desire to make a purchase or use the services of the facility, or a wish to work for the company to gain such access were all rendered criminal. According to the state, the prohibitions on lying in the ag-gag statute are not covered by the First Amendment because the statute does not regulate "falsity and nothing more," but rather targets the fact that one gains a benefit in the form of limited, consensual access, or perhaps the harm in the form of intrusion on private property interests, based on the deception.[119] Under this view, the falsity-plus (anything) view, nothing more than the falsehood is protected, and any benefit or burden produced by the lie takes it outside the scope of free speech.

Under this view, the defining feature of a lie that may be proscribed is that it "causes" any change in behavior or circumstances. Distilled to its essence, these arguments are really just tantamount to *Alvarez*'s limitation that the First Amendment protects only lies that produce no benefit and no harm or lies that do not in any way alter the status quo. And as we already have explained, every lie causes some harm or benefit, so no law prohibiting lies can ever be understood to regulate "falsity alone." As Justice Breyer illustrated, in his *Alvarez* concurrence, this is not the rule. In a timely, almost prescient example, Justice Breyer considered the problem of political messaging frauds and described their criminalization as "particularly dangerous." The concurrence did not dispute that lies by politicians or

---

this title, imprisoned not more than six months, or both." Stolen Valor Act, Pub. L. No. 109-437, 120 Stat. 3266 (2006). After *Alvarez*, that section was amended to add a requirement that the offender lied "with the intent to obtain money, property, or other tangible benefit." 18 U.S.C. § 704(b) (2015).

[118] IDAHO CODE § 18-7042(1)(a) (2017), held unconstitutional by *Otter*, 118 F. Supp. 3d at 1195, *aff'd in part, rev'd in part sub nom, Wasden*, 878 F.3d at 1184.

[119] Brief of Appellant at 17–22, Animal Legal Def. Fund v. Wasden, No. 15-35960, 2016 WL 1640034 (9th Cir. Apr. 20, 2016).

campaigns could change election outcomes by shaping voting behavior, but observed that such behavioral changes did not take the lies outside free speech protection. "In the political arena a false statement is *more likely to make a behavioral difference* (say, by leading the listeners to vote for the speaker) but at the same time criminal prosecution is particularly dangerous."[120]

There is a bit of a "tree falling in the forest" conundrum here. Arguing that only those lies that cause no harm or are false and nothing more are protected is the legal equivalent of saying that only those lies that no one hears or that have no effect on the behavior, emotions, or lives of anyone are protected. It cannot be that the speech protection of *Alvarez* protects only lies that generate no measurable impact or change in behavior, because that category of lies is essentially a null set. A lie will virtually always involve something more. Such a reading of *Alvarez* would mean that the Stolen Valor Act could be rewritten to say that anyone who falsely claims to have won the Medal of Honor, and by so doing hurts the feelings of another, impresses another, or is invited to a dinner party because of the lie, may be criminally punished. This not only would dilute the rule from *Alvarez* but would completely undermine it. Surely the Court could not endorse such a reading.

### 3.4.3 *Materiality as a Limiting Principle*

At several points, both the plurality and concurrence in *Alvarez* invoke terms that appear to limit the scope of harms that would exempt lies from First Amendment coverage. As discussed above, Justice Kennedy used the terms "legally cognizable"[121] and "material"[122] to limit the scope of relevant harms or gains, while Justice Breyer wrote of "specific"[123] harms as a limiting principle. We might surmise, then, that the state can regulate lies that cause cognizable or material harms to others and/or produce material benefits to the speaker, but there is little else to help us understand those modifiers. These terms are still relatively indeterminate.

Some clues can be discerned from the context in which the Justices use these terms. At one point, Justice Breyer focused on the idea that lies are exempt from First Amendment coverage when they cause "specific harm to identifiable

---

[120] *Alvarez*, 567 U.S. at 738 (Breyer, J., concurring) (emphasis added).

[121] *Alvarez*, 567 U.S. at 719.

[122] To be sure, at some points the *Alvarez* opinions focus on materiality as a modification of the *lie* as opposed to the resulting harm. *Id.* at 734, 738–39 (Breyer, J., concurring); *id.* at 747 (Alito, J., dissenting). One way of reading this is to infer that the Court is concerned about causation. That is, materiality here might suggest that the lie was sufficiently material to cause a change in the behavior of the listener. A materiality requirement applied to the falsehood itself would, of course, narrow the scope of such regulations, as Justice Breyer notes at several points. *Id.* at 734, 738–39 (Breyer, J., concurring). Our focus in this chapter is on materiality as a limit of the related harm or advantage.

[123] *Id.* at 736.

victims."[124] While this certainly helps to narrow the scope of lies that the state can regulate, it still offers relatively little guidance. Perjury, for example, which is universally accepted as a form of lying that is not covered by the First Amendment, can harm the parties involved in a lawsuit, and thereby affect "identifiable victims." But perjury is also understood to undermine the integrity of the justice system as a whole, which cannot be said to adversely affect individuals. In this respect, Justice Breyer's formulation is underinclusive. At the same time, because the opinion does not further elaborate on what it means by "specific," it may be overinclusive in that it might be understood to exempt lies that cause any harm that is articulable without regard to the degree or significance (i.e., the materiality) of that harm.

Another possible limitation on the types of harms that disqualify a lie from First Amendment protection can be gleaned from the plurality opinion. Justice Kennedy talks about the government interest in preventing speakers from securing a "material gain" in a manner that implies that he means some commercial benefit.[125] This makes some sense in that it is the type of harm associated with categorically uncovered speech, such as different types of fraud. When A lies to B to get B to give money to A under false pretenses, there is a direct and material commercial benefit to A.

But Justice Kennedy did not elaborate on what he meant by material gain or whether the false factual statement must be directly related to that gain. If one accepts this framework, then the material benefit factor might also be applied to allow regulation of a newspaper whose undercover journalist lies to gain access to groundbreaking information of public concern and produces a prize-winning article. The argument here would be that because the article helps sell more newspapers or generates more advertising revenue, the newspaper has materially benefited from its employee's lie. Similarly, the government might argue that such lies are not covered where the journalist themself gains a material benefit from their undercover work, such as winning a prestigious award, perhaps including cash,[126] or a raise or promotion.

In the context of political activists, we might see the same types of arguments. For example, an undercover activist who lies to gain access to private property, resulting in a widely publicized exposé that results in major legislative reform, may also increase publicity for the nonprofit organization for whom the activist works, and generate more donations from those inspired by the investigation. If that counts as material gain, then a substantial amount of important speech – what we have branded "high-value lies" or "investigative deceptions" – would fall outside the First Amendment's coverage.

---

[124] *Id.* at 734.
[125] *Id.* at 723 (plurality opinion).
[126] Winners of the Pulitzer Prize in journalism for most categories, for example, receive a $15,000 award. *Pulitzer Board Raises Prize Award to $15,000*, THE PULITZER PRIZES (Jan. 3, 2017), www .pulitzer.org/news/pulitzer-board-raises-prize-award-15000.

The post-*Alvarez* lower court decisions on lies do not provide considerably more guidance. In *United States v. Swisher*, the Ninth Circuit examined the constitutionality of another part of the Stolen Valor Act that criminalizes the act of *wearing* military medals one has not earned, as opposed to speaking about them.[127] The court held that the First Amendment prohibits the enforcement of this law because it was not limited to lies for which there was "proof of specific harm to identifiable victims."[128] Moreover, the court said, there was no requirement that the government show that "someone was deceived into following a course [of action] he would not have pursued but for the deceitful conduct."[129] Even this elaboration does not offer helpful insights into the harm requirement. Just as every lie causes some form of harm, many lies result in altered behavior – that is, the lie results in someone following a course of conduct that they would not have taken but for the lie. But just as not all harms should suffice to remove First Amendment coverage from the realm of falsehoods, it would be odd to suggest that any lie that plays a role in influencing one's behavior is beyond the Constitution's coverage. For example, the fact that a coworker wears a particular item of clothing to the office more frequently because a friend falsely told him it was stylish, or the fact that someone eats a particular diet because they rely on someone's lies about how good it makes them feel, ought not remove those lies from the First Amendment's coverage even though they produced changes in behavior (though as we discuss below, the value of that lie is also relatively low).

*Golb v. Attorney General New York* provides a useful illustration of the efforts of lower courts to grapple with this aspect of *Alvarez*.[130] In *Golb*, a prisoner petitioned for a writ of habeas corpus after being convicted in state court for criminal impersonation in the second degree and forgery in the third degree.[131] The petitioner had engaged in a bizarre and elaborate scheme to steal the identities of scholars who disagreed with his father's academic position on the origin of the Dead Sea

---

[127] 811 F.3d 299 (9th Cir. 2016). *But see* United States v. Hamilton, 699 F.3d 356, 373 (4th Cir. 2012) (upholding the medal-wearing provision of the Stolen Valor Act because the wearing of an unearned medal is more convincing evidence of actual attainment than words alone). A couple of other cases have upheld the application of laws against lying in contexts in which the harms were more readily identifiable. *See, e.g.*, United States v. Williams, 690 F.3d 1056, 1063–64 (8th Cir. 2012) (upholding statutes criminalizing hoax bomb reports because they criminalize "only those lies that are particularly likely to produce harm"); United States v. Gardner, 993 F. Supp. 2d 1294, 1307 (D. Or. 2014) (upholding as constitutional the Victim and Witness Protection Act, 18 U.S.C. § 1512, which criminalizes "knowingly engaging in misleading conduct towards another person with intent to hinder, delay and prevent the communication to a federal law enforcement officer of truthful information relating to the commission of a federal offense," because the statute regulates "speech integral to criminal conduct," a category of speech historically subject to regulation).

[128] *Swisher*, 811 F.3d at 315.

[129] *Id.* (alteration in original).

[130] No. 15 Civ. 1709 (KPF), 2016 WL 297726 (S.D.N.Y. Jan. 21, 2016), *aff'd in part and rev'd in part on other grounds*, 870 F.3d 89 (2d Cir. 2017).

[131] *Id.*

Scrolls.[132] Rather than use identity theft for the purpose of securing commercial gain, the petitioner used it to undermine the credibility of academic critics of his father's work.[133] He argued that under *Alvarez*, the state laws were unconstitutionally overbroad on the ground that the laws criminalized false speech designed to cause *intangible* (as opposed to "material") harm to someone's reputation.[134] In rejecting the petitioner's claim, the district court noted that

> Even if *Alvarez* could be read to suggest that it is impermissible to punish false speech unless the speaker intended to gain a "material" advantage or cause a "material" harm, the plurality in that case never equated "material" advantages or harms with tangible ones.... To the contrary, the plurality repeatedly suggested that harms and benefits can be "material" even if they are intangible.... For example, the plurality observed that perjury statutes are constitutional, even though they criminalize false speech, because perjury causes intangible harm to "the integrity of judgments that are the basis of the legal system.".... Thus, the *Alvarez* plurality clearly believed it was permissible to criminalize at least some false speech that has the potential to cause intangible injuries.[135]

But *Alvarez* is unclear on whether intangible harms to *individuals* as opposed to the government or the court system, which have historically proscribed lies that affect the functioning of government, can amount to a material harm sufficient to place the harm-causing lie outside the First Amendment. However, it is certainly true that there are different areas of the law in which intangible harms are deemed legally cognizable. For example, in the law of standing, the Supreme Court has recognized that in appropriate circumstances, Article III injuries may include not only tangible physical and economic harms, but also harms to aesthetic and recreational interests.[136] It is conceivable, then, that some injuries that are intangible might be sufficient to place certain types of lies beyond the concern of the free speech clause.

*Alvarez*'s lack of clarity as to what constitutes a material harm leaves lower courts as well as speakers in a state of confusion. Greater certainty is needed. Perhaps the determination about which injuries or benefits are caused by lying should be qualitative. That is, we could try to distinguish lie-based harms and gains by category, such as financial, emotional, or physical. But as the *Golb* case concludes, it is quite possible that some intangible or less tangible harms suffice, and, in any event, any division of the lies into qualitative categories neglects the fact that even within categories there can be large differences in the *degree* of harm, ranging from de minimis to devastating. This might lead one to conclude that the preferable approach is to focus on the quantitative differences in harms and benefits, focusing

[132] *Id.*
[133] *Id.*
[134] *Id.*
[135] *Id.* at *19 (citations omitted).
[136] Friends of the Earth, Inc. v. Laidlaw Envtl. Servs., Inc., 528 U.S. 167, 183 (2000).

on the degree of harm rather than the formal category of injury under which it falls. This too, however, proves unworkable as it leaves courts in the business of trying to figure out how much harm is "enough" to remove a category of lying from the scope of First Amendment coverage. It is doubtful, for example, that a fraud that results in the listener paying the liar only fifty cents would jettison that particular fraud from a type of nonspeech under *Chaplinsky*[137] to the category of fully protected speech under *Alvarez* merely because the harm is de minimis.

Even at a categorical level, this type of balancing seems problematic and unsatisfying. The problem with this approach to examining lie-based harms and benefits is that the law would require disaggregating lies into a potentially infinite set of subcategories determined by courts on a case-by-case basis, producing very little in the way of doctrinal coherence or predictability.

### 3.4.4 *Cognizable Harms That Might Suffice to Deprive an Investigative Lie of Protection*

Because of these flaws in *Alvarez*'s analysis, its application to government regulations of investigative deceptions is anything but straightforward. As we have argued, it is internally illogical to read *Alvarez* to mean that *any* harm or *any* benefit places a category of lies outside the First Amendment's reach. Accordingly, a full examination of the potential harms that investigative deceptions might cause is necessary. Scholars have identified two main categories of potential interests that might limit First Amendment protection for lies designed to secure truthful information. The first possible category of interests would include protecting the listener from "psychological or pecuniary harm" that the investigative deception caused "directly and independently."[138] These might be described as *direct harms* to legal interests. Second, states might argue that investigative deceptions potentially cause *indirect harms* from "the subsequent publication of the accurate information obtained as the result of the lie."[139] We discuss the possible claims based on these harms in the following section.[140]

### 3.4.4.1 Possible Direct Harms

There is not yet a lot of case law on the application of *Alvarez* to government efforts to impose criminal penalties on misrepresentations to gain access to business

---

[137] Recall that in *Chaplinsky*, 315 U.S. at 568, the Court held that categories of speech that have no or little value and also cause social harm are not even covered by the First Amendment.

[138] Varat, *supra* note 7, at 1122–23.

[139] *Id.* at 1123.

[140] In addition to the harms that might be caused by an investigator's deception, lawyers who counsel or advise such investigators and the organizations sponsoring the investigation may be in danger of violating professional ethics standards by facilitating investigative lies. For an argument that the First Amendment protects the rights of attorneys in this position, see Aviel & Chen, *supra* note 7.

operations, such as ag-gag laws, but the decisions to date have assessed whether the state may punish such lies to remedy direct harms inherent to such investigations. We can dismiss some types of harms at the outset. For example, where the investigator secures a job with the target to conduct an undercover investigation, the state might assert that it has an interest in protecting the employer from the purely psychic injury that flows from being fooled or tricked into hiring someone who doesn't like them or their way of doing business. But such harms are not the sort of cognizable harm that the Constitution recognizes as justifying restrictions on speech.[141] It would be absurd to criminalize an employee's false claims that she enjoys her boss's cooking or conversation. Likewise, an undercover investigator who seeks to expose and ultimately undermine a child sex trafficking ring or an investigator who seeks to show through an employment investigation that a childcare facility abuses children might both lack the sort of loyalty to the business that the owner might expect and desire. But non-loyalty of this sort – to the customer, the employer, or in other contexts – does not manifest itself in concrete financial or other injuries that take a lie outside the contours of free speech. That is not to say that there are no possible legal interests that might be implicated by investigative lies.

3.4.4.1.1 OBTAINING RECORDS One direct legal harm that the state might have the power to address is a protected interest in a business's records. To date, courts have accepted the notion that the use of lies to deprive another of their private records is a tangible harm, similar to other types of theft. At least one court of appeals has acquiesced to this limitation on investigative efforts, holding that the Idaho ag-gag law, which "criminalizes obtaining records of an agricultural production facility by misrepresentation," protects against a "legally cognizable harm associated with a false statement" and therefore survives constitutional scrutiny under *Alvarez*.[142] Under the court's reasoning, obtaining records is tantamount to a traditional crime of fraud, such as larceny by fraud or theft of records through misrepresentation. The court emphasized the long history of crimes prohibiting record theft, including theft by deception, and seemed to treat as material the difference between physically obtaining possession of the records of another and entering onto the property of another. As it explained, "Acquiring records by misrepresentation results in something definitively more than does entry onto land – it wreaks actual and potential harm on a facility and bestows material gain on the fibber."[143] And of course there is

---

[141] *See Alvarez*, 567 U.S. at 718–20 (cataloguing the types of cognizable harms that can justify regulation of lies without violating the First Amendment).

[142] *Wasden*, 878 F.3d at 1199.

[143] *Id.* at 1200 ("Obtaining records may also bestow a 'material gain' on the speaker. *See Alvarez*, 567 U.S. at 723 (plurality opinion). The records may contain confidential information, such as breeding histories of animals and livestock, and other proprietary research and development information valuable to those in the industry").

some difference between physically taking one's property (records) versus entering their property.

However, it is unclear how far this interest would extend to justify a state criminal prohibition on the deception itself as opposed to the theft of any tangible property. If a person walks into a retail store and falsely represents that they are an eager consumer, they have accessed that property under false pretenses. If they then steal an expensive item from the store, they may be punished for shoplifting, but the law does not address their dishonesty in posing as a customer as an independent crime.

Furthermore, it is not clear how far the state's interest in preventing theft of records would extend. There are multiple ways to obtain information from a business's records. First, one may steal the records in physical or digital form, which is akin to the theft of other tangible property. Second, one might record the contents of those records using a digital camera. The Idaho ag-gag law did not prohibit theft of records per se, but criminalized "obtaining records." If that case had involved an as applied challenge to the law where someone had photographed an agricultural facility's records on animal slaughter, would that action be punishable in the same way as a theft? Assuming that the information obtained from the records is a matter of public concern, rather than a legally protected trade secret, this poses a more complicated constitutional question. As we address in Chapter 4, photography and video recording are themselves acts of speech that might be protected under the First Amendment independently of the protection for investigative deceptions. Third, what if an investigator uses deception to secure employment at a business, and their job gives them access to the company's records? And what if the investigator then commits to memory the contents of the records, which reveal that the company's practices are illegal or inhumane? The states' ability to punish the investigative deception in that scenario as an act of "obtaining records" would be much more questionable in the face of a First Amendment defense.

Furthermore, there may be an important legal distinction between a law prohibiting obtaining records and a law prohibiting obtaining *access* to records. The former would, at least in the context of actual theft, be within the state's power to punish. But as we have already seen, there are multiple ways to access records without stealing them; an investigator might enter a property and look at or take a photograph of a record without stealing it. And it is not obvious that deception used to gain access to records is meaningfully different in terms of harms to the property owner's settled expectations than deception to gain access to real property. If the state has an interest in prohibiting access to records by first gaining access to private property through deception, that power could extend to a large number of scenarios.

3.4.4.1.2 TRESPASS: THE RIGHT TO EXCLUDE If obtaining access to records by deception can be prohibited, it is tempting to believe that a deceptive entry onto real property itself can also be criminalized or subject to civil liability as a trespass. The Restatement (Second) of Torts defines a trespass as follows:

One is subject to liability to another for trespass, irrespective of whether he thereby causes harm to any legally protected interest of the other, if he intentionally
  (a) enters land in the possession of the other, or causes a thing or a third person to do so, or
  (b) remains on the land, or
  (c) fails to remove from the land a thing which he is under a duty to remove.[144]

Trespass is commonly understood to protect property owners' possessory interest in their property and their right to exclude others. Although the property owner's consent is an affirmative defense to trespass, states and those targeted by undercover investigations have asserted that if persons secure entry to property by deception, they would be harming the same exclusive possessory interests of a property owner.[145] Indeed, trespass is perhaps the most common interest that states have advanced in support of laws restricting investigative deception.

To begin, it must be acknowledged that it is axiomatic under common law that civil trespass complainants need not show actual damages as a precondition of liability.[146] The landowner need not show that they were harmed in any manner by the trespass. A single footstep on the property of another is sufficient to impose liability; that a landowner suffers no actual or tangible harm from such an act is legally irrelevant. Liability for such a trespass, however, will presumptively result in the imposition of only nominal damages. Of course, if a trespasser does actual damage during the trespass, such as destroying or damaging property, that is compensable if the landowner can show the extent of actual damage.[147]

There are two relevant questions here, then. First, is entry to property by investigative deception a trespass? Second, even if such access is technically a trespass, is that a legally cognizable harm under *Alvarez* if there is no tangible harm to the property owner? That is, if the owner sued the investigator and could recover only nominal damages, is that the type of actual harm that *Alvarez* contemplates could remove First Amendment protection from the investigative lie?

---

[144] RESTATEMENT (SECOND) OF TORTS § 158 (1965).

[145] 17 WASH. PRAC., REAL ESTATE § 10.2 (2d ed. 2014) (consent can be a defense to trespass, "provided it was not obtained by fraud, misrepresentation, or duress"); Food Lion, Inc. v. Capital Cities/ABC, Inc., 951 F. Supp. 1217, 1222–23 (M.D.N.C. 1996); *see also* Laurent Sacharoff, *Constitutional Trespass*, 81 TENN. L. REV. 877, 882 (2014) (suggesting that trespass advances privacy interests).

[146] JOSEPH WILLIAM SINGER, PROPERTY 28 (3d ed. 2010).

[147] *See, e.g.,* IDAHO CODE § 18-7008(A)(9) (establishing a misdemeanor for "[e]ntering without permission of the owner or the owner's agent, upon the real property of another person which" is posted with proper signage indicating that the property is private and may not be trespassed upon). Interestingly, all other provisions of the Idaho criminal trespass statute entail actual tangible harm to the property. *Id.* § 18-7008(A)(1)–(8), (10). In contrast, it is common for statutory trespass actions to require actual damages. While some state criminal trespass laws may be enforced even without a showing of actual harm, the sort of privacy and property rights protected by trespass laws are simply not served by punishing someone who gains access through deception.

The majority of the courts that have addressed these questions to date seem reluctant to treat every entry predicated on a lie as a trespass, but there are some decisions that, at least partially, come out the opposite way.[148] We argue that the former decisions are correct as a matter of First Amendment law and the reasonable and most plausible application of *Alvarez*. That is to say, we think access to property by investigative deception may not even constitute a trespass under the law, which we will see is unclear under the weight of common law authority.[149] And even if one strains to categorize entry gained through deception as a trespass, the fact that most undercover investigations do not cause any tangible damage to the landowner means that it cannot be the type of legally cognizable harm that would remove First Amendment protection for such lies. Laws that try to criminalize or impose tort liability on undercover investigators violate the Constitution in the absence of actual harm.[150]

In *Desnick v. American Broadcasting Companies, Inc.*,[151] the US Court of Appeals for the Seventh Circuit agreed that the trial court properly dismissed a trespass claim brought by an eye doctor against a news station and its reporters, who conducted an undercover investigation revealing that his offices routinely prescribed and charged for cataract surgeries when the patients did not need them. As Judge Richard Posner explained in the court's opinion, entry into a business through deception where one wants or invites entry (but does not know the investigator's true purpose) is not a true trespass because in such cases there is no invasion of the "the specific interests that the tort of trespass seeks to protect."[152] More recently in striking down an Idaho ag-gag law that prohibited entry based on misrepresentations, another federal circuit court held that "a false statement made in order to access an agricultural production facility – cannot on its face be characterized as 'made to effect a fraud or secure moneys or other valuable considerations,'" so as to fall outside the scope of free speech protection.[153] In that case, *Animal Legal Defense Fund v. Wasden*, Idaho argued not that there was necessarily harm to the landowner but that the investigator received a material gain under *Alvarez*. In rejecting the state's contention, the court explained:

---

[148] One commentator has examined the cases involving deceptive entry and concluded, "Although advertised as the most important property right, [the right to exclude] is never given the weight it is meant to carry." Anthony Derron, *Trespass Plus: Ag-Gag and the Right to Exclude*, GEO. ENV'T L. REV. (forthcoming 2023).

[149] Desnick v. Am. Broad. Companies, Inc., 44 F.3d 1345, 1352 (7th Cir. 1995) (compiling authority).

[150] To the extent that some jurisdictions had previously suggested that harmless misrepresentations made in order to gain access were actionable as trespass, such cases must be revisited in light of *Alvarez*'s mandate that lies that do not cause cognizable harm are protected by the First Amendment.

[151] 44 F.3d at 1345.

[152] *Id.* at 1352.

[153] *Wasden*, 878 F.3d at 1194.

Idaho's argument that "the material gain to the person telling the lie is the entry to the property," is not supported by any authority and does not establish how entry onto the property and material gain are coextensive. Under the statute, any misrepresentation to gain entry could net a criminal prosecution. Take, for example, a teenager who wants to impress his friends by obtaining a highly sought after reservation at an exclusive pop-up restaurant that is open to the public. If he were to call the restaurant and finagle a reservation in the name of his mother, a well-known journalist, that would be a misrepresentation.[154]

Applying similar reasoning, in a challenge to a statute that treated entry onto agricultural properties as nonconsensual if the consent was obtained by deception, in *Animal Legal Defense Fund v. Kelly*, the Tenth Circuit reasoned that such laws function to "prohibit[] speech, such as a statement made to obtain the consent of the owner of an animal facility ... [and] thus regulate[] not only what ... investigators may or may not do, but what they 'may or may not say'";[155] in other words, the law directly regulated speech. Even more critically, the court reasoned that the fact that the statute limited its application to activities intended to cause harm to the facility did not save such speech-limiting prohibitions from unconstitutionality. The "intent to damage the enterprise requirement does not make the false speech here unprotected because not all intents to damage the enterprise of an animal facility are cognizable harms under *Alvarez*."[156] The court emphasized that the uncertainty of what "harms" count for purposes of *Alvarez* is enigmatic, but refused to agree that investigations that reveal wrongdoing give rise to the sort of harm contemplated by *Alvarez* as legally cognizable:

> The damage to the enterprise intended from [Animal Legal Defense Fund's] investigations does not flow directly from deceiving the animal facility owner into allowing entry. *Damage occurs only if the investigators uncover evidence of wrongdoing and share that information*, resulting in other actors choosing to take further actions. This is too attenuated from the false speech to be the sort of harm *Alvarez* is concerned with. It is not like defamation, where the false speech directly causes reputational harm; fraud, where the false speech causes someone to hand over a thing a value; or perjury, lies to the government, or impersonating a government official, where the speech itself harms our institutions. Rather, there are numerous further causal links between the false speech and the animal facility suffering damage.... Whatever legally cognizable harm is, it cannot be harm from protected, true, speech.[157]

---

[154] *Id.*
[155] 9 F.4th 1219, 1233 (10th Cir. 2021), *cert. denied*, 142 S. Ct. 2647 (2022) (citation omitted).
[156] *Id.* at 1234.
[157] *Id.* at 1234–35 (emphasis added). *Id.* at 1235 ("The damage Kansas fears is that animal facilities may face 'negative publicity, lost business[,] or boycotts.' Appellant Br. at 22. But these harms would be accomplished by ALDF disseminating true information – to the extent that information is injurious, it does not cause legally cognizable harm").

To be sure, the Tenth Circuit did not take a definitive position on the general question of whether access to private property by deception was in and of itself a trespass.[158] Nonetheless, the gist of these decisions is that either there is no trespassory harm, in the common law sense, when an investigator lies to gain access to private property, or, to the extent that harm may arise from the publication of negative information that is acquired only because of the investigative lie, the lie is not the legal cause of that harm. Those types of harms would be remediable only as publication damages, which we take up in our discussion of indirect harms, below.

But at least one federal appellate court in another ag-gag case reached a different conclusion. Reviewing an Iowa law that treats entry onto agricultural facilities based on misrepresentations as a crime, the Eighth Circuit in *Animal Legal Defense Fund v. Reynolds* concluded that "trespass to private property is a comparable 'legally cognizable harm,'" and treated lies told to gain access to a property as tantamount to trespass.[159] In the court's view, deception-based entries effect "a diminution of privacy and a violation of the right to exclude" that can be criminalized.[160] Following the same line of reasoning as the Eighth Circuit, dissenting judges in *Wasden* and *Kelly* argued that access to private property through deception constitutes a legally cognizable trespass, irrespective of whether any actual damages are incurred. Rather, they contended that the harm caused by a trespass is the interference with the owner's right to "exclusive possession of the land"[161] and "to control access to its property."[162]

Some academics agree with this analysis of laws prohibiting investigative deceptions. Professor Eugene Volokh has argued that when one uses a misrepresentation in order to facilitate an entry to private property and an accompanying investigation, there is "harm" sufficient to place such lies within the narrow category of lies that falls outside the First Amendment's scope.[163] The harm, Volokh posits, is an intrusion onto legitimate property interests.[164] As he puts it, "being duped into hiring someone, or into opening your property to someone, based on affirmative lies would indeed count as a specific harm, even in the absence of physical property

---

[158] *Id.* at 1234. The court instead held that the Kansas law discriminated based on viewpoint because access was punishable only if done with the "intent to damage" the agricultural enterprise, which the court found reflected the legislature's intent to protect animal facilities from criticism. *Id.* at 1233.

[159] 8 F.4th 781, 786 (8th Cir. 2021).

[160] *Id.*

[161] *Wasden*, 878 F.3d at 1206 (Bea, J., dissenting in part and concurring in part).

[162] *Kelly*, 9 F.4th at 1250 (Hartz, J., dissenting).

[163] Eugene Volokh, *Thoughts on the Court Decision Striking Down Idaho's "Ag-Gag" Law*, WASH. POST (Aug. 6, 2015), www.washingtonpost.com/news/volokh-conspiracy/wp/2015/08/06/thoughts-on-the-court-decision-striking-down-idahos-ag-gag-law/?utm_term=.c50182315390.

[164] *Id.*

damage caused by the employee or visitor."[165] In his view, the lie inflicts an injury on one's right to exclude others that is tantamount to fraud:

> Consider, for instance, going onto someone's property by consent when the consent has been gotten by intentional misrepresentation. State law could treat this as tortious trespass, and often does (even if state law could also sometimes choose not to treat it as a tort, for instance if the state wants to leave latitude for undercover newsgathering). The intrusion on someone's property is itself a harm, whether the intruder gets access to the property without consent – or with consent procured by lying. And if such actions can constitutionally be treated as a tort, they can constitutionally be treated as a crime, too.[166]

Volokh's claim also rests on the doctrinal premise that entry gained by deception is a trespass. Although the Restatement of Torts speaks in sweeping terms about deception vitiating consent,[167] that position has not been universally adopted by state courts. The reality is considerably more complicated.[168]

To courts and commentators who contend that a person who accesses private property through an investigative deception commits a trespass, we have three responses. First, state law about whether deception vitiates consent in trespass cases is in conflict, with an arguably more current trend of cases holding that it does not. Second, if it were truly the case that any access to private property under false pretenses constituted a trespass, this would extend to government the power to regulate an unfathomable range of activities that are widely understood to be socially acceptable (e.g., a restaurant critic disguising their identity while dining at a restaurant under review). Third, even if access to property by deception is uniformly understood to be a trespass, there is no actual harm to the landowner, independent of other consequences that might flow from the investigation. We contend that the

---

[165] *Id.*

[166] *Id.* For an interesting argument suggesting that trespass law ought to be modified from a strict liability regime to one that "would force courts to explicitly weigh the interests of society in access against the potential costs to property owners," thus accommodating some types of undercover investigations, see Benjamin Depoorter, *Fair Trespass*, 111 COLUM. L. REV. 1090, 1094 (2011).

[167] RESTATEMENT (SECOND) OF TORTS § 892B(2) (AM. L. INST. 1979) ("If the person consenting to the conduct of another is induced to consent by . . . the other's misrepresentation, the consent is not effective").

[168] *Food Lion, Inc.*, 194 F.3d at 518 ("Although the consent cases as a class are inconsistent, we have not found any case suggesting that consent based on a resumé misrepresentation turns a successful job applicant into a trespasser the moment she enters the employer's premises to begin work"). Deception may well vitiate consent when the deception goes to the very nature of the act in question. The classic examples here arise out of persons who pretend to be performing a medical procedure, but in fact are engaging in a sexual act. *See, e.g.*, People v. Quinlan, 596 N.E.2d 28, 31 (1992) ("D.S. consented to an invasive medical procedure, not to sexual acts. Since defendant's acts were not a medical procedure, the evidence proved beyond a reasonable doubt that D.S. did not give knowing consent"). Outside the line of cases sustaining sexual assault convictions when the consent is to a fundamentally different act, the common law notion that deception vitiates consent does not appear to have universal viability.

violation of a legally cognizable right that does not itself require the showing of actual harm cannot constitute the type of harm that the *Alvarez* Court excluded from free speech protection.

Turning to the state of trespass law, the issue of whether deception vitiates consent in trespass cases is in sharp conflict.[169] In a couple of states, courts have held that consent induced by deception, without regard to the liar's motive, is invalid and that the liar can be civilly or criminally liable for trespass.[170] But several federal and state courts have reached the opposite conclusion, holding that the consent to gain access to property does not become invalid if a person comes onto property under false pretenses.[171] A number of other state court decisions have touched on the consent issue only in dicta, discussed it in tangential contexts, or have grappled more with the scope of consent than the general question of whether deception automatically vitiates consent. But the vast majority of states have no published decision on this issue at all. Thus, it is hard to generalize about the state of the common law, the Restatement notwithstanding.

To the extent that looking back to the historical practice of courts in this area might be helpful to the analysis, one commentator recently noted that the common law courts often rejected the "very premise of trespass by misrepresentation."[172] This commentator criticized the Eighth Circuit's decision in *Reynolds* to the contrary, calling the decision overly "tidy" and that in concluding that "trespass is a legally cognizable harm" the court overlooked the "far messier question: whether the proscribed conduct constitutes trespass at all."[173]

If the law varies from state to state, or from circuit to circuit, this raises another problem with *Alvarez*'s analysis applied to investigative deceptions. If deception vitiates consent under one state's law, should federal appellate courts not apply the First Amendment to laws banning undercover investigations in that jurisdiction, but enforce it to invalidate laws in another jurisdiction within the same circuit where deception does not vitiate consent? This disuniformity over the scope of an important constitutional question seems undesirable at best and chaotic at worst. Moreover, the fact that such laws would be valid in some jurisdictions could lead

---

[169] *See* Med. Lab. Mgmt. Consultants v. Am. Broad. Companies, Inc., 30 F. Supp. 2d 1182, 1202 (D. Ariz. 1998) ("[T]respass cases involving fraudulently induced consent have reached contradictory results").

[170] Belluomo v. KAKE TV & Radio, Inc., 3 Kan. App. 2d 461 (1979); People v. Segal, 358 N.Y.S.2d 866 (Crim. Ct. 1974).

[171] *Food Lion, Inc.*, 194 F.3d at 518; *Desnick*, 44 F.3d at 1352; Baugh v. CBS, Inc., 828 F. Supp. 745, 756–57 (N.D. Cal. 1993); Keyzer v. Amerlink, Ltd., 173 N.C. App. 284 (2005), *aff'd*, 360 N.C. 397 (2006); Am. Transmission, Inc. v. Channel 7 of Detroit, Inc., 239 Mich. App. 695 (2000).

[172] *First Amendment – "Ag-Gag" Laws – Eighth Circuit Upholds Law Criminalizing Access to Agricultural Production Facilities under False Pretenses. – Animal Legal Defense Fund v. Reynolds*, 8 F.4th 781 (8th Cir. 2021), 135 HARV. L. REV. 1166, 1169 (2022).

[173] *Id.* (critiquing the court's misreading of the history of trespass and noting that "at both early and contemporary common law, fraudulently induced consent was, in some cases, sufficient to defeat a claim of trespass").

to a substantial chilling effect on investigators in other jurisdictions, particularly where no state court has yet addressed the issue.

Second, even if states uniformly held that deception vitiates consent in all trespass cases, that would not necessarily address the question of how *Alvarez* applies to government restrictions on investigative deceptions. If it did, then a variety of important legal questions would arise. As this book illustrates, investigative deceptions are used in a range of different contexts, all of which might constitute trespasses. Would governments then be able to criminalize or impose liability on civil rights testers, union salts, law enforcement officers, and journalists?[174] In the civil rights testing and union salting contexts, the property owners' trespassory interests have never even been asserted.[175] When it comes to law enforcement, some of their most celebrated actions have relied on the use of misrepresentations,[176] and existing statutory and constitutional law place very few limits on the ability of persons involved with law enforcement to use deceptive practices in order to conduct undercover investigations.[177] Not only could the government prohibit all of these types of investigative lies if those deceptions were to vitiate consent in all contexts, but it could go much further. The aforementioned restaurant critic would be committing a trespass. A customer falsely stating that they intend to buy a cup of coffee, but really just needing to use the restroom, would be a trespasser. A dinner host could sue the guest who lied about enjoying their company, when all the guest wanted was a delicious meal. The possibilities would be virtually limitless and the scope of government power frightening.

Third, what if access to property through an investigative deception is a trespass, but there is no tangible harm from that trespass? As we have seen, trespass under the

---

[174] Chen, *supra* note 3 (arguing that investigative deceptions should be properly viewed as a widespread, accepted social practice across all contexts, thus entitling it to the full protection of the First Amendment).

[175] *Id.*

[176] *See, e.g.,* Hoffa v. United States, 385 U.S. 293, 301 (1966); United States v. White, 401 U.S. 745, 775 (1971).

[177] For example, the Fourth Amendment has historically recognized a "false friend" doctrine, under which one loses any reasonable expectation of privacy in information shared with third parties if the third parties who obtain the information decide to share these details. One is said to run the risk that the person they trust with secrets is in fact a "false friend." Carpenter v. United States, 138 S. Ct. 2206, 2216 (2018) (one "takes the risk, in revealing his affairs to another, that the information [would] be conveyed by that person to the Government"); *id.* (narrowing the reach of this rule by holding that obtaining seven days' worth of location data from one's cellphone provider was a search). The Supreme Court has expressly rejected the notion that a criminal suspect's consent was vitiated by a government-placed informant's fraud, observing, "Whether an entry such as this, without any affirmative misrepresentation, would be a trespass under orthodox tort law is not at all clear," and thereby refusing to extend such a theory to the Fourth Amendment. Lee v. United States, 343 U.S. 747, 752 (1952). For arguments that the law permitting law enforcement agents to use deception should be, at the least, narrower, see Julia Simon-Kerr, *Public Trust and Police Deception*, 11 Nw. U. L. Rev. 625 (2019); Christopher Slobogin, *Deceit, Pretext, and Trickery: Investigative Lies by the Police*, 76 Or. L. Rev. 775 (1997).

common law is unique in that it explicitly allows for recovery based on unlawful entry *even though* there are no actual damages.[178] At the same time *Alvarez* states that the government may regulate or prohibit lies that cause a legally cognizable harm, and trespass with no actual damages is technically a legally recognized interest. This may be sensible policy in the realm of property law,[179] but not when there are countervailing federal interests – *constitutional* interests – at stake that must be balanced against the state's interests in imposing such broad liability. Such "no harm" legal violations should have no application in defining the contours of actual harms that are sufficient to justify leaving pure speech uncovered by the First Amendment.[180]

But let us take seriously for a moment the question of what harm a trespass causes if there are no actual damages. How has the property owner been negatively affected by the intrusion? The rights to dominion and control protected by the law of trespass are well settled; persons have a right to exclude anyone and everyone from their property.[181] The property owner can exclude persons because they seem untrustworthy, their attitude seems undesirable, or even if their speech is found to be annoying or boring. However, when the owner allows an investigator on to the property, they are fully aware that they have granted authority to *someone* to be present, even if they don't know that person's true identity, political or media affiliation, or motivation. As Judge Posner explained in the *Desnick* decision, when a person gains entry into a business through deception, where the business owner invites entry (but does not know the investigator's true purpose), the liar has not committed a true trespass because there is no invasion of "the specific interests [that] the tort of trespass seeks to protect."[182] Similarly, as the district court in the

---

[178] *See, e.g.*, Med. Lab. Mgmt. Consultants v. Am. Broad. Companies, Inc., 306 F.3d 806, 820 (9th Cir. 2002) (compiling cases about trespass as a nominal harm).

[179] The reason the common law did not require landowners to show actual damages in civil trespass actions was that the tort's underlying purpose was not compensation or deterrence (although actual damages could be proven and awarded), but disabling trespassers from asserting title or easement by adverse possession. *See* W. PAGE KEETON ET AL., PROSSER AND KEETON ON THE LAW OF TORTS 75 (5th ed. 1984) ("The plaintiff recovered nominal damages where no substantial damage was shown.... The action was directed at the vindication of the legal right, without which the defendant's conduct, if repeated, might in time ripen into prescription; and there was no room for the application of the maxim that the law does not concern itself with trifles") (footnotes omitted).

[180] Certainly, there are many scenarios where a deceptive entry may cause concrete, actual harm. For example, a wedding crasher who eats food and consumes drinks should be fully liable for the actual financial loss caused by his entry. It is also possible that entry into certain events or locations may deprive one of intimate privacy in a way that is harmful. But as a general rule, entry occasioned by deception is not itself a sufficient harm to justify excluding such lies from the coverage of the First Amendment.

[181] *See* David L. Callies & J. David Breemer, *The Right to Exclude Others from Private Property: A Fundamental Constitutional Right*, 3 WASH. U. J.L. & POL'Y 39 (2000); Thomas W. Merrill, *Property and the Right to Exclude*, 77 NEB. L. REV. 730 (1998).

[182] *Desnick*, 44 F.3d at 1352; *see also Baugh*, 828 F. Supp. at 756–57 ("In a case where consent was fraudulently induced, but consent was nonetheless given, plaintiff has no claim for trespass").

Idaho ag-gag case noted, "the limited misrepresentations [the animal rights organiza-
tion] says it intends to make – affirmatively misrepresenting or omitting political or
journalistic affiliations, or affirmatively misrepresenting or omitting certain educational backgrounds – will most likely not cause any material harm to the deceived
party."[183]

Thus, the harm that some courts recognize as flowing from deceptive entry is not
a violation of the right to exclude per se but of the right not to be lied to about
visitors' identity and motives when they are otherwise welcomed onto the premises.
That boils down to a right not be fooled. As we have already explained, *all* lies cause
some harms to the listener and produce some benefit for the liar. And this is no less
true here. Some type of injury, at the very least psychological harm, could flow from
deceptive entry. It is never pleasant to realize that you have been "duped," whether
the deception leads you to believe that someone is a true friend, a potential business
partner, or perhaps someone willing to donate money to your political campaign.
Although, of course, that harm would not manifest itself until the deception is later
revealed, or may never arise if the property owner never learns of the lie.

Such a capacious definition of the sort of "harm" that justifies excluding speech
from First Amendment protection swings wide open the back door to treating nearly
any posited government interest as a sufficient harm to justify restricting lies.
Trespass without any physical damage is truly the most nominal of harms. A world
where all deceptions that result in consequences or access are deemed unprotected
is, as Chief Judge Kozinski correctly observed in a lower court opinion in *Alvarez*,
chillingly dystopian.[184] In such a world, lies about one's feelings for another in order
to secure a social invitation could be criminalized.[185] Surely, if a lie about being a

---

This is not to say that in other contexts, deception might not vitiate consent. A fraud that
deceives one about the very nature of the acts in question, for example, pretending to be a
doctor providing medical care by engaging in otherwise unwanted touching, does vitiate
consent. Deception may not vitiate consent where "the mistake does not bear so directly and
immediately upon the conduct or the invasion it inflicts as to invalidate the consent itself and
permit a tort action as if it never had been given." RESTATEMENT (SECOND) OF TORTS § 892B
cmt. g. In the case of undercover journalists or investigators, while the property owner may not
be fully aware of the identity of that person, they are not mistaken as to the essential nature of
the act, which is consent for a person to enter onto the owner's land. For a thorough discussion
of the balancing of interests between the value of newsgathering and potential intrusions on
privacy, see Lyrissa Barnett Lidsky, *Prying, Spying, and Lying: Intrusive Newsgathering and
What the Law Should Do about It*, 73 TUL. L. REV. 173 (1998).

[183] *Otter*, 118 F. Supp. 3d at 1203–04; *see also* Animal Legal Def. Fund v. Herbert, 263 F. Supp. 3d
1193, 1205 (D. Utah 2017).
[184] *Alvarez*, 638 F.3d at 673 (Kozinski, C.J., concurring in the denial of rehearing en banc).
[185] Distinct concerns might arise if a law criminalized access or recording relating only to purely
private or intimate details, as opposed to commercial interests. Indeed, the First Amendment
provides heightened protection for speech-related activities that relate to matters of public, not
private, concern. *See, e.g.*, *Snyder*, 562 U.S. at 451–52; Dun & Bradstreet v. Green Moss
Builders, Inc., 472 U.S. 749, 759 (1985).

journalist so that one can document horrific workplace conditions could be criminalized, so can braggadocio used to earn love, affection, friendship, admiration, or respect.

The Supreme Court will eventually take up this question. But from a speech and privacy perspective, there is good reason to treat lies that facilitate access to matters of public concern in nonprivate settings (e.g., commercial establishments) as sufficiently rooted in the purpose of speech protection as to doubt the Eighth Circuit's conclusion in *Reynolds*.[186] We think the better reading of *Alvarez* is that the Court meant to limit the state's power to regulate a lie only where it causes an actual harm. As already explained, it would be perverse to imagine a First Amendment wherein the protection for "fake news" and for self-serving lies about things such as military honors were fully protected, but a lie that is used to facilitate investigative journalism on matters of public concern is not.[187]

3.4.4.1.3 INTERFERENCE WITH BUSINESS PRACTICES AND THE DUTY OF LOYALTY As we have seen, many, though by no means all, undercover investigations are employment based. That is, the investigator lies in order to secure a job with the target of the investigation, and that employment allows the investigator access to gather information on matters of public concern. In cases where an employment-based investigation takes place, states have asserted a couple of different interests that purportedly justify their prohibition of such lies. First, the state has an interest in protecting businesses from interference with their operations. Second, there is the state's interest in protecting employers from disruptions to their hiring practices, for example, by applicants engaged in résumé fraud. And finally, in some states there is a tortious action when an employee breaches the "duty of loyalty." We discuss each of these potential interests below.

Turning first to the state's legitimate power to protect a business's ability to lawfully carry out its operations, as with other laws meant to protect business operations from *tangible* harms, these would likely present no First Amendment problems. Thus, any misrepresentation that leads to direct interference with business operations, such as damaging equipment or deliberately slowing down processes, could be constitutionally punished. Similarly, as we have already acknowledged, the state has a legitimate interest in helping businesses protect trade

---

[186] Lies to reveal intimate, private details may present different questions. As Judge Posner has elaborated, "If a homeowner opens his door to a purported meter reader who is in fact nothing of the sort – just a busybody curious about the interior of the home – the homeowner's consent to his entry is not a defense to a suit for trespass." *Desnick*, 44 F.3d at 1352.

[187] Others have observed a parallel asymmetry in the First Amendment doctrine. Michael C. Dorf & Sidney G. Tarrow, *Stings and Scams: "Fake News," the First Amendment, and the New Activist Journalism*, 20 U. PA. J. CONST. L. 1, 8–10 (2017) (noting that the right of access and journalism do not receive special First Amendment protection vis-à-vis rights to tell outright lies).

secrets and other proprietary information that allows them to fairly compete in the economic marketplace.[188] Again, misrepresentations used to secure such information are within the state's authority to regulate because the harm prevented is concrete.

Even to the extent that the state's interests here are legitimate, however, some efforts to regulate investigative deception might still raise constitutional questions. If, as we assert, investigative deceptions are speech protected by the First Amendment, the government may regulate such speech only if it has a compelling interest and there is no less restrictive way to advance that interest. The fact that this type of business interference is likely covered by more specific available legal remedies means that these interests are satisfied by less restrictive alternatives than laws that categorically ban investigative deceptions. Furthermore, as we discuss further below, a state might run afoul of the First Amendment if it tried to regulate investigative deceptions on the grounds that publication of the information obtained during an investigation might interfere with a business's operations by harming its reputation. So long as that information is truthful, there would be no legitimate interest in protecting that reputation from such publication.

Another way of viewing the state's interest in protecting business operations is that lies in the employment context might interfere with a business's *hiring* practices, as opposed to its general operations. As the *Alvarez* plurality emphasizes, the First Amendment does not protect fraudulent speech, which may include lies made in order to "secure moneys or other valuable considerations, say *offers of employment*."[189]

But the matter is not as simple as the previous sentence suggests. Not all lies to gain employment are on equal footing. The passages in *Alvarez* regarding employment are dicta because the Court was not considering a lie used to get a job. To put the issue of employment-based investigative deceptions in context, consider again the precise lies told by Xavier Alvarez and their potential impact. Alvarez's lies about his military experience and honors were not generic puffery; instead, they were the sort of lies that are designed to gain credibility or at least reputational benefits for the speaker. Such lies, though perhaps not persuasive to many, were made, according to the Supreme Court, in order to "gain respect" from the public and his fellow board members.[190] In other words, the lie was made intentionally, and with the purpose of securing undeserved respect in the community, something that is not trivial to politicians. Yet because the lie did not cause any "legally cognizable injury" or "specific harm to identifiable victims," six Justices agreed it was

---

[188] *Desnick*, 44 F.3d at 1352 (explaining that "if a competitor gained entry to a business firm's premises posing as a customer but in fact hoping to steal the firm's trade secrets," that would be trespass) (citing Rockwell Graphic Sys., Inc. v. DEV Indus., Inc., 925 F.2d 174, 178 (7th Cir. 1991)).
[189] *Alvarez*, 567 U.S. at 723 (emphasis added).
[190] *Id.*

protected speech.[191] If a politician's lies about accomplishments, even military honors, are protected speech, then the range of lies that cause cognizable harm is arguably relatively small and a vast range of mistruths ought to be acknowledged as speech.

Imagine a scenario under which the state could prohibit all lies told in the process of an employment application. Lying to an employer by saying that he has beautiful kids, that you have always dreamed of working in a slaughterhouse, that you are a born-again Christian, or that you are an Iowa State football fan might very well affect the employer's decision to hire you. So, too, might lies about one's sexual orientation, love of sports, or marital status. In that sense these lies are relevant, and maybe even material, to the employment decision. But such lies are not the sort of harm-causing, material lies that fall outside the protection of the First Amendment. The Eighth Circuit in the *Reynolds* case struck down an Iowa law prohibiting lies told in order to gain employment (even as the same court treated as permissible a prohibition on lies told to gain access to property more generally). But the Court's rationale is a bit problematic. The court reasoned that many lies are told by job applicants that are not truly "capable of influencing an offer of employment,"[192] so the absence of any materiality requirement was the law's fatal flaw. In the words of the court, "Plausible scenarios abound: the applicant falsely professes to maintain a wardrobe like the interviewer's, exaggerates her exercise routine, or inflates his past attendance at the hometown football stadium."[193] Strikingly, the very sources the court cites for the idea that such lies are prevalent do *not* support the idea that the lies make no difference in the hiring outcome. A *Wall Street Journal* article cited by the court, for example, notes that many candidates lie about or omit "messy" backstories about prior jobs, and quotes a research study finding that applicants are more likely to lie "when they feel like they have a shot at being the winner, but coming out on top isn't a foregone conclusion."[194] By contrast, lying is less common in huge applicant pools or when the applicant thinks there is little chance of getting the job. In other words, persons are likely to lie in the ways the court identifies, particularly when doing so *would or could* make a difference; otherwise, there would be no reason to lie. The court was likely right to recognize constitutional protection for lies of this nature told to secure employment, but not because the lies don't matter or are irrelevant to the job-seeker's chances of being hired.[195]

---

[191] *Id.* at 719; *id.* at 734 (Breyer, J., concurring).

[192] *Reynolds*, 8 F.4th at 787.

[193] *Id.*

[194] Rachel Feintzeig, *The Lies We Tell during Job Interviews*, WALL ST. J., Jan. 11, 2021, at A11.

[195] It is hard to imagine a scenario in which the lies that the animal rights groups sought protection for would not be relevant to an employment decision. "The plaintiffs assert that their investigators would make misrepresentations that include omitting their affiliation with the Animal Legal Defense Fund [and] omitting their status as licensed private investigators...." *Reynolds*, 8 F.4th at 787.

However, the Ninth Circuit concluded that lies about one's identity or affiliation with an investigative entity are likely to influence employment decisions, and therefore held that when accompanied by an intent to harm the employer, misrepresentations told as part of the application process are not a form of protected speech. The court concluded that lies told in order to gain employment "fall squarely" within the category of lies that *Alvarez* held were unprotected, because the "subsection would [only] apply to an employee hired with an intent to harm the employer."[196] It did, however, caution that "[o]f course, this does not mean that every investigative reporter hired under false pretenses intends to harm the employer. That is a critical element that requires proof."[197]

This rule creates more circularity than clarity. Recall that the *Alvarez* decision holds that lies that do not cause cognizable harm are constitutionally protected. Rather than answering the question of whether offers of employment are a form of cognizable harm, the *Wasden* court said that where harm or an intent to harm inheres to a particular offer of employment, the lie made preceding the offer of employment may be criminalized. So as with *Alvarez* more generally, the critical question is: What kinds of harm flowing from the employment count? The harm of publicly exposing nondefamatory information discovered during the employment is not a cognizable harm.[198]

On the other hand, a wide range of employment-related lies might easily be characterized as falling outside the reach of the First Amendment. Lying by *overstating* one's qualifications for a job – falsely claiming to have a law degree, to have completed a surgical residency, to have been trained to operate heavy equipment, or to have other certificates or special skills – is a quintessential example of a lie that typically does not enjoy First Amendment protection, and is probably what the *Alvarez* plurality had in mind. These lies relate to the essential function or task of the job and can cause cognizable injury to employers by exposing them to liability risks and an unsafe or unqualified work force. Preventing work that is done less safely or less productively is a cognizable interest, and lies made to shield inexperience or lack of credentials, which according to experts are the types of lies most common among applicants who are not investigators, may impair those interests.[199] Such fraudulent representations might lead to actual and direct harm to a business's operations and perhaps to third parties, as in the case of an employee who creates safety risks because they are not trained in the way they represented.[200] But when the

---

[196] *Wasden*, 878 F.3d at 1201.

[197] *Id.* at 1202.

[198] *Desnick*, 44 F.3d at 1355 (recognizing that both the "broadcast" and the "production of the broadcast" are protected by the First Amendment and noting that the target of an undercover exposé has no legal remedy when misconduct is revealed even if the "investigatory tactics used by the network are surreptitious, confrontational, unscrupulous, and ungentlemanly").

[199] Feintzeig, *supra* note 194.

[200] Thus, where tangible harms result, the constitutional implications are different. *See* Cohen v. Cowles Media Co., 501 U.S. 663, 665–66 (1991) (rejecting newspaper's First Amendment

lie has no bearing on the requisite qualifications of the individual and no relation-ship to the ability of the individual to safely and effectively perform the work in question, free speech concerns are directly implicated.

One last point about employment investigations warrants mention. The reflexive reaction of some commentators might be that such lies are not protected speech because they are a form of fraud in that they yield wages that otherwise would not have been paid. It is classic fraud to steal wages based on lies. But on a closer analysis, the intuitive fraud framing makes little sense when applied to the employ-ment investigation. The lies told to earn employment are not harming the employer or defrauding them out of money, so long as the investigator-employee performs fully the employment duties they are being compensated to perform. If someone is paid to clean the bathrooms in a brothel, and they do so with diligence, it is hard to argue that the employer did not receive what they paid for even though the cleaner may have also worn a camera to reveal wrongdoing or exploitation. As the leading circuit court decision on this point explains:

> The question is what was the proximate cause of the issuance of paychecks to Dale and Barnett. Was it the resumé misrepresentations or was it something else? It was something else. Dale and Barnett were paid because they showed up for work and performed their assigned tasks as Food Lion employees. Their performance was at a level suitable to their status as new, entry-level employees. Indeed, shortly before Dale quit, her supervisor said she would "make a good meat wrapper." And, when Barnett quit, her supervisor recommended that she be rehired if she sought reemployment with Food Lion in the future. In sum, Dale and Barnett were not paid their wages because of misrepresentations on their job applications.[201]

In short, the run-of-the-mill lie about one's interest in the industry, an underselling of one's credentials, a lie about political or ideological beliefs, or a lie about investigative motives does not cause such harm, and as such these lies fall within the First Amendment protections recognized in *Alvarez*.[202]

Finally, there is one other employer interest that has been frequently asserted to allow governmental restrictions on investigative deceptions. Under the common

defense to suit by confidential source who claimed the newspaper breached its promise to protect his identity from public disclosure, resulting in the loss of his job).

[201] *Food Lion, Inc.*, 194 F.3d at 514 (holding that lost sales and profits were caused not by the undercover investigation but by the information disclosed by the publication of the investi-gation's findings).

[202] *Food Lion* stands for the proposition that the harms occasioned by investigative reporting are "caused not by [the Reporter's] conduct but by Food Lion's own labor and food handling practices." Symposium, *Panel I: Accountability of the Media in Investigations*, 7 FORDHAM INTELL. PROP. MEDIA & ENT. L.J. 401, 424 (1997). Moreover, in the age of mass media and the internet, the practical distinction between the media and non-media is crumbling, and so too must any doctrinal distinctions between the professional and amateur person engaged in publicizing an event. We are all to some degree, through Facebook, Twitter, YouTube, and the like, journalists now. *See* SCOTT GANT, WE'RE ALL JOURNALISTS NOW (2007).

law, some states have recognized a "duty of loyalty."[203] Where that duty is breached, employers can sue employees for damages under tort law. In this context, the argument is that whenever undercover investigators lie to obtain a job and perform the duties of that job while simultaneously conducting investigations, their divided loyalties themselves harm the employer's interests. Of course, an employee who lies to get a job and then causes the employer tangible harm could, as we have said, be held legally liable for such conduct. But what should the law be where employees both perform their job duties competently *and* carry out their investigation successfully?

First, as a matter of law, the duty of loyalty might not even apply to investigators. In some states, the duty of loyalty is limited to employees who have a fiduciary duty to the employer.[204] Most investigators who obtain jobs to conduct investigations are hired for at-will employment positions, which rarely if ever involve positions of trust.

But even in a state where the duty of loyalty was more broadly construed, it is not clear whether a violation of the duty of loyalty would represent legally cognizable harm within the meaning of *Alvarez*. Again, assuming the investigator performs the assigned job duties competently, it is unclear what harm the employer has suffered, other than the post hoc embarrassment that the employer was tricked into hiring that investigator. Loyalty to an employer's mission might make one a more desirable employee, but omissions or misrepresentations about political or ideological disagreement with the industry or employer cause no harm as a matter of law.

The relevant law regarding the duty of loyalty and undercover investigators is unclear because cases point in both directions. The Supreme Court has expressly rejected the duty of loyalty as a limitation on union salting. In *N.L.R.B. v. Town & Country Electric, Inc.*,[205] the Court denied an employer's claim that a salt was not an "employee" under federal labor law just because they were simultaneously working for a union and an employer. The employer's claim rested on the common law of agency, which is the basis of the duty of loyalty. The Court, however, held that the "hornbook rule" is that a "'person *may* be the servant of two masters . . . *at one time as to one act*, if the service to one does not involve *abandonment* of service to the other.'"[206] Indeed, in dicta the Court implied that the duty of loyalty would not be violated by an undercover law enforcement officer, either.[207]

In contrast, in the *Food Lion* case, the Fourth Circuit upheld a nominal damages verdict against two reporters who were hired by Food Lion stores, interpreting the

---

[203] *See generally* Marian K. Riedy & Kim Sperduto, *At-Will Fiduciaries? The Anomalies of a "Duty of Loyalty" in the Twenty-First Century*, 93 Neb. L. Rev. 267 (2014).

[204] *Id.* at 272.

[205] 516 U.S. 85 (1995).

[206] *Id.* at 94–95 (quoting Restatement (Second) of Agency § 226, at 498) (emphasis by the Court).

[207] *Id.* at 95.

laws of the states where they were employed to recognize a duty of loyalty where an employees' interests were "diametrically opposed" to the employer's interests.[208] The court turned out to be a poor predictor, however, as the North Carolina Supreme Court later rejected its interpretation of the North Carolina duty of loyalty.[209] As with many investigative deceptions under trespass law, however, it is completely unclear how the employer is tangibly damaged, other than from bad publicity, by hiring an undercover investigator. This is particularly so where the same court concluded that the reporters showed up to work and did their jobs competently.[210] Simply failing to disclose an investigative purpose does not cause (or amount to an intent to cause) legally cognizable injury any more than failing to disclose a desire to unionize a workplace.

3.4.4.1.4 PRIVACY AND AUTONOMY Finally, a law may legitimately protect reasonable expectations of individual privacy on commercial premises. Speech is always entitled to more protection if it is of public concern, and thus investigative deceptions may serve to facilitate politically important speech on issues relating to how certain industries are operating. But the importance of speech about an industry does not make everything that happens at its facilities politically significant. Thus, a law that forbade someone from lying to gain access to private information, such as individual income tax or health insurance records, or to areas of a commercial enterprise in which expectations of privacy are commonplace, such as workplace restrooms or employee locker/changing rooms, would advance valid personal privacy concerns. While many lies to gain access will cause no cognizable harm and are thus protected by the First Amendment, lies to gain access in ways that are harmful to personal dignity or to concrete business interests do not deserve constitutional sanction. Protection of personal privacy is a powerful interest that might be sufficient to rebut the claim that a lie to gain access is protected speech.[211]

### 3.4.4.2 Possible Indirect Harms Caused by Public Disclosure

While it may be challenging to identify a set of direct harms flowing from investigative deceptions, it is easier to recognize indirect harms flowing from an investigative reporting effort. One such harm from investigative deceptions is the reputational injury that results from the investigator's publication of an exposé.

---

[208] *Food Lion, Inc.*, 194 F.3d at 516.

[209] Dalton v. Camp, 548 S.E.2d 704, 709 (N.C. 2001) (noting that employers may introduce an employee's breach of the duty of loyalty only as a defense to a wrongful termination claim).

[210] *Supra* note 195 and accompanying text.

[211] Furthermore, privacy interests may dovetail with the trespass concerns we have already discussed. *See Kelly*, 9 F.4th at 1256 (Hartz, J., dissenting) (observing that privacy is one of the interests protected by trespass laws); Sacharoff, *supra* note 145, at 882. For a different view, see Lidsky, *supra* note 182, at 194 ("trespass is designed to protect property; it only incidentally protects privacy").

Businesses universally seek to ban undercover investigations because of the risk of backlash in the form of boycotts or bad publicity. The real sources of alleged injury in cases of undercover investigations are the reputational harms caused by the publication and distribution of truthful information or images obtained by deception. For instance, the harm that befalls a childcare facility exposed by an undercover investigation by *Dateline NBC* is the damage to the facility's reputation when the public witnesses the abusive treatment of children. The harm to a grocery store that is revealed by an investigator to have repackaged adulterated meat products is the public disclosure of its unsanitary practices, and potential loss of business as a result. Likewise, the harm to a business or a nonprofit organization from an undercover employment investigation is the public reaction to any unseemly or embarrassing revelations documented by the investigator, which could hurt its public standing and affect its future fundraising efforts.

We don't seek to diminish these injuries. These can be serious harms. But the harm that flows from public disclosure and debate about *nondefamatory* material is qualitatively different from direct harms to one's property or privacy interests.[212] When the harm sought to be avoided is the publication of *truthful* information of public concern, the First Amendment is uniquely implicated. First, harms borne of publication on issues of public concern, and the concomitant public discourse that follows, are harms that cannot fairly be traced to the lie that created the opportunity for the exposure.[213] Of course, it is true that without publication there would be no reputational harm, but the First Amendment cannot tolerate a state limitation on

---

[212] *Food Lion, Inc.*, 194 F.3d at 522 ("The publication damages Food Lion sought (or alleged) were for items relating to its reputation, such as loss of good will and lost sales").

[213] *But see* Dietemann v. Time, Inc., 449 F.2d 245, 250 (9th Cir. 1971) ("No interest protected by the First Amendment is adversely affected by permitting damages for intrusion to be enhanced by the fact of later publication of the information that the publisher improperly acquired"). A number of cases dating back to an era of very different and more robust expectations of privacy reach similar conclusions, extending the media's liability for newsgathering torts to damages arising from the ensuing publications. Andrew B. Sims, *Food for the Lions: Excessive Damages for Newsgathering Torts and the Limitations of Current First Amendment Doctrines*, 78 B.U. L. Rev. 507, 542 n.187 (1998) (compiling cases). These cases have been rightly and roundly criticized by the few commentators who have paid attention to them. *But see* Planned Parenthood Fed'n of Am., Inc. v. Newman, 51 F.4th 1125 (9th Cir. 2022) (citing *Dietemann* with approval). Taking a different view, one commentator observes,

> The *Dietemann* court erred in simply relying on the common law without incorporating First Amendment principles into its decision. Although Dietemann allegedly sought damages for invasion of privacy, the real harm, arguably, was his loss of reputation or esteem in the community resulting from the publication of the article and photographs disclosing his medical "quackery." Based on this theory, the court allowed Dietemann to recover damages coextensive with those awarded for a defamation claim without meeting the actual malice standard.

Jacqueline A. Egr, *Closing the Back Door on Damages: Extending the Actual Malice Standard to Publication-Related Damages Resulting from Newsgathering Torts*, 49 U. Kan. L. Rev. 693, 712–13 (2001).

lies simply because they may lead to the publication of information that is otherwise unavailable, at least not when the information is non-intimate, nondefamatory, and of great political importance. The harm of publication is caused not by the lie but by the bad acts that the investigator recorded or documented.[214] The lie itself facilitates access, and if one does poor work or appears disloyal, or overly snoopy, they can be fired at will; the lie is instrumental to publication but is not the true legal cause of the harms of publication. As one commentator has summarized the law:

> Courts have advanced several reasons why publication damages are not the proximate cause of newsgathering torts. Some follow the *Food Lion* district court's conclusion that the *acts of the plaintiff depicted in the publication are the real proximate cause* of publication damages, rather than newsgathering torts that merely facilitated access to learning about those acts. Others give no reason at all.[215]

As explained above, lies that do not implicate the essential qualifications or functions of the job, but rather omit or affirmatively conceal journalistic or investigative motives, do not proximately cause any legally cognizable harm by exposing unsavory or criminal acts thereafter observed as an undercover employee. Any reputational harm is not the product of a "natural and continuous sequence, unbroken by any efficient intervening cause."[216] If an investigator gains employment at a childcare facility and documents unsafe or criminal interactions with the children, neither the investigator nor their published report are the cause of the harm that will flow to the business; rather, the facility's practices are the cause of harm. To imagine otherwise would be to turn the First Amendment on its head insofar as the more newsworthy and politically salient the investigative publication – the more effective the investigation and the more damaging its revelations – the lower the speech protection and the more likely the state could regulate. By that logic, an undercover investigation

---

[214] Even those courts that have been willing to treat investigations as trespasses have recognized that damages flowing from the publication cannot fairly be traced to the trespass, and thus refused damages to the plaintiff flowing from the investigation. *See Med. Lab. Mgmt. Consultants*, 306 F.3d at 820.

[215] Nathan Siegel, *Publication Damages in Newsgathering Cases*, 19 COMM. LAW., Summer 2001, at 11, 15 (emphasis added) (footnote omitted). The author also notes that

> [o]ne reason the means by which raw information is obtained is not the proximate cause of publication damages is because that raw information harms no one. Rather, damage is caused by the way that information is subsequently presented in the publication, including the meaning that the publication ascribes to it editorially. Thus, the content and viewpoint of the ultimate publication, and the decisions made to express that content, are the proximate causes of publication damages.

*Id.; see also* Animal Legal Def. Fund v. Otter, No. 1:14-CV-00104-BLW, 2015 WL 4623943, at *6 (D. Idaho Aug. 3, 2015) ("[H]arm caused by the publication of true story is not the type of direct material harm that *Alvarez* contemplates").

[216] James Angell McLaughlin, *Proximate Cause*, 39 HARV. L. REV. 149, 199 n.99 (1925) (defining proximate cause).

showing that a business is an ongoing criminal enterprise would be less protected than an investigation that revealed no wrongdoing.[217]

More generally, if the injury flowing from the lie is reputational, then there are limits on the ability to protect against such harm. The Supreme Court has been steadfast in holding that the First Amendment limits on defamation actions apply to all tort or criminal actions that attempt to punish for reputational injuries.[218] If the ultimate harm flowing from the lie is damage to reputation caused by publication, then falsity of the publication and actual malice, among other things, ought to be constitutional prerequisites for liability.[219] To hold otherwise would be amount to an end-run around the Court's First Amendment defamation cases, which assume the speech at issue is false. Indeed, it is likely that the agricultural industry's push for ag-gag laws is a direct response to the fact that they are unable to seek relief under defamation law because the information revealed by undercover investigations is truthful.

Deceptions that serve as a predicate for undercover investigations can result in harm to the target of the investigation. But for the reasons expressed above, these reputational injuries are not typically cognizable. Moreover, the Court has recognized that the publication of truthful information about a matter of public significance, even if obtained unlawfully, may still be protected by the First Amendment.[220] In *Bartnicki v. Vopper*,[221] for example, the Court held that the

---

[217] Where an investigator also records the activity discovered (discussed in Chapter 4), some might argue that the true risk of undercover footage is that it will be edited or manipulated in a way that misleads viewers. But if the harm is from staged or unfairly edited videos, then "the real conduct being challenged ... is editorial conduct, not newsgathering [and] ... publication damages should only be permitted through the tort that challenges those decisions directly, defamation, rather than through fraud or trespass claims that have nothing to do with editorial content." Siegel, *supra* note 215, at 15.

> (*Dieteman*[n] was decided before much of the First Amendment jurisprudence related to publication damages was developed. Moreover, the question of whether publication damages should be rejected on proximate cause grounds was not raised or addressed. Thus, *Dieteman*[n] did not address the principal issues currently relevant to publication damages, and its authority may reasonably be questioned on that ground alone.).
> *Id.* at 16.

[218] *See, e.g.,* Time, Inc. v. Hill, 385 U.S. 374, 387–88 (1967); Hustler Mag. v. Falwell, 485 U.S. 46, 50–51 (1988).

[219] Arlen W. Langvardt, *Stopping the End-Run by Public Plaintiffs: Falwell and the Refortification of Defamation Law's Constitutional Aspects*, 26 AM. BUS. L.J. 665, 666 (1989) ("Recent years have witnessed attempts by plaintiffs to make an end-run around the obstacles posed by defamation law's harm to reputation element and its constitutional aspects" (footnote omitted)); Food Lion, Inc., 194 F.3d at 522 ("What Food Lion sought to do, then, was to recover defamation-type damages under non-reputational tort claims, without satisfying the stricter (First Amendment) standards of a defamation claim. We believe that such an end-run around First Amendment strictures is foreclosed by *Hustler*").

[220] Bartnicki v. Vopper, 532 U.S. 514, 534 (2001). Notably, in *Bartnicki* the publisher was not implicated in the illegal effort to acquire the information at issue.

[221] *Id.*

media's publication of the contents of a cellphone conversation regarding a highly contentious union negotiation was protected by the First Amendment, even when the media outlet had reason to believe that the conversation was illegally intercepted and recorded.

If lying is protected insofar as it does not cause cognizable injury, and if publication harms short of defamation are generally not cognizable, then lying for the purpose of facilitating a politically significant investigation will generally be protected speech.

## 3.5 AN ALTERNATE THEORY: LAWS LIMITING A SUBSET OF INVESTIGATIVE LIES

A question that is somewhat beyond the scope of this book, but likely to come up, is the extent to which content or viewpoint-based restrictions of unprotected lies are unconstitutional. That is, might laws prohibiting investigative deceptions be unconstitutional even if the courts find that they cause legally cognizable harm?

In *R.A.V. v. City of St. Paul*, the Supreme Court held that laws regulating even *unprotected* speech must be subjected to strict scrutiny if they discriminate within that category of unprotected speech on the basis of content.[222] In that case, the defendant was charged under a city ordinance that prohibited the display of a symbol that the defendant has reason to know "arouses anger, alarm or resentment in others *on the basis of race, color, creed, religion or gender*" after he allegedly burned a cross on the property of an African American family.[223] The state courts that had interpreted the ordinance had narrowed its construction to cover only conduct that was itself unprotected speech in the form of fighting words as defined by the Supreme Court in *Chaplinsky v. New Hampshire*.[224]

Notwithstanding the assumption that the ordinance only prohibited fighting words, the Court held that the ordinance was facially unconstitutional because "it prohibits otherwise permitted speech solely on the basis of the subjects the speech addresses."[225] As explained by Justice Scalia,

> What [the cases announcing categories of unprotected speech] mean is that these areas of speech can, consistently with the First Amendment, be regulated *because of their constitutionally proscribable content* (obscenity, defamation, etc.) – not that they are categories of speech entirely invisible to the Constitution, so that they may be made the vehicles for content discrimination unrelated to their distinctively proscribable content.[226]

---

[222] 505 U.S. 377, 383–84 (1992).
[223] *Id.* at 380 (emphasis added).
[224] *Id.* at 381.
[225] *Id.*
[226] *Id.* at 383–84.

The Court elaborated further by drawing on the example of unprotected defamation. "[T]he government may proscribe libel," it said, "but it may not make the further content discrimination of proscribing *only* libel critical of the government."[227] By similar reasoning, even if the government could criminalize lying in general (or lying to gain access more specifically), criminalizing lies to gain access to and expose the conduct in only a single industry must be subject to strict scrutiny because it results in content discrimination.

The regulation of investigative lies has in some instances contained distinctions based on whether the speaker intends harm to the owner of the investigated location. For example, the Kansas ag-gag law specified that it applied only when persons gained access under false pretenses with the "intent to damage" the facility. One might accept our preceding conclusions about lies used to conduct an undercover investigation as speech, but worry that the lies might fall out of the ambit of free speech if they are accompanied by an intent to cause harm. Surely an investigator whose lies are accompanied by an intent to see their investigative target suffer injury might be engaged in conduct that falls outside free speech.

Applying *R.A.V.*, however, the Tenth Circuit in *Kelly* held that "even unprotected speech may not "be made the vehicle[ ] for content discrimination," and thus held that even if it was "permissible to punish all entry onto private property by deception, the Act becomes impermissibly viewpoint discriminatory by choosing to punish only entry by deception with the intent to damage the facility."[228] This is not to say that an intent to harm one's property will not result in other charges; indeed, any direct harm such as theft or vandalism can and will be punishable even if it is undertaken for expressive purposes. But when the line between innocent and criminal speech is made to turn on one's reason for speaking, free speech concerns arise.

Similarly, a federal district court followed this reasoning in invalidating Iowa's second ag-gag law. It held that "as with many laws aimed at prohibiting trespassers at agricultural facilities, ... the [Iowa] law seeks to single out specific individuals for punishment based on their viewpoint regarding such facilities ... Iowa seeks to protect private property rights by singling out for punishment, at least in part, trespassers based on their disfavored viewpoint of agriculture. This is exactly what *R.A.V.* held to be impermissible."[229] The State of Iowa has appealed, so this issue is presently pending before the Eighth Circuit. It is important to watch for continuing legal developments on this issue.

The crux of this analysis is that while the government may suppress certain categories of speech because of the harms that are uniquely associated with their

---

[227] *Id.* at 384.
[228] *Kelly*, 9 F.4th at 1233–34.
[229] Animal Legal Def. Fund v. Reynolds, 591 F. Supp. 3d 397, No. 419CV00124SMRHCA, 2022 WL 777231, at *11 (S.D. Iowa Mar. 14, 2022), *appeal docketed*, No. 22-1830 (8th Cir. 2022).

expression, it may not discriminate within those categories because of its hostility toward its non-proscribable content or viewpoint. It is the exception that proves the rule that generally the greater power includes the lesser power. If it is permissible to criminalize all threats, it may still be impermissible to criminalize only threats based on a particular viewpoint. Likewise, even if we assumed that all lies to gain employment or access may be criminalized (though we believe they cannot be), laws prohibiting lies to gain employment in one particular industry, or lies told with an intent to harm the target by exposing and damaging that industry's reputation, would violate the First Amendment. As one leading First Amendment scholar has observed, "Singling out one or a small group of lies for government condemnation, while leaving others unregulated, signifies a 'realistic possibility that official suppression of ideas is afoot.'"[230]

* * *

Deception-based investigations have a long and storied, if controversial, role in American history. "[O]ur most cherished image of the press is the fearless reporter who uncovers matters we would prefer not to see or think about."[231] Lies play a surprisingly important historic role in uncovering truth. We contend that there is no tangible harm caused by such lies unless accompanied by some other unlawful act. Consent to enter based on deceptions is a contextual inquiry that necessarily considers whether the benefits to the public outweigh the harms to the landowner.[232] Once one considers the law's predilection for balancing and context, the strength of the claim that investigative deceptions are protected becomes clearer. Whatever the ultimate status of lies generally under the First Amendment, investigative deceptions used to access information of public import are *high-value lies*, and laws banning them should rarely be upheld.

---

[230] Varat, *supra* note 7, at 1118 (citing R.A.V. v. St. Paul, 505 U.S. 377, 390 (1992)).

[231] Bernard W. Bell, *Secrets and Lies: News Media and Law Enforcement Use of Deception as an Investigative Tool*, 60 U. Pitt. L. Rev. 745, 837 (1999).

[232] *See* David F. Freedman, *Press Passes and Trespasses: Newsgathering on Private Property*, 84 Colum. L. Rev. 1298, 1335 (1984); Saul Levmore, *A Theory of Deception and then of Common Law Categories*, 85 Tex. L. Rev. 1359, 1369 (2007) (recognizing trespass doctrine as flexible depending on the "social costs and benefits of deception").

# 4

# Free Speech Protections for Video Recordings

## 4.1 INTRODUCTION

The 2020 video recordings of Derek Chauvin killing George Floyd during an arrest for allegedly using a counterfeit twenty-dollar bill fundamentally challenged the American public's understanding of policing.[1] The footage was watched more than 1.4 billion times in the days immediately following Floyd's death, leading to national protests and unease over how policing is done in the country in a way that is simply unimaginable without the video footage. It is unlikely that there would have been national conversations about race and policing, much less the prosecution of Derek Chauvin, without the video recordings of the incident taken by bystanders. The source of the main recording viewed by the public and a key witness at Chauvin's trial was Darnella Frazier. The Pulitzer Prize board awarded her a special citation for "courageously reporting the murder of George Floyd, a video that spurred protests against police brutality around the world, highlighting the crucial role of citizens in journalists' quest for truth and justice."[2] The *New York Times* ran a headline noting that bystanders with cameras were now "Policing the Police." Unprecedented police accountability reforms became law in the wake of the videos and resulting protests.[3]

---

[1] *See* Sara Morrison & Adam Clark Estes, *How Protesters Are Turning the Tables on Police Surveillance*, Vox (June 2, 2020), www.vox.com/recode/2020/6/12/21284113/police-protests-sur veillance-instagram-washington-dc.

[2] Elahe Izadi, *Darnella Frazier, the Teen Who Filmed George Floyd's Murder, Awarded a Pulitzer Citation*, WASH. POST (June 11, 2021), www.washingtonpost.com/media/2021/06/11/darnella-frazier-pulitzer-george-floyd-witness/.

[3] "The story of police reform and of 'policing the police' has become the story of video and video evidence. 'Record everything to know the truth' has become the mantra." Howard M. Wasserman, *Police Misconduct, Video Recording, and Procedural Barriers to Rights Enforcement*, 96 N.C. L. REV. 1313, 1314 (2018).

In the same month that the video of George Floyd's execution would cause a reckoning about American policing, animal rights activists revealed a video from an undercover investigation demonstrating the extent of the cruel calculations that characterize modern meat production. In the midst of the global COVID-19 pandemic, meat from pigs was becoming unprofitable, so industry producers decided to engage in mass killings of animals instead of continuing to feed sentient beings that were not commercially valuable. The chosen method of "depopulation" was ventilation shutdown, or the practice of sealing off barns so there is no fresh air, and pumping extreme levels of heat and humidity into the barns until all of the animals died. The terrified animals are cooked to death, and the process would have been a secret if not for video recordings obtained by activists who had secretly installed cameras in the barn to record the extermination.[4] Without such video evidence, the public would have no idea about the practices on factory farms.

Video recordings have emerged as one of the most critical vehicles for obtaining some measure of political or public accountability relating to police misconduct, political corruption, and corporate abuses. The opportunity for virtually all people to gather and disseminate images, facilitated by easy access to inexpensive camera phones and other handheld recording devices, decentralizes political power in transformative ways. Recordings empower bystander accounts with a degree of credibility and an ease of transmission that was unthinkable in previous decades. No longer are police, school officials, politicians, and others trusted because of their positions of power; instead, ubiquitous video footage upends their claimed entitlement to blind trust.[5] Apart from spontaneous video recordings, audiovisual recordings can also be an important component of undercover investigations, as we began to discuss in Chapter 3.

Of course, increased transparency through video recordings is not an idea welcomed by everyone.[6] The use of video recording devices can impose significant

[4] Glenn Greenwald, *Hidden Video and Whistleblower Reveal Gruesome Mass-Extermination Method for Iowa Pigs amid Pandemic*, THE INTERCEPT (May 29, 2020), https://theintercept .com/2020/05/29/pigs-factory-farms-ventilation-shutdown-coronavirus/.

[5] *See, e.g.*, Ryan J. Foley, *Video Evidence Disproves Police Narratives Time and Again*, COURTHOUSE NEWS SER. (June 10, 2020), www.courthousenews.com/video-evidence-disproves-police-narratives-time-and-again/; Azi Paybarah, *How a Teenager's Video Upended the Police Department's Initial Tale*, N.Y TIMES (June 25, 2021), www.nytimes.com/2021/04/20/us/ darnella-frazier-floyd-video.html; Audra D. S. Burch & John Eligon, *Bystander Videos of George Floyd and Others Are Policing the Police*, N.Y. TIMES (Nov. 24, 2021), www.nytimes .com/2020/05/26/us/george-floyd-minneapolis-police.html?referringSource=articleShare.

[6] As of this writing, some state legislatures are actively considering or have already enacted legislation that would deter citizens from recording police officers. For example, an Oklahoma law makes it a crime to post videos of law enforcement with an "intent to threaten," but allows police or prosecutors the discretion to decide when the improper intent might be present and press charges. OKLA. STAT. ANN. tit. 21, § 1176 (2022); Deon Osborne, *Oklahoma Bill Makes It Illegal to Post Photos of Police with "Threatening Intent,"* BLACK WALL ST. TIMES (Jan. 24, 2022), https://theblackwallsttimes.com/2022/02/24/oklahoma-bill-makes-it-illegal-to-photo-or-film-police-dems-vote-yes/. Arizona recently enacted a law that forbids bystanders to record

intrusions on property rights and personal privacy. For teachers forced to record classes and participate in discussions over Zoom, it is no surprise to learn that persons may behave differently (or not at all) if they are aware they are being recorded. Perhaps the risk of being recorded will chill certain interactions or relationships altogether. We might think this is a good thing when it comes to police taking more care to avoid harm or insults, or when it deters factory farms from deploying particularly cruel methods of husbandry. But more positive, intimate interactions might also be discouraged, such as a comforting embrace among factory farmworkers who are caught in a web of immigration and labor laws that sometimes cause emotional breakdowns,[7] or an intimate moment between a politician and her partner.

Recording, then, creates a substantial set of dilemmas for policy makers and theorists who care about both free speech and privacy. This chapter examines constitutional theory and doctrine as applied to emerging government regulations of video image capture and proposes a framework that will promote free speech to the fullest extent possible without facilitating unnecessary intrusions into legitimate privacy interests.

Laws governing video image capture are already commonplace in many contexts. The US Supreme Court and the state courts in many jurisdictions forbid video recording of court proceedings.[8] Restrictions on videotaping live artistic performances are widespread, whether by statute, contractual agreement, or federal copyright law.[9] Additionally, video recording bans are becoming more common across a number of different regulatory regimes. For example, several years ago the Federal Aviation Administration fined a documentary filmmaker for violating its regulations when he flew a drone from which he recorded and disseminated a video image.[10]

---

videos within eight feet of police activity. Ariz. Rev. Stat. Ann. § 13-3732; Amanda Holpuch, *Arizona Law Bans People from Recording Police within Eight Feet*, N.Y. Times (July 9, 2022), www.nytimes.com/2022/07/09/us/arizona-recording-police-8-feet.html. However, a federal district court has entered a preliminary injunction barring enforcement of the law on the grounds that the plaintiffs are likely to succeed in showing that the law violates the First Amendment. Ariz. Broad. Ass'n v. Brnovich, ___ F.Supp.3d ___, No. CV-22-01431-PHX-JJT, 2022 WL 4121198, at *1 (D. Ariz. Sept. 9, 2022). *See also* Am. Civ. Liberties Union of Ill. v. Alvarez, 679 F.3d 583 (7th Cir. 2012) (finding Illinois statute criminalizing recording police officers in public likely violates First Amendment).

7   Timothy Pachirat brilliantly captures the difficulties facing primarily undocumented workers in factory farms. Timothy Pachirat, Every Twelve Seconds: Industrialized Slaughter and the Politics of Sight (2011).

8   *See, e.g.*, D.C.Colo.LCivR. 83.1; Fed. R. Crim. P. 53; *Visitor's Guide to Oral Argument*, Sup. Ct. of the U.S., www.supremecourt.gov/visiting/visitorsguidetooralargument.aspx (last visited Nov. 15, 2022). *See also* 1 Fed. Jury Prac. & Instructions § 2.5 n.7 (6th ed.).

9   *See, e.g.*, 17 U.S.C. §1101 (subjecting those who videotape artistic performances to same civil remedies as copyright infringers).

10  Marc Jonathan Blitz et al., *Regulating Drones under the First and Fourth Amendments*, 57 Wm. & Mary L. Rev. 49, 83 (2015). We take up in more detail the issue of drones and recording in Chapter 5.

Similarly, Idaho enacted a law prohibiting any person from using drones "to intentionally conduct surveillance of, gather evidence or collect information about, or photographically or electronically record specifically targeted persons or specifically targeted private property."[11] In a very different context, lawmakers have criminalized surreptitious, nonconsensual recording of another's private body parts and sexual conduct through video voyeurism laws.[12] And a number of federal courts continue to grapple with the issues raised by anti-abortion groups' efforts to take and release undercover videos purported to reveal misconduct by Planned Parenthood officials.[13]

Another important context in which video image capture is being targeted as "wrongful" conduct[14] is ag-gag laws,[15] which have become a leading legislative priority of commercial food producers across the country.[16] The model legislation

---

[11] IDAHO CODE ANN. § 21-213 (2014). For comprehensive treatment of the regulation of drone recordings, see Blitz et al., *supra* note 10 (discussing constitutional implications of regulation of drones); Margot E. Kaminski, *Regulating Real-World Surveillance*, 90 WASH. L. REV. 1113 (2015) (discussing potential constitutional challenges to drone regulation and identifying government's interest in such regulations). *See also* Chapter 5, *infra*.

[12] *See* 18 U.S.C. § 1801 (criminalizing nonconsensual image capture of another's private area). This chapter distinguishes these laws, which directly regulate the act of recording, from so-called revenge porn laws, which regulate the distribution of sexually intimate video images that were recorded, but not disseminated, with the consent of the recorded parties. These laws raise important constitutional and public policy questions, but because they do not focus on the initial recording, this chapter does not evaluate them as implicating the right to record. For a comprehensive examination of such laws, see Danielle Keats Citron & Mary Anne Franks, *Criminalizing Revenge Porn*, 49 WAKE FOREST L. REV. 345 (2014) (advocating for trend toward criminalization of revenge porn and discussing potential First Amendment implications).

[13] *See* Nat'l Abortion Fed'n v. Ctr. for Med. Progress, No. 21-15953, 2022 WL 3572943, at *1 (9th Cir. Aug. 19, 2022) (upholding permanent injunction barring anti-abortion group from releasing contents of secretly recorded videos); Planned Parenthood Fed'n of Am., Inc. v. Newman, 51 F.4th 1125 (9th Cir. 2022) (affirming $2.425 million jury award against anti-abortion group that conducted undercover investigation); Planned Parenthood Fed'n of Am., Inc. v. Newman, No. 20-16068, 2022 WL 13613963 (9th Cir. Oct. 21, 2022) (same). This chapter briefly discusses the Planned Parenthood video dispute, which is still the subject of ongoing litigation, below. *See infra* notes 40–42 and accompanying text.

[14] Defendant Wasden's Response to Motion for Partial Summary Judgment Filed on November 18, 2014, at 15, Animal Legal Defense Fund v. Otter, 2014 WL 7530410 (D. Idaho Nov. 18, 2014), ECF No. 88 ("The statute's objective is 'to protect agricultural production facilities from interference by wrongful conduct'") (citing Statement of Purpose, S.B. 1337, 62nd Leg., 2nd Reg. Sess. (Idaho 2014), https://legislature.idaho.gov/wp-content/uploads/sessioninfo/2014/legislation/S1337SOP.pdf).

[15] The term "ag-gag" was originated by food writer Mark Bittman. Mark Bittman, *Who Protects the Animals?*, N.Y. TIMES (Apr. 26, 2011), https://archive.nytimes.com/opinionator.blogs.nytimes.com/2011/04/26/who-protects-the-animals/.

[16] *See* Dan Flynn, *Farm Protection Is Not "Ag-Gag,"* Says Animal Ag Spokeswoman, FOOD SAFETY NEWS (Jan. 30, 2013), www.foodsafetynews.com/2013/01/call-it-farm-protection-not-ag-gag-says-animal-ags-spokeswoman/ (explaining agricultural industry's push for ag-gag laws in various states); *Debate: After Activists Covertly Expose Animal Cruelty, Should They Be Targeted with "Ag-Gag" Laws?*, DEMOCRACY NOW! (Apr. 9, 2013), www.democracynow.org/2013/4/9/

drafted by the American Legislative Exchange Council (ALEC)[17] criminalizes the act of nonconsensual audio or video recording on the premises of slaughterhouses, factory farms, and other industrial meat operations, and state statutes tend to follow this template.[18] The first ag-gag laws were enacted in the early 1990s by Kansas, Montana, and North Dakota.[19] Montana's law was largely limited to conduct that was already criminalized, but Kansas and North Dakota included precursors to more recent laws by prohibiting nonconsensual video recordings.[20] In all, ten states currently have ag-gag laws on the books (including the ones that have already been enjoined).[21] These ag-gag laws are striking in the scope of their recording prohibitions, many of which criminalize the act of recording conduct or activities that one is otherwise lawfully able to observe from a location they are otherwise lawfully permitted to be.

A number of important constitutional questions are implicated by the state regulation of video image capture. For example, if recording bans such as ag-gag

---

debate_after_activists_covertly_expose_animal (demonstrating agricultural sector's advocacy for ag-gag legislation).

[17] It has been reported that ALEC was integrally involved in the drafting of model ag-gag legislation. Will Potter, *"Ag Gag" Bills and Supporters Have Close Ties to ALEC*, GREEN IS THE NEW RED (Apr. 26, 2012), www.greenisthenewred.com/blog/ag-gag-american-legislative-exchange-council/5947/.

[18] *See, e.g.,* UTAH CODE ANN. § 76-6-112 (2012); IDAHO CODE ANN. § 18-7042 (2014). Federal courts have enjoined the enforcement of all or parts of ag-gag laws in Idaho, Iowa, Kansas, North Carolina, and Utah. Animal Legal Def. Fund v. Wasden, 878 F.3d 1184 (9th Cir. 2018); Animal Legal Def. Fund v. Reynolds, 8 F.4th 781 (8th Cir. 2021); Animal Legal Def. Fund v. Kelly, 9 F.4th 1219 (10th Cir. 2021), *cert. denied*, 142 S.Ct. 2647 (2022); People for the Ethical Treatment of Animals, Inc. v. Stein, ___ F.4th ___, 2023 WL 2172219 (4th Cir. Feb. 23, 2023); Animal Legal Def. Fund v. Herbert, 263 F. Supp. 3d 1193, 1205 (D. Utah 2017). There is also litigation pending in Arkansas, Animal Legal Def. Fund v. Vaught, 8 F.4th 714, 721 (8th Cir. 2021) (remanding case to district court for further proceedings). In addition, litigation regarding a second ag-gag statute in Iowa is ongoing. Animal Legal Def. Fund v. Reynolds, 591 F. Supp. 3d 397 (S.D. Iowa 2022), *appeal docketed*, No. 22-1830 (8th Cir. 2022).
   As we discussed extensively in Chapter 3, another common feature of these laws is the criminalization of misrepresentations as a means of gaining access to those places for the purpose of taking audio or video images. A third provision required in some states is that any videotape of unlawful activity recorded in these locations must be turned over to the state within twenty-four hours after it is obtained. *See* MO. ANN. STAT. § 578.013 (2012).

[19] KAN. STAT. ANN. §§ 47-1825–1830 (2015); MONT. CODE ANN. §§ 81-30-101–105 (2015); N.D. CENT. CODE ANN. §§ 12.1-21.1-01–05 (2015) (generally prohibiting nonconsensual entry to animal facilities).

[20] KAN. STAT. ANN. §§ 47-1827(c)(4) (2015) (prohibiting nonconsensual entry to animal facility to take pictures by photograph or video camera); MONT. CODE ANN. §§ 81-30-103(2)(e) (2015) (prohibiting nonconsensual entry to animal facility to take pictures "with the intent to commit criminal defamation"); N.D. CENT. CODE ANN. §§ 12.1-21.1-02(6) (2015) (prohibiting nonconsensual entry to animal facility to use or attempt to use camera, video camera, or other video or audio recording equipment).

[21] *Ag-Gag Laws*, ANIMAL LEGAL DEF. FUND, https://aldf.org/issue/ag-gag/ (last visited Nov. 15, 2022).

laws are constitutionally permissible, it is foreseeable that any number of indus-tries and business operations would seek similar government controls on surrep-titious video recordings that might expose misconduct in other areas of the private sector, such as commercial childcare facilities, senior care homes, hos-pitals, and industrial factories. Such laws represent a unique incidence of legal regulation – private commercial interests coopting state legislatures to take sides in distorting discourse by chilling the speech on only one side of an important public debate.

This chapter seeks to provide answers to four primary questions. First, is the act of video image capture a form of speech, or an intrinsic precursor to speech, and thereby covered by the First Amendment? Second, if video image capture is speech, does that include all such recordings, or only those that occur in public or with the consent of the persons recorded?[22] Although the First Amendment does not ordinarily apply to expression occurring on private property, state laws that criminalize recording on private property based on the recording's content necessarily implicate constitutional concerns about public speech. Third, if video recording is covered by the First Amendment, is that coverage limited to recording matters of public concern that facilitate public discourse? Fourth, and finally, if video image capture is speech, what standard of review ought to apply to its regulation? Are the default doctrinal First Amendment rules – including strict scrutiny of content-based limits – adequate to protect important speech while maintaining sensitivity to legitimate property and privacy concerns? Only by addressing these questions can lawyers and courts competently provide answers to some of the most vexing and undecided questions of free speech law, such as the constitutionality of laws banning drone recordings or criminalizing secret videos by undercover animal welfare investigators.

## 4.2 VIDEO RECORDING AS SPEECH

As we explained in Chapter 3, a fundamental element of speech doctrine involves determining what, beyond the obvious category of spoken or written words, "counts" as speech, and therefore is potentially entitled to First Amendment protection. The so-called coverage question of the First Amendment asks what types of conduct are sufficiently related to the values underlying free speech so as to warrant constitutional scrutiny. Scholars have debated the range of conduct that is close enough to expression to warrant

---

[22] *See* Seth F. Kreimer, *Pervasive Image Capture and the First Amendment: Memory, Discourse, and the Right to Record*, 159 U. Pa. L. Rev. 335 (2011) (discussing tension between privacy and First Amendment protections for image capture).

coverage,[23] and the Supreme Court itself has confronted several coverage issues in its decisions over the past decades.[24]

In this chapter, we argue that video recording, whether on public or private property, promotes the values often associated with free speech, and is a form of expression covered by the First Amendment. We then carefully lay out the relevant factors for determining whether and in what circumstances the act of recording is also constitutionally protected.[25]

### 4.2.1 *The First Amendment Values of Video Recording*

As we laid out in Chapter 3, the most common justifications for protecting expression under free speech law typically turn on three major instrumental claims: free speech promotes democratic self-governance, facilitates the search for broader truths beyond the political world, and advances important interests in individual self-realization and autonomy.

First Amendment theory supports recording's inclusion as speech because this form of speech activity advances all three of these interests. The capacity for individual citizens to make audiovisual recordings has been around since at least the latter part of the twentieth century.[26] But the advancement of digital technology and the relative ease with which one can acquire a recording device has now made video recordings so widely available as to be virtually ubiquitous.[27] Coupled with the

---

[23] *See, e.g.*, John Greenman, *On Communication*, 106 MICH. L. REV. 1337 (2008) (defining communication under free will theory from viewpoint of listener); R. George Wright, *What Counts as "Speech" in the First Place?: Determining the Scope of the Free Speech Clause*, 37 PEPP. L. REV. 1217 (2010) (exploring boundaries of scope of First Amendment protections); Mark Tushnet, *Art and the First Amendment*, 35 COLUM. J.L. & ARTS 169 (2012) (exploring First Amendment doctrine as applied to artwork); Jane Bambauer, *Is Data Speech?*, 66 STAN. L. REV. 57, 63–64 (2014) (arguing that data is form of protected speech as it serves the purpose of knowledge creation); Joseph Blocher, *Nonsense and the Freedom of Speech: What Meaning Means for the First Amendment*, 62 DUKE L.J. 1423 (2014) (detailing First Amendment protection for nonsense, or meaningless words); Genevieve Lakier, *Sport as Speech*, 16 U. PA. J. CONST. L. 1109 (2014) (arguing that sports are speech and thus covered by First Amendment); Ashutosh Bhagwat, *Producing Speech*, 56 WM. & MARY L. REV. 1029, 1035 (2015) (arguing that, although not absolute, conduct associated with producing speech should be protected by First Amendment); Alan K. Chen, *Instrumental Music and the First Amendment*, 66 HASTINGS L.J. 381, 385 (2015) (arguing "instrumental musical expression is constitutionally equivalent to speech"). *See also* KENT GREENAWALT, SPEECH, CRIME, AND THE USES OF LANGUAGE 54 (1989) (distinguishing speech from conduct conveying no message).

[24] *See, e.g.*, Texas v. Johnson, 491 U.S. 397 (1989) (flag burning); Hurley v. Irish-Am. Gay, Lesbian & Bisexual Grp. of Bos., 515 U.S. 557 (1995) (parades); Virginia v. Black, 538 U.S. 343 (2003) (cross burning); Brown v. Ent. Merchs. Ass'n, 564 U.S. 786 (2011) (video games).

[25] Our analysis focuses on the free speech implications of restrictions on video recordings; however, in many instance audio recording is an essential part of a video. Our free speech analysis, accordingly, necessarily applies to both audio and visual recordings. See infra note 31, and notes 40–44. There is no principle of free speech that would provide preferential protection to visual as opposed to audio recording.

[26] Kreimer, *supra* note 22, at 339–40 (discussing emergence of digital and cellphone cameras).

[27] *Id.* at 337.

advent of the internet, the expansion of video recording technology has made it possible to broadcast images widely, inexpensively, and instantaneously.[28] This creates transformative ways for individuals to express themselves as individuals, participate in democracy, and inform public discourse about not only political and social issues, but also broader understandings about the truths of the universe, including complex moral questions.

Although it is not the strongest argument in support of speech protections for recording, it is hard to dispute that there is also an autonomy-based rationale for treating video recording as speech. There are persons who devote themselves to recording different topics and using a variety of styles. Persons make a living by recording videos for platforms like Tik Tok or Instagram that range from random to political. There are persons who specialize in recordings in remote travel destinations, others who capture funny moments in public, and others who focus on the acts of public servants such as police officers. It could be argued that the freedom to engage in such video recording allows individuals to express themselves and develop their thoughts, ideas, and other mental faculties in a manner that helps them evolve as autonomous human beings. The problem with this argument, as with other autonomy justifications, is that it is difficult to draw the line between video recording and other forms of conduct that advance autonomy but are more clearly not speech. But in the age of social media, it seems hard to dispute that persons creating and sharing videos on nonpolitical, seemingly frivolous topics, who seek to influence popular culture or become a type of celebrity of sorts, are not engaged in speech. And while concepts like democratic self-governance may be broad enough to capture such ideas, it still seems meaningful to reserve space for cat videos and social media influencing efforts as a category of expression primarily associated with nonpolitical, autonomy-defining aspects of life.[29]

An easier case can be made that recording serves interests in self-governance.[30] Video has become an important part of both public official accountability and effective citizen participation in public dialogue. Official campaign videos, of course, now play a prominent and central role in electoral politics, whether they are broadcast on television or over the internet.[31] But with the proliferation of image

---

[28] *Id.*

[29] But perhaps the difference here is primarily semantic. Scholars have noted that "we also have reason to communicate with like-minded others regarding nonpolitical values having to do with art, religion, science, philosophy, sex, and other important aspects of personal life," and still conclude that the "chief problem with 'autonomy'" as a justification for speech protection "is that it is commonly understood in too many different ways." T. M. Scanlon, *Why Not Base Free Speech on Autonomy or Democracy*, 97 Va. L. Rev. 541, 544, 546 (2011).

[30] Kreimer, *supra* note 22, at 341.

[31] *See, e.g.*, Ted Cruz, *Ted Cruz for President*, YouTube (Mar. 23, 2015), www.youtube.com/watch?v=cEOKJRkhpxg (showing Republican presidential candidate Ted Cruz's campaign video); Hillary Clinton, *Getting Started | Hillary Clinton*, YouTube (Apr. 12, 2015), www.youtube.com/watch?v=ouY7gLZDmn4 (showing Democratic presidential candidate Hillary Clinton's campaign video).

capture technology, unofficial videos, too, have entered the scene. One of the biggest stories of the 2012 US presidential campaign emerged when Scott Prouty, a catering company waiter, secretly video recorded a speech by Republican candidate Mitt Romney at a private fundraising event.[32] The nonconsensually recorded video shows Romney talking to wealthy donors about what he characterized as the 47% of Americans who believe they are "victims" and "believe the government has a responsibility to take care of them."[33] Not surprisingly, President Obama later used these remarks to argue that Romney was out of touch with mainstream, average Americans.[34] Of course, the revelations of video recordings are bipartisan. As Professor Seth Kreimer noted, President Obama himself was captured on video talking about "bitter" Pennsylvanians at a private fundraising meeting during his first presidential campaign.[35] Undercover investigations or candid moments caught on video that portray politicians in a poor light have become commonplace. Former President Trump was caught making sexist "jokes" that he later dismissed as locker room talk, and one of his top lawyers, Rudy Giuliani, was caught in a compromising situation by comedian Sacha Barron Cohen in a *Borat* film.

Aside from political groups or candidates, video recordings may be valuable and effective tools that can provide information to the public eye and be persuasive on a wide range of issues from all points on the political spectrum:

> Image capture can document activities that are proper subjects of public deliberation but which the protagonists would prefer to keep hidden and deniable. Animal rights activists regularly seek to record and publicize what they regard as graphic examples of animal abuse. Conservative activists seek to capture and publish images of their opponents engaged in activities that the activists believe the public would oppose. Human rights campaigners document violations of humanitarian norms. News organizations place dubious police tactics on the public record.[36]

And video recording is a speech tool used across the political spectrum. Progressives have investigated prisons, asylums, and far-right political rallies. Social conservatives have documented events at brothels, union leadership meetings, and abortion facilities. On the political left iconic investigations have enjoyed celebrity support, and been carried out by nonprofit organizations. On the political right churches have funded investigations, and it has even been reported that Ginni Thomas, wife of Justice Clarence Thomas, planned to use secret recordings of political figures that

---

[32] David Corn, *Meet Scott Prouty, the 47 Percent Video Source*, MOTHER JONES (Mar. 14, 2013), www.motherjones.com/politics/2013/03/scott-prouty-47-percent-video.

[33] Jim Rutenberg & Ashley Parker, *Romney Says Remarks on Voters Help Clarify Position*, N.Y. TIMES (Sept. 18, 2012), www.nytimes.com/2012/09/19/us/politics/in-leaked-video-romney-says-middle-east-peace-process-likely-to-remain-unsolved-problem.html.

[34] Mark Landler, *Obama Hits Romney over 47 Percent Remark*, N.Y. TIMES (Sept. 20, 2012), http://thecaucus.blogs.nytimes.com/2012/09/20/obama-hits-back-at-romney-on-47-percent-remark/.

[35] Kreimer, *supra* note 22, at 345 n.27.

[36] *Id.* at 345.

she and others suspected of being insufficiently supportive of then President Trump.[37]

These investigations can potentially have an enormous impact on social consciousness and public policy. For example, in 2008 the Humane Society of the United States released video footage from the Hallmark slaughterhouse in Chino, California, that showed workers "kicking cows, ramming them with the blades of a forklift, jabbing them in the eyes, and applying painful electrical shocks in attempts to force these sick or injured animals to walk to slaughter."[38] As we discussed in Chapter 1, reaction to the video's public disclosure of this abusive conduct was so strong that it produced four significant, concrete results: criminal charges against a slaughterhouse manager, the largest beef recall in US history, a $500 million False Claims Act judgment, and state legislation mandating better treatment of injured animals.

Another example comes from the labor movement. The National Labor Relations Board (NLRB) reported in a ruling against the Whole Foods grocery chain that employees may legitimately use video devices for "recording images of protected picketing, documenting unsafe workplace equipment or hazardous working conditions, documenting and publicizing discussions about terms and conditions of employment, documenting inconsistent application of employer rules, or recording evidence to preserve it for later use in administrative or judicial forums in employment-related actions."[39] Such recordings can be valuable in facilitating enforcement of the law and generating political support and sympathy for union activities. Thus, even a private company's ban on recording by its employees implicated federal concerns, leading the NLRB to strike down Whole Foods' categorical ban on nonconsensual recordings by its workers.[40]

In addition to using deception to gain access to reproductive freedom groups, the undercover investigation by the Center for Medical Progress (CMP) also employed secret video recording as a tool. Recall that CMP alleged that the reproductive freedom groups it investigated sold fetal tissue in violation of federal law. It claimed its videos showed officials from those groups discussing fetal tissue sales, and its reports prompted some elected officials to call for an investigation of Planned

---

[37] Jane Mayer, *Is Ginni Thomas a Threat to the Supreme Court?*, THE NEW YORKER (Jan. 21, 2022), www.newyorker.com/magazine/2022/01/31/is-ginni-thomas-a-threat-to-the-supreme-court. Ginni Thomas is a particularly good example of the fact that undercover investigations benefit all political stripes; this article notes that not only was she involved in coordinating investigations of persons who might hold anti-Trump views, but she was herself also the target of investigations.

[38] Lisa Acho Remorenko, *Downed Cow Disgrace: The Truth about Dairy Cow Abuse*, SANTA BARBARA INDEP. (Feb. 29, 2008), www.independent.com/2008/02/29/downed-cow-disgrace/.

[39] Whole Foods Mkt., Inc., 363 NLRB No. 87, slip op. at 3 (Dec. 14, 2015).

[40] *Id.*

Parenthood.[41] However, it appears that the group may have edited the video of these conversations in a way that misrepresents the doctor's statements – leaving out a portion of the interview in which the doctor reiterated that the fees cover only the clinic's actual expenses.[42] As we previously discussed, the reproductive freedom groups have thus far successfully sued CMP for an injunction and a substantial damages award as a result of CMP's investigation.[43]

Another high-profile example of the use of undercover videos is the 2009 investigation of a progressive organization, the Association of Community Organizations for Reform Now (ACORN), by conservative activist James O'Keefe, the founder of the controversial conservative organization Project Veritas.[44] O'Keefe and another activist visited an ACORN office and secretly recorded a conversation in which they pretended to be seeking help to facilitate a plan to smuggle underaged girls into the United States for the purposes of prostitution.[45] Although the ACORN employee immediately reported the "plan" to law enforcement authorities, O'Keefe released an edited version of the video that was broadcast publicly and appeared to show the ACORN employee offering support for parts of the plan.[46] This led to an investigation of ACORN and its eventual demise.[47] While this example may give some observers pause, particularly when they are sympathetic to the persons or organizations who are targeted for investigation, it is difficult to dispute that these recordings potentially contributed to public discourse.[48]

---

[41] Jackie Calmes, *Planned Parenthood Videos Were Altered, Analysis Finds*, N.Y. Times (Aug. 27, 2015), www.nytimes.com/2015/08/28/us/abortion-planned-parenthood-videos.html.

[42] The Editorial Board, *The Campaign of Deception against Planned Parenthood*, N.Y. Times (July 22, 2015), www.nytimes.com/2015/07/22/opinion/the-campaign-of-deception-against-planned-parenthood.html.

[43] *See supra* note 13.

[44] *ACORN Workers Caught on Tape Allegedly Advising on Prostitution*, CNN (Sept. 11, 2009), www.cnn.com/2009/POLITICS/09/10/acorn.prostitution/. To be sure, O'Keefe has been accused of unsavory practices. *See* Catherine Thompson, *Ex-Staffer Slams James O'Keefe: He Crossed a Line with Vile "Kill Cops" Stunt*, Talking Points Memo (Mar. 20, 2015), http://talkingpointsmemo.com/muckraker/james-okeefe-kill-cops-script. And he has even been convicted of breaking into a US Senator's office. *See* Christina Wilkie, *ACORN Filmmaker James O'Keefe Sentenced in Sen. Mary Landrieu Break-In*, The Hill (May 26, 2010), http://thehill.com/capital-living/in-the-know/100105-filmmaker-okeefe-sentenced-in-sen-mary-landrieu-break-in. But the basic point remains – his video recordings constituted profoundly powerful political speech.

[45] *Vera v. O'Keefe*, No. 10-CV-1422-L MDD, 2012 WL 3263930, at *1 (S.D. Cal. Aug. 9, 2012).

[46] *Id.* at *2.

[47] *Id.*

[48] In O'Keefe's case, as with the CMP, note that there were claims that the video recordings were edited in ways that might have actually misrepresented the interactions he recorded. Conor Friedersdorf, *Still Making an Innocent Man Look Bad*, The Atlantic (Dec. 29, 2010), www.theatlantic.com/daily-dish/archive/2010/12/still-making-an-innocent-man-look-bad/177964/. Cal. Dep't of Just.: Off. of the Att'y Gen., Report of the Attorney General on the Activities of ACORN in California 14–15 (Apr. 1, 2010).

Like CMP, O'Keefe and Project Veritas have been under close scrutiny because their practices have gone beyond what others engaged in investigative video recordings have done. There have been claims that some of O'Keefe's secret video recordings were edited in ways that misrepresented the interactions he recorded.[49] Indeed, independent investigations concluded that the ACORN video was edited in a way that created a misleading view of the ACORN employee's actions.[50] To the extent that this was the case, while we would still regard the recording as an act of speech, and therefore covered by the First Amendment, the recording's exhibition might not be protected to the extent that it conveyed false or defamatory information. O'Keefe and some of his colleagues were arrested for posing as telephone company repairpersons to access the office of a US Senator, for which he was sentenced to three years' probation.[51] And in 2016 O'Keefe found himself embarrassed by a recording of himself when he made a call to George Soros's Open Society Foundations (OSF) posing as a foundation representative interested in the OSF's support for "European values," but neglected to hang up the phone while he continued to plot with his colleagues, revealing their plans in detail on the OSF's voicemail system.[52] But shorn of these questionable and problematic embellishments of secret recordings, O'Keefe's actions might otherwise be considered protected expression under the First Amendment.

The utility of video recordings may also manifest itself through spontaneous acts of recording, as well as deliberate ones. As the George Floyd video illustrates, citizens have increasingly used cell phones to record police officers' conduct as they carry out their official duties. The use of video recordings to memorialize police misconduct has stretched from a bystander video recording of police officers beating Rodney King in Los Angeles in the early 1990s[53] to multiple incidents in recent years, mostly involving what almost seems like an epidemic of incidents where police have killed or injured young black men. Citizen video recordings of police

---

[49] Friedersdorf, *supra* note 47. Project Veritas continues to be embroiled in a number of different challenges to not only its practices but also its work environment. Colin Moynihan & Jonah E. Bromwich, *In Lawsuits, Ex-Employees Offer Harsh Portrait of Project Veritas*, N.Y. TIMES (Aug. 8, 2022), www.nytimes.com/2022/08/08/nyregion/project-veritas-employees-lawsuits.html?referringSource=articleShare. It is worth noting that at the time that article was published, Project Veritas had a pending defamation suit against the *New York Times*.

[50] CAL. DEP'T OF JUST.: OFF. OF THE ATT'Y GEN., *supra* note 47.

[51] Jane Mayer, *Sting of Myself*, THE NEW YORKER (May 20, 2016), www.newyorker.com/magazine/2016/05/30/james-okeefe-accidentally-stings-himself.

[52] *Id.*

[53] Sa'id Wekili, *Police Brutality: Problems of Excessive Force Litigation*, 25 PAC. L.J. 171, 181–82 (1994); Jim Kavanagh, *Rodney King, 20 Years Later*, CNN (Mar. 3, 2011), www.cnn.com/2011/US/03/03/rodney.king.20.years.later/.

misconduct can also serve as an important vehicle for rebutting the false claims of officers and enhancing police accountability.[54]

Police videos are equally powerful even beyond the function of providing evidence. As Professor Jocelyn Simonson has put it, "civilian filming of the police is not only a tool of police accountability, but also a method of power transfer from police officers to the populations that they police."[55] Commentators have elaborated that even secretly made recordings of police warrant First Amendment protection, explaining that a "legal regime that would draw ... distinctions between secret and open recordings" is unintelligible.[56] In this view, "[t]he secret recording of the police is a particularly crucial tool, as it enables the public reporting of police activity in a way that exposes police misconduct, better informs public discourse, and makes democratic redress and reform possible, free from fear of police retaliation or legal sanction."[57]

As Professor Simonson also notes, in addition to being a method of acquiring power for activists, the act of recording can in and of itself be expressive.[58] The very act can be an expression of dissent. Professor Scott Skinner-Thompson elaborates on this idea, arguing, "The act of recording operates as an assertion of the recorder's agency toward the object being filmed – often the government – establishing the recorder's independence through the communicative act of recording qua resisting."[59]

Video recording's unique ability to accurately document interactions can provide individuals with evidence that may contradict official accounts of an event, or perhaps deter ex ante any official misconduct from occurring[60] simply by its availability. On the other side, some police departments and policy makers have advocated requiring officers and their vehicles to be equipped with mounted video

---

[54]   Foley, *supra* note 5.

[55]   Jocelyn Simonson, *Beyond Body Cameras: Defending a Robust Right to Record the Police*, 104 Geo. L.J. 1559, 1561 (2016); *id.* at 1562–63 ("there has been strong resistance to civilian recording of police officers from police departments around the country, based in large part on accusations that civilian filming 'interfere[s]' with police work, places officers in danger, or makes officers hesitant to engage in meaningful police work for fear of being filmed").

[56]   Aidan J. Coleman & Katharine M. Janes, *Caught on Tape: Establishing the Right of Third-Party Bystanders to Secretly Record the Police*, 107 Va. L. Rev. Online 166, 191 (2021).

[57]   *Id.*

[58]   Simonson, *supra* note 54, at 1568, 1573.

[59]   Scott Skinner-Thompson, *Recording as Heckling*, 108 Geo. L.J. 125, 140 (2019). *See also* Laurent Sacharoff, *Cell Phone Buffer Zones*, 10 U. St. Thomas J.L. & Pub. Pol'y 94, 97 (2016).

[60]   Simonson, *supra* note 54, at 1564 (explaining that recording of police does serve "public discourse and self-government" values but noting that one should not "discount the equally important value of promoting the ability of civilians to challenge government authority and contest government practices – to dissent"). In this way, "[a] jurisprudence of the right to record should account for both the benefits to public discourse *and* the in-the-moment communication to officers that can be found when civilians record the police." *Id.*

cameras to protect themselves from inaccurate or fabricated allegations of their own conduct.[61]

The expressive value of recording is not limited to partisan politics or public policy controversies. Video recording also functions as a manner of revealing broader truths, ranging from the pragmatic, such as law enforcement and journalistic investigations, to the aesthetic and moral, such as promoting discourse about the manner in which our society treats animals.

Law enforcement and other government investigators often engage in secret video recordings as part of their investigations of criminal and other unlawful private conduct. Of course, when government agents use such tactics, they typically must comply with constitutional and statutory limits on their investigation derived from the Fourth Amendment. But when an undercover officer makes a video recording of a suspect who permits the officer to be present, it is not considered to be a search or seizure subject to Fourth Amendment restrictions because the suspect does not have a reasonable expectation of privacy in the recorded acts.[62] The lower federal courts have applied a more stringent standard, however, when government officials seek a warrant under Rule 41 of the Federal Rules of Criminal Procedure to plant a surveillance video camera at the location of suspected criminal activity.[63] Under that rule, courts have suggested that in order to balance the need for video recording with the intrusiveness of the search, officials must show that all other "reasonable" investigatory methods would not suffice in a particular investigation.[64]

Nonetheless, the courts have recognized that in many types of investigations, video recording is a far superior tool for fact finding than conventional methods. For example, the Tenth Circuit held that video recording was a necessary tactic for investigating a counterfeiting operation because the machinery used would drown out a mere audio recording and because counterfeiting is a form of criminal activity that can take place without any verbal communication.[65] Similarly, a decision by the Second Circuit noted that videos were an essential investigative method to uncover illegal loan sharking because "[l]ike much of organized crime, it operated

---

[61] *See, e.g.*, Mark Potter & Tim Stelloh, *Michael Brown's Death in Ferguson Renews Calls for Body Cameras*, NBC NEWS (Aug. 17, 2014, 5:54 PM), www.nbcnews.com/storyline/michael-brown-shooting/michael-browns-death-ferguson-renews-calls-body-cameras-n182751 (discussing police use of body cameras). For similar reasons, there have been increasing calls from both the law enforcement community and the criminal defense bar to videotape police interrogations. THOMAS P. SULLIVAN, POLICE EXPERIENCES WITH RECORDING CUSTODIAL INTERROGATIONS (2004); *see generally* Thomas P. Sullivan, *Electronic Recording of Custodial Interrogations: Everybody Wins*, 95 J. CRIM. L. & CRIMINOLOGY 1127 (2005). Having a video recording of the questioning can both deter police misconduct and either confirm or rebut suspects' claims that officers used coercive interrogation techniques.

[62] United States v. White, 401 U.S. 745, 751 (1971).

[63] United States v. Mesa-Rincon, 911 F.2d 1433, 1443–44 (10th Cir. 1990).

[64] *Id.*

[65] *Id.* at 1444.

behind an enforced wall of secrecy."[66] Moreover, from "a law enforcement perspective, video surveillance not only enhances investigative capabilities, but also decreases the strain on limited investigative resources."[67]

Investigative journalists, too, have used video recordings, often surreptitiously obtained, to inform the public about issues of grave public concern.[68] As we have already discussed at length, one investigation that has received great attention from legal scholars is the work of two reporters from the ABC News program *Primetime Live* to investigate the grocery store chain Food Lion.[69] The reporters obtained jobs with two different Food Lion stores, and thereafter used hidden video cameras to document and confirm what sources had initially reported – that Food Lion's food handling practices were highly unsanitary and probably illegal.[70] The broadcast included, for example, videotape that appeared to show Food Lion employees repackaging and redating fish that had passed the expiration date, grinding expired beef with fresh beef, and applying barbeque sauce to chicken past its expiration date in order to mask the smell and sell it as fresh in the gourmet food section. The program included statements by former Food Lion employees alleging even more serious mishandling of meat at Food Lion stores across several states.[71]

Though investigations such as this may lead to concrete policy debates, and therefore also support democratic self-governance, they may also provoke thought and expression about larger moral questions, such as business ethics.

### 4.2.1.1 The Unique Contributions of Recording to Enhancing Truth and Promoting Public Discourse

As we discuss in Chapter 6, there are active scholarly debates about the extent to which transparency will drive social change or public policy. Exposing misdeeds may not generate public interest or law reform in many circumstances. It is also possible that transparency can be commodified such that corporations can profit from it without making substantial changes to their status quo practices. But audiovisual evidence has the power to change the course of public and legal debate. Many criminal defense lawyers have had a client who likely would have been

---

[66] United States v. Biasucci, 786 F.2d 504, 511 (2d Cir. 1986).

[67] Mona R. Shokrai, *Double-Trouble: The Under Regulation of Surreptitious Video Surveillance in Conjunction with the Use of Snitches in Domestic Government Investigations*, 13 RICH. J.L. & TECH. 3, 16 (2006).

[68] *See, e.g.*, Desnick v. Am. Broad. Companies, Inc., 44 F.3d 1345 (7th Cir. 1995) (uncovering ophthalmic clinic's overuse of cataract surgery for guaranteed Medicare payment); Med. Lab'y Mgmt. Consultants v. Am. Broad. Companies, Inc., 30 F. Supp. 2d 1182, 1185 (D. Ariz. 1998), *aff'd*, 306 F.3d 806 (9th Cir. 2002) (discussing undercover investigation into medical laboratory's errors in pap smear readings).

[69] Food Lion, Inc. v. Cap. Cities/ABC, Inc., 194 F.3d 505, 510 (4th Cir. 1999).

[70] *Id.*

[71] *Id.* at 511.

incarcerated if not for the fact of a video that proved their innocence or refuted a police officer's account.[72] The US Supreme Court has recognized that when video evidence is available, the video becomes central to summary judgment analysis.[73]

To be sure, persons caught on video engaging in misconduct will often claim that the video does not tell the entire story, or they may seek to recharacterize what is seen on the video.[74] But the factual depictions in the video fundamentally frame the debate and limit the scope of possible denials. A police officer caught on camera striking an unarmed man may offer context about what is happening off camera that is mitigating. A factory farm may claim that a gruesome act of animal suffering is uncharacteristic of their business. But the officer cannot deny hitting the person, nor can the farm deny the animal suffering. And this base level of consensus, though it is not all that matters, is an important orientation about debates over the incidents that follow.[75]

Put plainly, audio-video recording has at least two particular advantages over other communication media: availability and accuracy. In terms of the former, technological advances have made video recording more accessible to a broader range of people than conventional forms of expression and have done so at a relatively low cost. As Professor Kreimer argues, the advent of video recording means that "the marginal cost of the physical composition and transmission of speech has dropped to close to zero."[76] The second advantage of recording is that video records of events and behavior are likely to be much more accurate than other forms of documenting information.[77] Not only do these speech acts inform public discourse, but they do so

---

[72] *See, e.g.*, Sasha Goldstein, *Police Dash Cam Video Exonerates New Jersey Man, Leads to Indictment of Cops*, N.Y. DAILY NEWS (Feb. 25, 2014), www.nydailynews.com/news/crime/police-dash-cam-video-exonerates-nj-man-implicates-cops-article-1.1701763.

[73] Scott v. Harris, 550 U.S. 372 (2007).

[74] *See, e.g.*, Tim Mak, *Weeks before Virus Panic, Intelligence Chairman Privately Raised Alarm, Sold Stocks*, NPR (Mar. 19, 2020), www.npr.org/2020/03/19/818192535/burr-recording-sparks-questions-about-private-comments-on-covid-19 (stating US Senator Richard Burr was secretly recorded and he later claimed, "NPR knowingly and irresponsibly misrepresented [his] speech").

[75] Of course, it is also possible that one could allege that the video in question is doctored or fabricated. Such claims can usually be demonstrably rebutted, however, and are unlikely to limit the utility of valid video evidence in most instances. We discuss the emerging issue of deepfake videos in Chapter 5.

[76] Kreimer, *supra* note 22, at 386.

[77] *See* Marshall Zelinger, *Civil Rights Attorney Says Body Cams Have Become "Best Invention to Stop Police Brutality,"* 9NEWS (June 1, 2020), www.9news.com/article/news/local/next/civil-rights-attorney-says-cameras-have-become-best-invention-to-stop-police-brutality/73-39f4f1ad-bb30-46be-bcdf-5908c0c98968 (stating that video recordings have been more beneficial to police brutality cases than police testimony). However, the review of such footage must be conducted with a discerning eye. Some observers have warned that bodycam footage may provide an incomplete account of a particular incident because it provides only the law enforcement officers' point of view. Albert Fox Cahn, *How Bodycams Distort Real Life*, N.Y. TIMES (Aug. 8, 2019), www.nytimes.com/2019/08/08/opinion/bodycams-privacy.html.

in an unusually effective way.[78] Video provides to courts and the public a sort of instant replay of real world events. As the Supreme Court has explained, when a "videotape quite clearly contradicts the version of the story told by" one party, it is legal error to ignore the facts presented in the video and instead to rely on a version of events that is a "visible fiction."[79]

### 4.2.2 *Video Recording as a Component of Expression*

From a doctrinal standpoint, understanding video recording as speech must begin with a look at the manner in which the exhibition and viewing of such recordings communicate. While the First Amendment protects the freedom of "speech," the concept of speech is not self-defining. Rather, the Supreme Court has struggled for decades to provide a sound analytical framework for determining which activities count as speech and which do not. Some forms of conduct indisputably count as expression, such as giving a speech or publishing and distributing a pamphlet bearing a printed message. In cases involving nontraditional forms of expression, however, the inquiry is more complex. Typically, though not always, the Court focuses on whether a speaker is engaged in conduct that demonstrates that the speaker has the intent to convey a specific message that is likely to be understood by listeners.[80] The focal point of the doctrinal coverage analysis is the communicative nature of the conduct. The following discussion breaks down video recording into the distinct elements involved in the acts of making and watching the recordings and explains the communicative aspects of each. It then analyzes how, under current First Amendment doctrine, video recording is more like speech than conduct.

### 4.2.2.1 Recording Videos as Expression

Some videos depict a classic form of recognized expression, such as a speech by a political candidate. Such videos are tantamount to a pamphlet, a flyer, or perhaps just a more easily transferable version of presenting a speech. In some ways the video that can be posted and viewed on YouTube or social media is tantamount to the modern-day public soapbox.

---

[78] Professor Kreimer makes the point in this way: "images are often more salient than verbal descriptions. Their apparently self-authenticating character gives them disparate authority, and their rhetorical impact encompasses the proverbial 'thousand words.'" Kreimer, *supra* note 22, at 386.

[79] *Harris*, 550 U.S. at 378.

[80] Spence v. Washington, 418 U.S. 405, 410–11 (1974). *But see* Chen, *supra* note 23, at 389–90 (arguing that the Court does not apply this test consistently and that it does not adequately address many free speech problems, such as abstract art and instrumental music).

But, of course, a video can also display images that do not involve verbal communication. Some such recordings of this type would clearly constitute expression, and others seemingly would not. Imagine, for example, a store's security camera, which records the comings and goings of customers over the course of an ordinary business day. The images exhibited provide information about what actually occurred during that day, but are not expressive in the ordinary sense. Perhaps the camera might catch a conversation or two between clerk and customer, but even then, the spoken words are likely to be incidental, rather than central, to whatever we interpret the video to communicate. By contrast, a video can exhibit art in concrete or abstract forms, and even without any verbal language, that video is still communicative. The art may convey subtle messages, be symbolic, or just satisfy a particular aesthetic style. Abstract forms of cinematic art may convey something or nothing at all.[81]

Several Supreme Court cases have expressly or implicitly recognized that the *exhibition* of video recordings is a form of speech covered by the First Amendment, and the reasoning informs the conclusion that recording itself is often an expressive activity. In *Joseph Burstyn, Inc. v. Wilson*, the Court reviewed a commercial film distributor's constitutional challenge to a state agency's revocation of its license to exhibit a controversial motion picture on the ground that the film was sacrilegious.[82] Rejecting earlier decisions in which it had suggested that commercial film exhibitions were not on par with speech by the press or expression of public opinion, the Court held for the first time that movies are covered by the First Amendment. As it observed, motion pictures are a significant medium for the communication of ideas. They may affect public attitudes and behavior in a variety of ways, ranging from direct espousal of a political or social doctrine to the subtle shaping of thought which characterizes all artistic expression."[83] In short, "[t]he importance of motion pictures as an organ of public opinion is not lessened by the fact that they are designed to entertain as well as to inform."[84] Such reasoning forecloses any argument that either the commercial or entertainment aspect of a movie's exhibition dilutes its expressive value or claim to First Amendment protection.[85]

---

[81] *See* MUSEUM OF MOD. ART, www.moma.org/ (last visited Aug. 10, 2015) (noting point of Andy Warhol's film *Empire* was to "see time go by"); Erin Whitney, *17 Andy Warhol Films You Probably Haven't Heard of but Should Know*, HUFFINGTON POST (Aug. 6, 2015), www.huffingtonpost.com/2014/08/06/andy-warhol-films_n_5652672.html (providing brief summaries of seventeen Andy Warhol films that are all abstract or symbolic artistic representations). *Cf.* Blocher, *supra* note 23 (describing First Amendment protections given to meaningless or abstract works); Tushnet, *supra* note 23 (exploring First Amendment protections given to artwork).

[82] 343 U.S. 495 (1952).

[83] *Id.* at 501.

[84] *Id.*

[85] *See also* Citizens United v. Fed. Election Comm'n, 558 U.S. 310 (2010) (recognizing the difficulty in drawing a line between limiting corporate funding of political ads, and corporate-funded films about a political candidate).

### 4.2.2.2 Watching Videos as a Component of Speech

It is not just the filmmaker's speech rights that are implicated. Government restrictions of video recordings implicate the First Amendment rights of their audiences no less than their producers. In *Stanley v. Georgia*, the Court invalidated the conviction of a man for the possession of obscene films in his home.[86] Although the films were conceded to be obscene, and therefore otherwise censorable under the law, the Court noted that the government cannot legitimately reach into the privacy of one's home to control what people choose to watch.[87] It viewed the law as a restriction not only on speech but on the autonomy of thought.[88] "If the First Amendment means anything," the Court explained, "it means that a State has no business telling a man, sitting alone in his own house, what books he may read or what films he may watch."[89] Indeed, to the extent that the Court's cases have consciously and categorically excluded legally obscene movies from constitutional protection, its decision in *Stanley* implies that movies are speech.[90] That is, there is no dispute that even obscene films have a communicative element.[91]

The point here is that video recordings express content in ways that are communicative and that watching, listening to, and consuming video recordings is covered by the First Amendment such that government regulation of their exhibition or viewing implicates free speech concerns.[92]

### 4.2.2.3 Recording Video as Fully Protected Speech, Not Mere Conduct

To say that the exhibition and viewing of video recordings is covered by the First Amendment does not necessarily lead to the conclusion that the regulation of the act of video recording – the *creation* of the video – also implicates constitutional free speech concerns. Indeed, the argument that video recording is a form of speech is counterintuitive insofar as this conduct involves receiving or gathering information, rather than producing, editing, or disseminating the recording's content.

---

[86] 394 U.S. 557 (1969).

[87] *Id.* at 564.

[88] *Id.* at 565.

[89] *Id. But see* Osborne v. Ohio, 495 U.S. 103 (1990) (upholding law criminalizing possession alone of child pornography).

[90] *See, e.g.,* Jacobellis v. Ohio, 378 U.S. 184, 186 (1964) (noting that although "[m]otion pictures are within the ambit of the constitutional guarantees of freedom of speech and of the press[,] ... obscenity is not subject to those guarantees").

[91] Paris Adult Theatre I v. Slaton, 413 U.S. 49, 58 (1973).

[92] The same arguments would attach to the argument that other forms of recording, as well as their later display, implicate free speech concerns. So, for example, this chapter's arguments would extend to characterizing still photography, audio recording, drawings of sketches, or taking of notes as forms of expression covered by the First Amendment.

Under First Amendment doctrine, it is axiomatic that the Constitution's protections apply to speech and not to mere conduct. But the notion that recording is conduct and not speech seems to fail under closer scrutiny. As many First Amendment theorists have observed, however, *all* speech is conduct – whether it involves writing words on a page, carrying a picket sign, shouting a protest chant, or burning a flag.[93] Recognizing this, the Supreme Court has embraced the notion that nonverbal conduct can sometimes have a significant communicative component. In *United States v. O'Brien*, a case involving whether burning a US flag was a form of speech, the Court held that nonverbal conduct may not be covered by the First Amendment when "the governmental interest [in regulating that conduct] is unrelated to the suppression of free expression."[94] The key, it has suggested, is whether the government is regulating the conduct because of its expressive aspects or for another reason not related to communication.[95] Determining First Amendment coverage requires a precise analysis about the purpose of the government's regulation, the values underlying the protection of speech, and the function of the particular conduct.

One argument for counting video recording as speech is that, in nearly all circumstances, the government's only conceivable reason for regulating such recording must necessarily be to prevent the recording's contents from being viewed, either by the recorder or by third parties. As some First Amendment theorists have argued, the freedom of expression can best be understood by examining the government's reasons for regulation.[96] Professor Larry Alexander suggests, for example, that "[f]reedom of expression is implicated whenever an activity is suppressed or penalized for the purpose of preventing a message from being received."[97] On this view, the upstream suppression of recording in order to diminish the opportunity for downstream exposés is intolerable from a constitutional standpoint.

The Supreme Court cases dealing indirectly with the question of recording's status under the First Amendment tend to confirm this view. For example, the Court struck down as overbroad under the First Amendment a statute that targeted the

---

[93] *See, e.g.*, Edward J. Eberle, *Cross Burning, Hate Speech, and Free Speech in America*, 36 Ariz. St. L.J. 953, 964 (2004) ("[Q]uintessential speech actions like reading and writing, speaking and listening involve certain physical motor conduct").

[94] 391 U.S. 367, 377 (1968).

[95] United States v. O'Brien, 391 U.S. 367, 377 (1968).

[96] *See, e.g.*, Elena Kagan, *Private Speech, Public Purpose: The Role of Governmental Motive in First Amendment Doctrine*, 63 U. Chi. L. Rev. 413 (1996) (noting true purpose of the content-based inquiry is to discern improper, speech-suppressing motives). *See also* Alan K. Chen, *Statutory Speech Bubbles, First Amendment Overbreadth, and Improper Legislative Purpose*, 38 Harv. Civ. Rts.-Civ. Liberties L. Rev. 31, 85–87 (2003) (urging courts to utilize First Amendment overbreadth analysis to determine government's motive for regulations).

[97] Larry Alexander, Is There a Right of Freedom of Expression? 9 (2005). *See also* Andrew Koppelman, *Veil of Ignorance: Tunnel Constructivism in Free Speech Theory*, 107 Nw. U. L. Rev. 647, 722 (2013).

creation, selling, or possession of images of certain types of animal cruelty.[98] Likewise the Court struck down prohibitions on the possession of "virtual child pornography" that involves adult actors pretending to be minors on video, or the use of computer technology.[99]

Likewise, the Supreme Court has held that conduct that creates information is a form of expression that is governed by First Amendment principles in a couple of other contexts. In *Sorrell v. IMS Health Inc.*,[100] the Supreme Court invalidated a Vermont law prohibiting the sale of information about physicians' past prescription practices to pharmaceutical manufacturers, who would use the information to allow their representatives to target and refine their sales presentations to doctors based on their history of prescribing drugs. The state asserted that the statute was justified by its police powers interest in protecting medical privacy and reducing the chance that the prohibited marketing would influence doctors to prescribe medications that were not in their patient's best interests. The Court rejected the state's arguments in support of the law, noting that the law directly "imposed a restriction on access to information in private hands" and that "the creation and dissemination of information are speech within the meaning of the First Amendment."[101]

*Sorrell* reaffirmed the Court's commitment to the idea that free speech protections extend not only to ideas but also to information. Thus, regulation of the gathering, organization, and analysis of such information, and not just its dissemination, is subject to the First Amendment. As the Court further noted, "[f]acts, after all, are the beginning point for much of the speech that is most essential to advance human knowledge and to conduct human affairs."[102]

In *Brown v. Entertainment Merchants Association*,[103] the Court examined the constitutionality of a state law prohibiting the sale or rental of violent video games to minors. In responding to the claim that prohibiting the sale of such games did not interfere with their creation, the majority noted that drawing this distinction would be fraught with First Amendment concerns. It pointed out that recognizing this difference would "make permissible the prohibition of printing or selling books – though not the writing of them," adding that "[w]hether government regulation applies to creating, distributing, or consuming speech makes no difference" for First Amendment purposes.[104] In doing so, the Court was strongly indicating that speech creation is fundamentally protected by the free speech clause.

To be sure, there will be limited circumstances in which the government might have a non–speech-related interest in banning some forms of recording. For

---

[98]  United States v. Stevens, 559 U.S. 460 (2010).
[99]  Ashcroft v. Free Speech Coal., 535 U.S. 234 (2002).
[100]  564 U.S. 552 (2011).
[101]  *Id.* at 568, 570.
[102]  *Id.* at 570.
[103]  564 U.S. 786 (2011).
[104]  *Id.* at 792 n.1.

instance, suppose that the government prohibited flash photography at a publicly owned theater, not to protect the property rights in the performance (which would be speech)[105] but to prevent the performers from being injured because they were distracted by the light. Or suppose a wildlife agency prohibited any visual recording of an endangered bird species because the disruption caused by video or still cameras would in itself be upsetting to the birds in ways that caused them harm. Or perhaps recording in a courtroom is inherently damaging to the decorum of the courtroom. Arguably, the First Amendment would not protect such recordings from governmental limits, because the government interest can be completely separated from the communicative element of the image capture. The reasoning for this conclusion can be derived from the Court's symbolic expression cases.

Applying *O'Brien* to the examples in the previous paragraph, the government is regulating image capture not because of its communicative element but because of the impact of the very act of recording, regardless of its communicative aspects. Removing the expressive element of recording, the conduct is the distraction of performers, scaring of birds, or interference with court proceedings. Even when the government regulates recording for these non-expressive reasons, while such restrictions receive less than full protection, they will still be reviewed under intermediate scrutiny.[106]

An interesting problem may arise from universities' attempts to regulate secret recordings on campus. Yale Law School, for example, recently announced such a policy, which prohibits "surreptitious recording of meetings and activities on Law School property or sponsored by the Law School or by an official Law School organization."[107] As a private university, Yale is not bound by the First Amendment, but if a public university adopted an identical code, it is fair to consider how might courts analyze such a ban. According to Yale, the policy is designed "to foster a spirit of trust and promote the open exchange of viewpoints and ideas within the Law School community."[108] Thus, the policy arguably promotes free speech by reducing the inhibitions on discourse a potential secret recording might create. Is this a regulation directed at the communicative content of the video, which would be subject to heightened scrutiny under the First Amendment, or is it more like the regulation of recording for its noncommunicative outcomes, such as distracting performers? It is unlikely that one could enjoy a reasonable expectation of privacy in their statements or actions during a law school speech or event, but one can still appreciate the idea that ubiquitous recording could change behavior or chill speech.

---

[105] It is axiomatic that a live performance is a form of speech. *See, e.g.*, Schact v. United States, 398 U.S. 58, 62–63 (1970) (holding that a live theatrical performance is speech). *See infra* Part II.C.1 (describing potential private property interests in regulating video recording).

[106] O'Brien, 391 U.S. at 377.

[107] YALE LAW SCHOOL, POLICY REGARDING RECORDINGS BY FACULTY MEMBERS, STAFF, STUDENTS, AND INVITED GUESTS (2022), https://law.yale.edu/sites/default/files/area/depart ment/studentaffairs/document/law_school_recording_policy_091722.pdf.

[108] *Id.*

In any event, in most instances the government's reasons for banning or limiting recording, however tangible, have to do with its concerns about the content and communication of the video recordings. When the government penalizes or prevents the creation or dissemination of a message via video or otherwise, the First Amendment is implicated.

Not surprisingly, then, there is a strong scholarly and lower court consensus that recording is itself a form of speech.[109] Speaking about the recording of police, one scholar has posited that "the fact that the act of visible recording feels disruptive to police officers, even from afar, supports its inclusion as the kind of speech that must be protected precisely because it 'invite[s] dispute' and causes 'public inconvenience' and 'unrest.'"[110] Although for different reasons, nearly every lower court to directly address the issue has recognized that recording limits implicate free speech concerns.[111]

An important category of these cases holds that the act of recording the conduct of public officials, including law enforcement officers performing their duties[112] and officials conducting public meetings,[113] is covered by the First Amendment. In addition, public photography for artistic projects has been found to fall within the umbrella of free speech protection.[114] Such cases rule in favor of the party asserting a right to record, but do so on narrow grounds focused on the public nature of the recording.[115] As one court summarized this view, "several of our sibling circuits have

---

[109] *See, e.g.*, Clay Calvert, *The Right to Record Images of Police in Public Places: Should Intent, Viewpoint, or Journalistic Status Determine First Amendment Protection?*, 64 UCLA L. Rev. Discourse 230, 251 (2016) (arguing that distinctions in the protection between credentialed and citizen-journalists are untenable as a doctrinal matter).

[110] Simonson, *supra* note 54, at 1573.

[111] *But see* D'Amario v. Providence Civic Ctr. Auth., 639 F. Supp. 1538, 1541 (D.R.I. 1986) (stating that plaintiff's desire to film did not implicate First Amendment because it was "conduct, pure and simple"), *aff'd without opinion*, 815 F.2d 692 (1st Cir. 1987).

[112] *See, e.g.*, Glik v. Cunniffe, 655 F.3d 78, 82 (1st Cir. 2011) ("The First Amendment issue here is, as the parties frame it, fairly narrow: is there a constitutionally protected right to videotape police carrying out their duties in public? Basic First Amendment principles, along with case law from this and other circuits, answer that question unambiguously in the affirmative"); Irizarry v. Yehia, 38 F.4th 1282, 1292 (10th Cir. 2022) ("Based on First Amendment principles and relevant precedents, we conclude there is a First Amendment right to film the police performing their duties in public.").

[113] *See, e.g.*, Blackston v. State of Alabama, 30 F.3d 117, 120 (11th Cir. 1994) (finding plaintiffs stated claim that prohibition of filming public committee was First Amendment violation); Iacobucci v. Boulter, 193 F.3d 14, 25 (1st Cir. 1999) (explaining that plaintiff journalist did nothing wrong when he filmed public meeting: "he was in a public area of a public building; he had a right to be there; he filmed the group from a comfortable remove; and he neither spoke to nor molested them in any way").

[114] Tunick v. Safir, 228 F.3d 135, 137 (2d Cir. 2000).

[115] Even in the context of public recording, courts continue to disagree about whether the right to record is clearly established so as to overcome qualified immunity and allow officials to be held civilly liable for infringing on the right to record. *See, e.g.*, Fields v. City of Philadelphia, 862 F.3d 353 (3d. Cir. 2017); Turner v. Lieutenant Driver, 848 F.3d 678 (5th Cir. 2017). The Supreme Court has not yet sought to resolve this circuit split.

held that the First Amendment protects the recording of officials' conduct in public."[116]

Among the cases holding that the right to record applies to persons engaged in public duties, lower courts have emphasized that the recording right is not limited to *consensual* public recording. As the First Circuit recently held, "a citizen's audio recording of on-duty police officers' treatment of civilians in public spaces while carrying out their official duties, even when conducted without an officer's knowledge, can constitute newsgathering every bit as much as a credentialed reporter's after-the-fact efforts to ascertain what had transpired."[117]

Cases holding that recording protections apply to public recordings reflect a necessary element of speech protection, but we contend that they do not sufficiently reflect the full breadth of the right to record. A second category of decisions recognizes that recording is speech and acknowledges that it does not cease to become speech, or less protected speech, because the recording is of private parties or on private property. An example of this reasoning is the Seventh Circuit decision *Desnick v. American Broadcasting Companies*, which we also discussed in Chapter 3. *Desnick* reviewed tort claims brought against a national television program for its investigation of a commercial ophthalmological surgery center that allegedly encouraged and conducted unnecessary cataract surgeries.[118] In addressing the plaintiffs' claims, the court recognized that both the "broadcast" and the "production of the broadcast" are protected by the First Amendment.[119] The logic of *Desnick* is that there can be no meaningful distinction between the recording, editing, and ultimate dissemination of a video recording. It also supports the notion that the journalists did not lose that constitutional protection even though the recording took place on the premises of a private business (albeit one that was open to any willing customers) and the employees who were filmed did not consent.

As of the time this book is published, the leading cases in this realm of recording on private property involve challenges to ag-gag laws in Kansas, Idaho, and Utah, which criminalized the recording of agricultural production operations. Holding that nonconsensual recording still implicates the First Amendment, the Ninth Circuit Court of Appeals laconically observed that the limit "regulates speech protected by the First Amendment."[120] Giving short shrift to the argument that recording is conduct rather than expression, the Court explained:

> We easily dispose of Idaho's claim that the act of creating an audiovisual recording is not speech protected by the First Amendment. This argument is akin to saying that even though a book is protected by the First Amendment, the process of writing

[116] W. Watersheds Project v. Michael, 869 F.3d 1189, 1196 (10th Cir. 2017).
[117] Project Veritas Action Fund v. Rollins, 982 F.3d 813, 833 (1st Cir. 2020), *cert. denied*, 142 S. Ct. 560 (2021).
[118] *Desnick*, 44 F.3d 1345.
[119] *Id.* at 1355.
[120] *Wasden*, 878 F.3d at 1203.

the book is not.... It defies common sense to disaggregate the creation of the video from the video or audio recording itself. The act of recording is itself an inherently expressive activity; decisions about content, composition, lighting, volume, and angles, among others, are expressive in the same way as the written word or a musical score.... Because the recording process is itself expressive and is "inextricably intertwined" with the resulting recording, the creation of audiovisual recordings is speech entitled to First Amendment protection as purely expressive activity.[121]

The Tenth Circuit's decision in the Kansas ag-gag case similarly held that a law prohibiting a person from entering an animal facility "to take pictures by photograph, video camera, or by any other means" "implicates speech"[122] and therefore is subject to First Amendment scrutiny.

A federal district court in Utah reached the same conclusion in striking down a similar provision, which criminalized the nonconsensual recording of agricultural operations. The court noted that the idea that speech becomes non-speech when it occurs on private property "finds no support in the case law." And with good reason. A law that criminalized the recording of police officers when they are on private property, for example, would not be more constitutionally tolerable than a general prohibition on such recording. Whether on the street, in a restaurant, or in one's home, recording is expressive conduct. On this point, the judge in the Utah case explained:

> [I]t appears the consensus among courts is that the act of recording is protectable First Amendment speech. And this court agrees. Were the law otherwise, as the State contends, the State could criminalize, for example, creating music videos, or videos critical of the government, or any video at all, for that matter, with impunity. In other words, the State could do indirectly what the Supreme Court has made clear it cannot do directly. Because recordings themselves are protected by the First Amendment, so too must the making of those recordings be protected.[123]

Not only are the courts correct that recording is a form of expression, but they are also almost certainly right in concluding that recording is no less a form of speech

---

[121] Id. at 1203–04; See also Anderson v. City of Hermosa Beach, 621 F.3d 1051, 1061–62 (9th Cir. 2010) ("neither the Supreme Court nor [the Ninth Circuit] has ever drawn a distinction between the process of creating a form of pure speech (such as writing or painting) and the product of these processes (the essay or artwork) in terms of the First Amendment protection afforded ... The process of expression through a medium has never been thought so distinct from the expression itself that we could disaggregate Picasso from his brushes and canvas, or that we could value Beethoven without the benefit of strings and woodwinds").

[122] Kelly, 9 F.4th at 1235–56.

[123] Animal Legal Def. Fund v. Herbert, 263 F. Supp. 3d 1193, 1208 (D. Utah 2017). See also W. Watersheds Project, 869 F.3d at 1191 (treating activities such as photography as protected acts of expression).

when it occurs on private property.[124] As a recent court of appeals decision relying on the ag-gag cases states the rule, "[t]he First Amendment protects the right to photograph and record matters of public interest."[125]

Public regulation of expression in private spaces surely implicates the Constitution. Imagine that a commercial dairy included a non-disparagement clause in its employment contract that barred employees from criticizing the dairy whether they were at work or away from work. Violation of such a provision could provide a basis for terminating an employee. But if the dairy successfully lobbied for the enactment of a state criminal law forbidding dairy industry employees from criticizing their employers, whether on the public sidewalk in front of the dairy's headquarters or to their closest friends over dinner in their own homes, strict constitutional scrutiny surely is warranted. The restriction on private speech, no less than the restriction on public speech, implicates the First Amendment. The disparagement of a company or a politician does not become less speech-like just because it occurs in private.[126] An activity does not lose its speech characteristics depending on where the speech occurs, though it may lose its First Amendment protection under the relevant scrutiny.

Secret recordings of private conversations can be a critical vehicle for transparency in government and government affairs as well. Although the cases about recording public officials have been about recordings in the public space, two recent incidents illustrate how such recordings can inform the public. In early 2020, National Public Radio reported that it had obtained a secret recording made of Senator Richard Burr's private meeting with a small group of wealthy constituents.[127] At that meeting, Senator Burr warned them about the seriousness of the coming Covid-19 crisis in ways that may have benefited them financially, as this information might have led them to sell off stock holdings that would drop in value when the pandemic hit the United States. His warnings about Covid-19 in this private meeting were much more foreboding than his public statements to his constituents. His statements are unequivocally a matter of public concern.

---

[124] One federal appellate court noted that "even if the recordings ... are unprotected speech because they occur on private property," when a law is "viewpoint-discriminatory," it will still be an unconstitutional restriction on speech. *Kelly*, 9 F.4th at 1240. *Id.* at 1236 ("Even if Kansas may ban recordings on private property or trespass-through-deception, it may not limit the scope of the prohibition due to favor or disfavor of the message. R.A.V., 505 U.S. at 391, 112 S.Ct. 2538").

[125] *Askin v. U.S. Dep't of Homeland Sec.*, 899 F.3d 1035, 1044 (9th Cir. 2018).

[126] The dairy industry has a right to restrict workplace speech that interferes with its business, but a law that criminalizes such speech is not a protection of privacy or a forum selection limitation; instead, it is a content-based law targeting speech activities. This reasoning is at least as true for recording bans. A company also has a right to be free from untruthful and harm-causing disparagement, but this is already protected by defamation law, subject to the constraints of the First Amendment.

[127] Mak, *supra* note 73.

In another incident of private nonconsensual recording, representatives of the Environmental Investigation Agency (EIA), an environmental advocacy group, secretly recorded a Zoom meeting with executives from a company that hoped to build a large gold and copper mine in an environmentally sensitive site in Alaska.[128] The EIA representatives posed as potential investors in the mine, and the mining executives boldly boasted about the amount of power they had over Alaska's US Senators and that they could speak with the White House Chief of Staff about the project any time they wanted to, implying that they had strong influence over the project's approval, even as these officials publicly expressed concerns about it. Stories such as these illustrate the direct role that secret recordings even in private places can play in the promoting transparency and public discourse.

### 4.2.3 *Video Recording as Conduct Essentially Preparatory to Speech*

Even if one were to reject the claim that recording is expressive activity, there is equally strong support for the argument that image video capture is conduct that is an essential precursor to speech, and is therefore covered by the First Amendment. This argument is largely subsumed in the reasoning of the lower courts quoted immediately above. Essentially, the obliteration of the means of producing expression endangers free expression no less than the destruction of the speech itself. In prior centuries, this might have involved destruction of printing presses;[129] today, it might involve smashing video recorders.[130]

[128] Juliet Eilperin, *In Secret Tapes, Mine Executives Detail Their Sway over Leaders from Juneau to the White House*, WASH. POST (Sept. 30, 2020), https://www.washingtonpost.com/climate-environment/2020/09/22/pebble-mine-secret-tapes/.

[129] As Justice Scalia has remarked,

> In any economy operated on even the most rudimentary principles of division of labor, effective public communication requires the speaker to make use of the services of others. An author may write a novel, but he will seldom publish and distribute it himself. A freelance reporter may write a story, but he will rarely edit, print, and deliver it to subscribers. To a government bent on suppressing speech, this mode of organization presents opportunities: Control any cog in the machine, and you can halt the whole apparatus. License printers, and it matters little whether authors are still free to write. Restrict the sale of books, and it matters little who prints them. Predictably, repressive regimes have exploited these principles by attacking all levels of the production and dissemination of ideas. See, e.g., Printing Act of 1662, 14 Car. II, ch. 33, §§ 1, 4, 7 (punishing printers, importers, and booksellers); Printing Act of 1649, 2 Acts and Ordinances of the Interregnum 245, 246, 250 (punishing authors, printers, booksellers, importers, and buyers).

McConnell v. Fed. Election Comm'n, 540 U.S. 93, 251 (2003) (Scalia, J., concurring in part and dissenting in part), *overruled by* Citizens United v. Fed. Election Comm'n, 558 U.S. 310 (2010).

[130] As Jack Balkin has observed,

> Old-school speech regulation is normally directed at (1) people, (2) spaces, and (3) predigital technologies of mass distribution. The state arrests, detains, or deports people;

Indeed, the Supreme Court has recognized that conduct preparatory to speech is often deserving of full First Amendment protection. This means that even conduct that is not itself speech, such as spending money to purchase ink and paper,[131] spray paint,[132] or to support a political candidate,[133] is itself treated as speech. Thus, in *Citizens United v. FEC*, the Court observed that "laws enacted to control or suppress speech may operate at different points in the speech process."[134] The Court's campaign spending cases are all predicated to some degree on the notion that restrictions on fundraising and spending are limited by the First Amendment because they facilitate subsequent political speech.[135] While the bare act of passing money to another is not in itself expressive, the Court has recognized that by protecting spending as a non-speech *means*, the political speech *ends* are also safeguarded.[136]

The analytical premise of these decisions is that expressive activity typically takes place along a continuum of actions that include not only direct expression, but also much of the conduct that is a necessary precursor to speech. At one end of the continuum or spectrum lie the most basic elements of conduct that are necessary to engage in expression: the purchase of paper, ink, paint, and so on. At this end, many things will fall completely off the speech spectrum and will not be covered by the First Amendment. For example, buying clothes to wear to a political rally or gasoline for the vehicle that a protestor drives to that rally are both antecedent to speech, yet are too attenuated from the actual expressive activity to implicate the First Amendment. At the other end of the spectrum is the directly communicative

---

it controls access to public spaces for assembly and protest; and it monopolizes, regulates, seizes, or destroys capacities and technologies for publication and transmission like printing presses, broadcast facilities, movie projectors, videotapes, handbills, and books.

Jack M. Balkin, *Old-School/New-School Speech Regulation*, 127 HARV. L. REV. 2296, 2306 (2014).

[131] Kreimer, *supra* note 22, at 381.

[132] *Id.* (noting lower courts have also invalidated on First Amendment grounds ordinances criminalizing purchase or possession of spray paint). *See, e.g.*, Vincenty v. Bloomberg, 476 F.3d 74, 78 (2d Cir. 2007) (affirming district court's grant of preliminary injunction finding that statute criminalizing the possession of spray paint, even for legitimate purposes, violates First Amendment).

[133] *Citizens United*, 558 U.S. at 365 (finding corporate expenditures are entitled to First Amendment protection).

[134] *Id.* at 336. Campaign expenditures are protected and are analyzed under strict scrutiny because "[a]ll speakers, including individuals and the media, use money amassed from the economic marketplace to fund their speech. The First Amendment protects the resulting speech." *Id.* at 351.

[135] *See, e.g.*, Buckley v. Valeo, 424 U.S. 1, 19 (1976) ("A restriction on the amount of money a person or group can spend on political communication during a campaign necessarily reduces the quantity of expression by restricting the number of issues discussed, the depth of their exploration, and the size of the audience reached").

[136] *Id.*

element of the expressive process – shouting through a megaphone, exhibiting a painting, displaying a video.

In her important work focusing on whether data is speech, Professor Jane Bambauer has written persuasively to debunk the distinction between conveyance and collection of information, explaining that "[i]f the dissemination of mechanical recordings receives First Amendment protection (which it does), then the creation of those same recordings must have First Amendment significance, too."[137] More recently, Professor Ashutosh Bhagwat has cogently observed that the conduct of "producing speech," as distinct from actual communication, falls within the penumbral protection of the First Amendment's press clause.[138] As he explains, "[r]egulation of the press is thus regulation of the production of communication rather than of communication itself, and so the Press Clause by its terms protects the production of written speech."[139] The scholarly commentary is increasingly clear that the protection of the essential precursors of expression is necessary to the protection of expression itself.

Lower federal courts, too, have recognized that First Amendment protections must attach to government actions restricting conduct that is necessarily preparatory to speech. In *ACLU v. Alvarez*, the Seventh Circuit reversed the denial of a preliminary injunction against an Illinois eavesdropping law, which made it a felony to record a conversation without the consent of all parties to the conversation.[140] In doing so, the court held that the "act of making an audio or audiovisual recording is necessarily included within the First Amendment's guarantee of speech and press rights *as a corollary* of the right to disseminate the resulting recording."[141] According to that court, a recording is not necessarily speech, but it is nonetheless an essential and protected antecedent step in the process of expression.

One recent decision considers a city ordinance providing that in city parks, "[n]o person shall intentionally take a photograph or otherwise record a child without the

---

[137] Bambauer, *supra* note 23, at 61. To the extent that the collection of data through recording is speech, as this chapter argues, one has to identify a limiting principle. Is all data collection speech? Is all data collection done for the purpose of communicating (or communicating on a matter of public concern) speech? These issues are not of merely idle interest. The state of Wyoming enacted civil and criminal laws prohibiting the "collection of resource data" such as soil samples or water samples from public as well as private land, WYO. STAT. ANN. § 40-27-101 (2015); WYO. STAT. ANN. § 6-3-414 (2015), though some parts of those laws have been invalidated. W. Watersheds Project v. Michael, 869 F.3d 1189 (10th Cir. 2017). Although that question is beyond the scope of this project because this chapter argues that recording is clearly on the expressive side of that line, there is need for additional research and thought on this point.

[138] Bhagwat, *supra* note 23, at 1054–58.

[139] *Id.* at 1057. This chapter focuses its analysis on the speech clause, but as Professor Bhagwat's insightful analysis demonstrates, similarly forceful claims might be leveled against recording restrictions under the Press Clause.

[140] 679 F.3d at 597.

[141] *Id.* at 595 (emphasis added).

consent of the child's parent or guardian." A woman who was alleging overuse of the parks by day camps and schools challenged the statute as an infringement of her efforts to document this problem, and a federal appellate court agreed. "If the act of making a photograph or recording is to facilitate speech that will follow, the act is a step in the 'speech process,' and thus qualifies itself as speech protected by the First Amendment.... If the photography or recording is unrelated to an expressive purpose, ... then the act of recording may not receive First Amendment protection."[142] Emphasizing that the speech protection was arguably contingent on the individual's intention to use the videos for political purposes, the Court held that the First Amendment applied:

> Ness's photography and video recording is speech. Ness wants to photograph and record the asserted "noncompliant and overuse of Smith Park" by the Center and Success Academy, and she wants to post those photographs and videos to an internet blog and a Facebook page "in order to inform the public" about the controversy. Thus, her photography and recording is analogous to news gathering. The acts of taking photographs and recording videos are entitled to First Amendment protection because they are an important stage of the speech process that ends with the dissemination of information about a public controversy.[143]

Such reasoning is in accord with Professor Kreimer's central premise:

> One might try to dissect the medium into its component acts of image acquisition, recording, and dissemination and conclude that recording is an unprotected "act" without an audience. But this maneuver is as inappropriate as maintaining that the purchase of stationery or the application of ink to paper are "acts" and therefore outside of the aegis of the First Amendment.[144]

Essentially, the point is that protecting speech at the end point of the continuum, when it is communicated to others, is insufficient if the state can circumvent that protection by preventing the speech's creation. No one would doubt that live-streaming an event is an act of speech; the proposition that recording that same event for later broadcast or consumption is not covered by the First Amendment is untenable. Editing the footage before distributing it to media or to fans cannot make the recording less speech-like than live-streaming.

## 4.3 FROM COVERAGE TO RIGHT: THE CONTOURS OF A CONSTITUTIONAL RIGHT TO VIDEO IMAGE CAPTURE

We have argued that audiovisual recording is the pen and paper for twenty-first century Upton Sinclairs. Recording observations, no less than (and maybe even

---

[142] Ness v. City of Bloomington, 11 F.4th 914, 923 (8th Cir. 2021).
[143] *Id.*
[144] Kreimer, *supra* note 22, at 381.

more than) taking notes about those observations, preserves facts and information for engagement in political, social, or moral discourse and informing the public. Government bans on recording therefore interfere with one's ability to create a record of otherwise lawful observations, and when such restrictions impede the creation of a self-authenticating communication, they must be carefully scrutinized.

But First Amendment coverage is not tantamount to protection. As Professor Schauer has noted, "when we say that certain acts, or a certain class of acts, are covered by a right, we are not necessarily saying that those acts will always be protected."[145] That is, activity such as obscenity is not even covered by the First Amendment, and because it simply does not "count" as speech no further analysis is warranted.[146] But an activity that is covered, such as defamation of a public official, may or may not be protected, depending on whether the government's interests outweigh the speaker's interests in communication.[147] Accordingly, if this chapter has established that video recording is speech or conduct preparatory to speech, it must next make the case that state regulation of private individuals engaging in such activity may violate the First Amendment – that there is sometimes a constitutional right to record.

In this section, we show that the First Amendment will often, but not always, protect individuals from being criminally punished or civilly sanctioned for recording videos. But the protection of recording as speech activity, particularly on private property, is not self-evident as a doctrinal matter.

### 4.3.1 *Lawful Access*

It is a canonical principle of First Amendment doctrine that there is no "right to use private property owned by others for speech."[148] Laws of general applicability that protect property interests are not typically understood to implicate free speech interests. Thus, one cannot claim, for example, to be immunized from generally applicable trespass laws out of an interest in gaining access to valuable recordings.[149]

---

[145] Frederick Schauer, Free Speech: A Philosophical Enquiry 90 (1982); *see also* Frederick Schauer, *The Boundaries of the First Amendment: A Preliminary Exploration of Constitutional Salience*, 117 Harv. L. Rev. 1765, 1768 (2004).

[146] *See* Miller v. California, 413 U.S. 15, 23 (1973) (holding obscenity is not covered by First Amendment).

[147] *See* N.Y. Times Co. v. Sullivan, 376 U.S. 254, 270–71 (1964) (imposing limitations, but complete ban, on libel claims brought by public officials).

[148] Erwin Chemerinsky, Constitutional Law: Principles and Policies, § 11.4.3 (4th ed. 2011).

[149] *See* Zemel v. Rusk, 381 U.S. 1, 16 (1965); *id.* at 3: "On January 16 (1961) the Department of State eliminated Cuba from the area for which passports were not required, and declared all outstanding United States passports (except those held by persons already in Cuba) to be invalid for travel to or in Cuba 'unless specifically endorsed for such travel under the authority of the Secretary of State'"). If one could assert immunity from trespass law in order to engage in important speech activities, then the laws of private property would mean very little. As the

Moreover, it is accepted doctrine that the "First Amendment does not guarantee the press a constitutional right of special access to information not available to the public generally,"[150] and there is "no basis for the claim that the First Amendment compels others ... to supply information."[151] One might surmise from these principles that even if video recording is a category of speech within the meaning of the First Amendment, the government may still restrict or regulate such recording in appropriate circumstances.

An important illustration of this general limitation is the Sixth Circuit's decision in *S.H.A.R.K. v. Metro Parks*.[152] In *S.H.A.R.K.*, the court addressed plaintiffs' claims that government officials' removal of cameras they had placed in a public park to detect and expose mistreatment of wildlife, and the subsequent deletion of the recordings from those cameras, violated the First Amendment. Central to the court's holding that the city's actions did not violate the First Amendment was the conclusion that because the cameras were left at the park to record activities during hours when the park was closed, there was no public access to the images captured by the recording devices.[153] The court emphasized that there is no general right of access to private areas, and noted that when the state closes an area off to the public, such action, unless driven by an improper, content-based motive, generally will not offend the First Amendment.[154]

Such reasoning illustrates how broadly the right to record can be limited by government or private actors. A municipality can apparently shield its unsavory tactics – perhaps relating to animal culling, or homeless encampment removal, for example, by simply closing off the park or public space to public access. While Yellowstone National Park's logo includes a bison, because the large animals compete with cattle for precious grazing land when they roam out of the park, Yellowstone has agreed to "manage" the population, and conducts nearly annual culling events within the national park boundaries. But the culling roundups are generally not viewable by the public or interested parties because park officials close off that part of the national park while the culling is occurring.[155] One might imagine that a right to record should include reasonable access to *public spaces*. But at present the officials in charge of the park in *S.H.A.R.K.* and Yellowstone

Court explained in rejecting a right of access claim, "[t]here are few restrictions on action which could not be clothed by ingenious argument in the garb of decreased data flow." *Id.*

[150] Branzburg v. Hayes, 408 U.S. 665, 684 (1972); D'Amario v. Providence Civic Ctr. Auth., 639 F. Supp. 1538, 1542 (D.R.I. 1986), aff'd, 815 F.2d 692 (1st Cir. 1987) (quoting *Branzburg*).

[151] *Branzburg*, 408 U.S. at 684.

[152] 499 F.3d 553 (6th Cir. 2007).

[153] *Id.* at 561.

[154] *Id.* at 560–61 (recognizing government's right to block access to information so long as it does not "selectively [ ] delimit the audience") (alteration in original).

[155] Ketcham v. U.S. Nat'l Park Serv., No. 16-CV-00017-SWS, 2016 WL 4269037, at *1–3 (D. Wyo. Feb. 5, 2016).

National Park appear within their rights to preclude recording by denying access to the areas in question during the relevant times.

On the other hand, if a person engaged in recording is lawfully present, video recording can be understood as little more than the technological enhancement of their individual powers of observation. The right to record is essentially a right to memorialize or enshrine one's interactions or observations. Surely it would be unconstitutional for the government to punish someone who was in a place where they had a lawful right to be present for observing something and committing it to memory or jotting down handwritten descriptions in a notebook. The state could not require such a person to take steps, perhaps through hypnosis or drugs, to forget what they had seen or to require the destruction of their notes. This is no less true with acts of audiovisual recording. A recording provides a self-authenticating and easily reproduced memorialization of one's encounters or experiences.

As we conceive the First Amendment right to record, as long as the person engaged in recording has a right to be in the place where they record, the conduct of recording cannot be categorically prohibited by the state.[156] The access may be the result of a variety of different legal statuses, including an employment relationship, another type of contractual agreement, or a guest or invitee relationship. Access may even be the result of subterfuge, as gained through an investigative deception, as long as the person engaged in the recording has permission to be on the property. At least on this criterion, then, the right to record would extend to video recording in a public park; at a parade; in a store, restaurant, or other place of public accommodation; at one's place of employment; or even in a private home where one is an invited guest.

Many government regulations of recording would affect recording that meets this threshold requirement, even if there are other arguments for permitting such regulation. Ag-gag laws categorically ban recording in the physical spaces where an employee is not only entitled, but required, to be present. Bans on recording in courtrooms would also implicate this first threshold, assuming that the proceedings are otherwise open to members of the public. Likewise, the making of a consensual private sex tape would fall within this first requirement because the participants are lawfully present and aware of the recording, even if, for privacy reasons, the right might not attach to the tape's later dissemination. Regulations of recordings made from privately operated drones might, or might not, meet this requirement, depending on where the drone is flown.[157]

---

[156] *See* Marc Jonathan Blitz, *The Right to Map (and Avoid Being Mapped): Reconceiving First Amendment Protection for Information-Gathering in the Age of Google Earth*, 14 COLUM. SCI. & TECH. L. REV. 115, 185 (2012) (discussing public forum doctrine and broad right not only to receive but also to acquire information).

[157] Nat'l Press Photographers Ass'n v. McCraw, No. 1:19-CV-946-RP, 2022 WL 939517, at *8–9 (W.D. Tex. Mar. 28, 2022) (recognizing that drone photography is speech protected by the First Amendment), *appeal filed*, No. 22-50337 (5th Cir. May 3, 2022). *See also* Blitz et al., *supra* note

Thus, as a threshold matter, it cannot be overemphasized that the power of recording in documenting everything from the mundanity of life to atrocities in a slaughterhouse does not carry with it a corollary right of access. But neither does recording make entry that is otherwise permitted a trespass. As the Tenth Circuit Court of Appeals explained in striking down a Wyoming law, "[a]lthough trespassing does not enjoy First Amendment protection, the statutes at issue target the 'creation' of speech by imposing heightened penalties on those who" would engage in photography or videography, and thus run afoul of the First Amendment.[158] That is, the law could not withstand constitutional scrutiny because it restrained recording by people in places where they had a lawful right to be present.

The power of a recording, no more than the importance of Upton Sinclair's notepad, does not justify uninvited entry into any area of public or private property. Thus, for example, the First Amendment right to record would not attach to a person who breaks into a private residence or the Oval Office to record a video, even if the content relates to a matter of great public concern. Likewise, trespass onto private property even in the service of compelling exposures of the greatest public concern is not legally justified.[159] The right to record is a right to record only that which one is lawfully and consensually present to observe.[160]

## 4.3.2 *Recording in Public and Private Settings*

Even if the above points are accepted, there will still be doctrinal resistance to recognizing recording as a form of protected First Amendment activity. This is particularly true with regard to recording on private property. Because the stakes of the right to record may be different depending on the location of the recording, the right may be articulated into two broad categories. First, this section addresses the right to record in public places, or in private places where the person engaged in recording has the consent of the property owner. Second, this section defines the right to record on private property without the owner's consent.

---

11 (arguing that act of recording using unmanned aircrafts in public navigable airspace should enjoy First Amendment protection). For a thoughtful examination of the constitutional implications of government-imposed limits on computer-generated digital mapping, such as those created by large search engine companies, see Blitz, *supra* note 155 (discussing First Amendment implications of digital mapping).

[158] W. *Watersheds Project*, 869 F.3d at 1192.

[159] On the other hand, trespass laws that are motivated by a desire to chill speech, including recording, might implicate First Amendment concerns.

[160] It also bears noting that some courts might seek to limit the right to record by pointing out that the Supreme Court has concluded that there is no right to engage in First Amendment activities on private property, even when that private property is otherwise open to the public. For example, there is no constitutional right to use shopping malls or their respective parking lots for protests, leafleting, or other First Amendment activity. Hudgens v. N.L.R.B., 424 U.S. 507 (1976).

### 4.3.2.1 Recording on Public or Private Property with Consent

The First Amendment protects individuals from government regulation of audio-visual recordings made in publicly accessible spaces, subject to reasonable, content-neutral time, place, or manner restrictions. Government restrictions on recording political demonstrations or parades or the everyday plight of a city's homeless population would infringe the right to record. As would a prohibition on video recording everyday activities on the street or in a public park, even if they were not directly connected to a political or artistic objective.

The right to record would also extend to protect recordings made on one's *own* private property and to recordings made on another's property *with* their consent and knowledge. Thus, recording oneself, one's family, or pets is speech subject to constitutional protection from government constraints. This might include every-thing from recording of commonplace activity such as home movies to self-recorded instructional videos to be posted on YouTube to private sex tapes. If another person invites the recorder into his home and consents to the recording, the act of making those recordings would be constitutionally protected as well.

The right to record in public or in private with consent should be afforded First Amendment protection for at least two important reasons. First, outside a few narrow circumstances, there will seldom be any legitimate reason for the state to ban recording in these settings. To the extent the government wishes to ban public recordings, its reasons are likely, though not always, related to prohibiting exposure of matters that it would prefer to hide from public scrutiny and not to advance any legitimate police power concern. Moreover, it is difficult to imagine many circum-stances in which the state might have a legitimate, much less compelling, reason to ban private, consensual video recordings. This is not to suggest that all such recording will be protected. For example, one area in which this has been highly controversial is when parents have been criminally charged for taking private photographs or video recordings of their minor children in the nude.[161]

### 4.3.2.2 Recording on Private Property without Consent

As discussed earlier, video image capture on private property, even without consent, is no different from video recording in public in terms of its qualities as speech as understood under First Amendment theory. Thus, a constitutional right to free speech should also extend to some nonconsensual recordings on private property. This section addresses the skepticism about this view under existing case law, and also suggests some important limitations on the right to nonconsensual video recordings on private property that will ameliorate concerns that the government

[161] *See* Amy Adler, *The Perverse Law of Child Pornography*, 101 COLUM. L. REV. 209 (2001) (collecting cases).

might have in regulating them. First, with respect to nonconsensual recordings on private property, the right to record should be limited to recordings about *matters of public concern*. Second, these types of recordings, while protected, must still be examined in light of the appropriate First Amendment doctrinal test, depending on how the regulation operates.

4.3.2.2.1 COMMENTARY AND CASE LAW Prior to the recent federal court decisions in the ag-gag cases, the limited scholarly and judicial treatment of video recording or photography under the First Amendment typically assumed that any constitutional protections for recording were limited to acts of public recording. And as Professor Bambauer has explained, even in the limited cases that have confronted the question of a right to record, "with one exception, the right was crafted narrowly, as a right to record public officials performing their public duties."[162] Other leading scholars have wondered whether when one engages in the activities on private property the recorder may have "waived [her] First Amendment rights to capture images."[163]

Lower courts considering assertions of a right to record had traditionally been similarly guarded. A 1970s state court of appeals case addressing various privacy torts elaborates on this view. In reviewing the scope of privacy, the court explains, "[i]t seems to be generally agreed that anything visible in a public place can be recorded and given circulation by means of a photograph, to the same extent as by a written description, since this amounts to nothing more than giving publicity to what is already public and what anyone present would be free to see."[164]

More recently, a Seventh Circuit decision illustrates that the increasing prevalence of recording technologies has not entirely eroded the entrenched private/public dichotomy.[165] In *ACLU v. Alvarez*, the case involving a First Amendment challenge to a law that required consent in order to record another person, the court struck down the statute on the basis that there is a constitutional "right to record."[166] However, it emphasized that the recordings the plaintiff sought to produce were of officials "performing their duties in traditional *public fora*."[167] The reasoning of the decision stresses that the recordings in question were not "of a private communication" and instead were of actions and utterances "occur[ing] in public."[168] The court stopped short of holding that recording is speech only when it occurs in

---

[162] Bambauer, *supra* note 23, at 84; *id.* at n.117 (compiling cases on this point).
[163] Kreimer, *supra* note 22, at 403 (citing Andrew J. McClurg, *Kiss and Tell: Protecting Intimate Relationship Privacy through Implied Contracts of Confidentiality*, 74 U. CIN. L. REV. 887, 916–17 (2006), and Neil M. Richards & Daniel J. Solove, *Privacy's Other Path: Recovering the Law of Confidentiality*, 96 GEO. L.J. 123, 177–80 (2007)).
[164] Hollander v. Lubow, 277 Md. 47, 57–58 (1976).
[165] *Alvarez*, 679 F.3d at 586.
[166] *Id.* at 595.
[167] *Id.* at 594.
[168] *Id.* at 595.

public, but this decision explicitly addresses only public recording. Other federal decisions have also implicitly suggested a distinction between private and public recording. For example, it is commonplace for courts to recognize a right to record "on public property"[169] or to record "public meetings."[170]

Perhaps no case stands more clearly for the proposition that recordings made outside the public sphere may offend notions of privacy than the fifty-year-old, and arguably outdated, Ninth Circuit decision in *Dietemann v. Time*.[171] A. A. Dietemann was practicing some form of "healing" out of a home office when a reporter from *Life* magazine pretended to be an interested patient in order to obtain audio and image recordings for a story called "Crackdown on Quackery."[172] Dietemann alleged that his privacy was violated and the Ninth Circuit agreed, holding that the "First Amendment has never been construed to accord newsmen immunity from torts or crimes committed during the course of newsgathering."[173]

The *Dietemann* rule, if read broadly, is largely incompatible with a conception of a First Amendment right to record outside of purely public realms. If states can criminalize or impose civil penalties for all variety of nonpublic recordings, then recording is protected speech *exclusively* in public domains or private domains with consent. But *Dietemann* does not portend such a First Amendment rule, and in fact a close reading of the case leads to the conclusion that it may now be outdated. There are at least a couple of important features of *Dietemann* that limit its persuasiveness in the context of secret recordings made as part of undercover investigations. First, the court faults the media defendant for intruding on reasonable expectations of privacy, but privacy expectations looked much different when *Dietemann* was decided.[174] Because of both changes in the law and changes in technology, it is fair to say that expectations of privacy in 1971 were more capacious than they are today.[175]

---

[169] Smith v. City of Cumming, 212 F.3d 1332, 1333 (11th Cir. 2000).

[170] Iacobucci v. Boulter, 193 F.3d 14, 25 (1st Cir. 1999); *see also* Blackston v. Alabama, 30 F.3d 117, 120 (11th Cir. 1994).

[171] 449 F.2d 245 (9th Cir. 1971).

[172] *Id.*

[173] *Id.* at 249.

[174] *Compare Dietemann*, 449 F.2d at 249 (explaining that while invitee assumes risk that "visitor may repeat all he hears and observes when he leaves[,] ... [he] should not be required to take the risk that what is heard and seen will be transmitted by photograph or recording") *with* United States v. Davis, 326 F. 3d 361, 366 (2d Cir. 2008) (holding that video recordings made by invited guest did not violate Fourth Amendment where "hidden camera did not capture any areas in which Davis retained a privacy interest").

[175] For example, citizens do not hold a reasonable expectation of privacy in the phone numbers they dial, Smith v. Maryland, 442 U.S. 735, 742 (1979), or in their bank records, United States v. Miller, 425 U.S. 435, 443 (1976), because they take the risk their information, when revealed to another individual, "will be conveyed by that person to the government." *Id.* In some circumstances, individuals also have a lower expectation of privacy in shared premises. *See* Illinois v. Rodriguez, 497 U.S. 177, 188–89 (1990) (explaining that warrantless search does not violate Fourth Amendment when police obtain consent from persons whom they reasonably

Second, many courts have emphasized that the reasoning of *Dietemann* is limited to an intrusion into one's *private home*, where Dietemann happened to also engage in his healing practices, and not a commercial office or workplace.[176] Moreover, four of the laws limiting recording at private, agricultural facilities – ag-gag laws – have been resoundingly struck down by lower courts. The Ninth Circuit struck down Idaho's restriction on video recording of private, agricultural facilities, stating, "Problematically, Idaho has effectively eliminated the subject matter of any audio and visual recordings of agricultural operations made without consent and has therefore 'prohibit[ed] public discussion of an entire topic.'"[177] Rejecting the state's efforts to justify the law, the Court reasoned, "agricultural production facility owners can vindicate their rights" to privacy "through tort laws against theft of trade secrets and invasion of privacy," and to the extent there are claims of fabricated videos, farmers "can turn to defamation actions for recourse."[178] Better yet, if you want to combat undercover videos, engage in your own speech, said the Court, "not, as Idaho would like, the suppression of that speech."[179]

Not surprisingly, other circuits have readily distinguished or rejected *Dietemann*.[180] The Ninth Circuit has sent mixed signals, sometime distinguishing or limiting *Dietemann*[181] while more recently seeming to reembrace it.[182] But we maintain that the weight of authority and logic reject the underlying assumption that recording necessarily loses its status as constitutionally protected speech if it is done in private.

believe to have authority to grant consent); Fernandez v. California, 571 U.S, 292,301–02 (2014) (holding warrantless search valid where third party consented after defendant's lawful arrest).

[176] *Desnick*, 44 F.3d at 1352–53; Med. Lab. Mgmt. Consultants v. Am. Broad. Companies, Inc., 306 F.3d 806, 818 n.6 (9th Cir. 2002). *But see* Planned Parenthood Fed'n of Am., Inc. v. Newman, 51 F.4th 1125 (9th Cir. 2022) (citing *Dietemann* with approval).

[177] *Wasden*, 878 F.3d at 1204.

[178] *Id.*

[179] *Id.* at 1205.

[180] *See, e.g., Desnick*, 44 F.3d at 1352–53 (distinguishing public ophthalmic clinic from private "quackery" at issue in *Dietemann*).

[181] *See, e.g., Med. Lab. Mgmt. Consultants*, 306 F.3d at 818 n.6 (distinguishing the private nature present in *Dietemann* from a workplace interaction). Professor Bambauer has also provided a stinging critique of *Dietemann*'s reasoning:

> A right to access information (or, more precisely, a right to be free from government restraint on access to information) is at odds with *Dietemann* and other cases that presume the First Amendment imposes absolutely no constraint on the tort of intrusion upon seclusion. But [such an] approach seems necessary. If access to knowledge were not a constitutionally protected right, the intrusion tort could be boundless. At the extreme, the government could prohibit a person from recording anything at all without conflicting with the First Amendment. This cannot be right.

Bambauer, *supra* note 23, at 85.

[182] *Planned Parenthood, supra* note 175.

4.3.2.2.2 A PUBLIC CONCERN LIMITATION ON THE RIGHT TO NONCONSENSUAL
RECORDING ON PRIVATE PROPERTY Under our conception, the right to engage in
nonconsensual video recordings on private property (but not on public property or
on private property with consent) would be limited to protecting recordings that
pertain to a matter of public concern or at least have a strong connection to public
discourse. That is, the recordings must somehow relate to a general matter of
political, social, or moral significance that is an appropriate subject of public debate.
Another relevant consideration ought to be whether the person engaged in
recording is motivated by a political, journalistic, or investigative purpose, which
would receive greater First Amendment protection, or a purely commercial purpose
or purely private/personal reason, which would be less protected.[183]

This focus on recordings relating to matters of public concern ties the right to
make audiovisual recordings directly to the underlying purposes of the First
Amendment, which include the promotion of democratic self-governance and the
search for truth. As the Supreme Court has repeatedly declared, "[s]peech on
'matters of public concern' ... is 'at the heart of the First Amendment's protection.'"[184] That is because "speech concerning public affairs is more than self-
expression; it is the essence of self-government."[185] Accordingly, "speech on public
issues occupies the highest rung of the hierarchy of First Amendment values, and is
entitled to special protection."[186]

As the Court has defined it, speech deals with matters of public concern when it
can "'be fairly considered as relating to any matter of political, social, or other
concern to the community,' ... or when it 'is a subject of legitimate news interest;
that is, a subject of general interest and of value and concern to the public,' ... The
arguably 'inappropriate or controversial character of a statement is irrelevant to the
question whether it deals with a matter of public concern.'"[187] Limiting the
right to make nonconsensual recordings on private property to matters of public
concern further helps sort out some of the government regulations of recording that
are the subject of current controversy. Like public recordings, video recordings on
private property may substantially inform public discourse. Again, many of the
illustrations of important recordings already discussed involve recordings on

---

[183] Motive is not a controlling feature of the public concern inquiry in other areas of First
Amendment doctrine, but it often plays a nontrivial role in the manner in which the
Supreme Court decides whether to categorize something as speech. *But see* Snyder
v. Phelps, 562 U.S. 443, 471 (2011) (Alito, J., dissenting) (faulting majority for deciding that
funeral protests were entitled to First Amendment protection because speech "was not motivated by a private grudge").
[184] *Snyder*, 562 U.S. at 451–52 (citations omitted).
[185] *Id.*
[186] *Id.*
[187] *Id.* at 453.

private property, such as at private political fundraisers, at a conference, or at a restaurant or bar.

In addition, it is worth pointing out that to a certain extent the recording of another person or another person's property will always pit some assertions of privacy (well-founded or not) against the speech rights attached to recording.[188] In this regard, any such privacy concerns are much less likely to be deemed a significant, let alone a compelling interest, when the matters sought to be revealed are matters of public concern.[189] This is not to suggest that all restrictions on recordings of nonpublic concern should be upheld. Certainly, a ban on making videos of one's own cat from within the privacy of the home, while perhaps serving a significant government interest in avoiding workplace distractions broadcast over YouTube,[190] would not be permissible. On the other hand, the recording of another's cat without permission while on someone else's private property would be entitled to less protection than other recording bans or limitations because the recording is unrelated to a matter of public concern. Likewise, a narrowly tailored ban on videotaping a business's operations to appropriate trade secrets would not implicate the right to record because that is a matter of private concern. Bans on drone recordings to reveal the conduct of industrial polluters would be at risk for invalidation, but not bans on the use of drones to spy on nude sunbathers. On balance, a recording related to a matter of public concern cuts in favor of the recorder, and against limits on such recording.

Critics of this approach might raise at least two legitimate objections to the public concern requirement. First, it may import administrability problems into this area of First Amendment doctrine. Disputes about the definitions of public concern have plagued First Amendment employee speech doctrine,[191] and the same thing might

---

[188] *See, e.g.*, Nicky Woolf, *Hulk Hogan v Gawker: $100m Lawsuit Puts First Amendment to the Test Again*, The Guardian (Dec. 19, 2017), www.theguardian.com/media/2016/mar/06/hulk-hogan-gawker-lawsuit-first-amendment-trial. In 2012, Terry Bollea (Hulk Hogan) filed an invasion of privacy lawsuit against the media outlet Gawker for releasing a nonconsensual video recording to the public of Bollea having an affair. *Hulk Hogan v. Gawker: Invasion of Privacy & Free Speech in a Digital World*, First Amend. Watch, https://firstamendmentwatch.org/deep-dive/hulk-hogan-v-gawker-invasion-of-privacy-free-speech-in-a-digital-world/ (last visited Nov. 18, 2022). Gawker argued Bollea's right to privacy was superseded by the First Amendment and public interest – which applied in the case as Bollea had publicly denied the affair and he should not have had an expectation of privacy. *Id.* This trial emphasized the ongoing tension between freedom of the press and the right to privacy. *Id.*

[189] To be sure, public concern is not self-defining, but we are comfortably saying all nonprivate, non-intimate details are generally public.

[190] Lucia Peters, *Does the Internet Make Us Less Productive at Work?*, Bustle (Dec. 31, 2014), www.bustle.com/articles/56315-pew-survey-reveals-the-internet-doesnt-distract-us-from-our-jobs-no-matter-how-many-cat; Hadley Freeman, *So This Is How the World Ends: With Us Distracted by Cute Cats*, The Guardian (Nov. 29, 2017), www.theguardian.com/commentisfree/2015/mar/04/cute-cats-internet.

[191] *See, e.g.*, Stephen Allred, *From Connick to Confusion: The Struggle to Define Speech on Matters of Public Concern*, 64 Ind. L.J. 43, 75 (1988) (explaining inconsistency in lower federal

occur here. Indeed, as the Court has candidly acknowledged, "the boundaries of the public concern test are not well defined."[192] Nonetheless, the Court has, of course, elaborated on the standard at some length.

A second critique of tying the protection of recording in private to the question of public concern also relates to the lack of a clear dividing line between recordings about matters of public concern and recordings that do not relate to public discourse. Because there is ambiguity as to exactly what constitutes a matter of public concern, such a standard could have a chilling effect. Persons engaged in video activism[193] might consider making a recording that would be valuable, but its public significance may be unclear or ambiguous, or perhaps not yet apparent. While there will be some level of uncertainty in the application of this standard, it need not be fatal. Other areas of First Amendment doctrine have provided robust protection for speech even where the boundaries of the right are not crystal clear. We do not pretend that the public concern limitation is a flawless limiting principle, but it is surely a workable one.

### 4.3.3 *Addressing Potential Barriers to a Right to Record in Private under Existing First Amendment Doctrine*

#### 4.3.3.1 The Absence of a General Newsgatherer's Privilege

One objection to the argument that video recording is protected expression under the First Amendment might be that the Supreme Court has heretofore failed to embrace the idea of a constitutional newsgatherers' privilege. In *Branzburg v. Hayes*, the Court rejected the First Amendment claim of newspaper reporters who refused to appear before grand juries to testify about information they had acquired from confidential informants.[194] The reporters claimed that they should have some protection from having to testify because revealing confidential sources and information would seriously impair their ability to gather information for news stories.[195] The Court found that no citizen has immunity from a grand jury investigation and that there is no right for journalists to have any sort of special exemption just because of their association with the press.[196] More generally, it has noted that the enforcement of general laws does not "offend the First Amendment simply because

---

courts arising from their discretion in determining scope of public employees' free speech rights); Michael L. Wells, *Section 1983, the First Amendment, and Public Employee Speech: Shaping the Right to Fit the Remedy (and Vice Versa)*, 35 GA. L. REV. 939, 960–61 (2001) (same).

[192] San Diego v. Roe, 543 U.S. 77, 83 (2004).

[193] *See generally* THOMAS HARDING, THE VIDEO ACTIVIST HANDBOOK (2d ed. 2001) (describing how to effectively capture and disseminate video images to promote social justice).

[194] 408 U.S. at 665.

[195] *Id.* at 679–80.

[196] *Id.* at 682–83.

their enforcement against the press has incidental effects on its ability to gather and report the news."[197]

Although the Court rejected the claim for a newsgatherers' privilege from grand jury subpoenas, it clarified that this conclusion did not mean that "news gathering does not qualify for First Amendment protection; without some protection for seeking out the news, freedom of the press could be eviscerated."[198] However, the Court has never elaborated on the precise scope of such protection. Thus, the absence of a narrowly defined newsgatherers' privilege does not necessarily lead to the conclusion that there is no broader right to record.

To reiterate, one need not advocate for any sort of journalistic exceptionalism for recording, and in any event, the right to record should not be limited to professional newsgatherers. As Darnella Frazier's video of the police killing of George Floyd patently demonstrates, some of the most important video recordings that have informed public debate have been by political activists, amateur hobbyists, and undercover government investigators.[199] Moreover, with the expansion of internet avenues for conveying information, the line between professional journalists and citizen activists is becoming less clear, making a right contingent on one's professional credentials difficult both to administer and to justify.[200] In any event, a right to record in private without consent is not in direct conflict with the long-standing view that there is no general newsgatherers' privilege.

### 4.3.3.2 Protection of Captive Audiences

A distinct line of First Amendment cases permits the state to limit speech in private spaces, and even some public spaces, to the extent that the speech interferes with individual liberty by forcing people to be "captive" audiences.[201] The captive audience cases recognize a right to be free from uninvited speech activities in the

---

[197] Cohen v. Cowles Media Co., 501 U.S. 663 (1991).

[198] *Id.* at 681.

[199] *See generally* Adam Cohen, *The Media That Needs Citizens: The First Amendment and the Fifth State*, 85 S. CAL. L. REV. 1 (2011) (discussing ways in which amateur videographers have contributed to public debate).

[200] *See* Bhagwat, *supra* note 23, at 1053 (arguing First Amendment should protect more than just "institutional press" in an age where the broader public regularly engages in information gathering).

[201] *See, e.g.*, Frisby v. Schultz, 487 U.S. 474 (1988) (upholding ordinance banning picketing in front of targeted residences based on government's interest in protecting residential privacy); Hill v. Colorado, 530 U.S. 703 (2000) (upholding Colorado statute prohibiting any person from approaching within eight feet of another person near healthcare facilities based, in part, on state's desire to protect listeners from unwanted communication). For a critique of the Court's extension of the captive audience doctrine to public sidewalks in *Hill*, see Chen, *supra* note 95, at 60.

zone of privacy of one's own property.[202] For example, the Court has upheld a law allowing persons to prevent the delivery of salacious mailings to their homes[203] and an ordinance prohibiting picketing "before or about" any particular individual's residence.[204] On this basis, the Court has even upheld laws limiting door-to-door commercial sales.[205]

In short, the unwilling listener line of cases bespeak a foundational principle: "Even protected speech is not equally permissible in all places at all times."[206] Focusing on "the place of ... speech" is a staple of First Amendment analysis.[207] This protection of "unwilling listeners" might suggest another barrier to recognizing a right to record on private property.

On reflection, however, the captive audience cases do not have any application in the recording context because while recording on private property is part of the spectrum of expressive activity, it is not immediately communicative to those present during the recording.[208] As explained in the context of distinguishing the right of access cases, recording is not tantamount to protesting, chanting, soliciting, leafleting, or otherwise communicating on private property. The captive audience doctrine is designed to protect individuals from having their private space intruded on with unwelcome messages or disturbing communications. In the case of secret recordings, there is no risk of speech being thrust upon an unwilling listener. The property owner is not the target audience for the recorder. Thus, arguments by states like Kansas defending private property bans in this way are unpersuasive. In defending its ag-gag law, Kansas argued, "individuals generally do not have a First Amendment right to engage in speech on the private property of others."[209]

One might counter that recordings, or the threat of being recorded, may change behavior or chill relationships. A group of activists (or politicians) might interact differently if they are afraid they are being recorded, by either law enforcement or private infiltrators. And this potential to change behavior should be considered. But

[202] The phrase "unwilling listener" is closely associated with the "captive audience" doctrine. *See, e.g., Snyder*, 562 U.S. at 459 ("As a general matter, we have applied the captive audience doctrine only sparingly to protect unwilling listeners from protected speech").

[203] Rowan v. Post Off. Dept., 397 U.S. 728, 736–38 (1970) (considering challenge to a portion of "Postal Revenue and Federal Salary Act ... under which a person may require that a mailer remove his name from its mailing lists and stop all future mailings to the householder").

[204] *Frisby*, 487 U.S. at 488.

[205] Breard v. City of Alexandria, 341 U.S. 622 (1951). *But see* Vill. of Schaumburg v. Citizens for a Better Env't, 444 U.S. 620, 641 (1980) (abrogating *Breard* by distinguishing between ordinances that deal "not with the dissemination of ideas, but rather with the solicitation of money" and noting that ordinance banning only commercial activity, as in *Breard*, might survive constitutional scrutiny).

[206] Cornelius v. NAACP Legal Def. & Educ. Fund, Inc., 473 U.S. 788, 799 (1985).

[207] *Frisby*, 487 U.S. at 479; *id.* at 485 ("[W]e have repeatedly held that individuals are not required to welcome unwanted speech into their own homes").

[208] Recording that is live streamed is arguably speech, but for an audience different from those who are the subject of the recording.

[209] *Kelly*, 9 F.4th at 1240.

such concerns raise the question of whether new doctrinal limits should be created. It is not the case that the captive audience cases create a generic and invariable right to privacy against those you have invited to be present on your property. For example, if a Walmart employee secretly records a conversation with their boss that documents demeaning or inappropriate behavior, it may be embarrassing for the supervisor or the company, but it is not forcing the supervisor to be an unwilling audience to speech,[210] nor is it impeding or coercing their private behavior. Because recording is not actively communicating to the persons present, the concerns about interruption of a captive audience are generally nonexistent.

There will be circumstances when recording (or even the risk of being recorded) could disrupt official proceedings, such as in a courtroom, as discussed below. There may also be times when a recording of intimate, private details from one's home or from a restroom invades privacy concerns so fundamental as to exceed First Amendment protection.[211] So there will be recording that is unprotected, perhaps in both the private and the public spheres. But the core rationales behind doctrines protecting nonpublic and private forums from speech – the captive audience doctrine – cannot be reasonably extended to non-interruptive audiovisual recording of non-intimate acts.

### 4.3.3.3 Public Forum Doctrine

A third doctrinal area that is possibly in tension with the right to record in private, at least by analogy,[212] is the Court's public forum doctrine.[213] It is a common wisdom that "[t]he greatest [First Amendment] protection is provided for traditional public fora."[214] Speech in these locations enjoys the strongest constitutional protection, and content-based limits are therefore subject to the most exacting scrutiny.[215] Stated simply, there is one set of (greater) speech protections for places that constitute traditional public forums for speech, and a separate (and lesser) set of protections for government-owned forums that are not open to speech or that are open to speech only by certain groups or on certain subjects.[216]

---

[210] In Snyder v. Phelps, the Court emphasized that observing replays of speech on news or other media sites does not itself raise captive audience concerns. *Snyder*, 562 U.S. at 459–60.
[211] Kreimer, *supra* note 22, at 395 ("These justifications often suffice to justify bans on peeping Toms with cameras or surreptitious image capture of intimate conduct").
[212] Of course, it is only by analogy. The public forum doctrine has nothing at all to say about the regulation of speech that does not occur on public property.
[213] *See* Perry Educ. Ass'n v. Perry Local Educators' Ass'n, 460 U.S. 37, 45–46 (1983) (explaining public forum doctrines).
[214] Victory through Jesus Sports Ministry Found. v. Lee's Summit R-7 Sch. Dist., 640 F.3d 329, 334 (8th Cir. 2011).
[215] *Perry Educ. Ass'n*, 460 U.S. at 44.
[216] *Compare Frisby*, 487 U.S. at 481 (holding residential street was public forum) *with* Int'l Soc'y for Krishna Consciousness, Inc. v. Lee, 505 U.S. 672, 680 (1992) (holding speech in airport terminals is not subject to First Amendment protection because they are not public forums).

But, like the right of access and captive audience cases, the public forum doctrine does not apply to the distinction between private and public recording. First, the government's legitimate interest in regulating speech on public property relates to its authority to manage those spaces for use by multiple users and to prevent uses of public property that may interfere with its intended purposes.[217] Competing demands for use of public spaces for First Amendment activity can result in chaos and disruption, and inhibit both the exercise of speech and the use of the property for other nonspeech reasons, such as Little League baseball games and picnics. Similarly, limits on speech at schools are designed to ensure that the educational mission is not impaired;[218] solicitation limits at airports are intended to avoid hassles for already frenzied airline travelers;[219] and limits on courtroom protests are designed to maintain the dignity of the forum and protect the due process rights of participants.[220] As the Supreme Court has observed, "[a]lthough a silent vigil may not unduly interfere with a public library ... making a speech in the reading room almost certainly would. That same speech should be perfectly appropriate in a park. The crucial question is whether the manner of expression is basically incompatible with the normal activity of a particular place at a particular time."[221]

None of these governmental interests in preventing speech to avoid interference or inconvenience with the present use of an area apply to the act of recording. It simply makes no sense to treat a noncommunicative act of expression as raising the same concerns as a protest or a concert; the latter forms of expression will cause immediate interference with the contemporaneous use of the forum, the very problem that the public forum doctrine was designed to address. But making a surreptitious video recording is not inherently incompatible with the activity being recorded, which can proceed uninterrupted.

* * *

In short, there are a variety of important doctrinal considerations under the First Amendment that, at least by analogy, suggest that recording in private is less protected than recording in public. But on close examination, none of these limits hold up to careful scrutiny. The concerns that undergird various location-related limits on speech – the newsgatherer's privilege, the captive audience cases, the

---

[217] *See, e.g.*, Pleasant Grove City v. Summum, 555 U.S. 460, 480 (2009) (explaining that accepting every monument donation into park would inevitably lead to closing of park); *Perry Educ. Ass'n*, 460 U.S. at 46.

[218] *See, e.g.*, Bethel Sch. Dist. No. 403 v. Fraser, 478 U.S. 675, 685 (1986) (explaining that student's "vulgar and lewd speech ... would undermine the school's basic educational mission").

[219] *See, e.g.*, *Int'l Soc'y for Krishna Consciousness, Inc.*, 505 U.S. at 682 (finding that airports may limit solicitation practices in order to "provide services attractive to the marketplace").

[220] *See, e.g.*, Press-Enterprise Co. v. Superior Ct. of Cal. for Riverside Cnty, 478 U.S. 1, 9 (1986) (balancing public's right of access with right to fair trial).

[221] Grayned v. City of Rockford, 408 U.S. 104, 116 (1972).

public forum doctrine, and the right of access that we discussed earlier in this chapter – are all inapplicable to an act of recording done in a location where one is otherwise lawfully permitted to be.

### 4.3.4 *Governmental Interests and the Right to Record*

As the opportunities for individuals to record videos have expanded, governments have identified reasons to regulate recordings.[222] Examination of state action that interferes with the right to record is subject to application of the basic infrastructure of First Amendment doctrine. Thus, viewpoint and content-based restrictions on recording would be highly suspect, and would be evaluated under traditional strict scrutiny; the laws would have to be narrowly tailored to advance a compelling governmental interest, and the state would have to show that no less speech-restrictive alternative was available to serve that interest.[223] In contrast, content-neutral regulations of video recording would be subject to intermediate scrutiny. Under that standard, laws must be "narrowly tailored to serve a significant governmental interest" and must "leave open ample alternative channels for communication of the information."[224] Below we consider some of the commonly asserted interests that governments use to justify limiting the First Amendment right to video image capture under either strict or intermediate scrutiny.

#### 4.3.4.1 Tangible Property Interests

In certain contexts, the state will be able to assert a compelling interest in protecting tangible property rights. However, it is important to note that the mere assertion of a property interest is not sufficient to overcome a ban on recording, either in public or in private. An undifferentiated assertion of private property protection as a government interest is simply too generalized, just as an assertion that the state enacted this law to "make our state a better place" could not suffice as a compelling or significant interest. The very purpose of heightened scrutiny is to require a close judicial examination of the state action and its rationales. A vague assertion of property rights is insufficiently concrete to be considered a compelling government interest.

Framed at a greater level of specificity, however, there are a considerable number of tangible property interests that might be raised in support of state regulation of the

---

[222] *See, e.g.*, Alex, *Livestreaming Ban in Tennessee House Shows How Power Can Limit the Right to Record*, E Pluribus Unum (Jan. 30, 2019), https://e-pluribusunum.org/2019/01/30/livestream ing-ban-in-tennessee-house-shows-how-power-can-limit-the-right-to-record/?fbclid= IwAR1EwCChH_2wrvsgbije3hcx1s6dqYEj8cNkguGx7KsFVEBuhKCsmQ3i-PE.

[223] Turner Broad. Sys., Inc. v. FCC, 512 U.S. 622, 641–42 (1994).

[224] Ward v. Rock against Racism, 491 U.S. 781, 791 (1989). *See also* McCullen v. Coakley, 573 U.S. 464, 476–77 (2014) (applying standard articulated in *Ward* to speech on public sidewalks).

right to record. First, there could be legitimate concerns about the misappropriation of intellectual property. For example, a government regulation that prohibited taking video recordings of copyrighted performances at a publicly owned theater might be justified on that ground. Similarly, laws that prohibit video recordings used to steal a business's trade secrets will surely be tolerated, so long as trade secrets are not defined in similarly vague ways, because there is a state interest in protecting those secrets and promoting innovation as a matter of public policy.

Another legitimate interest might be the imposition of penalties for physical damage to property resulting from a person's video recording. For instance, tort liability for damage to property caused by the use of large video recording equipment would not necessarily be invalid even if the recording met the other requirements of the right to record. Similarly, if an undercover investigator caused personal injury or some other tangible harm to property arising from the act of recording, they could be held criminally or civilly liable. Or efforts to limit recording in order to avoid spoliation or contamination concerns, if properly focused, could be legitimate government interests. If a laboratory employee takes risks with certain research samples in order to get high-quality video footage, but in the process damages the research samples, this is a serious concern. By the same token, persons investigating factory farms could be accused of presenting biosecurity or food safety concerns if they did not comply with the same standards for safety as employees and others who enter the facility.[225]

What these interests have in common is that they are identifiable and tangible. By contrast, in the absence of such tangible harms, the act of recording does not intrinsically cause any legally cognizable harm to property interests. As the trial court judge in the Idaho ag-gag case concluded:

> Other than physical damage to property, the most likely loss that would flow from a violation of section 18-7042 [Idaho's ag-gag law] would be losses associated with the publication of a video critical of an agricultural facility's practices. In fact, the more successful an activist is in mobilizing public opinion against a facility by publishing a video or story critical of the facility the more the activist will be punished. Moreover, agricultural operations will be able to collect the same damages as in a libel action without satisfying the constitutional defamation standard, which the Supreme Court has expressly prohibited.[226]

Making a recording itself does not typically interfere with a property interest in any meaningful way. It is a concept foreign to law to argue, for example, that one enjoys a property right to be free from the very *presence* of an invited guest who later turns

---

[225] Kelsey Piper, *"Ag-Gag Laws" Hide the Cruelty of Factory Farms from the Public. Courts Are Striking Them Down.*, Vox (Jan. 11, 2019), www.vox.com/future-perfect/2019/1/11/18176551/ag-gag-laws-factory-farms-explained.

[226] Animal Legal Def. Fund v. Otter, 44 F. Supp. 3d 1009, 1024 (D. Idaho 2014).

out to be a civil rights tester or whistleblower.[227] And, to the extent that a company suffers a loss of business because of the reputational effects of the exposure of its illegal or otherwise unsavory conduct, that harm cannot fairly be said to have been caused by the person revealing the conduct. The true cause of the loss is the company's own behavior. As one commentator has suggested, "One reason *the means by which raw information is obtained* is not the proximate cause of publication damages is because that raw information harms no one."[228] We discussed the issue of publication damages more extensively in Chapter 3, and the same logic applies here.

Put bluntly, a bare desire to avoid reputational injury flowing from the unwanted disclosure of matters of public concern is not a cognizable property interest. If the harm alleged was grounded on damage caused by *false* factual statements, then there is no question that common law defamation torts would be adequate to address their harms. Likewise, intrusions on the intimate details of one's life might properly be remedied under state privacy torts. There is no constitutional right to become a Peeping Tom or to maliciously doctor or manipulate video footage. But recent legislative efforts, including the ag-gag laws, evince a willingness to punish persons who record matters of public concern, based on business harms caused by their *truthful* broadcasts.[229]

### 4.3.4.2 Personal Privacy Interests

In addition, an interest closely related to the protection of private property is safeguarding personal privacy.[230] An important debate among contemporary First Amendment theorists involves the tension between speech and privacy, a potential conflict that has not surprisingly emerged in full blossom as new technologies

---

[227] *See, e.g., Desnick*, 44 F.3d at 1353 ("'Testers' who pose as prospective home buyers in order to gather evidence of housing discrimination are not trespassers").

[228] Nathan Siegel, *Publication Damages in Newsgathering Cases*, 19 COMM. LAW. 11, 15 (2001) (emphasis added).

[229] "Whatever legally cognizable harm [from an undercover investigation] is, it cannot be harm from protected, true, speech. The damage Kansas fears is that animal facilities may face 'negative publicity, lost business[,] or boycotts.'... But these harms would be accomplished by ALDF [Animal Legal Defense Fund] disseminating true information – to the extent that information is injurious, it does not cause legally cognizable harm." *Kelly*, 9 F.4th at 1235.

[230] The privacy interests of business entities themselves, while recognized, are not nearly of the same order as individual privacy. The Court

> has recognized that a business, by its special nature and voluntary existence, may open itself to intrusions that would not be permissible in a purely private context.... When a dealer chooses to engage in this pervasively regulated business and to accept a federal license, he does so with the knowledge that his business records, firearms, and ammunition will be subject to effective inspection.

*See* G. M. Leasing Corp. v. United States, 429 U.S. 338, 353–54 (1977) (distinguishing between entity and individual's sense of privacy).

make data collection, transfer, and dissemination (like video recording) easy and inexpensive.

It is beyond debate that advances in technology create substantial impediments to efforts to safeguard individual privacy. But as with an overly broad articulation of property rights, a generic reference to the importance of personal privacy cannot categorically defeat all claims to a right to record. Privacy, like any other government interest, must be specifically articulated in terms of what particular privacy goals the law or government action will serve.[231] The privacy interests in the open areas of a large, commercial workplace are quite different from the privacy interests in one's bathroom or bedroom. Thus, while government interests in privacy are different in public than they are in private, defining expectations of privacy in this context purely in terms of whether the recording is in public or private is overly simplistic and analytically incomplete.

On the most basic level, the argument that private recording *always* violates privacy rights rests on an assumption that the First Amendment right to record on private property would necessarily imply a right of access to private property in order to record. As previously explained, the former does not imply the latter; the right to record should be limited to those who already have lawful access to the place where the recording occurs. Thus, although the *recording* is a secret, the *presence* of another person on one's property is not. Of course, this raises a set of interesting questions. For example, what rights should one have to recordings they create while *unlawfully* present in a location? Does the antecedent illegal entry render the possession rights in the recording a nullity? If someone trespassed into a nursing home and captured a video of a resident being physically abused, or even murdered by staff, would anyone really think the video (and the right to destroy it) belongs to the nursing home?[232]

Regardless, the point is that one cannot enter someone else's home, even a politician's, just because they think the occupants might be talking about something

---

[231] *See, e.g.*, *Alvarez*, 679 F.3d at 595 (finding government failed to adequately articulate privacy concern that would outweigh right to speech in statute banning audiovisual recordings of police officers).

[232] Although the Court has not answered this question, *Bartnicki v. Vopper*, 532 U.S. 514 (2001), is instructive. In that case the Court considered the "clash" between an unlawful privacy intrusion and the publication of materials obtained. The federal wiretapping law at issue contained penalties for disclosing the contents of an illegally intercepted communication. Radio broadcasters disclosed the contents of an illegally intercepted cellphone conversation. The Court held the information disclosed concerned a matter of public interest and that neither the state's interest in protecting the privacy of its citizens nor its interest in deterring the unlawful interception of communications justified punishing the truthful publication of the lawfully obtained information. *See* Ex parte Metzger, 610 S.W.3d 86, 94 (Tex. App. 2020), *petition for discretionary rev. refused* (Jan. 27, 2021) ("The United States Supreme Court has never held that truthful expression that invades privacy 'in an intolerable manner' categorically loses its First Amendment protection or that intent to invade privacy converts protected expression into unprotected conduct").

interesting or newsworthy. A desire to record is not a ticket to enter. On the other hand, if a person is invited to a location, as a guest, an employee, in some other capacity, or even as a result of an investigative deception, the privacy interest in keeping secret any non-intimate details revealed to that party is not as substantial. The host is on notice that a person is in their home. The interest in privacy for things one does not keep private from others is not very great. If a politician invites a constituent into their office and uses illegal drugs in that constituent's presence, for example, that politician can hardly claim a privacy violation if the constituent later writes a journal entry or a newspaper column about the encounter.[233] The politician may resent that it is not just their word against the witness's, but the reliability of a video and its ability to confirm the witness's observations should not be a reason to discount the right to record.

Likewise, the childcare manager who is caught on tape abusing children by a *Dateline* NBC investigator might regret that she hired or invited an undercover reporter into her workplace, but she did not have a reasonable expectation of privacy in avoiding the observation – she knew that another person witnessed her abuse. Her interest is not in privacy per se, but in preventing the public distribution of the recording, and a law that facilitates such an interest directly suppresses expression regarding a matter of public concern. A child abuser or law-breaking politician might claim that video recordings violate their privacy. But in reality the video simply enhances the truth-finding ability of public debate beyond rhetoric and press campaigns.

Stated differently, the privacy intrusion narrative is often a canard. The person who is observed (or observed and recorded) is not arguing that the observation itself was improper, for she consented to the observation by a third party. Rather, she is attempting to prevent "evidence of dubious or potentially embarrassing actions" from being conveyed "to a wider audience."[234] Photographs are said to be worth a thousand words, and videos worth millions of online views.[235] The unimpeachable and rapidly transmittable nature of the modern video images ought to make recording more, not less, valuable than the hand-scribbled retellings of a firsthand observation.

A cautionary tale on the investigations-versus-privacy debate comes from abroad. In litigation brought by the Farm Transparency Project to challenge the Surveillance Device Act, which prohibits the use or possession of footage or audio

---

[233] When we first wrote out this scenario, it was simply a hypothetical to illustrate the point. Since then, it has become a reality. Jenny Gross, *Lord Sewel Resigns after Drug Claims*, WALL ST. J. (July 28, 2015), www.wsj.com/articles/lord-sewel-resigns-after-drug-claims-1438069487.

[234] Kreimer, *supra* note 22, at 383.

[235] Scott MacFarland, *If a Picture Is Worth a Thousand Words, What Is a Video Worth?*, HUFFINGTON POST (May 19, 2014), www.huffingtonpost.com/scott-macfarland/if-a-picture-video-production_b_4996655.html (arguing shift in paradigm from "picture is worth a thousand words" to "moving picture is worth a million people").

obtained from a listening device or hidden camera, the highest court in New South Wales, Australia, recently ruled that the law did not pose too great a burden on free speech.[236] The court's decision relied on the state's interest in protecting privacy and on the fact that the law could be used to punish those who had unlawfully trespassed to obtain the footage.

Of course, there will sometimes be a compelling government interest in regulating recordings even by persons who are lawfully present when they make the recording because the recording violates tangible and concrete privacy interests. The hotel housekeeper who in good faith enters a bathroom to clean it and comes upon a guest in a state of undress has surely intruded on protected privacy if they record the images.[237] Even though the housekeeper is lawfully present, the state has an interest in protecting the guest's personal privacy. By the same reasoning, nothing in the First Amendment would prevent the enactment of laws banning so-called up-skirt videos or photos,[238] which can many times be taken from a vantage point where the recorder or photographer is lawfully present. In contrast to secret recordings made as part of an undercover investigation, such speech has little social value and the harm to privacy is potentially great.

The government will also have a relatively more powerful claim to regulating recordings when they take place in a private home, as opposed to a commercial workplace. The Court's admonition in the Fourth Amendment context that "all details of the home"[239] are intimate and therefore entitled to a reasonable expectation of privacy, while not dispositive with respect to First Amendment claims, certainly has a strong bearing on the extent to which someone's asserted right to record on private property can overcome a prohibition on in-home recordings.

By contrast, "in light of the regulatory framework governing his business and the history of regulation of related industries," the Supreme Court has recognized significantly limited privacy interests in businesses.[240] Similarly, several years ago

---

[236] Christopher Knaus, *Activists Lose Challenge to NSW Laws Banning Secret Filming of Animal Cruelty*, THE GUARDIAN (Aug. 10, 2022), www.theguardian.com/law/2022/aug/10/animal-rights-activists-lose-challenge-to-nsw-laws-banning-secret-filming-of-animal-cruelty.

[237] Because this would constitute a nonconsensual recording on private property, the theory of the right to record would impose a public concern limitation. Thus, in addition to the privacy considerations, the value of the speech here would be extremely low because it does not touch on a matter of public concern. On balance, the harm is great and the value is low, so bans on such recordings would likely be upheld.

[238] *See, e.g.*, 720 ILL. COMP. STAT. ANN. 5/26-4(a-10) ("It is unlawful for any person to knowingly make a video record or transmit live video of another person under or through the clothing worn by that other person for the purpose of viewing the body of or the undergarments worn by that other person without that person's consent").

[239] Kyllo v. United States, 533 U.S. 27, 38 (2001); *id.* at 48 ("[T]he Fourth Amendment draws 'a firm line at the entrance to the house'"). *Id.* at 37 ("In the home ... all details are intimate details").

[240] New York v. Burger, 482 U.S. 691, 707 (1987); *see also* Minnesota v. Carter, 119 S. Ct. 469 (1998) (recognizing that a private home used occasionally for business purposes may have reduced expectations of privacy that extend to commercial properties).

the National Labor Relations Board ruled that Whole Foods' rules prohibiting employees from engaging in all nonconsensual video recording in the workplace violated federal labor law because it tended to chill employees in the exercise of their labor rights.[241] To the extent that law enforcement agents or informants remain free to infiltrate and make recordings of truly private information in the commercial context, it would be perverse to recognize an untethered common law privacy right that broadly trumps the First Amendment interests of private parties interested in engaging in audiovisual recording where they are lawfully present. This does not mean that all workplace recordings are without privacy protections. But the expectations of privacy in highly regulated businesses are diminished.

* * *

By examining the history and purpose of free speech, this chapter presents the claim that there is a right to record and that it extends to some recordings on private property. More specifically, there is a right to record even on private property without consent if the recording relates to a matter of public concern and if the person making the recording is otherwise lawfully present at the location the recording is made. This is a key to the ongoing success of undercover investigations, which we argue throughout this book are integrally related to promoting transparency on important public matters.

American democracy has a history of being informed by rebellious and sometimes unpopular recordings. Upton Sinclair documented food safety and labor concerns by watching, remembering, and then writing up his notes in his room at the end of each day of investigation. Today, the ubiquity and relatively inexpensive nature of recording devices has resulted in a fundamental shift in our ability to document and authenticate the wrongdoing observed by an individual reporter, investigator, or activist. Video recordings are uniquely able to shape public debate; they are verifiable, easily disseminated to a wide audience, and frequently more powerful than words alone. When addressing these issues, courts ought to explicitly recognize that recording is a form of speech, and grapple with the harder questions of how to apply the relevant constitutional scrutiny to the particular context in question.

---

[241] Whole Foods Mkt., Inc., *supra* note 38. Although the employer argued that the purpose of its rule was to promote open communication in the workplace, the NLRB found that it was overly broad. *Id.* at 4. Moreover, the Board did not even discuss any countervailing employer privacy concerns.

# 5

# Undercover Investigations and New Technologies

## 5.1 INTRODUCTION

In Chapter 4, we showed that even nonconsensual video recording may be a form of protected speech or speech-creating activity that is covered by the First Amendment. Conceptually, such claims could also apply to less technologically sophisticated forms of nonconsensual memorialization of information observed by the investigator, including still photography, audio recordings, or even taking handwritten notes. But the landscape of undercover investigations has been transformed, and will probably continue to be transformed, by the development of new and less expensive forms of news and information gathering made possible by technological innovation. And, of course, whatever information is gathered can now be communicated to a wide audience through the availability of the internet. This chapter examines some more recent technological developments, including changes in the video recording technology discussed in Chapter 4, that are likely to be employed by undercover investigators going forward, while also discussing some potential social problems associated with such technologies.

Over the past few generations, American society has witnessed speech evolve as a social practice in ways that have been heavily influenced and shaped by emerging technologies, from radio to broadcast television to cable to the internet.[1] As Professor Eugene Volokh observed at a very early stage of this era, until the availability of the internet, speech was heavily controlled by powerful and well-resourced intermediaries, such as major radio, television, and cable broadcasting networks.[2] The availability of the internet changed the communications landscape by allowing individuals and smaller institutions to *distribute* speech without having to work

---

[1] On the concept of understanding speech as a social practice, focusing more on its context than its substance, see generally Robert Post, *Recuperating First Amendment Doctrine*, 47 STAN. L. REV. 1249, 1250 (1995).

[2] Eugene Volokh, *Cheap Speech and What It Will Do*, 104 YALE L.J. 1805, 1834 (1995).

through these intermediaries. But what has also made speech more accessible is the expansion and wide availability of devices that make it easy and inexpensive to engage in a range of expressive activity involving the *creation* of speech.

In Chapter 4, we discussed video recordings as a form of speech creation. We elaborate on the definition of speech creation here because it is important not only to understand communicative value of such activity, but also in determining to what extent other new ways of creating speech count as speech under the First Amendment. By speech creation, we mean to describe a set of social practices that begin with the internal intellectual, inquisitive, deliberative, and creative processes of the human mind; the acquisition of information and images; and the early manifestation of that process into a tangible form of expression, often before it is even conveyed to an audience. People who keep a journal in which they memorialize their most intimate thoughts are creating speech. The same is true for someone who writes a poem, novel, screenplay, or political speech; composes a piece of music; choreographs a dance; or draws images for an animated film.[3] Sometimes, the creations of the mind are externalized and are exercised by the manipulation of technology to enhance, alter, and transform the artistic work into something that cannot be simply created by the human hand.

Creation of speech also involves the process of engaging in practices that facilitate future engagement in speech, including the creation, gathering, and processing of data and the recording or other memorialization of events or information. For example, carrying out many of the basic practices of journalism or newsgathering involves speech creation. Newsgathering entails a range of activities that include doing research, interviewing witnesses and sources, gathering documentary evidence, observing events firsthand, and memorializing information.[4] It might also entail the acquisition and analysis of tangible objects, such as water, air, and soil samples, as well as data derived from the collection of such materials.

As we previously discussed, speech creation can also be understood to include conduct that facilitates speech in more concrete ways, such as spending money to buy a printer and paper, tattoo ink, or paint, or to support a political candidate or ballot initiative. These might also be described as conduct that is a necessary precursor to speech, but if so, that is because, like the other activities described

---

[3]   For a comprehensive treatment of artistic creation as speech, see generally Mark V. Tushnet, Alan K. Chen, & Joseph Blocher, Free Speech beyond Words: The Surprising Reach of the First Amendment (2017).

[4]   The law offers no single definition of newsgathering. While the Supreme Court has recognized that "[newsgathering] is not without its First Amendment protections," Branzburg v. Hayes, 408 U.S. 665, 707 (1972), it has never elaborated on the scope of that right, much less the definition of what it covers. Some states have enacted shield laws that protect the privilege of news media organizations to protect their confidential sources but define news media as organizations that are engaged in newsgathering, without defining the latter term. See, e.g., Wash. Rev. Code Ann. § 5.68.010 (2020) (defining news media simply as "any entity that is in the regular business of [newsgathering] and disseminating news or information to the public by any means").

here, they directly facilitate its creation. Understanding the transformation of speech creation over the past generation requires a brief discussion of important changes to both technology and information acquisition practices.

American society has recently witnessed unprecedented transformations in political speech and professional newsgathering, as well as the emergence of citizen journalism, in ways that have highlighted how we create speech. In the realm of political speech, particularly in the time of the COVID-19 pandemic,[5] everyone from a presidential candidate to a grassroots political activist can employ modern technology to produce a planned or spontaneous moment using widely available digital recording technology. No professional film crew with its expensive equipment is needed. Consider the way that Elizabeth Warren's 2020 presidential campaign leveraged "selfies" with the candidate to mobilize support.[6] It wasn't just the production of the selfie that was speech, but its ability to allow her to connect with voters. As Warren herself noted, "That's 100,000 hugs and handshakes and stories.... Stories of people struggling with student loan debt, stories of people that can't pay their medical bills, stories from people that can't find child care."[7] State representative Wendy Davis became nationally famous by live-streaming her thirteen-hour filibuster against a Texas abortion bill, mobilizing Texas voters to pressure their representatives to reject the proposed law.[8]

As we have already described extensively, professional journalists have frequently used secret video-recording equipment to document information as part of their newsgathering activities.[9] Though this practice has been controversial even within the journalism community, one cannot deny that the practice of journalists surreptitiously recording for stories has on multiple occasions revealed information of profound public concern. And these practices have now been adopted by nonprofessional journalists engaged in traditional newsgathering practices. While in past generations newsgathering had been almost exclusively the bailiwick of professional journalists, in the contemporary era we have seen the proliferation of the so-called

---

[5]   *See generally* COVID-19, CTRS. FOR DISEASE CONTROL & PREVENTION, www.cdc.gov/corona
       virus/2019-ncov/index.html (last visited Jan. 27, 2021) (providing a centralized repository of all
       information and official reporting regarding the COVID-19 pandemic).
[6]   *See* Rebecca Jennings, *Why Selfie Lines Are Crucial to Elizabeth Warren's Campaign*, VOX
       (Dec. 20, 2019), www.vox.com/the-goods/2019/9/19/20872718/elizabeth-warren-2020-selfie-line.
[7]   *Id.*
[8]   *See* Tracey Welson-Rossman, *Politics in the Age of Technology-Enabled Campaigning*, FORBES
       (Sept. 24, 2018), www.forbes.com/sites/traceywelsonrossman/2018/09/24/politics-in-the-age-of-
       technology-enabled-campaigning/.
[9]   Because secret video recordings are, by definition, nonconsensual, there is implicit deception
       in their very use. But it is also true that in order to gain access to areas in which such recordings
       can be made, investigators may need to lie about their identities as journalists or activists prior
       to recording. *See, e.g.*, Med. Lab. Mgmt. Consultants v. ABC, Inc., 30 F. Supp. 2d 1182, 1185
       (D. Ariz. 1998) (describing a television news show's undercover investigation that used decep-
       tion to gain access to business, in which secret recordings were used to reveal misconduct),
       *aff'd*, 306 F.3d 806 (9th Cir. 2002).

citizen journalist.[10] The emergence of citizen journalists has generated interesting doctrinal questions, such as who "counts" as the press for the purposes of the First Amendment's Press Clause.[11] But the actual world of on-the-ground newsgathering does not follow neat legal boundaries. Furthermore, as discussed below, some individuals and organizations have adopted the information-acquisition practices of undercover journalists as a form of political advocacy to promote social movements.

Political speech, undercover investigations by professional journalists, and newsgathering by citizen journalists have all been rendered even more effective by technological innovations, as discussed next. These innovations have expanded the opportunities for all types of information gatherers to document their findings.

## 5.2 TECHNOLOGICAL CHANGES

### 5.2.1 Compact Digital Video Recorders

Perhaps the most salient example of a technological development that facilitates undercover newsgathering is the digital video recorder. In the past, video recording involved cumbersome and expensive equipment as well as sizable recording media such as large videocassettes. Use of such recording equipment would be obvious, and therefore unlikely to capture any images or sounds that the target of an investigation wished to hide from public view. As with other electronic equipment,[12] digital video recorders today are smaller, less expensive, and more easily capable of being obscured from observation. Some video recorders are specifically designed to be small and undetectable. As just one example, one can currently purchase a portable, digital high-definition, spy camera that is less than one square inch and has night

---

[10] *See* SCOTT GANT, WE'RE ALL JOURNALISTS NOW 3 (2007) ("The lines distinguishing professional journalists from other people who disseminate information, ideas, and opinions to a wide audience have been blurred, perhaps beyond recognition, by forces both inside and outside the media themselves").

[11] Despite the express text of the First Amendment, the Supreme Court has generally not recognized freedom of the press as a right distinct from the freedom of speech. *See* Sonja R. West, *Awakening the Press Clause*, 58 UCLA L. REV. 1025, 1027–28 (2011). Though scholars have argued that this approach substantially diminishes the constitutional importance of a free press, there has been an ongoing and contested discussion about how to define the press for these purposes. *See id.* at 1029–30 (discussing the problematic nature of defining the press and providing a voluminous list of scholarly attempts to do so). *But see* Ashutosh Bhagwat, *Producing Speech*, 56 WM. & MARY L. REV. 1029, 1053 (2015) (arguing the First Amendment should protect more than just "institutional press" in an age where the broader public regularly engages in information gathering).

[12] *See, e.g.*, A. Bruno Frazier, Robert O. Warrington, & Craig Friedrich, *The Miniaturization Technologies: Past, Present, and Future*, 42 IEEE TRANSACTIONS ON INDUS. ELECS. 423, 423 (1995) (discussing examples of the "miniaturization" in the context of other electronic devices).

vision capability for less than $30.[13] For about $10 or $15 more, the buyer can add Wi-Fi capability and secure the ability to watch live video feeds on a smartphone.[14] In contrast, less than thirty years ago, major electronics companies were selling home digital camcorders in the range anywhere from $400 to $3,000, though even by then, these devices were "[a]bout the size of a paperback novel."[15] Today's miniature spycams can be employed in planned undercover investigations to document things ranging from industrial pollution to labor law violations to incriminating statements.

Moreover, today's camcorders are more useful for undercover work because rather than using cumbersome tapes or discs, they record digitally and allow one to upload video files to the cloud quickly and easily. Editing technology has also improved, so one can not only gather the digital information inexpensively, but also easily produce a professional quality video, shaped by one's own editorial sensibilities. As with questions about professional journalism standards, the editing of videos may sometimes raise questions about the value and accuracy of video recordings. It is one thing for an editor to use technology to present information professionally (e.g., editing out extraneous, irrelevant material), but a completely different thing for the editing process to result in intentionally misleading images about the events or actions recorded.[16]

But dedicated camcorders are no longer even necessary to create high-quality digital still images and videos because of the wide availability of cellphone cameras. In 1995, only 22% of Americans had cell phones.[17] By 2016, 75% of people had smartphones while another 18% had non-smart cellphones.[18] Cellphone digital video cameras are now ubiquitous and, as we all know, can be used to capture unplanned, spontaneous events of public interest.[19]

---

[13] *See Mini Spy Camera 1080P Hidden Camera*, AMAZON, www.amazon.com/Mini-Camera-1080P-Hidden-Built/dp/B07X1YLC2L (last visited Nov. 14, 2022).

[14] *See Smallest Wireless WiFi Camera*, AMAZON, www.amazon.com/dp/B09WMDMBNJ/ref= syn_sd_onsite_desktop_96?ie=UTF8&psc=1&pd_rd_plhdr=t (last visited Feb. 18, 2023).

[15] Dennis Hunt, *Low-End Camcorders, High-End Features*, L.A. TIMES (Dec. 16, 1994), www .latimes.com/archives/la-xpm-1994-12-16-ca-9822-story.html (placing camcorder costs between $400 and $1,000); Rich Warren, *Digital Camcorders among Best Products of 1995*, HARTFORD COURANT (Dec. 28, 1995), www.courant.com/news/connecticut/hc-xpm-1995-12-28-9512270035-story.html (reporting camcorder costs from $2,200 to $3,000). In either case, the costs are much lower today.

[16] Video footage that is altered so as to deliberately mislead viewers can expose those who release such footage to defamation liability. Just as one who misrepresents facts in a written or oral narrative can be legally responsible for resulting damage, so too can persons who alter (or republish) videos that misrepresent events.

[17] Reuben Fischer-Baum, *What "Tech World" Did You Grow Up In?*, WASH. POST (Nov. 26, 2017), www.washingtonpost.com/graphics/2017/entertainment/tech-generations/.

[18] *Id.*

[19] *See* Seth F. Kreimer, *Pervasive Image Capture and the First Amendment: Memory, Discourse, and the Right to Record*, 159 U. PA. L. REV. 335, 344 (2011).

As discussed earlier, the use of cellphone videos to document the tragically commonplace incidents of law enforcement officers' shootings, frequently of young Black men, has become seemingly ubiquitous.[20] Building on this phenomenon, organizations such as Cop Watch and the American Civil Liberties Union (ACLU) have developed apps that allow such video recordings to be uploaded to the internet instantaneously in case the cellphones are destroyed or confiscated before the videos can be posted.[21] These videos have helped generate broader public support for Black Lives Matter and related social movements and political organizers.[22] Moreover, similar recordings have made acquittals possible in cases in which a conviction would otherwise have turned on jurors believing police officer accounts over those of eyewitnesses. In short, police accountability is much more plausible in an era of ever-present recording. There could hardly be a matter that fits more directly within the definition of matters of public concern.

The same tools that benefit journalists and other citizens have also been adopted by political activists to carry out undercover investigations that are linked to their causes. By providing information that sparks public discourse and democratic responses to documented social problems, the creation of speech through these videos advances basic principles underlying the freedom of speech.

It is worth adding a note of caution about these transformative new technologies and free speech. The same technical ability to gather information for journalistic or political purposes can be employed by the government to monitor the activities of lawful political organizations. That type of governmental spying can, in turn, chill constitutionally protected speech by private actors. Whether limitations on such surveillance come from the Constitution or from federal and state law, the emergence of these technologies ultimately may require the development of some sorts of legal or professional standards to ensure that the resulting gains to free expression are not outweighed by the costs. The precise contours of protections for recording are discussed in other parts of the book, but it suffices here to note that there can be material privacy interests at stake, and we are skeptical of claims that government actors should have more power than private actors to take advantage of emerging technology to facilitate investigations.

---

[20] *See* Nicol Turner Lee, *Where Would Racial Progress in Policing Be without Camera Phones?*, Brookings (June 5, 2020), www.brookings.edu/blog/fixgov/2020/06/05/where-would-racial-pro gress-in-policing-be-without-camera-phones/.

[21] *See* Farhad Manjoo & Mike Isaac, *Phone Cameras and Apps Help Speed Calls for Police Reform*, N.Y. Times (Apr. 8, 2015), http://nytimes.com/2015/04/09/technology/phone-cameras-and-apps-help-speed-calls-for-police-reform.html (discussing Cop Watch and interviewing its creator); Tom McGhee, *Witness Police Wrongdoing? There's an App for That*, Denv. Post (Oct. 29, 2015), www.denverpost.com/news/ci_29043137/witness-police-wrongdoing?-theres-an-app-for-that (describing Mobile Justice Colorado app).

[22] *See* Adam Serwer, *The New Reconstruction*, Atlantic (Oct. 2020), www.theatlantic.com/magazine/archive/2020/10/the-next-reconstruction/615475/. *See generally* Black Lives Matter, https://blacklivesmatter.com/ (last visited Jan. 24, 2021) (providing background information and resources related to the Black Lives Matter organization and movement).

### 5.2.2 *Drones*

A related technological development has been the proliferation of drones, a shorthand term for unmanned aerial vehicles (UAVs). Originally created for military use, drones have become widely available to consumers for a number of personal uses, with around two million sold in 2016:[23] "[T]here is a wide array of nonmilitary applications for UAVs: firefighting and disaster recovery, precision agriculture and ranching, pipeline and other utility inspection, weather forecasting, newsgathering, mapmaking, real estate, amateur and professional photography and videography, filmmaking, sports broadcasting, tourism, prevention of poaching and other unwanted behaviors, search and rescue, and shipping and transport."[24] But for both individual and commercial uses, a significant utility for drones is to serve as flying cameras.[25]

In one reported incident, a hobbyist flying a drone in Texas recorded images of a creek near his home that had turned red, later learning that he had inadvertently captured evidence that a local meat processing plant was engaged in illegal dumping.[26] A few years ago, activists used drones to monitor protests at the Dakota Access Pipeline in Standing Rock, North Dakota, capturing aerial images of police shooting high-pressure water cannons at protestors when temperatures fell well below freezing.[27] Reporters who cover environmental issues have used drones to document rising waters and other signs of climate change that are not observable from the ground.[28] In 2020, a professional photojournalist used a drone to document the mass burial of people who died of COVID-19 on Hart Island in New York. New York police then seized his drone and charged him with a misdemeanor for violating an "avigation" law, prohibiting aircraft from taking off or landing outside the city's airports.[29]

---

[23] As one report indicates, however, the technologies used for consumer drones are drawn not from military systems, but from hobbyists' radio-controlled aircraft and smartphones. Tom Standage, *Taking Flight: Civilian Drones*, Economist (June 8, 2017), https://www.economist .com/technology-quarterly/2017-06-08/civilian-drones.

[24] Marc Jonathan Blitz et al., *Regulating Drones under the First and Fourth Amendments*, 57 Wm. & Mary L. Rev. 49, 54 (2015).

[25] Standage, *supra* note 23.

[26] Colleen Curry, *Drone Eyed by Paparazzi, J-School Teaching Reporters How to Fly Them*, ABC News (Mar. 21, 2013), https://abcnews.go.com/US/drones-eyed-paparazzi-school-teaching-reporters-operate/story?id=18782432.

[27] Janus Kopfstein, *Police Are Making It Impossible to Use Drones to Document Protests*, Vocativ (Jan. 27, 2017), www.vocativ.com/396662/police-drone-journalists-protests/.

[28] *See Taking Visual Journalism into the Sky with Drones*, N.Y. Times (May 2, 2018), www .nytimes.com/2018/05/02/technology/personaltech/visual-journalism-drones.html.

[29] New York University, *NYPD Seizes Photojournalist's Drone after He Documented Mass-Burials*, First Amend. Watch (Apr. 22, 2020), https://firstamendmentwatch.org/nypd-seizes-photojournalists-drone-after-he-documented-mass-burials/. This case was spontaneously dismissed months later. Kara Murphy, *Case Dismissed against George Steinmetz, Whose Drone Was Confiscated for Documenting Mass Burials*, Digit. Photography Rev. (Aug. 17, 2020), www

The possibilities of drone-based journalistic investigations have not been lost on the profession. Several news media companies, including CNN, have established drone divisions.[30] Supported by the Knight Foundation, two professors at the University of Nebraska, Lincoln, have developed a drone journalism lab as well as a procedures manual for carrying out such work.[31] The Poynter Institute for Media Studies provides training for journalists who want to incorporate drones into their fact finding.[32] And the National Press Photographers Association and Poynter have teamed up with other organizations to develop a drone journalism code of ethics.[33]

While drones therefore are another example of technologically driven cheap speech creation, they can also be used to interfere with speech and other political activity. Like miniature video cameras, drones paradoxically present the opportunity for cheap speech creation that can promote democracy by securing information that is of great public importance while also creating the possibility of both ominous and ubiquitous government surveillance of private citizens. Government regulation that addresses both of these concerns has already begun to emerge.[34]

In response to the expanded use of drones for a range of private uses, the federal government and many states have enacted several laws. As of the end of 2019, according to the Federal Aviation Administration (FAA), consumers had registered over a million recreational drones.[35] At the federal level, the applicable regulations depend on the user. Recreational drone pilots must register their drone and mark it with a registration number.[36] Furthermore, they must keep their drones within their line of sight and may not fly them above 400 feet.[37] There are other limitations pertaining to where recreational users may fly drones.[38]

---

.dpreview.com/news/7618724976/case-dismissed-against-george-steinmetz-drone-confiscated-for-documenting-mass-burials?utm_source=Twitter-tweet&utm_medium=mobile-social-bar&utm_campaign=social-sharing.

[30] Benjamin Mullin, *CNN Just Launched a New Drone Division. Here's What They Plan to Do with It*, POYNTER (Aug. 19, 2016), www.poynter.org/tech-tools/2016/cnn-just-launched-a-new-drone-division-heres-what-they-plan-to-do-with-it/.

[31] Matt Waite, *Drone Journalism Lab Publishes Operations Manual to Guide Newsrooms*, KNIGHT FOUND. (Sept. 1, 2016), https://knightfoundation.org/articles/drone-journalism-lab-publishes-operations-manual-guide-newsrooms/.

[32] *Drone Journalism*, PONYTER, www.poynter.org/tag/drone-journalism/ (last visited Jan. 16, 2021).

[33] Al Tompkins, *Help Journalism Grow Responsibly*, NAT'L PRESS PHOTOGRAPHERS ASS'N, https://nppa.org/magazine/drone-code-ethics (last visited Nov. 19, 2022).

[34] We do not address concerns about government use of drones for surveillance. For a comprehensive evaluation of constitutional limitations on government drone use and government regulation of private drone use, see Blitz et al., *supra* note 24, at 49.

[35] *UAS by the Numbers*, FED. AVIATION ADMIN. (Dec. 10, 2019), https://web.archive.org/web/20200103181022/https://www.faa.gov/uas/resources/by_the_numbers/.

[36] *See* 14 C.F.R. § 48.100(c) (2020).

[37] *See id.* § 107.51(b)(2) (2020).

[38] *See generally* 14 C.F.R. §§ 107.37–107.51 (codifying operating rules for small, unmanned aircraft systems).

In 2016, the FAA issued regulations permitting journalists to use drones, though they must be operated by someone who has obtained a remote pilot certificate and has passed a background security check.[39] The regulations also impose limits on the size of drones and where they can be flown, and require that they be kept in the operator's line of sight.[40] Since then, the FAA has issued additional regulations that permit journalists in some circumstances to fly drones over people and at night, which had previously been prohibited, provided that the operators undergo additional training and that such drones bear a marker so they can be identified during flight.[41]

State laws vary widely. Many states have no drone regulations. Some states regulate only government use of drones.[42] Many states regulate drone flights to protect public safety. Several states limit the locations where drones may be flown, including some restrictions that could have free speech implications. Idaho law establishes a civil tort remedy for anyone who is the subject of drone surveillance or nonconsensual photography or recording from a drone for the purpose of publishing or otherwise publicly disseminating the images recorded.[43] A few states prohibit flying drones above "critical infrastructure facilities."[44] These resemble other laws that restrict protests that might interfere with such facilities, as several states enacted in the wake of the protests at the Dakota Access Pipeline construction site.[45]

Law enforcement agencies can chill speech through the use of drones that monitor protest activity and identify potential targets of prosecution, so drones are not always speech-enhancing tools.[46] When helicopters (though not drones) were used to cover news about protests in Ferguson, Missouri, after the killing of Michael Brown, the FAA agreed to a request by local police to impose a temporary no-fly

---

[39] 14 C.F.R. § 107.7 (2016).

[40] 14 C.F.R. § 107.3, 107.51, 107.31.

[41] 14 C.F.R. § 107.39, 107.29.

[42] *See, e.g.,* H.B. 255, 28th Leg., Reg. Sess. (Alaska 2014) (regulating law enforcement use of drones); ME. REV. STAT. tit. 25, § 4501 (2020) (regulating law enforcement use of drones); UTAH CODE ANN. § 72-14-203 (2020) (regulating law enforcement use of drones).

[43] IDAHO CODE § 21-213 (2020). Like some of the ag-gag laws discussed in this book, the Idaho law also specifically prohibits conducting drone surveillance of "[a] farm, dairy, ranch or other agricultural industry, or commercial or industrial property, without the written consent of the property owner." *Id.*

[44] H.B. 1027, Reg. Sess. (Fla. 2017); *see* H.B. 1770, 90th Leg., Reg. Sess. (Ark. 2015); H.B. 195, 148th Leg., Reg. Sess. (Del. 2016); H.B. 2599, 55th Leg., Reg. Sess. (Okla. 2016); S.B. 2106, 109th Leg., Reg. Sess. (Tenn. 2016); H.B. 1481, 84th Leg., Reg. Sess. (Tex. 2015). New Jersey allows operators of critical infrastructure to apply to the FAA to forbid or limit drone use near their facilities. S.B. 3370, 217th Leg., Reg. Sess. (N.J. 2018).

[45] *See* S.B. 151, Reg. Sess. (S.D. 2020); H.B. 4615, 84th Leg., Reg. Sess. (W.V. 2020).

[46] *See* John D. McKinnon & Michelle Hackman, *Drone Surveillance of Protests Comes under Fire*, WALL ST. J. (June 10, 2020), www.wsj.com/articles/drone-surveillance-of-protests-comes-under-fire-11591789477.

zone over the city.[47] Sources reported, however, that the purpose of the ban was to keep news stations away from covering the protests.[48] Similarly, in 2020 the Department of Homeland Security used drones to monitor demonstrators protesting the death of George Floyd in fifteen cities.[49]

California has one of the most restrictive drone laws, prohibiting all use of drones to record another person without their consent.[50] That law resembles, in important ways, some of the ag-gag laws discussed in previous chapters. Other laws are more narrowly tailored to more specific government interests, and prohibit drone use that invades privacy and/or involves "video voyeurism."[51]

### 5.2.3 *Data Creation and Acquisition*

Thus far, the discussion has focused on advancements in audiovisual recording technology as the primary examples of contemporary speech creation. But acquisition of data or other types of information can also be a form of speech creation. Collecting information can take place through traditional methods, including personal observation, use of scientific methods (such as gathering of soil or water samples to identify contamination), or employment of technological methods (such as programs that can scrape data from websites). Data can be critical evidence that documents the violation of environmental regulations, civil rights statutes, or other laws.

In *Western Watersheds Project v. Michael*,[52] the Tenth Circuit addressed the constitutionality of a state law that prohibited certain types of data collection on public and private lands, and implicated citizen scientists' efforts to monitor government and private actions. In that case, the plaintiffs challenged the constitutionality of a Wyoming law that subjected anyone who crosses private property to access adjacent land to collect "resource data" to criminal penalties and tort liability.[53]

---

[47] Associated Press, *Police Targeted Media with No-Fly Zone over Ferguson, Tapes Show*, N.Y. TIMES (Nov. 2, 2014), www.nytimes.com/2014/11/03/us/police-targeted-media-with-no-fly-zone-over-ferguson-tapes-show.html.

[48] *Id.*

[49] Zolan Kanno-Youngs, *U.S. Watched George Floyd Protests in 15 Cities Using Aerial Surveillance*, N.Y. TIMES (June 19, 2020), www.nytimes.com/2020/06/19/us/politics/george-floyd-protests-surveillance.html?referringSource=articleShare.

[50] CAL. CIV. CODE § 1708.8 (2020).

[51] H.B. 1349, 90th Leg., Reg. Sess. (Ark. 2015) (privacy & voyeurism); FLA. STAT. § 934.50 (2020) (privacy) (Florida also authorizes local governments to adopt drone restrictions to prohibit voyeurism, *see* H.B. 1027, Reg. Sess. (Fla. 2017)); H.B. 635, Reg. Sess. (La. 2016) (voyeurism); S.B. 992, 98th Leg., Reg. Sess. (Mich. 2016); S.B. 80, Reg. Sess. (S.D. 2017). Interestingly, Utah exempts drone users from liability for what would otherwise be a privacy violation if they are employing the drone for a commercial or educational purpose. *See* S.B. 111, 59th Leg., Reg. Sess. (Utah 2017) (voyeurism).

[52] 869 F.3d 1189, 1191–92 (10th Cir. 2017).

[53] *Id.* at 1191. The lower court had dismissed the challenge, along with challenges to two other parts of the statute that prohibited entry on to private land for the purpose of collecting resource

Under the law, "collect" meant "to take a sample of material, acquire, gather, photograph, or otherwise preserve information in any form and the recording of a legal description or geographical coordinates of the location of the collection."[54] "Resource data" was defined as "data relating to land or land use, including, but not limited to data regarding agriculture, minerals, geology, history, cultural artifacts, archeology, air, water, soil, conservation, habitat, vegetation or animal species."[55] The law was challenged by, among others, environmental organizations that collected these types of data to uncover information that would assist them in advocating for public policy reforms regarding water quality and endangered species.[56] In defending the statute, Wyoming contended that the prohibited activity was not speech, but only conduct on public lands. As discussed below, the Tenth Circuit ultimately concluded that the collection of resource data constituted the "creation of speech."[57]

There is also a close connection between speech and the creation of data. For example, some of the sample materials that were prohibited from collection by the Wyoming law were not in and of themselves communicative, but had to be subjected to further testing to create information. As with other types of suppressing speech creation, cutting off the inputs effectively prohibited the speech outputs. Collection led to testing, which created data, which was then used to inform the public.

While the expressive activities at issue in the *Western Watersheds* case were not solely technologically based, there are other, more advanced tools for acquiring data that also can be importantly and effectively used to create speech. One example comes from the contemporary investigation of civil rights violations. When it comes to face-to-face transactions, illegal discrimination can sometimes be detected by civil rights testers, which we have discussed in previous chapters. But proving online discrimination is even more elusive.

Many major parts of commerce, including real estate, employment, and consumer purchases, have moved to web-based transactions, but there has been increasing concern that it will be harder to detect discrimination against marginalized groups by such e-commerce enterprises. The volume and the impersonal nature of transactions make it easier to obscure discriminatory conduct or effects because these sites may discriminate through the algorithms they employ rather than by direct consumer contact. These algorithms use consumers' data in ways that might

---

data and actually doing so. W. Watersheds Project v. Michael, 196 F. Supp. 3d 1231, 1242-45 (D. Wyo. 2016) (upholding WYO. STAT. ANN. § 6-3-414 (a)–(b) (2020)), *rev'd in part*, 869 F.3d 1189 (10th Cir. 2017). The plaintiffs did not appeal the dismissal of those claims.

[54] WYO. STAT. ANN § 6-3-414 (e)(1).

[55] *Id.* § 6-3-414 (e)(iv).

[56] *See W. Watersheds Project*, 869 F.3d at 1195. The other plaintiff was the National Press Photographers Association, an organization whose members engage in photojournalism. NAT'L PRESS PHOTOGRAPHERS ASS'N, https://nppa.org/ (last visited Mar. 7, 2021).

[57] *W. Watersheds Project*, 869 F.3d at 1195–96.

direct them toward or away from certain transactions or enable unlawful class-based price discrimination.[58] Thus, in the same ways that cheap speech has made targeted advertising beneficial to consumers by directing them to books or music similar to the ones they have previously purchased, it also enables sellers to identify consumers by characteristics that can be used to discriminate.[59] The discrimination might be purposeful or it may be unintentional with a substantially disparate impact on members of protected classes.[60]

Researchers have recently developed two methods of online auditing that allow users to acquire data from websites, creating an inexpensive and effective way of accessing information that is worthy of public concern. The two methods are "sock puppet" audits and "scraping" audits, both of which may be used to identify whether a website has engaged in discriminatory conduct. As described in a recent article,

> In a "scraping" audit, a researcher uses a bot to impersonate users of various backgrounds; the bot then issues repeated queries to see how an algorithm functions in response and subsequently collects the responses it receives. A "sock puppet" audit essentially replicates a traditional testing scenario online: Researchers imitate users of various backgrounds with fake accounts or preprogrammed data profiles to test whether any differential treatment occurs.[61]

This sort of investigation allows researchers to examine how a website's algorithms respond to certain information provided by the program, such as race or gender, thus making it possible to detect the very type of discrimination that has historically been identified by in-person civil rights testers. As discussed below, there may be legal barriers to the use of these technological auditing programs, which in turn may implicate the First Amendment to the extent that such restrictions interfere with data-based speech creation.

## 5.3 DOCTRINAL RECOGNITION FOR SPEECH CREATION

At the same time the aforementioned rapid technological developments were occurring, federal courts and legal scholars became more focused on the doctrinal and theoretical underpinnings that would evaluate the constitutional limits on regulating the expressive functions of these technologies. Building on earlier cases that implicitly recognized that government restrictions on the creation of speech at the front end of the speech continuum could effectively censor speech at the back

---

[58] Komal S. Patel, *Testing the Limits of the First Amendment: How Online Civil Rights Testing Is Protected Speech Activity*, 118 COLUM. L. REV. 1473, 1477–82 (2018). *See generally* Solon Barocas & Andrew D. Selbst, *Big Data's Disparate Impact*, 104 CAL. L. REV. 671, 692–93 (2016) (explaining the potential for data mining to "indirectly determine individuals' membership in protected classes and unduly discount, penalize, or exclude such people accordingly").

[59] Patel, *supra* note 58, at 1477.

[60] *Id.* at 1477–82.

[61] *Id.* at 1474.

end,[62] these claims about the breadth of First Amendment coverage have become more commonplace, and have in large measure facilitated the effective use of these technologies.

Before discussing these legal developments, it is worth noting that, as with other historical shifts in First Amendment doctrine that were tied to technological developments such as radio and television broadcasting,[63] there are complex "chicken or egg" questions about causality. Did the technological changes compel the Supreme Court and other federal courts to come up with new First Amendment rules or were the courts simply adapting preexisting principles to slightly new circumstances?

As we explored in greater detail in Chapter 4 regarding video recording for undercover investigations, much First Amendment doctrine already lays the foundation for a right to create speech. As the Supreme Court acknowledged in *Sorrell v. IMS Health Inc.*, laws that interfere with "the creation and dissemination of information are speech within the meaning of the First Amendment."[64] *Sorrell* is premised on the notion that the Constitution's free speech protections extend to obtaining or creating information, and not simply to distributing it. To the extent that new technologies reconstruct the way that we gather, organize, and analyze such information, regulation of those technologies triggers First Amendment coverage. And even if the courts were to reject the argument that creation of information and knowledge is speech, cases such as *Citizens United v. Federal Election Commission*[65] and *Minneapolis Star & Tribune Co. v. Minnesota Commissioner of Revenue*[66] recognize that, at the very least, the First Amendment's protections are implicated by laws that regulate activities that are antecedent to actual expression.

As we have seen in previous chapters, decisions from multiple lower courts also provide solid doctrinal foundation for the claim that creation of speech through new technologies is protected by the First Amendment. First, there are the numerous federal courts that have recognized the right to record police officers when they are in public and carrying out their job duties, even without the officers' consent.[67] Second, there are several cases invalidating state ag-gag laws that conclude that there

---

[62] *See* Minneapolis Star & Tribune Co. v. Minn. Comm'r of Revenue, 460 U.S. 575, 585 (1983) (striking down state use tax on the cost of paper and ink products used in the production of newspapers). There, the Court noted that the threat of burdensome taxes on newspapers "can operate as effectively as a censor to check critical comment by the press, undercutting the basic assumption of our political system that the press will often serve as an important restraint on government." *Id.* at 585.

[63] David S. Han, *Constitutional Rights and Technological Change*, 54 U.C. Davis L. Rev. 71, 77 (2020) ("[I]n the First Amendment context, the Court has dealt with the development of sound amplification, the rise of radio and television, and the emergence of motion pictures and video games") (footnotes omitted).

[64] 564 U.S. 552, 570 (2011). *See also* Brown v. Ent. Merchants Ass'n, 564 U.S. 786 (2011).

[65] 558 U.S. 310, 466 (2010).

[66] 460 U.S. at 591.

[67] *See, e.g.*, Am. Civ. Liberties Union of Ill. v. Alvarez, 679 F.3d 583, 588, 608 (7th Cir. 2012); Fields v. City of Philadelphia, 862 F.3d 353 (3d Cir. 2017).

is a First Amendment right to record matters of public concern even on private property.[68]

Case law is also beginning to emerge surrounding some of the new technologies discussed in this chapter. First, we may well witness further legal recognition of the right to record in the context of regulations on drones. In one of the first lawsuits challenging a state's drone regulations, the National Press Photographers Association and other plaintiffs sued to invalidate provisions of a Texas law that imposed criminal and civil penalties on any person who "uses an unmanned aircraft to capture an image of an individual or privately owned real property in [Texas] with the intent to conduct surveillance on the individual or property contained in the image."[69] The plaintiffs also challenged the law's no-fly provision, which barred flying UAVs over a "Correctional Facility, Detention Facility, or Critical Infrastructure Facility" as well as over any "Sports Venue." The law's definition of critical infrastructure facility included animal feeding operations, oil and gas drilling sites, and chemical production facilities. Though the statute provided for some exemptions to the no-fly provision, such as using drones to capture images for commercial purposes, its prohibitions fully applied to news media entities.[70]

In 2022, a federal district court granted summary judgment to the plaintiffs in this case, concluding that the regulation violated the First Amendment.[71] The court first entertained the plaintiffs' arguments about the speech-creating value of drone photojournalism. The plaintiffs submitted evidence of the increasing value of acquiring UAV images in contemporary journalism, noting that drone photography can "add additional information and important perspective for the reader – particularly where, for example, a story covers a large area that would be difficult to visualize or understand without an aerial perspective."[72] The court also acknowledged the plaintiffs' assertion that because drones can fly at low altitude, they "can allow for better images to be made and can provide more information to the viewer," that their "maneuverability 'enables better and clearer photography,'" and that they are "more economically feasible than helicopters for freelance journalists and news organizations."[73]

Although the state argued that the right asserted by the plaintiffs "is found nowhere in the First Amendment," the court observed that "the process of creating ... images [through drone photojournalism] finds just as much protection in the First Amendment as the images themselves do."[74] The court further found

---

[68] *See, e.g.*, Animal Legal Def. Fund v. Wasden, 878 F.3d 1184, 1203, 1205 (9th Cir. 2018); Animal Legal Def. Fund v. Kelly, 9 F.4th 1219, 1235 (10th Cir. 2021), *cert. denied*, 142 S. Ct. 2647 (2022).

[69] TEX. GOV'T CODE ANN. § 423.003 (2019).

[70] TEX. GOV'T CODE ANN. §§ 423.0045–423.0046 (2019).

[71] Nat'l Press Photographers Ass'n v. McCraw, No. 1:19-CV-946-RP, 2022 WL 939517 (W.D. Tex. Mar. 28, 2022), *appeal docketed*, No. 22-50337 (5th Cir. May 3, 2022).

[72] *Id.* at *3.

[73] *Id.*

[74] *Id.* at *8.

that the Texas drone law restricted the plaintiffs' ability to use drones to "record the news," which correspondingly restricted their right to disseminate that news. Furthermore, it concluded that budgetary and other constraints made it impossible for news organizations to gather some information in the absence of drones.[75]

Because it found the law to be a content-based restriction on speech, the court applied strict scrutiny to the law and struck it down because it found that the state had not demonstrated that the law was "actually necessary" to serve its interests in protecting private property, individual privacy, and the safety of critical infrastructure facilities.[76] It pointed out that the law was both substantially overinclusive and underinclusive to address the state's purported interests.[77] Finally, the court noted in dicta that the law was also invalid because it was unconstitutionally vague in its definitions of "surveillance" and "commercial purposes," causing it to create a chilling effect for journalists uncertain of its potential application to their newsgathering.[78] The state has now appealed the case to the Fifth Circuit, however, so the state of the law on this topic will continue to evolve.

Doctrinal developments in the area of data acquisition are promising as well. In the *Western Watersheds Project* case, in which plaintiffs challenged the Wyoming data trespass law discussed earlier, the state contended that collection of resource data is conduct, not speech. Rejecting this claim, the Tenth Circuit held that "[a]n individual who photographs animals or takes notes about habitat conditions is creating speech in the same manner as an individual who records a police encounter."[79] Furthermore, although collection of water or soil samples is further afield from typical speech creation than, say, engaging in video recording, the court noted that because the law's prohibitions coupled such collection with the recording of either a legal description or the geographical coordinates of where the collection took place, the regulated conduct was nevertheless at the front end of the speech continuum.[80] Consistent with the Supreme Court's cases acknowledging the dangers of state regulation of speech-creating activity, the Tenth Circuit acknowledged that "[i]f the creation of speech did not warrant protection under the First Amendment, the government could bypass the Constitution by 'simply proceed[ing] upstream and dam[ming] the source' of speech."[81]

Returning to scraping audits and sock puppet audits, the two computer tools used to detect unlawful discrimination on websites, the law here is developing as well. One impediment to using such tools to gather data is the federal Computer Fraud

---

[75] *Id.* at *9.

[76] *Id.* at *11.

[77] *Id.* at *11–12.

[78] *Id.* at *12.

[79] *W. Watersheds Project*, 869 F.3d at 1196 (citing *Am. Civ. Liberties Union of Ill.*, 679 F.3d at 595–96).

[80] *Id.* at 1197.

[81] *Id.* at 1196 (alteration in original) (quoting *Buehrle v. City of Key West*, 813 F.3d 973, 977 (11th Cir. 2015)).

and Abuse Act (CFAA),[82] which prohibits fraudulent access to computers or access that exceeds the scope of authorized permission by imposing both criminal penalties and civil liability. Some courts have applied CFAA to persons who have violated a site's terms of service on the grounds that such access may be without, or has exceeded, the user's authorization.[83] Not surprisingly, many websites' terms of service prohibit using data scraping tools or creating fake user profiles, and using the auditing tools might therefore well violate CFAA.[84]

In *Sandvig v. Sessions*,[85] several researchers and a media organization who wished to use computer auditing tools to identify discrimination on commercial websites sued the US Attorney General seeking a decision that CFAA violated their First Amendment rights and an injunction against their prosecution under the act. Specifically, the plaintiffs challenged the CFAA provision that imposes punishment on anyone who "intentionally accesses a computer without authorization or exceeds authorized access, and thereby obtains ... information from any protected computer."[86] The government moved to dismiss the case on the grounds that the plaintiffs lacked standing and had failed to state a valid First Amendment claim.[87] The federal district court rejected the motion, concluding that computer tools used to access data on a website are analogous to devices used to make recordings.[88] The court expanded on this analysis as follows:

> That plaintiffs wish to scrape data from websites rather than manually record information does not change the analysis. Scraping is merely a technological advance that makes information collection easier; it is not meaningfully different from using a tape recorder instead of taking written notes, or using the panorama function on a smartphone instead of taking a series of photos from different positions. And, as already discussed, the information plaintiffs seek is located in a

---

[82] 18 U.S.C. § 1030 (2018).
[83] *See, e.g.*, United States v. Lowson, No. CRIM. 10-114 KSH, 2010 WL 9552416, at *5, 8 (D.N.J. Oct. 12, 2010) (denying motion to dismiss an indictment on CFAA charges when the alleged conduct involved violations of the website's terms of service). *But see, e.g.*, United States v. Drew, 259 F.R.D. 449, 464 (C.D. Cal. 2009) (holding that CFAA prosecution for violation of terms of service agreement violated void for vagueness doctrine). For a discussion of the potentially problematic scope of CFAA, see Orin S. Kerr, *Cybercrime's Scope: Interpreting "Access" and "Authorization" in Computer Misuse Statutes*, 78 N.Y.U. L. REV. 1596, 1598, 1628–34, 1648–60 (2003).
[84] Airbnb's terms of service, for example, prohibit the use of "bots, crawlers, scrapers, or other automated means to access or collect data or other content from or otherwise interact with the Airbnb Platform." *Terms of Service*, AIRBNB (Feb. 10, 2022), www.airbnb.com/help/article/2908/terms-of-service. ZipRecruiter's terms of service forbid any job seeker to "post or submit any inaccurate, incomplete, or false biographical information or another person's information." *Global Terms of Use Agreement*, ZIPRECRUITER (Aug. 26, 2022), www.ziprecruiter.com/terms#s1.
[85] 315 F. Supp. 3d 1 (D.D.C. 2018).
[86] *Id.* at 8 (quoting 18 U.S.C. § 1030(a)(2)(C)).
[87] *Id.* at 11.
[88] *Id.* at 15–16, 34.

public forum. Hence, plaintiffs' attempts to record the contents of public websites for research purposes are arguably affected with a First Amendment interest.[89]

In a later decision, the court ruled that CFAA is not implicated by a violation of the terms of service alone and dismissed the case as moot.[90] But this case and others like it are likely to shape an important aspect of First Amendment doctrine as it pertains to automated data collection.

In *Van Buren v. United States*,[91] the Supreme Court reviewed the scope of CFAA, albeit not in a free speech context. There, the defendant was a police officer who had been convicted under CFAA for receiving payment for using his lawful access to a police database of state-issued license plates for a reason not related to law enforcement. The United States charged him with violating CFAA's provision making it a crime "to access a computer with authorization and to use such access to obtain or alter information in the computer that the accesser is not entitled so to obtain or alter."[92] The lower courts had concluded that Van Buren violated this provision because he accessed the license plate database for an "inappropriate reason," but the Court rejected that interpretation and overturned his conviction. In an opinion written by Justice Barrett, the Court concluded that Van Buren did not violate the terms of the statute because he was authorized both to access the computer and to use it to obtain information about the identity of a person based on her license plate number.[93]

While the Court's conclusion was based primarily on its reading of the statutory language and the statute's legislative history, it also expressed alarm at the potential breadth of the government's interpretation of CFAA. Noting that the United States had essentially argued that Van Buren was guilty because his conduct violated the police department's computer-user policy, the Court observed that such a reading would mean that any employee who accessed their personal email accounts or a news site from their work computer could be prosecuted under the law.[94] And further, the Court warned, if the violation of an employer's policy about its employees' use of their work computers constituted a violation of CFAA, so too would a computer user's access to a website or service that violated that site's terms of service.[95] If that were the case, the government's reading would "criminalize everything from embellishing an on-line dating profile to using a pseudonym on Facebook."[96]

---

[89]  *Id.* at 16.
[90]  *Sandvig v. Barr*, 451 F. Supp. 3d 73, 76 (D.D.C. 2020). The decision was initially appealed, but that appeal was later dismissed. 2021 WL 2525027 (D.C. Cir. June 10, 2021).
[91]  141 S. Ct. 1648 (2021).
[92]  18 U.S.C. § 1030.
[93]  *Van Buren*, 141 S. Ct. at 1662.
[94]  *Id.* at 1661.
[95]  *Id.*
[96]  *Id.*

Though the plaintiffs in the *Sandvig* case, discussed above, were researchers, data scraping tools can also be a valuable form of speech creation for journalists. And indeed, the Reporters Committee for Freedom of the Press (RCFP) and other media entities, as well as those engaged in online civil rights testing, filed amicus briefs in *Van Buren*. In the RCFP amicus brief, the journalists challenged the government's broad interpretation of CFAA, arguing that it would chill journalists from using web scraping tools, which it noted are an "increasingly common data-journalism technique."[97] The RCFP identified multiple examples of journalistic uses of such tools to gather information on important matters of public concern and reporting that information to the public. For instance, it noted, "journalists have used web-scraping techniques to identify doctors nationwide that have continued to practice after being caught sexually abusing patients – a reporting feat that was not practically feasible through traditional means," and to "evaluate prison conditions," "to reveal to the public that the National Park Service had removed from its website 'politically inconvenient environmental information related to efforts to reduce carbon emissions,'" and to carry out an ongoing project "identifying new or changed missing person cases."[98]

The plaintiffs from the *Sandvig* case, along with the ACLU, the Knight First Amendment Institute, and other parties, also filed an amicus brief in *Van Buren*. Their brief mentioned the importance of using computer data tools to engage in the modern equivalent of civil rights testing. As they argued, "[c]ivil rights enforcement in the twenty-first century relies on audit techniques and basic research methods that bear no resemblance to hacking, but are nonetheless commonly prohibited by exceptionally broad terms of service" on many websites.[99] They explained that because people seeking loans, jobs, housing, and other things must now do so online, they are subject to potential discrimination through algorithms that can "enable intentional and unintentional discrimination."[100] Accordingly, it is necessary for those seeking to identify such discrimination to use outcomes-based audit testing, which "is a way to determine whether users are experiencing discrimination in transactions covered by civil rights laws on the basis of their protected class status."[101] To carry out these investigations, researchers sometimes create fictitious profiles for fictitious job seekers, using them to acquire information in the same way as paired testers have long used in person to uncover discrimination. These amici then catalogued a range of research studies employing these techniques to identify discrimination on websites advertising housing, payday lending, insurance, and

---

[97] Brief for the Reporters Committee for Freedom of the Press et al. as Amicus Curiae in Support of Petitioner at 4, Van Buren v. United States, 141 S. Ct. 1648 (2021) (No. 19-783).
[98] *Id.* at 14 (citations omitted).
[99] Brief for Kyratso Karahalios, et al. as Amicus Curiae in Support of Petitioner at 4, Van Buren v. United States, 141 S. Ct. 1648 (2021) (No. 19-783).
[100] *Id.* at 7–8.
[101] *Id.* at 10.

education, and to show biases in facial recognition technologies used by law enforcement, just to name a few.[102] And these studies not only have led to enforcement of the laws but also have contributed to legal reforms and public policy debates.

Finally, an amicus brief from the National Whistleblower Center illustrated how a broad reading of CFAA would undermine federal laws protecting whistleblowers. Whistleblowers could be chilled by the potential that their employers could bring civil actions against them for violating the employers' computer-use policies in accessing information they then turned over to law enforcement authorities or other government agencies.[103]

Although the Supreme Court has yet to fully acknowledge the notion of speech creation as within the First Amendment's scope, contemporary circumstances suggest that it will have to address the issue at some point in the near future. It's worth noting that rejecting the claim that speech creation or production is "speech" would fundamentally undermine the protection of essential components that rest on the speech continuum. Displaying a photograph would be speech, but not taking one. Writing in a diary would not be speech unless there was an intended audience. Attending a protest might be speech, but not buying the materials to create or creating a banner or protest sign.

Furthermore, the implications for newsgathering, whether by professional journalists or citizens, would be severe. The Supreme Court has held that journalists are not exempt from otherwise generally applicable laws, but it has somewhat opaquely suggested that this does not mean "that [newsgathering] does not qualify for First Amendment protection."[104] It has acknowledged that "without some protection for seeking out the news, freedom of the press could be eviscerated."[105] Yet the Court has never expounded on the scope or extent of such protection. As discussed above, newsgathering itself is an important component of speech creation. Some newsgathering activities, such as interviewing a source, are unambiguously speech. But much journalism involves collecting, digesting, and organizing information and data and recording events, images, and sounds. That process continues with refinement, confirmation, writing, and editing, all before the speech is ever published. At a time when public trust in the press is waning,[106] it is critical to protect newsgathering as a form of speech creation as a way of bolstering the ability of the news media to discover and publish factually accurate information to promote public interest and deliberation.

---

[102] *Id.* at 12–13.
[103] Brief for the National Whistleblower Center as Amicus Curiae in Support of Petitioner at 2–3, Van Buren v. United States, 141 S. Ct. 1648 (2021) (No. 19-783).
[104] Branzburg v. Hayes, 408 U.S. 665, 681 (1972).
[105] *Id.*
[106] *See* Lee Rainie, Scott Keeter, & Andrew Perrin, *Trust and Distrust in America*, PEW RSCH. CTR. (July 22, 2019), www.pewresearch.org/politics/2019/07/22/trust-and-distrust-in-america/.

## 5.4 SOME CHALLENGES AND LOOKING AHEAD

As with most technological developments, the availability of inexpensive speech-creating tools has some negative externalities as well. It is worth exploring what those might be and addressing how the First Amendment can be deployed to protect speech that advances the goals of free expression while allowing some room for restriction of the most harmful instantiations of speech creation. This section addresses a few of the most obvious costs of cheap speech creation: the abuse of the right to record by misleading editing and display, making a video appear to show something that it does not and the related problem of deep fake videos;[107] the apparent proliferation of "fake news";[108] and the documented privacy harms caused by "revenge porn."[109]

### 5.4.1 *Misleading Editing and Manipulation of Images*

The ability to inexpensively create socially valuable speech also, not surprisingly, makes it easy to create expression that is less valuable or, worse, produces significant social harms.[110] With the same tools that a citizen journalist can use to create an independent newsletter, another person can design a masthead for a fictional newspaper and simply make up and publish false news stories that may mislead its readers.

The First Amendment value of speech creation is largely dependent on such actions resulting in a form of expression that is accurate and truthful.[111] At least with regard to political speech, there may be problems associated with audiovisual

---

[107] Deepfake videos have been described "as shorthand for the full range of hyper-realistic digital falsification of images, video, and audio." Bobby Chesney & Danielle Citron, *Deep Fakes: A Looming Challenge for Privacy, Democracy, and National Security*, 107 CAL. L. REV. 1753, 1757 (2019).

[108] There is at least some evidence that the problem of fake news, while commanding the public's attention more than ever before, has not had a great influence on American politics or elections. *See, e.g.*, Andrew Guess, Brendan Nyhan, & Jason Reifler, *Exposure to Untrustworthy Websites in the 2016 Election*, 4 NATURE HUM. BEHAV. 472 (2020).

[109] Danielle Keats Citron & Mary Anne Franks, *Criminalizing Revenge Porn*, 49 WAKE FOREST L. REV. 345, 346 (2014) (advocating for criminalization of revenge porn and discussing potential First Amendment implications).

[110] In this section, we touch on some of the major concerns, as well as some preliminary responses to those concerns, but do not mean our analysis to represent a comprehensive response to these challenges.

[111] Alan K. Chen, *Free Speech, Rational Deliberation, and Some Truths about Lies*, 62 WM. & MARY L. REV. 357, 362 (2020) (noting that "a central claim that underlies much First Amendment theory" is that "speech's value is primarily connected to its ability to facilitate rational deliberation in its audience, thus advancing the goals of promoting democracy and truth finding"). There are, however, other theories about the values of free speech that are not dependent on factual truth, such as the notion that the First Amendment's function should be to promote individual self-realization. *See* Martin H. Redish, *The Value of Free Speech*, 130 U. PA. L. REV. 591, 593 (1982).

recordings, photographs, or other images that have been manipulated in ways that undermine their reliability. In many contexts, video recordings can be even more reliable than other tools for creating speech, such as note taking or dictation. Rather than having whatever is observed be filtered through the speaker's own biases and faulty memory, the recording is in some ways self-authenticating and therefore more reliable.

But as the United States in particular enters what some consider a "post-truth" era in which lies and deception dominate political discourse, there is reason for caution. When the political party of law and order that campaigns against reducing the size of police forces spins the federal investigation of former President Trump as a justification to "defund the FBI," then one must expect that persons confronting an unfavorable video exposure will simply claim that the video is doctored or misleading. But, of course, sometimes a video image *can* be manipulated. In recent years, we have witnessed a couple of incidents of secret video recordings by conservative activists affiliated with Project Veritas[112] and some anti-abortion groups in which the accuracy of the published recording has been seriously challenged.[113] There is, of course, no ideological valence for accuracy, so the same thing could occur with progressive activists. As we discussed in Chapter 4, Project Veritas and its founder, James O'Keefe, have been called out for inaccuracies in the way they have edited videos produced by their investigations.[114] In his infamous investigation of ACORN, in which O'Keefe pretended to engage an ACORN employee in a plan to smuggle underage girls into the United States for prostitution, O'Keefe published an edited version of the video that appeared to show that employee offering support for parts of the plan.[115] The controversy contributed to ACORN's dissolution.[116]

We also reported in Chapter 4 that the anti-abortion group Center for Medical Progress (CMP) secretly recorded conversations with individuals who worked with Planned Parenthood and the National Abortion Federation, but those organizations argued that the videos were edited in such a way that misled viewers regarding the substance of the conversation.[117]

---

[112] PROJECT VERITAS, www.projectveritas.com/ (last visited Jan. 15, 2021).

[113] *See* Jackie Calmes, *Video Accuses Planned Parenthood of Crime*, N.Y. TIMES (July 15, 2015), www.nytimes.com/2015/07/15/us/video-accuses-planned-parenthood-of-crime.html.

[114] *See, e.g.*, Conor Friedersdorf, *Still Making an Innocent Man Look Bad*, ATLANTIC (Dec. 29, 2010), www.theatlantic.com/daily-dish/archive/2010/12/still-making-an-innocent-man-look-bad/177964/ (emphasizing "misleading" nature of O'Keefe's videos, making "innocent man look as if he was complicit in a plot to traffic underage girls across the border"); Alexander Nazaryan, *James O'Keefe: Meet the Man Who Makes the Fake News*, NEWSWEEK (Jan. 17, 2018), www.newsweek.com/2018/02/02/james-okeefe-project-veritas-american-pravda-fake-news-781964.html (criticizing O'Keefe for purposefully and grossly misrepresenting facts in several videos that purport to uncover and reveal wrongdoing).

[115] Vera v. O'Keefe, No. 10-CV-1422, 2012 WL 3263930, at *961 (S.D. Cal. Aug. 9, 2012).

[116] *Id.*

[117] Calmes, *supra* note 113.

While these are surely concerning incidents, it is also important to note that the target of an investigation can also lie about the accuracy of the videos to protect its reputation. For example, it was common when undercover investigations of factory farms first appeared on publicly available video platforms for the targeted corporation to suggest or state that the video was manipulated or did not present a fair picture.[118]

Though there is little doubt that the issues that were the subject of the recordings in these disputes were matters of public concern and would otherwise be of First Amendment value, the manipulation and editing of videos in ways that communicate something that is objectively not true raise important questions about the limits on the right to record. Although the Supreme Court has recognized that false statements of fact are not categorically exempt from First Amendment coverage, it has also stated that lies that cause legally cognizable or tangible harms are not protected as speech.[119] If false representations of fact through manipulation of videos causes such harms, constitutional protection from their regulation may no longer apply.[120]

Similarly, it is not just the editing of videos that can make them misleading, and therefore potentially harm causing. A video might also be misleading if it reflects anecdotal, unrepresentative, or selective information about the activities recorded, thus not fairly depicting the events it purports to have documented. A video's accuracy might also be affected by camera angles or production choices.

One might take from the above discussion that any editing or incomplete disclosure of video footage risks forfeiting legal protection. But that is not the point being made. On the contrary, it is important to recognize that editing itself can be a form of speech in that it is an important component of the ultimate communicative project. In a highlight video of a soccer player's career, it may appear that the player is flawless, and constantly scoring goals, which of course would be an exaggeration. But the point of the compilation is to highlight some of the athlete's greatest moments, and it does not purport to show every minute, or even the standard or average minutes of the player's career. Likewise, a film highlighting only the worst moments of child abuse during many hours of video footage at a daycare would not be misleading insofar as the video was the only tangible evidence of wrongdoing caught on tape, and not suggesting that the abuse occurred constantly.

---

[118] *See, e.g.*, Elizabeth Lee, *USDA Probes PETA Claim against Tyson*, ATLANTA J. & CONST., Jan. 18, 2008.

[119] *See* United States v. Alvarez, 567 U.S. 709, 719 (2012) (plurality opinion) ("[T]he knowingly false statement and the false statement made with reckless disregard of the truth, do not enjoy constitutional protection" (quoting Garrison v. State of Louisiana, 379 U.S. 64, 75 (1964))); *see also id.* at 734 (Breyer, J., concurring in the judgment).

[120] Some state courts have considered editing videos to create misleading communications to be defamatory. *See, e.g.*, Nguyen v. Taylor, 723 S.E.2d 551, 558 (N.C. Ct. App. 2012).

Simply put, in films, editing is an art form worthy of recognition by the relevant artistic community. For political videos, editing can highlight key aspects of the information documented and can present them in informative, but also persuasive, ways, as in a documentary film. It seems that the development of some sorts of editorial standards is necessary to draw distinctions between editing that has speech value and editing that is tantamount to fraud. One key feature of any such standards would be a focus on what the video purports to show, and whether the clip can be viewed as fairly conveying the events recorded. A video of Lionel Messi's greatest soccer bloopers, no less than a video showing his greatest goals, would be protected speech. But a video that was edited so as to suggest that something happened that did not or that claimed facts not substantiated by the footage would be deceptive.

A related, but slightly different and perhaps even more pernicious problem arises from the proliferation of so-called deepfake videos. Deepfake videos employ advanced digital technology and artificial intelligence to create and manipulate video images in ways that display images of a person saying or doing something that in reality was never said or done.[121] These images may be a more powerful communication vehicle that is even more difficult to rebut than false statements of fact, yet they are also capable of causing tangible and perhaps even tragic harms. For example, as Professors Chesney and Citron have argued,

> In addition to the ability of deep fakes to inject visual and audio falsehoods into policy debates, a deeply convincing variation of a long-standing problem in politics, deep fakes can enable a particularly disturbing form of sabotage: distribution of a damaging, but false, video or audio about a political candidate. The potential to sway the outcome of an election is real, particularly if the attacker is able to time the distribution such that there will be enough window for the fake to circulate but not enough window for the victim to debunk it effectively (assuming it can be debunked at all).[122]

While many deepfake videos that have appeared have been relatively innocuous or intended as parody, we have begun to witness the exhibition of deepfake videos that, if not detected, or detected in time, could cause substantial harms. For example, in 2022, shortly after the Russian invasion of Ukraine, someone hacked into a Ukrainian television station and broadcast a deepfake video of President Volodymyr Zelenskyy ordering his troops to surrender to Russia.[123] Needless to say, wrongful information conveyed to military troops during an active war could have tragic consequences. It isn't difficult to imagine that widespread deepfake videos could cause unwarranted panic (or unwarranted *calm*) in the face of a natural

---

[121] *See* Chesney & Citron, *supra* note 107.
[122] *Id.* at 1778. *But see* Glenn Bow, *Deepfakes Are Bad – Deepfakes Are Good*, FORBES (Sept. 11, 2020), www.forbes.com/sites/glenngow/2020/09/11/deepfakes-are-baddeepfakes-are-good/?sh=22e1ee964ba0 (suggesting that there can be socially beneficial uses of deepfake videos).
[123] *Heads of States, Celebrities Targeted by Deep Fake videos*, NEWS INT'L (PAK.), Oct. 13, 2022.

disaster. They could be used to perpetuate false impressions about politicians' statements during an election.

One response to these problems might be narrowly targeted regulations to check fraudulent editing of real videos and the creation of deepfake images. Even if the First Amendment does and should protect the creation of truthful video images on matters of public concern, that should not forbid legal sanctions for misrepresentation of images. There is no right to mislead or provide false impressions through video recording. No one could reasonably assert a right to record and cause damage through the presentation of untruthful (or substantially untrue) broadcasts. This consideration may cause courts to look differently at situations in which the video is alleged to be edited or otherwise presented in a way that conveys untruthful information.

Furthermore, in addition to making these misleading video images possible, technology can also expand the possibilities for responding to deepfake or other altered and edited videos. One example comes from a report about city council candidate Alicia Roth Weigel in Austin, Texas:

> [W]hen a conservative pundit recently edited an interview with [Weigel] for a YouTube channel and used it in a paid media campaign, she began receiving hate mail. Weigel fought back by re-editing the piece with her own core messages intact and turning it into a counter piece that resonated with her base. That familiarity with tech, aided by an understanding of voter interests and her learned marketing skills, allowed her to turn a potentially bad moment into a positive one.[124]

Of course, the opportunity to rebut these videos may require sufficient notice and time, so corrective measures may not always be an adequate solution. There are increasing efforts to design systems that will help detect deepfake videos. But some reports suggest that in what has emerged as something of an arms race, those who develop fake video technology far outnumber those working on tools to detect deepfake videos.[125]

### 5.4.2 *Fake News*

Another negative externality of the inexpensiveness of speech creation and distribution (though other conditions are relevant as well) is the proliferation of fake news. Many years ago, Professor Volokh predicted that the expanded availability of the internet would mean that speakers would no longer have to rely on speech intermediaries such as the professional media, which would lead to the dissemination of less trustworthy speech. Individual speakers, he wrote, "might not be willing to hire

---

[124] Welson-Rossman, *supra* note 8.

[125] Drew Harwell, *Top AI Researchers Race to Detect "Deepfake" Videos: "We Are Outgunned,"* Wash. Post. (June 12, 2019), www.washingtonpost.com/technology/2019/06/12/top-ai-research ers-race-detect-deepfake-videos-we-are-outgunned/.

fact checkers, or might not be influenced enough by professional journalistic norms, or might not care enough about their long-term reputation for accuracy," though he also said it was not clear how significant the "magnitude of the greater inaccuracy would be."[126]

The apparent proliferation of "fake news" in our contemporary speech and political climate would seem to validate this part of Volokh's prediction, not only for speakers unwilling to conform to professional journalistic norms but also for those who intentionally wish to mislead the public. The problem in addressing fake news is that there are strong arguments why its regulation might violate the First Amendment, particularly in light of the Supreme Court's decision in *United States v. Alvarez*.[127] As we discussed at length in Chapter 3, *Alvarez* invalided the Stolen Valor Act, a federal statute making it a crime to lie about having received certain military honors from the United States.[128] The plurality of the Court, coupled with a concurring opinion, suggested that the government can prohibit false factual statements only when they cause a tangible harm or produce an undeserved material gain on the part of the liar, as in the case of fraud.[129] Many lower courts have distinguished *Alvarez*'s application based on the context of the particular lie. When the false statement is made in the context of an undercover investigation, for example, but causes no harm to the listener, courts have held the lies to be protected by the First Amendment.[130] But it has always been the case that lies that cause tangible harms to others may be subject to government regulation.[131]

Beyond limited regulations of harm-causing lies, effective and constitutional responses to fake news, therefore, are more likely to come from nonrestrictive measures that facilitate the ability of consumers to detect information provided from questionable sources, technological tools that help to detect fake news, and from the widespread and rapid dissemination of fact-checking platforms.[132] These same tools might help address the deepfake videos problem. Furthermore, there may be narrowly drawn regulations of fake news that can withstand First Amendment scrutiny when the speech causes tangible harms to readily identifiable victims.[133]

---

[126] Volokh, *supra* note 2, at 1838.

[127] 567 U.S. 709.

[128] *Id.* at 730. Justice Breyer's concurring opinion agrees with this holding. *Id.* at 736 (Breyer, J., concurring in the judgment).

[129] *Id.* at 734–36.

[130] *See, e.g., Wasden*, 878 F.3d at 1194–99 (emphasizing how entry to property is the only material gain in this context, but that entry in itself is not a cognizable harm).

[131] *See, e.g.,* Illinois, ex rel. Madigan v. Telemarketing Assocs., Inc., 538 U.S. 600, 612 (2003) (emphasizing that the First Amendment "does not shield fraud").

[132] *See* Chen, *supra* note 111, at 425–27.

[133] *Id.* at 418–19.

### 5.4.3 *Revenge Porn*

The cheapness of speech creation also has made it possible for unscrupulous people, almost always men, to record intimate sexual encounters with their partners and distribute them on the internet without the partner's consent.[134] Even if the original encounter and video recording is done with the partner's consent, the distribution is most frequently not, thus causing deep and indelible privacy concerns. Here, legislative enactments of criminal or civil penalties for distribution of nonconsensual pornography or "revenge porn" have been, for the most part, upheld by the courts that have examined them against First Amendment challenges, though on different theories.[135] A complete discussion of the constitutionality of revenge porn prohibitions would require a great deal more time and space. For now, we make the following observations.

First, there are important distinctions between the decision of private individuals to *create* a consensual video of their intimate sexual encounters and the act of one of those involved to *publish* the video without the other's consent. The consensual creation of a sex video itself can be an important and valuable form of speech creation, made for the private use of those involved. Just as memorializing one's most intimate thoughts in a diary or in private correspondence with another person are speech, so too is the act of creating a private sex video.[136] Thus, the distinction that some courts have drawn about the constitutionality of revenge porn being that the recordings involve purely private activity rather than matters of public concern[137] could arguably be used to justify prohibitions of the creation of consensual sex videos.

But there are two other critical distinctions between revenge porn videos and the types of valuable, speech-creating videos discussed in this chapter. First, revenge porn laws regulate not speech creation, but speech *distribution*, and therefore do not need to influence our understandings about the degree of the right to record per se.[138] Second, and more critically, to the extent that government restrictions on the

---

[134] *See* Citron & Franks, *supra* note 109, at 348–49. For a comprehensive resource about the state of laws and litigation regarding revenge porn, see CYBER CIV. RTS. INITIATIVE, https://cybercivilrights.org/ (last visited Nov. 20, 2022).

[135] *See, e.g.*, State v. Katz, 179 N.E.3d 431, 456–60 (Ind. 2022) (concluding that revenge porn is speech, but that the law was narrowly tailored to serve a compelling governmental interest and therefore not facially unconstitutional); State v. Casillas, 952 N.W.2d 629, 644 (Minn. 2020), *cert. denied*, 142 S. Ct. 90 (2021) (same); State v. VanBuren, 210 Vt. 293, 323 (2019) (same); People v. Austin, 155 N.E.3d 439, 456, 475 (Ill. 2019) (upholding state revenge porn law on the grounds that it was a content-neutral time, place, and manner restriction and also regulated a purely private matter).

[136] *Cf.* Danielle Keats Citron, *Intimate Privacy's Protection Enables Free Speech*, 2 JOURNAL OF FREE SPEECH LAW 3, 8 (2022) ("After we have been secretly recorded having sex or our nude image is shared online in betrayal of our trust, intimate expression can seem dangerous, almost foolhardy, lest it be weaponized against us again.").

[137] *See VanBuren*, 210 Vt. at 321.

[138] Of course, as we have noted, limits on speech can be placed upstream from the speech, such as at the stage of preventing a recording. Likewise, limits on the downstream display or distribution of recordings could also implicate free speech concerns.

distribution of speech are constitutionally suspect, so long as those measures are narrowly tailored to target revenge porn and not chill socially valuable speech, it would seem hard to dispute that protection of privacy in this context is a compelling state interest.[139] Therefore, though revenge porn probably counts as speech under the First Amendment, its regulation is likely to survive even the most rigorous form of constitutional scrutiny. And such regulation can likely be carried out without prohibiting or chilling speech that has social value.

\* \* \*

In the next chapter, we turn our attention to public attitudes and opinions about the value and credibility of undercover investigations based on our empirical research.

---

[139] *See Katz*, 179 N.E.3d at 456–60; *VanBuren*, 210 Vt. at 317–23. It is hard to conceive of reasoned arguments in favor of protecting the nonconsensual disclosure of intimate videos, and scholars have certainly made a strong case for protecting such privacy. *See, e.g.*, Danielle Citron, *Restricting Speech to Protect It*, *in* Free Speech in the Digital Age (Susan J. Brison & Katharine Gelber eds., 2019). But one might argue that there is something of a slippery slope problem afoot. For many persons the disclosure of intimate images may be the most damaging privacy invasion imaginable. But for others, at least in some circumstances, non-video revelations of intimate secrets or indiscretions could be far worse. For some, a verbal report disclosing a public kiss with a secret acquaintance or coworker might be more devastating than would any image. An audio clip speaking poorly about one's boss or revealing one's most deeply held, intimate secrets might be subjectively worse than an image showing a sexual act. The point here is not to diminish the privacy invasions inherent to revenge porn, but to note that it cannot be that the absence of consent to disclose intimate matters alone creates a freestanding, categorical limit on what counts as speech.

# 6

## Public Perceptions of Undercover Investigations

### 6.1 INTRODUCTION

The material in this book has thus far argued that undercover investigations are an important tool for professional journalists, citizen journalists, and political activists to gain access to information of public concern and then disseminate that information widely. The assumption throughout these discussions has been that the publication of such information may promote public awareness and influence public opinion, and thereby materially enhance democracy. That assumption is itself based on two distinct premises: first, that such investigations will be generally viewed as credible and reliable by the general public, and second, that the information revealed by investigative journalism and whistleblowing (which sometimes, but does not always, involve undercover investigations) does, in fact, influence public opinion. The latter question has been the subject of social science research, which we discuss below.

To date, however, there is very little research on the first question – how the general public feels about undercover investigations when they reveal truthful and valuable information. Indeed, there has been virtually no empirical research about undercover investigations at all. Understanding public views about these investigations is important for its own sake, but also relates to the legal and policy conversations about how society might respond to these tactics. In this chapter we consider whether the public is generally receptive to the idea of undercover investigations. We further explore the degree to which such acceptance is path dependent. Do an investigator's political motives diminish public acceptance of an investigation? Does political party (and thereby ideology) influence receptivity to undercover investigations? Will the investigation be received differently depending on who the messenger is, or who the investigative target is? For example, are Democrats less likely to trust investigations that serve Republican interests, and vice versa?

As previous chapters have emphasized, support for undercover investigations has varied over time. At certain points in history, investigators have been heralded as national heroes and their investigations have spurred political action. At other times, or in other conditions, investigators seem to be villainized and their efforts labeled as unethical conduct, privacy intrusions, property rights violations, political theater, or worse. Some of these variations are no doubt a result of cyclical historical patterns regarding the conditions that make the public amenable to investigative efforts, factors beyond the control of an undercover investigator. But in our view, a thorough study of undercover investigations would be deficient if it failed to account for the possibility that demographic factors or politically motivated reasoning might, at least partially, explain the public response to different investigations. This chapter reports on a unique set of experiments that may help us better understand public perceptions of undercover investigations.

We seek to provide the most comprehensive account to date of the factors impacting the public perceptions of undercover investigations on matters of public and political concern. Through a series of nationally representative studies, we sought to better understand US adults' support for and opposition to undercover investigations generally, and under specific conditions that describe the nature of the investigating entity, the investigative target, or the investigated behavior. Given the heavily partisan nature of contemporary Americans and the controversies surrounding undercover investigations, we expected that public approval of such investigations might vary depending on how closely the respondents' views related to the ideology of the investigator, the ideology of the investigative target, and the subject matter of the investigation. Instead, as detailed below, we found surprisingly widespread support for undercover investigations across partisan divides in ways that may not have been previously understood. Our study also found that, with one exception, even investigations done by politically motivated entities with an expectation of good publicity and financial gain do not diminish public confidence in undercover investigations.

## 6.2 INVESTIGATIVE JOURNALISM, WHISTLEBLOWING, AND UNDERCOVER INVESTIGATIONS

Before discussing both prior research and our own study, we need to be precise about what we are studying as well as what past researchers have studied. There are three overlapping and related categories relevant to transparency in this context: whistleblowing, investigative journalism, and undercover investigations. We have focused our study on the discrete topic of undercover investigations, which we defined in Chapter 1 as follows:

> [T]he investigations . . . involve the investigator engaging in some form of deception toward the investigation's target, either affirmatively misrepresenting the investigator's identity, background, and motives or at least omitting information that would cause the target to turn them away. Second, the investigation uses the

deception or other tactic to access private property, information, or people. Third, the investigations reveal conduct that is unlawful, unethical, or immoral, or otherwise a matter of considerable public interest. Fourth, all of these investigations involve documenting the information discovered, whether by handwritten notes made while the investigator cannot be observed or by using hidden digital recording equipment, such as cameras, audio recorders, or video recorders. Finally, in each case the investigation targets seek to keep the information that is sought from public scrutiny, thus making it difficult if not impossible to obtain without an undercover investigation.[1]

By contrast, both investigative journalism and whistleblowing are categories that are distinct from undercover investigations, although there is important overlap. Investigative journalism is both broader and narrower than undercover investigations. It is broader, because as we discuss in Chapter 2 it involves a range of exhaustive investigative methods, including culling through documents (often acquired through freedom of information laws), interviewing sources, securing leaks from anonymous sources, and other dogged tactics not traditionally associated with more conventional journalism. Some investigative journalists engage in undercover investigations, but many do not. Investigative journalism is narrower than undercover investigations because it is usually associated with professional journalists affiliated with news media outlets. But as we have explained, undercover investigations may be conducted by professional journalists, citizen journalists, and political activists.

Whistleblowing is a term not necessarily linked to undercover investigations because it frequently involves some sort of insider, usually an employee or former employee, revealing something of public concern about their workplace. That is, whistleblowers are frequently people who are already in place, rather than those who set out to investigate another entity from the outside. Indeed, state and federal statutes sometimes define whistleblowing in this manner.[2] However, the definition is not always limited to employees. For example, the Dodd-Frank Wall Street Reform and Consumer Protection Act defines a whistleblower as "any individual who provides ... information relating to a violation of the securities laws to the [Securities and Exchange] Commission."[3] Thus, under that law, a whistleblower might be a non-employee who secured their information by an undercover investigation.

We do not endeavor here to clearly demarcate the boundaries of what constitutes whistleblowing or investigative journalism, but it is necessary to clarify that our original research is focused specifically on undercover practices that are a subset of these larger, umbrella concepts.

---

[1]   Chapter 1, at 18.
[2]   *See, e.g.*, 49 U.S.C. § 30172 (defining a whistleblower as "any employee or contractor of a motor vehicle manufacturer").
[3]   15 U.S.C. § 78u-6(a)(6).

In addressing the connection between investigations and public opinion and policy, there are two interesting empirical questions. First, does information provided to the public through investigative reporting and whistleblowing (whether by undercover investigation or not) shape the public's conscience and opinions, and perhaps then influence public policy, or does it simply reinforce and further entrench preexisting values? The prior literature that we describe here has something to say about this question.[4]

The second question, and what we set out to study in this chapter, is whether the public's perception of the value of undercover investigations in particular vary by the subject matter of the investigation, the political priors of the audience, the type of wrongdoing exposed by the investigation, the ideology or identity of the investigator, or the ideology or identity of the investigation's target. This is important because if opinions about undercover investigations differ based on these variables, this may in turn affect the prior question – whether investigations influence public opinion. If the investigation is not viewed as credible, ethical, or legal, that may in turn dilute its impact on public opinion. And if that effect differs by the variables we study, it may mean that public opinion is only *selectively* influenced by investigations. Despite the intuition that investigations are important, there has been surprisingly little quantitative research on the public reaction to investigative exposures. Indeed, prior research has almost entirely failed to engage directly with the question of how the public perceives undercover investigations, and instead has jumped to the question of whether any type of investigative journalism shapes public opinion.

## 6.3 PRIOR RESEARCH ON WHETHER INVESTIGATIONS GENERALLY INFLUENCE PUBLIC OPINION

For all three categories of information gathering and dissemination – investigative reporting, whistleblowing, and undercover investigations – there are important questions about whether and how they affect public opinion. In 2012, Brook Kroeger published one of the definitive accounts of undercover reporting, *The Truth about Deception*.[5] The book examines the intersection of undercover investigations and social change, noting, for example, that while undercover investigations have often been sensational, many of the investigators were doing the work not for "sensation's sake," but in pursuit of "a clear civic or social agenda."[6] Quite often

---

[4]  David Protess et al., The Journalism of Outrage: Investigative Reporting and Agenda Building in America 19 (1991) (noting that the link between investigative reporting and policy changes is often "weak and unreliable"). *Id.* at 20 (explaining that instead of public opinion creating changes, such changes may be the result of collaboration between journalists or investigators and key policymakers). In this vein, an apt summary of the relationship might be that "reporters and officials are like professional wrestlers – competing and cooperating in the performance of their jobs." *Id.* at 23.

[5]  Brooke Kroeger, The Truth about Deception (2012).

[6]  *Id.* at 195.

investigations are undertaken in order to "focus public attention on important social issues, to invite a wide public conversation, and to *have impact*."[7] Indeed, most persons who engage in undercover investigations would likely cite the actual social, political, legal, or attitudinal impacts of the disclosure of information as their primary motivation and their yardstick for measuring the success of an investigation. Kroeger's project provides numerous examples of undercover investigations that preceded and contributed to social reform. But the causal link between the investigations and subsequent law reform or social change is sometimes attenuated or assumed.

There may be something of a mythology around the impact of investigative journalism, whistleblowing, and undercover investigations that assumes that public opinion necessarily changes following an investigation of import, and that shift in public opinion leads inexorably to policy change. Viewed this way, muckrakers like Upton Sinclair and Nellie Bly helped change public opinion and thereby drove law reform agendas. And there is likely some truth to these narratives, but perhaps less so than is assumed. For starters, scientific measurements of public opinion were not available in the early twentieth century, so we don't really know how the public was responding to investigations of the day beyond the often anecdotal information available in the public record. A social scientist would surely wonder whether the very "societal conditions that bred muckraking journalism" also fueled "citizen outrage" and engagement in a way that was unique to the historical period.[8] The directional arrows of influence between the public and journalists, in other words, are perhaps a little more nuanced than the conventional narrative assumes.

Among political scientists and journalism scholars, the extent to which investigative journalism has actually generated civic engagement is hotly debated. It is often observed that voter turnout actually declined during the muckraking eras.[9] Perhaps agenda-setting or policy change occurred because investigators were savvy in leveraging direct relationships with politicians interested in the issue under investigation. Or perhaps investigators have pursued investigations on topics that were already on the radar of the public and policymakers. For example, in the stories crediting Sinclair with prompting the passage of the Pure Food and Drug Act, it is rarely mentioned that a version of the bill was pending in Congress prior to the publication of *The Jungle*.[10]

---

[7]  *Id.* at 63.

[8]  PROTESS ET AL., *supra* note 4, at 40. *See also id.* at 41 ("the rise of muckraking journalism and changes in public opinion are most likely the product of mutually reinforcing conditions"). It seems clear that some policy impacts were demonstrably linked to investigative journalism, but was it public opinion or investigations or both that "caused" these policy reforms? *Id.* (criticizing the overly tidy view of policy change as a linear progression from investigation to public opinion changes to policy changes).

[9]  Richard Harwood, *The Alienated American Voter: Are the News Media to Blame*, THE BROOKINGS INST., Sept. 1, 1996 ("Voter turnout fell 40 percent from 1896 to 1920").

[10]  PROTESS ET AL., *supra* note 4, at 42.

The point here is not to suggest that investigations cannot impact public opinion. Rather, the point is that the public reaction to information revealed through investigative journalism, whistleblowing, and undercover investigations (and any connection between public sentiment and law reform)[11] is an important empirical question.[12] A noteworthy limitation here is that the prior academic literature focuses not specifically on undercover investigations but on the broader categories of investigative journalism and whistleblowing (which, as we have explained, may or may not include an undercover component).

Before turning to our own research, it is worth exploring what prior research has found about the first question: Does information revealed by investigative journalists or whistleblowers meaningfully influence public opinion? The research about investigations' impact on public opinion is limited, and unfortunately not terribly revealing. One problem is that research on the importance of investigative journalism is "based largely on normative and anecdotal accounts."[13] Prior scholarship describes investigative reporting as capitalizing on "the journalism of outrage," yet concludes that the degree of journalism's influence on actual reforms is unclear.[14] Rather, the power they hold is the power to "engage the public's sense of right and wrong."[15]

For example, in one case study from 1996, Mary Bernstein and James Jasper described the role that whistleblowing and transparency played in triggering stricter government regulations of nuclear power.[16] As with similar case studies in this field, the research has a compelling narrative but lacks much by way of controls or hard evidence to show a causal link between the investigations and a shift in public opinion. Moreover, if public opinion and law reform were spurred by a particular investigation, then why have so many other investigations enjoyed less success?

---

[11] We must acknowledge, particularly in the midst of conversations about the antidemocratic nature of the Senate and the Supreme Court, that one might question whether changes to public opinion are even relevant to electoral politics. It is possible, both because of the structures of state and federal government and because of the disconnect between public opinion and public mobilization, that efforts that do shape public opinion might still not directly impact law and policy.

[12] *See also* PROTESS ET AL., *supra* note 4 (concluding that rather than shaping the public agenda, investigative journalism tends to reaffirm a developing public consensus or policy agenda). Ultimately, the authors of the Protess study conclude that investigative reporting plays a central role of media in developing and advancing a policy agenda, based on interviews with journalists and on case studies. Other researchers have noted the "scant attention ... paid to the question of how the audience perceives investigative reporting." Lars Willnat & David H. Weaver, *Public Opinion on Investigative Reporting: Has Anything Changed since the 1980s?*, 75 JOURNALISM & MASS COMMC'N Q. 449, 450 (1998).

[13] PROTESS ET AL., *supra* note 4, at 4.

[14] *Id.* at 4–6, 11, 15–20.

[15] *Id.* at 4.

[16] Mary Bernstein & James M. Jasper, *Interests and Credibility: Whistleblowers in Technological Conflicts*, 35 SOC. SCI. INFO. 565 (1996).

One of the most promising sources of information involved a group of researchers who creatively studied investigative journalism by gaining access to investigative journalism projects before they went public and by conducting public opinion surveys both before and after the public release of the investigation (the "Protess study").[17] Even at the time of the book's publication documenting this research in 1991, the research was somewhat dated, as all the studies focused on investigative journalism projects conducted in the 1980s. But the findings of public impact are nonetheless striking. The researchers documented a number of instances where persons who were exposed to media coverage of an investigation had a heightened sense of corruption or injustice regarding the specific investigated conduct relative to the control groups.[18] At least in some instances, the investigation appeared capable of changing public opinion. But many of the investigations studied did not measurably impact public opinion.

Another limitation for our purposes is that the Protess study examined investigative journalism more broadly, and did not focus on undercover investigations (though some of the investigations studied did use such tactics). The researchers did not distinguish between investigations that used undercover techniques such as deception and secret recording and other investigative techniques like open records research. In fact, that study called undercover investigations "perhaps the least commonly used, but most controversial" form of investigative journalism.[19] The research, in short, leaves one uncertain about what conclusions to draw about the public reaction to investigative journalism more generally, and really does nothing to advance the study of undercover investigations in particular.

Other studies, however, have attempted to study the narrower topic of undercover investigations. We have already explored at great length the ABC News investigation of the Food Lion grocery chain that revealed problems with sanitation and food handling, ultimately leading to litigation against the news network. A survey was conducted in the 1990s following that investigation. That survey found that about half of the persons who had heard of the investigation supported ABC News, while around 21% sided with the supermarket chain.[20]

---

[17] PROTESS ET AL., *supra* note 4, at 65 (describing their special access to the journalists that made such research possible).
[18] *See, e.g., id.* at 86, 133 (detailing changes in public opinion based on viewing a news segment on fraud in the home healthcare field and changes in opinion based on an investigation of police abuse). *But see id.* at 109 (noting that an investigative project around claimed under-enforcement by police of sexual assault laws did not "increase the salience of those issues to the public"). Notably, even investigations that do not produce changes in public opinion, when used strategically, can result in policy shifts. Indeed, several of the investigations documented by Protess and his colleagues do not show the traditional model of journalism shaping public opinion and thereby generating law reform, and thus the reforms that were achieved raise questions about this linear view of social change.
[19] PROTESS ET AL., *supra* note 4, at 217.
[20] Willnat & Weaver, *supra* note 12, at 450.

At one level, these findings are reassuring to those who endorse undercover investigations as a tool for change. But are these reactions idiosyncratic? Does the public hold ABC News, a mainstream news media outlet, in particularly high regard, thus skewing the results in a favorable direction? Or is the public inclined to support an investigation like this one because it is relevant to public health or basic consumer protection that affects ordinary shoppers? Or does the public find an employment-based investigation uniquely unethical, such that the results were *less* favorable than they would have been for most any other kind of investigation? Would the results have looked radically different if an activist organization had done the investigation instead of ABC, particularly if the activists had a vested political interest in making the Food Lion chain look bad?[21]

It is worth pausing to note that prior research has taken for granted that an investigator's bias or self-interest will undermine public confidence in the investigation.[22] It has been assumed that the public perception of self-serving or politically motivated investigations will be viewed materially less favorably than those conducted by a neutral reporter. Such a conclusion is consistent with the nascent body of research finding that how an investigation is framed or described affects the public reaction to the revelations. For example, if someone is called an investigator or a whistleblower, we might expect a markedly different public reaction to their disclosures than if they are called a leaker, an activist, or an infiltrator.[23] Prior research finds that public perception of disclosures varies based, in part, on the terms used to describe the disclosure, and the "public generally favors those" who are said to be engaging in "whistleblowing over those who leak" information.[24]

---

[21] In thinking about undercover investigations and the credibility of claims made about facts uncovered through such tactics, one must be mindful of the theory that there is "an automatic skepticism built into how we listen to others," such that claims are discounted by most audiences if the message tends to align with the speaker's agenda. Bernstein & Jasper, *supra* note 16, at 565 ("every claim put forward by a group or individual is discounted by most audiences according to how much it furthers the speaker's interests").

[22] *See, e.g.*, Milton Heumann et al., *Public Perceptions of Whistleblowing*, 18 PUB. INTEGRITY 6, 6–24 (2016).

[23] Note that even the term "whistleblower" is given varying definitions, some of which create a hierarchy that prioritizes investigations or revelations by persons who are already part of the entity being investigated, as opposed to outsiders who take a job or gain entry in order to expose wrongdoing. Other commentators disagree, suggesting that this clean binary between insider and outsider whistleblowing is artificial. *See* Brian K. Richardson & Johny Garner, *Stakeholders' Attributions of Whistleblowers: The Effects of Complicity and Motives on Perceptions of Likeability, Credibility, and Legitimacy*, 59 INT'L J. BUS. COMMC'N 334, 336 (2019) ("[A]s long as wrongdoing is being exposed, whistleblowers' motivations are irrelevant"). For purposes of this chapter it suffices to note that factors diminishing the perceived legitimacy of a whistleblower probably apply with equal or even greater force to an undercover investigator from the outside, whom some might consider something other than a true whistleblower.

[24] Michael R. Touchton et al., *Whistleblowing or Leaking? Public Opinion toward Assange, Manning, and Snowden*, RSCH. & POL. 1, 7 (2020) (noting, however, that this framing effect might apply only if the disclosure harms a person in the opposing political party); *id.* (observing a willingness to forgive leakers when the information "hurts the opposing party"). These

Likewise, prior scholarship tends to argue that undercover investigations carried out by partisan or activist organizations will be of substantially diminished value in the eyes of the public. For example, an investigation of housing discrimination, according to this view, will be received very differently by the public depending on whether the investigation was conducted by a journalist or an antidiscrimination nonprofit organization.[25] And this theory has support in a prior empirical study of public perceptions of whistleblowing, which found that as persons engage in investigations or whistleblowing that can be "viewed as more self-interested," the confidence in the investigation declines.[26] The conclusion drawn by at least one prior research paper was that any acts that "tainted the[] sense of the purity of the employee's motivation" resulted in a reduction in the positive view of the investigation.[27]

Such findings are consistent with a closely related conclusion drawn by scholars studying whistleblowing, and assessing what makes whistleblowing effective. These researchers have argued that only certain whistleblowing projects are effective in attracting public and political support, and have advanced the argument that the public's perception about the legitimacy and credibility of investigators is key to understanding the public's reaction.[28] Attribution theory posits that persons frequently attribute causes to particular behavior, and researchers have concluded that these "attributions affect judgments."[29] The public's trust or valuation of an investigation, according to this logic, is dictated by whether the investigator is viewed as "reporting for altruistic or selfish reasons."[30] And selfish motives have been defined broadly to include efforts to seek "fame, notoriety, and monetary rewards."[31]

---

researchers noted the limits of their study, but posit that "in the real world," partisanship may overwhelm the question of how an investigator or whistleblower is perceived because they may receive their news from partisan news outlets. *Id.* at 8.

[25] Richardson & Garner, *supra* note 23, at 346 (noting the study found that an "altruistic whistleblower [is] more likeable, trustworthy, legitimate, and higher in goodwill than the selfish whistleblower"). Scholars such as Bernstein and Jasper go some distance to perpetuate this theory of differential credibility. In an article about the importance of whistleblowers, however, they ignore the impact of their own framing of investigations. They use the pejorative term "infiltrator" to distinguish persons who engage in whistleblowing while affiliated with a social movement. Bernstein & Jasper, *supra* note 16, at 573. The connotation of an infiltrator as one with hostile or improper motives tends to confirm the theory that investigations by such persons might be perceived less favorably by the public. *Id.* at 585 (declaring that whistleblowers associated with social movements "lose credibility").

[26] Heumann et al., *supra* note 22, at 19, 20.

[27] *Id.* At the same time, researchers found that there was no impact on the perceptions of a whistleblower based on factors such as the gender of the whistleblower, the stakes of the investigation, or where the whistleblower was employed. *Id.* at 13.

[28] Richardson & Garner, *supra* note 23, at 2 (noting that the public will "make judgments about the whistleblower and his or her motives").

[29] *Id.* at 5.

[30] *Id.*

[31] *Id.* at 6.

Although research on these questions is thin,[32] there has been an overriding trend in favor of assuming that one's motive for whistleblowing could be of particular relevance to public perception in cases alleging or revealing "severe wrongdoing."[33]

Prior research has also often been too specific or too general. Some researchers have tended to study one particular investigation, without the ability to control for factors unique to that precise investigation that might have affected the public perceptions the researchers were measuring. Alternatively, another set of researchers has tended to study investigations in a general, noncontextualized way without any connection to concrete facts or definitions. For example, a 2002 CNN poll asked, "In general, do you think whistleblowers are heroes who help uncover crimes, or traitors who betray their company or government department?" Fifty-nine percent responded that they considered them heroes.[34] Other researchers have also studied general public reactions to investigative techniques, without anchoring the study in concrete facts or circumstances.[35] It is unclear what, if anything, these general findings reveal.[36] Indeed, one article suggests that surveys measuring general public support for investigative practices are more a reflection of confusion than anything else, with persons not actually understanding the definition of investigative reporting and equating any news coverage to an investigation.[37]

Our research reported in the remainder of this chapter seeks to build on this prior body of work by studying more comprehensively the factors that influence the public perception of undercover investigations in particular, including the influence

[32] *Id.* at 11–12 (discussing results and noting mixed results for questions such as whether selfish versus altruistic motives diminished the perceived trustworthiness or legitimacy of a whistle-blower). Notably, the study did find that being perceived as "innocent" – that is, not complicit in the wrongful conduct – is reliably linked to the perceived credibility of a whistleblower. *Id.* at 13 ("those who participated in wrongdoing were tainted by their complicity" and not seen as likable or credible).

[33] *Id.* at 14. It should be noted that this theory could be criticized as a post-hoc explanation for inconsistent results. The findings are based not on differences in opinion within the same samples but rather on comparisons between a study of students and a study of alumni at a university.

[34] One of the few modern academic studies on the topic found broad support for the idea that whistleblowers help the public (83%), and found that "Women (p < 0.05), Democrats (p < 0.1), and those in union households (p < 0.1) are all more likely to think whistleblowers protect the public (the positive view), while Republicans and independents (p < 0.1), the less educated (p < 0.05) and, interestingly, respondents aged 30–44 are all more likely to take the cynical view of whistleblowers." Heumann et al., *supra* note 22, at 11.

[35] Susan K. Opt & Timothy A. Delaney, *Public Perceptions of Investigative Reporting, in* THE BIG CHILL: INVESTIGATIVE REPORTING IN THE CURRENT MEDIA ENVIRONMENT 81, 88–89 (M. Greenwald & J. Brent eds., 2000) (noting that more affluent and better-educated persons tend to have a more favorable view of investigative reporting); *id.* (citing research concluding that "rural respondents were less likely to approve investigative reporting").

[36] Heumann et al., *supra* note 22, at 8.

[37] Opt & Delaney, *supra* note 35, at 83.

of perceived bias or self-serving motives. Though in some ways our research is more limited, it yields more concrete conclusions. We don't ask sweeping questions about whether public opinion was or was not changed by an investigation, but instead measure public perceptions about the importance and credibility of such investigations, and the type of political or demographic factors that might affect public opinion on this question. Our research seeks to avoid the risks of overclaiming and overgeneralizing. We do not claim to be able to show whether public opinion is definitively altered because of investigations. Nor do we draw sweeping conclusions from a single investigation with its particular details. Rather, we look at the antecedent questions: When does the public trust an investigation? What factors tend to enhance or reduce the credibility of an investigation? Such questions ultimately may have relevance to social change, at least insofar as an undercover investigation that is perceived negatively by the public is unlikely to be a successful lever of social change.[38]

Our primary goal is not to make sweeping claims about social change, but rather to contribute to the understanding of public perceptions of undercover investigations. Those perceptions, in turn, may factor into whether undercover investigations are likely to influence public opinion and whether they will be viewed as politically, ethically, and legally acceptable going forward into the remainder of the twenty-first century.

## 6.4 ORIGINAL EMPIRICAL RESEARCH REGARDING PUBLIC REACTIONS TO UNDERCOVER INVESTIGATIONS

Researchers have asserted that "relatively little is known about how the public perceives the whistleblower."[39] The same might be said of public opinions about undercover investigations, because there is a notable gap in modern research specific to such investigations. In this section we detail our original empirical research studying the factors that impact public perceptions of undercover investigations. Through a series of experiments, we studied the factors that influence the public views about the value and legitimacy of undercover investigations – what makes them more or less credible, or more or less important, in the eyes of the public.

---

[38] PROTESS ET AL., *supra* note 4, at 251. To paraphrase a useful metaphor developed by other scholars to make this point: the public is a bit like the audience at a play. It is not as though the audience (ordinarily) has any direct say in what the cast does on stage, other than perhaps flourishes at the margin, but the scriptwriters certainly keep in mind public perception as they choose how and when to pursue different social change agendas. *Id.* at 248 (noting that even when the media leapfrogs public opinion and goes straight to policy makers, it should not be doubted that "policy makers have the public in mind" when they set agendas).

[39] Heumann et al., *supra* note 22, at 7.

### 6.4.1 *Research Methodology*

To study public reactions to undercover investigations we ran a series of five individual surveys.[40] Rather than running a single study, which is harder to monitor for compliance with nationally representative standards and risks creating some confusion in the data, the decision was made to divide the key research questions into five studies. Each survey was conducted within the same period of time in late 2021,[41] and all subjects received the same introductory statement that defined undercover investigations. In addition, each study included identical survey questions asking about general attitudes about such investigations. Accordingly, we compare results across the surveys, as the separate surveys are essentially just different conditions of an experiment. The five surveys were as follows:

- **Survey 1. Baseline Support for Undercover Investigations.** This survey measured the baseline support for undercover investigations. Respondents were given a generic description of undercover investigations, and then asked a series of questions regarding their attitudes about the importance and legality of undercover investigations and the integrity of investigating journalists or investigators.
- **Survey 2. Impacts of Varying the Investigating Entity.** This survey tested the effect of changing the investigating entity. Does public opinion about undercover investigations change when all of the details regarding the investigation are held constant but the identity of the investigator is varied (Fox News, the *New York Times*, or a nonpartisan nonprofit organization)? Subjects read and responded to one randomly assigned vignette. Each vignette contained an identical description of an investigation, except that the identity of the investigating entity was randomly varied.
- **Survey 3. Impacts of Varying the Political Identity of the Person Investigated.** This survey tested the effect of changing the political orientation of the investigative target. Does public opinion about undercover investigations change when all of the details regarding the investigation (and investigator) are held constant, except that the identity of the investigative target varies from a Republican, Democrat, or an Independent politician? Subjects read and responded to one randomly assigned vignette. Each vignette contained an identical description of the

---

[40] Our research was preregistered, our methods and hypotheses clearly defined, before we circulated the surveys, and posted to the Open Science Foundation, https://osf.io/urqnm (last visited Nov. 27, 2022).

[41] All surveys were conducted between November and December 2021. The fifth survey was completed last in time and was completed by December 20. The other surveys were all completed no more than three weeks earlier.

investigating entity and the investigation except that the political party of the person investigated was randomly varied.

- **Survey 4. Nature of the Conduct Investigated.** This survey tested the effect of altering the subject matter of the investigated behavior. Does public opinion about undercover investigations change when all of the details regarding the investigator are held constant, but the nature of the investigated conduct is varied (political corruption, sex trafficking, dog-fighting, farm animal cruelty, and abortion)?[42] Each subject was randomly assigned a vignette. The vignettes were identical in terms of the person investigated and the investigative entity, but the underlying conduct investigated was randomly varied.

- **Survey 5. Impacts of Investigator Motives and Consequences for the Investigated Party.** This survey tested the impact of investigations in which the investigator was working for a nonprofit organization with a particular mission related to the practice being investigated (e.g., an animal rights nonprofit), and the nonprofit organization expected to gain some positive publicity and enhance fundraising potential from the investigation. In addition, the stakes of the investigation were made clear as it was specified that the target of the investigation might face criminal charges. Each subject was randomly assigned the same vignettes from Survey 4, except this time the nature of the investigator was specified as an interested group (such as an animal rights group or a pro-life group).

For all five surveys in the study, we used Prolific[43] to source online respondents.[44] We sought to obtain representative samples of the US adult population based on age, gender, and ethnicity, consistent with US Census Bureau data.[45] We removed respondents for failing consistency or attention checks.[46]

---

[42] The original survey failed to include the abortion investigation vignette. When this was realized, a separate survey that randomly assigned persons to the abortion survey was conducted. All of the questions and conditions remained identical, but the abortion investigation portion of the survey was conducted approximately three weeks later than the other conditions.

[43] PROLIFIC, www.prolific.co/ (last visited Nov. 27, 2022).

[44] Our methods and study design were informed by a rigorous process involving multiple sources of feedback. We obtained and incorporated input from experts at the UCLA Animal Law and Policy Program, https://law.ucla.edu/academics/centers/animal-law-policy-program (last visited Nov. 27, 2022), and Faunalytics (a nonprofit social science organization providing research for animal advocates), https://faunalytics.org/ (last visited Nov. 27, 2022). We also submitted the project to the University of Denver for IRB approval and received exempt status. This study was also preregistered with the Open Science Framework; for additional details about the study and to see the full survey instruments, visit https://osf.io/urqnm.

[45] We achieved this for Surveys 1, 3, and 4. For Survey 2, Prolific's representative sampling tool experienced an error and the sample for this survey is somewhat younger, whiter, and more liberal than the other surveys.

[46] *See* OSF registration, *supra* note 44, for details.

TABLE 6.1. *Number of participants*

|  | Total | Condition 1 | Condition 2 | Condition 3 | Condition 4 | Condition 5 |
|---|---|---|---|---|---|---|
| Survey 1 | 751 | – | – | – | – | – |
| Survey 2 | 655 | 225 | 215 | 215 | – | – |
| Survey 3 | 589 | 210 | 212 | 167 | – | – |
| Survey 4 | 894 | 216 | 222 | 228 | 228 | 271 |
| Survey 5 | 1,151 | 228 | 227 | 218 | 243 | 235 |

For Survey 1, which is the baseline survey on general opinions about undercover investigations, our sample size was 751 individuals, which equates to an error margin of $\pm$ 3.6%. Table 6.1 shows the final sample sizes for each survey and condition.[47] In Surveys 2–5, respondents were randomly assigned to one of the three, four, or five conditions. Within each survey, the demographic profile of respondents in different conditions are generally well balanced and comparable. However, we feel it important to acknowledge that the respondents to these surveys skew Democrats/liberals (~45–50% of our sample vs. ~28–31% of the adult population), with a smaller percentage of Republicans/conservatives.[48] This appears to be inherent with Prolific. Where relevant to our analysis, we explain how we considered this factor.

### 6.4.2 *Overview of Findings*

One of the clearest findings from our study is that the public today tends to view undercover investigations as an indispensable tool to address corruption or malfeasance. There is an overwhelming baseline of public support for undercover investigations, even when it is made clear that the investigators may employ lies, nonconsensual recording, or both. As a baseline, over 90% of respondents found that undercover investigations are either somewhat or very important, and the vast majority of respondents rejected the idea that undercover investigations should be made illegal. Similarly, about twice as many people concluded that persons who engage in undercover investigations have very high integrity rather than low integrity, notwithstanding that they use deception to conduct the investigations.

Another interesting finding, as discussed in more detail below, is that public support for undercover investigations *increases* from the baseline level of support as soon as persons are given a concrete example of an undercover investigation, as

[47] For our experimental Surveys 2–4, we used G*Power to determine our sample to be able to detect a minimum effect size of d = 0.35 (using a two-tailed t-test with 80% power and alpha corrected for false discovery rate).

[48] As a comparison, the political affiliation of the general population, recent polls suggest that about 28–31% of people identify as Democrats, 25–28% as Republicans, and about 40–44% as Independents. Jeffrey M. Jones, *U.S. Political Party Preferences Shifted Greatly during 2021*, Gallup (Jan. 17, 2022), https://news.gallup.com/poll/388781/political-party-preferences-shifted-greatly-during-2021.aspx.

opposed to just a standard definition of undercover investigations. That is, whenever a person was confronted with concrete facts about an investigation (relating to political corruption, animal welfare, human trafficking, etc.), regardless of the seeming political cause served by the investigation, there was virtually always an increase in the support for undercover investigations relative to the baseline support for such investigations. The one exception, discussed below, was an investigation of an abortion provider. We intentionally studied undercover investigations of abortion providers because, as we have discussed throughout the book, in recent years a number of pro-life advocacy groups such as the Center for Medical Progress have conducted high-profile and controversial investigations that have been widely covered in the media, discussed by policy makers, and the subject of federal litigation.[49] Our findings are that abortion is *the* exception to the rule that regardless of the topic of the investigation, support for investigations always go up when details of the investigation are revealed. When it comes to investigations in the abortion context, there is no difference in the public support for investigations compared with the baseline.[50]

Equally striking, whereas prior researchers have tended to assume that partisan bias in the form of motivated reasoning or motivated cognition[51] would dominate other considerations when it came to investigative reporting in general, our findings tend to undermine this presumption in the more specific context of undercover investigations. According to earlier researchers, investigative reporting and whistle-blowing will be viewed positively by persons who see the investigation as harming their political enemies, and negatively to the extent it harms their political allies.[52] But our study contradicts these reflexive assumptions in the context of undercover investigations, and suggests that persons are more nuanced in their thinking, not cartoonish, political caricatures. Instead, a substantial portion of the public responds with interest and concern to undercover investigations regardless of whether the investigation tends to support their preexisting political views. Republicans are less likely than others to say investigations are "very" important and slightly more likely to agree that they should be illegal. Republicans also tend to have a greater willingness to change their views of investigations depending on whether a Democrat or Republican is the target of the investigation. But overall, the differences between parties and the extent of motivated, partisan reasoning are considerably less than prior scholarship seems to have presumed. Our findings suggest that when it comes

---

[49] *See generally* Sabina Tavernise, *Planned Parenthood Awarded $2 Million in Lawsuit over Secret Videos*, N.Y. TIMES (Nov. 15, 2019), www.nytimes.com/2019/11/15/us/planned-parenthood-lawsuit-secret-videos.html.

[50] *See infra* note 67 and accompanying text.

[51] "Motivated reasoning refers to the unconscious tendency of individuals to process information in a manner that suits some end or goal extrinsic to the formation of accurate beliefs." Dan M. Kahan, *Foreword: Neutral Principles, Motivated Cognition, and Some Problems for Constitutional Law*, 125 HARV. L. REV. 1, 19 (2011).

[52] Touchton et al., *supra* note 24, at 8 (positing this thesis but noting the need for specific research studying "partisan motivated reasoning" in this context).

to investigations on matters of public concern, support for undercover investigations may be a bipartisan value in ways that have not been previously understood. Transparency may transcend political party.

### 6.4.3 *Detailed Findings Based on Each Survey*

#### 6.4.3.1 Study 1: Baseline

In Survey 1, we set out to examine baseline views about undercover investigations. Prior research has suggested that the best predictor of whether someone supports investigative journalism is one's general attitude toward the press.[53] Much has been written in recent years about a diminished confidence in the media more generally,[54] and in particular there is a sense that persons on the political right have a generally less favorable view of the media.[55] Accordingly, one might hypothesize that there would be a strong correlation between one's political identity and their support for undercover investigations. Our findings, however, do not support this thesis, but rather show widespread bipartisan support for undercover investigations.

To measure the baseline support for undercover investigations we deliberately did not provide any specific factual context. Nonetheless, before asking the survey questions that were standardized across all of our experiments, unlike prior studies, we provided a general definition of undercover investigations to each respondent. That definition made very clear what we meant by undercover investigations and was intended to state that definition in neutral terms. Each respondent was provided the following statement:

> This survey is about undercover investigations. An undercover investigation is a secret operation by a journalist or political activist that can include deception or misrepresentation about the investigator's identity. This is done to gain access to important information that would not be available if the person disclosed their true objectives. Undercover investigators may use electronic equipment to make a video or audio recording to document what they discover during the investigation. These recordings are made without the consent of the people being investigated.

We provided this statement in order to improve on prior research that had asked general opinion questions regarding whistleblowing or investigative reporting without any context. By making clear that we were interested in "secret operations," and investigative tools that may include deception and surreptitious audio or video

---

[53] Willnat & Weaver, *supra* note 12, at 459.

[54] Megan Brennan, *Americans' Trust in Media Dips to Second Lowest on Record*, Gallup (Oct. 7, 2021), https://news.gallup.com/poll/355526/americans-trust-media-dips-second-lowest-record .aspx.

[55] Jeffrey Gottfried & Jacob Liedke, *Partisan Divides in Media Trust Widen, Driven by a Decline among Republicans*, Pew Rsch. Ctr. (Aug. 30, 2021), www.pewresearch.org/fact-tank/2021/08/ 30/partisan-divides-in-media-trust-widen-driven-by-a-decline-among-republicans/.

recording, we limited the risk that persons would conclude that undercover investigations were desirable without focusing on their more controversial aspects. In contrast, prior researchers had found that while people "approve of investigative reporting techniques in general," they are "much less likely to support specific investigative reporting techniques such as the use of hidden cameras or microphones."[56]

In short, Survey 1 provides the most detailed look at baseline public perceptions of undercover investigations to date. Our sample is generally representative of the population on a number of metrics, but the population skews left of center for politics, something we controlled for in the adjusted findings discussed below.

**PROFILE:** Survey 1 sample demographics:
- 51% female
- 32% age 18–34; 33% 35–54; 34% 55+
- 76% white; 14% Black; 8% Asian
- 58% with bachelor's degree or higher education
- 51% liberal; 26% moderate; 20% conservative
- 45% Democrats; 18% Republicans; 28% Independents.

The study shows overwhelming baseline support for undercover investigations. As Table 6.2 indicates, about 92% of all persons surveyed think that undercover investigations are either very or somewhat important. This finding is particularly striking in a political climate where laws prohibiting undercover investigations, such as ag-gag laws, have seen increased political support.[57] When the investigations relate to matters of public concern, our findings show that only about 3% of US adults think that undercover investigations are very or somewhat unimportant for "revealing unknown truths about organizations or individuals." These investigations, even when it is specified that they will deploy deception and nonconsensual recording, enjoy considerable public support.

Despite this clarity in the support for undercover investigations, our findings also reveal some tensions in the way persons think about the investigators. For example, Table 6.2 shows that although 92% of persons indicated that undercover investigations are very or somewhat important, 20% of persons think that undercover *investigators* have very (5%) or somewhat (15%) low integrity. Another interesting finding is that although only 4% of persons strongly agree that undercover investigations should be illegal, only 33% strongly disagree with making them illegal. The baseline public perception appears to be that investigations are important, but there is not a consensus about whether the investigations are moral, or even whether the law should definitively protect them. Of course, it is not entirely implausible that

---

[56] Willnat & Weaver, *supra* note 12, at 451. *Id.* at 454 (finding that in 1997 only about 33.3% of persons supported investigations where reporters did not identify themselves). As we discussed in Chapter 2, many professional journalists share this same ambivalence.

[57] Depending on how such laws are defined, about ten states have enacted ag-gag laws, though as discussed in other chapters, lawsuits have halted the enforcement of several of these laws. *Ag-Gag Laws*, ANIMAL LEGAL DEF. FUND, https://aldf.org/issue/ag-gag/ (last visited Nov. 27, 2022).

TABLE 6.2. *The importance of undercover investigations: Findings from the baseline condition* (n = 751)

Panel A: How important are undercover investigations for revealing unknown truths about organizations or individuals?

| Very unimportant | Somewhat unimportant | No opinion | Somewhat important | Very important |
|---|---|---|---|---|
| 1% | 2% | 5% | 42% | 50% |

Panel B: How important are undercover investigations for informing people about important political and social issues?

| Very unimportant | Somewhat unimportant | No opinion | Somewhat important | Very important |
|---|---|---|---|---|
| 2% | 5% | 9% | 41% | 43% |

Panel C: How would you rate the integrity of journalists or activists who engage in the kinds of undercover investigations you just read about?

| Very low integrity | Somewhat low integrity | No opinion | Somewhat high integrity | Very high integrity |
|---|---|---|---|---|
| 5% | 15% | 37% | 31% | 13% |

Panel D: Do you agree or disagree that undercover investigations should be illegal in the United States?

| Strongly disagree | Somewhat disagree | Neither agree nor disagree | Somewhat agree | Strongly agree |
|---|---|---|---|---|
| 33% | 37% | 17% | 8% | 4% |

people might simultaneously believe that undercover investigations are important, but should nevertheless be illegal. That is, they might believe that the harms outweigh the benefits.

Our findings show that persons with lower levels of formal education are much more likely to simultaneously hold these conflicting views, and notably, Republicans are about 50% more likely to say that journalists have low integrity compared with both Democrats and Independents. Future researchers may wish to further examine the tensions between valuing undercover investigations and simultaneously villainizing the investigator.[58]

---

[58] Interestingly, this tension is sometimes reflected in the law as well. The Supreme Court has sometimes distinguished the legality of publishing information that may have been unlawfully

TABLE 6.3. *The importance of undercover investigations by gender, age, education, and political party: Findings from the baseline condition*

| | Very important for revealing unknown truths | Very important for informing people | High integrity[a] | Should be illegal[b] | (n) |
|---|---|---|---|---|---|
| Gender | | | | | |
| Male | 50% | 43% | 42% | 12% | (380) |
| Female | 50% | 44% | 44% | 13% | (367) |
| Age | | | | | |
| 18–24 | 46% | 39% | 37% | 11% | (103) |
| 25–34 | 52% | 46% | 43% | 12% | (141) |
| 35–44 | 51% | 45% | 46% | 11% | (121) |
| 45–54 | 53% | 47% | 47% | 12% | (129) |
| 55–64 | 49% | 41% | 43% | 14% | (166) |
| 65+ | 47% | 40% | 41% | 14% | (91) |
| Race | | | | | |
| White | 48% | 41% | 44% | 13% | (520) |
| Person of color | 56% | 49% | 43% | 12% | (223) |
| Education | | | | | |
| High school degree (or less) | 51% | 44% | 45% | 16% | (80) |
| Some college | 53% | 45% | 40% | 11% | (171) |
| Associate's degree | 50% | 50% | 32% | 13% | (62) |
| Bachelor's degree | 51% | 44% | 46% | 13% | (284) |
| Graduate degree | 44% | 36% | 44% | 11% | (150) |
| Political party | | | | | |
| Democrat | 51% | 44% | 46% | 12% | (353) |
| Independent/no preference | 51% | 45% | 43% | 10% | (249) |
| Republican | 45% | 38% | 37% | 16% | (139) |

[a] Combines somewhat high integrity and very high integrity.
[b] Combines somewhat agree and strongly agree.

We also assessed baseline support for undercover investigations based on political party, Table 6.3. While Democrats and Independents are slightly more likely than Republicans to think that undercover investigations are important, the differences by political party are minimal. We found that 93% of Democrats and 92% of Independents regard undercover investigations as somewhat or very important, compared with 90% of Republicans. Notably, a much higher percentage of Republicans (39.5% compared with 17% of Democrats and 19% of Independents)

obtained, which is generally protected under the First Amendment, from the government's power to punish the individuals who obtained that information, who do not benefit from such protection. *See, e.g.,* Bartnicki v. Vopper, 532 U.S. 514 (2001); N.Y. Times Co. v. United States, 403 U.S. 713 (1971).

responded that they thought investigators were of very or somewhat low integrity. This finding might suggest that Republicans tend to support investigations in general, but their moral unease with the practice may make their support more fickle when the investigations conflict with their preexisting beliefs, such as a belief about the importance of private property rights.

Our findings suggest that one's race may also affect reaction to undercover investigations. Persons of color were more likely than white respondents to think that undercover investigations were important for revealing underlying truths (56% vs. 48%) and very important for informing people about political issues of consequence (49% vs. 41%). Neither gender nor higher levels of education correlate with higher levels of support for undercover investigations.

### 6.4.3.2  Study 2: Investigating Entity

Having established baseline support for investigations, our second study was designed to test the public perception of investigations when the source of the investigation is varied. In particular, the study examines whether persons respond differently to an identical investigation when it is conducted by a journalistic entity identified with the political left (*New York Times*),[59] a journalistic entity identified with the political right (Fox News), or a neutral nonpartisan nonprofit organization. Our hypothesis was that the identity of the messenger would tend to undermine or bolster the message to different audiences.

To test this question, we again provided every respondent with the definition of undercover investigations used in the baseline study. In addition, each participant was asked the same questions as participants in the baseline study about their views of undercover investigations. The only difference with this survey was that before answering the questions, the participants in this second experiment were randomly assigned to one of three fact patterns. The fact pattern, reproduced immediately below, was identical for each participant other than the fact that the identity of the investigator was varied (*New York Times*/Fox News/nonpartisan nonprofit).

(*New York Times*/Fox News/nonpartisan nonprofit) recently sent a reporter undercover to investigate corruption by a prominent politician who is the mayor of a large city. During the course of the investigation, the reporter used deceptive practices, including posing as a prospective intern with the mayor's office and secretly recording coworkers while training for the new job. The reporter learned that the

---

[59] Public opinion polls have shown that there is a fairly broad belief that the *New York Times*'s news coverage leans liberal. *New York Times, Washington Post, and Local Newspapers Seen as Having Liberal Bias*, RASMUSSEN REPS. (July 15, 2007), www.rasmussenreports.com/public_content/politics/current_events/media/new_york_times_washington_post_and_local_news papers_seen_as_having_liberal_bias; Tim Groseclose & Jeffrey Milyo, *A Measure of Media Bias*, 120 Q. J. ECON. 1191 (2005). As we discussed in Chapter 2, however, the *New York Times* does not allow its reporters to engage in investigative deceptions.

mayor used city funds to lease an expensive car for personal use. The mayor also used their city-issued credit card to charge tens of thousands of dollars' worth of extravagant meals, spa massages, and personal items. While this was happening, the mayor closed two public parks and a public health clinic because of budget concerns. The reporter left the mayor's office and provided this footage to (*New York Times*/Fox News/nonpartisan nonprofit) to air on national television as part of an exposé revealing the mayor's corruption.

As with the other surveys, we monitored participation in order to ensure a nationally representative sample of respondents.

**PROFILE:** Survey 2 sample demographics:
- 61% female
- 44% age 18–34; 44% 35–54; 12% 55+
- 81% white; 10% Black; 7% Asian
- 55% with bachelor's degree or higher education
- 58% liberal; 23% moderate; 16% conservative
- 52% Democrats; 17% Republicans; 24% Independents.

The key unadjusted finding is that the perceived importance of undercover investigations varies only slightly based on who conducts the investigation. The only variation of note, before controlling for potentially confounding variables, is that persons exposed to an undercover investigation by the *New York Times* were more likely to feel that investigations are very important than persons exposed to investigations by Fox News or a nonpartisan nonprofit. A full 69% of persons exposed to an investigation conducted by the *New York Times* regard undercover investigations to be very important in revealing hidden truths, compared with 57% of persons exposed to an investigation by a nonpartisan nonprofit, and 50% of persons exposed to an investigation by Fox News. Similarly striking, 22% of persons who were told of an investigation by the *New York Times* believed that undercover investigators had very high integrity, compared with 17% who had the nonpartisan nonprofit fact pattern, and 11% were told the investigation was by Fox News.

A skeptical reader might assume that these differences are driven by the left-leaning political orientation of our study population. But the story is more complicated, and less driven by political orientation, than we had hypothesized. First, it is important to note that support for investigations by *any* entity was consistently quite high. It is not the case that investigations conducted by one source cause support for investigations to decline from the baseline.

In order to more closely examine variation in support for undercover investigations based on political party, we focused on the respondents who characterized undercover investigations as very important to revealing underlying truths, and compared those persons and their political ideology with all others.

There are a number of critical findings detailed below, but by way of a broad-brush overview, a few points jump out. First, we find that no matter who is

TABLE 6.4. *The importance of undercover investigations: Young Republicans diverge from expectations*

| | Very important for revealing unknown truths | Very important for informing people | High integrity | (*n*) |
|---|---|---|---|---|
| Young Republicans (under 45) | | | | |
| Fox News condition | 28% | 24% | 36% | (25) |
| *New York Times* condition | 56% | 61% | 50% | (18) |
| Old Republicans (45 and older) | | | | |
| Fox News condition | 60% | 40% | 67% | (15) |
| *New York Times* condition | 58% | 50% | 67% | (12) |

investigating, Democrats are more likely than Republicans to conclude that undercover investigations are very important. Second, the entity doing the investigation is a better predictor of public perception than the political party of the individual surveyed. Both Democrats and Republicans were more likely to think that undercover investigations were very important when they were presented with an investigation by the *New York Times*. Republicans have a more favorable perception of investigations by the *New York Times* than by Fox News by a notable margin. How could it be that Republicans favor investigations by the *New York Times*? Table 6.4 illustrates there is an interesting divergence between young Republicans and those who are older. Whereas persons who are forty-five or older and Republican tend to value investigations from either the *New York Times* or Fox News in roughly equal measure, persons who are under forty-five tend to diverge from this view and instead tend to credit investigations from the *New York Times* at much higher rates. The numbers here are too small to make claims of statistical significance, but the pattern is striking: young Republicans appear to treat undercover investigations by the *New York Times* as more credible than investigations by Fox News. This finding may be important to the degree it bears on the receptivity of future generations of Republicans to undercover investigations in general.

To provide a more complete examination of the factors influencing public perceptions of undercover investigations when the source of the investigation is varied, we compared the results of Survey 2 with our baseline findings from Survey 1, and we controlled for potentially confounding variables.

As noted above, the baseline view of undercover investigations – meaning those who were not presented with an experimental condition – is that 50% feel undercover investigations are very important for revealing hidden truths. We were interested in whether this baseline support increased or decreased when one was presented with a concrete, factual investigation from one of three sources (*New York Times*, Fox News, nonprofit).

Our findings indicate that when a person is presented with the Survey 2 investigation and told that it was done by Fox News, the support for undercover investigations (as very important) does not change much from baseline (50.2% vs. 49.9%). Essentially, support for undercover investigations remains constant between a generic baseline and in situations when one is presented with an investigation conducted by Fox News. By contrast, when presented with a nonpartisan nonprofit investigation, there is a modest change from the baseline public perception (57.2% vs. 49.9%), and when persons are presented with the New York Times condition, we can see a substantial change in support for investigations from baseline – about 19 percentage points (from 49.9% to 69.3%).[60]

To further explore how varying the investigating entity affects public perception, we conducted further regression analyses. Using odds ratios, we found that the odds of seeing an undercover investigation as very important for revealing underlying or hidden truths are 2.3 times greater in the New York Times condition as compared with the baseline condition ($p < .001$). By contrast, the odds of seeing an undercover investigation as very important are 1.4 times greater than the baseline when persons are exposed to an investigation by a nonpartisan nonprofit organization ($p < .05$).[61] But the odds ratio for Fox News is 1.05, meaning the baseline view of the importance of undercover investigations and the view of investigations when conducted by Fox News is indistinguishable ($p$ value is nonsignificant).

Stated succinctly, an identical investigation will generate different public reactions to undercover investigations depending on who conducted the investigation. A New York Times investigation is far more likely to lead to very positive perceptions of investigations more generally.[62] An investigation by a nonpartisan entity tends to have a positive impact on the public perception of undercover investigations relative to the baseline, whereas an investigation by Fox News has no impact on public perception.

We also examined all of the control variables in order to see whether demographic factors might explain the varying support for undercover investigations. For the most part, demographics do not predict support for undercover investigations. But there is one exception: race. Specifically, the odds of seeing undercover investigations as very important are 1.5 times greater for people of color than white people, with a $p$ value less than .01 ($p$ value is .002).

---

[60] The chi-square value of 27.455 is significant at p < .001 (reads .000).

[61] Exact $p$ value is .029. For the reader unfamiliar with statistics, it is worth a simple reminder that $p$ value can be multiplied by 100 to generate percentage: .05 = 5% chance of Type 1 error; .01 = 1% chance of Type 1 error; .001 = .1% chance of Type 1 error. So, a $p$ value of .029 means that there is a 2.9% chance that something other than the nature of the investigative entity is explaining the different outcome.

[62] In the logistic regression (LR) model, we would also rotate the comparison group. The odds of seeing an undercover investigation as very important are significantly greater in the New York Times condition than even the nonpartisan nonprofit condition (as opposed to comparing the Times with the baseline). This means that public perception is different in a statistically significant way even when the New York Times is contrasted with a nonprofit investigating entity, as compared with the baseline.

TABLE 6.5. *The importance of undercover investigations by investigative entity*[a]

| | Very important for revealing unknown truths | Very important for informing people | High integrity | Should be illegal | (n) |
|---|---|---|---|---|---|
| Baseline | 50% | 43% | 43% | 13% | (751) |
| New York Times | 69%*** | 66%*** | 63%*** | 9% | (215) |
| Fox News | 50% | 42% | 48% | 8% | (225) |
| Nonpartisan nonprofit | 57%* | 53%** | 59%*** | 8% | 215) |

[a] Statistical significance: *$p$ < .05; **$p$ < .01; ***$p$ < .001. This table is based on four cross-tabulations. Each cross-tabulation includes four conditions (baseline, *New York Times*, Fox News, nonpartisan nonprofit) predicting a binary outcome. In a 4 × 2 cross-tabulation, chi-square provides an omnibus test of statistical significance. Thus, the $p$ value for the cross-tabulation indicates the probability of committing a Type I error if one rejects the null hypothesis of equal treatment across conditions (Franke et al. 2012). The $p$ value for the cross-tabulation does not indicate whether specific differences are significant (e.g., baseline vs. *New York Times* on the question of whether undercover investigations are very important for revealing unknown truths). To address the issue, we estimated four logistic regression models. The logistic regression models control for the respondent's gender, age, race, and education. The baseline condition serves as the comparison group. So statistical significance is based on the logistic regression models (available on request), as such models allow specific comparisons. Here, each condition is compared with the baseline. Todd M. Franke, Timothy Ho, & Christina A. Christie, *The Chi-Square Test: Often Used and More Often Misinterpreted*, 33 AM. J. EVALUATION 448 (2012).

Table 6.5 illustrates another compelling finding from Survey 2. The public perception of undercover investigators as persons of integrity, and the question of whether such investigations should be illegal, varies considerably based on who has done the investigation. The baseline survey found that 43% of respondents see undercover investigators as having very or somewhat high integrity.

When persons are presented with an investigative scenario conducted by Fox News, there is no statistically significant change in the view that investigators have somewhat or very high integrity (48%). By contrast, when a nonpartisan nonprofit is credited with the investigation, there is a moderate impact on the public perception of investigator integrity (59%), and an investigation by the *New York Times* generates a substantial positive change in the public's perception of the investigator as having somewhat or very high integrity (63%). A logistical regression confirms this finding. Compared with the baseline, the odds of seeing an investigator as having a somewhat or very high level of integrity were 2.3 times greater for persons exposed to an investigation done by the *New York Times* and 1.9 times greater for those exposed to an investigation done by a nonpartisan nonprofit.

Likewise, whereas the baseline study found that about 13% of persons thought that undercover investigations should be illegal, that number drops to less than 10% once an investigation (by any entity) is introduced in Survey 2.

### 6.4.3.3 Studies 3 and 4: Investigative Target

Our third and fourth studies were designed to test the public perception of investigations when the target of the investigation is varied. The question is whether public support for investigations varies depending on the political party of the person investigated or the type of information that is revealed by an investigation. Scholars have previously observed that there is a "difference between general sentiment" in support of investigative journalists and "support of press performance in specific cases."[63] Surveys 3 and 4 focus on the possibility that public support may not remain constant when the conduct or the target of the investigation varies.

As with the other surveys, we monitored participation in order to ensure a nationally representative sample of respondents.

**PROFILE:** Survey 3 sample demographics:
- 51% female
- 31% age 18–34; 35% 35–54; 33% 55+
- 77% white; 14% Black; 7% Asian
- 59% with bachelor's degree or higher education
- 53% liberal; 23% moderate; 21% conservative
- 49% Democrats; 20% Republicans; 26% Independents.

**PROFILE:** Survey 4 sample demographics:
- 51% female
- 32% age 18–34; 35% 35–54; 33% 55+
- 78% white; 13% Black; 8% Asian
- 54% with bachelor's degree or higher education
- 52% liberal; 26% moderate; 19% conservative
- 46% Democrats; 18% Republicans; 28% Independents.

The two surveys each started with the same general definition of undercover investigations and asked each participant the same set of survey questions. The only difference was that persons were randomly selected to receive different fact patterns describing an investigation.

In Survey 3, each person received the fact pattern below, with the only difference being that persons were randomly assigned to Democrat, Republican, or Independent investigative targets.

A major television network recently sent a reporter undercover to investigate corruption by a prominent politician (a Republican/Democrat/Independent) who is the mayor of a large city. During the course of the investigation, the reporter used deceptive practices, including posing as a prospective intern with the mayor's office and secretly recording coworkers while training for the new job. The reporter

---

[63] PROTESS ET AL., *supra* note 4, at 14.

learned that the mayor used city funds to lease an expensive car for personal use. The mayor also used their city-issued credit card to charge tens of thousands of dollars' worth of extravagant meals, spa massages, and personal items. While this was happening, the mayor closed two public parks and a public health clinic because of budget concerns. The reporter left the mayor's office and provided this footage to the network to air on national television as part of an exposé revealing the (Republican/Democrat/Independent) mayor's corruption.

Contrary to our hypothesis, public support for undercover investigations does not vary significantly based on the political orientation of the investigated target. Again, the baseline survey finds that about 50% of respondents believe that undercover investigations are very important. That number goes up if the respondent is presented with a target: 59% for investigations of Democrats, 58% for investigations of Republicans, and 65% for investigations of Independents. A logistic regression, detailed in Table 6.6, controlling for gender, age, education, and race, confirms that exposure to an investigation of a politician of any (or no) party produces more support for undercover investigations than the baseline (all $p$ values less than .05). Strikingly, our studies find that both Democrats and Republicans are more likely to view undercover investigations as important, controlling for demographic variables, even when the investigation was focused on a member of their own political party.

This is not to say that there is no difference in reactions to undercover investigations between Democrats and Republicans who are exposed to investigations of someone from their own party or the opposite party. Indeed, there was a statistically significant increase in support for undercover investigations among Democrats and Republicans when the investigative target was a politician from the opposite party. Support for investigations is more constant than we expected, but it is still to a certain degree contingent on who exactly is being investigated and exposed. Strikingly, for persons who identify as Independents, the investigations that they view as the most important are investigations of their own in-group; Independents favor investigations of other Independents over investigations of either Republicans or Democrats.

As Table 6.6 illustrates, 57% of Democrats see undercover investigations as very important if the investigative target is a Democrat, but that figure rises to 64% if the investigative target is a Republican. Among Republicans, 49% see undercover investigations as very important if they are told that the investigative target is a Republican, but that number rises to 61% if the investigative target is a Democrat. Among respondents who are Independents, 58% view undercover work as very important if the target is a Republican, 59% if the target is a Democrat, and if the target of the investigation is an Independent, the number jumps to 67%.

For Democrats and Republicans, this sort of in-group bias was expected, but it is far less than we anticipated, and much less than prior commentators have suggested. These same patterns held for the public's assessment of the integrity of an investigator. Our research suggests that there is a strong, bipartisan support for undercover

TABLE 6.6. *The importance of undercover investigations depends on whether target is in-group or out-group*[a]

| | Very important for revealing unknown truths | (n) |
|---|---|---|
| Respondent is a Democrat | | |
| Baseline | 51% | (353) |
| Investigative target in-group: Democrat | 57% | (108) |
| Investigative target out-group: Republican or Independent | 64%** | (182) |
| Respondent is a Republican | | |
| Baseline | 45% | (139) |
| Investigative target in-group: Republican | 49% | (41) |
| Investigative target out-group: Democrat or Independent | 61%* | (80) |
| Respondent is an Independent | | |
| Baseline | 51% | (249) |
| Investigative target in-group: Independent | 67%+ | (43) |
| Investigative target out-group: Democrat or Republican | 59% | (130) |

[a] Statistical significance: $^+p < .10$; $^*p < .05$; $^{**}p < .01$; $^{***}p < .001$. As noted above, $p$ values are based on logistic regression models (estimated separately for respondents who are Republicans, Democrats, and Independents). The models control for the respondent's gender, age, race, and education. The baseline condition serves as the comparison group.

investigations that does not vary overwhelmingly depending on partisan-motivated cognition.

In Survey 4, we studied whether the public perception of undercover investigations depends on the nature of the misconduct revealed. Whereas Survey 3 examines political corruption by a politician with an identified political party, Survey 4 considers whether partisan-motivated thinking will influence public perception when the investigation targets vary. Some of the investigative topics, we imagined, would be relatively politically neutral (e.g., corruption, human trafficking), and others we anticipated would appeal to particular political groups more than others (e.g., abortion, animal rights).

To study the impact of the type of investigation conducted on public perception, persons received a randomized fact pattern, and this time the facts were identical except for the details of what was investigated. There were five investigative scenarios: human trafficking, political corruption, dogfighting, farm animal cruelty, and abortion.[64] The core fact pattern was identical, and below is the text of the human trafficking investigation and the abortion investigation.[65] As you can see, even for

[64] As noted *supra* note 42, the abortion scenario was run slightly after the completion of the other four scenarios.

[65] The other fact patterns were all preregistered and are available at https://osf.io/r9qev/.

radically different investigative revelations, we strove to maintain consistency across the fact patterns.

> A major television network recently sent a reporter undercover to investigate sex trafficking by a prominent politician who is the mayor of a large city. During the course of the investigation, the reporter used deceptive practices, including posing as a prospective intern with the mayor's office and secretly recording coworkers while training for the new job. The reporter learned that the mayor was involved in a sex trafficking ring. The mayor worked with others to illegally transport women and children from other countries to the U.S. for the purpose of sexual exploitation. While this was happening, the mayor cut the budgets of both the local women's shelter and the local police division in charge of investigating sex crimes. The reporter left the mayor's office and provided this footage to the network to air on national television as part of an exposé revealing the mayor's involvement in sex trafficking.

> A major television network recently sent a reporter undercover to investigate a prominent politician (the mayor of a large city) who previously ran a local abortion clinic. During the course of the investigation, the reporter used deceptive practices, including posing as a prospective intern with the mayor's office and secretly recording coworkers while training for the new job. The reporter learned that the mayor, while acting as head of the abortion clinic, may have violated federal and state laws. It was discovered that the clinic had been selling fetal tissue to research laboratories in other states, which is against the law. While this was happening, the mayor (who was then running for office) focused their campaign on protecting young children and improving the health of infants. The reporter left the mayor's office and provided this footage to the network to air on national television as part of an exposé revealing the mayor's involvement in illegally selling fetal tissue.

We found strong support for the investigations across these subject matter contexts. In all five of the scenarios we randomly presented, more than 50% of the respondents concluded that undercover investigations were very important to revealing hidden truths. And in all but the abortion scenario, over 60% of persons concluded that undercover investigations were very important. The exposure to an investigation on a matter of public concern revealing possible wrongdoing, no matter the topic, appears to be sufficient to convince the majority of the public that undercover investigations are very important. Investigations in every setting (including abortion) led to the respondents concluding that investigations were very or somewhat important more than 90% of the time. There was some variation – for example, about 97% of persons exposed to sex trafficking investigations concluding that undercover investigations were important, compared with about 92% of persons exposed to abortion investigations. Likewise, support for making investigations illegal was consistently low across all five groups.

TABLE 6.7. *The importance of undercover investigations of farm animal cruelty depends on respondent's political party*[a]

|  | Very important for revealing unknown truths | (n) |
|---|---|---|
| Respondent is a Democrat |  |  |
| Baseline | 51% | (353) |
| Farm animal cruelty | 67%* | (105) |
| Respondent is a Republican |  |  |
| Baseline | 45% | (139) |
| Farm animal cruelty | 45% | (42) |
| Respondent is an Independent |  |  |
| Baseline | 51% | (249) |
| Farm animal cruelty | 65%* | (77) |

[a] Statistical significance: $*p < .05$; $**p < .01$; $***p < .001$. As noted above, $p$ values are based on logistic regression models (estimated separately for respondents who are Republicans, Democrats, and Independents). The models control for the respondent's gender, age, race, and education. The baseline condition serves as the comparison group.

The support for investigations across all five scenarios was much higher than prior scholarship in the area would have anticipated,[66] and much broader than theories of motivated cognition would have predicted. Our study finds much less motivated cognition than might be expected in the realm of evaluations of undercover investigations.

Nonetheless, in examining the results in Survey 4, we realized that although there was strong support across party lines for all investigations, when one focuses on who thinks undercover investigations are very important for revealing unknown truths (for all of the behaviors investigated), Democrats are more likely than Republicans to conclude that undercover investigations are very important. But strikingly, the difference between Democrats and Republicans is only statistically significant for one category of investigations: farm animal cruelty investigations. For sex trafficking, political corruption, dogfighting, and even abortion, there are no statistically significant differences between the views of persons of different political parties when it comes to their opinions about the importance of undercover investigations. But for reasons that future research should further unpack, our data illustrate that when it comes to factory farming, there is a significant difference between Democrats (65% say undercover investigations are very important), and Republicans (45% say undercover investigations are very important). See Table 6.7. Support for undercover investigations dramatically increases among Democrats and Independents between the baseline support and support after being exposed to a farm animal investigation, but the same is not true for Republicans. When it comes to Republicans, there

[66] Again, we emphasize that the prior scholarship has been focused on investigative journalism and whistleblowing more generally, and not solely on undercover investigations.

appears to be a form of factory-farm exceptionalism such that every other type of investigation improves the baseline perception of investigations, but not when it comes to factory farms.

In order to contextualize the findings in Survey 4, as we did with each of the other surveys, we compared the support for undercover investigations in each of these novel investigative contexts with the baseline support for investigations identified in Survey 1. In other words, we assessed whether exposure to investigations in any of the five areas studied (human trafficking, abortion, dogfighting, political corruption, and farm animal cruelty) increased or decreased favorable public opinion of undercover investigations relative to the baseline perceptions of investigations.

Interestingly, our findings on this point suggest that the content of the message (or nature of the conduct investigated) does less to impact public perception of undercover investigations than might commonly be assumed. There are no drops in support for investigative practices when the public is exposed to investigations about a topic that persons may not care about as much or may be reluctant to have investigated in the abstract. We compared the baseline odds of the general public perceiving undercover investigations as very important for revealing underlying truths with the respondents who received one of the five different investigative scenarios. In four of the five experimental conditions, the view that undercover investigations were very important *increased* relative to the baseline. An undercover investigation of an abortion provider is the one exception to the rule. For the abortion investigation scenario, when persons were exposed to an abortion investigation, support for investigations did not increase. But it also did not decrease, remaining indistinguishable from the general baseline support for undercover investigations (Table 6.8).

Of course, the natural question is whether the political orientation of the respondents is what is actually driving the different views about undercover investigations. We ran a logistic regression that asked whether support for undercover investigations depends on a combination of what is investigated and the respondent's political party. Table 6.9 illustrates our findings, several of which are worth highlighting.

- One type of investigation always increases support for undercover investigations regardless of political party: sex trafficking.
- One type of investigation never increases support for undercover investigations regardless of political party: abortion.
- The three other investigations (farm animal cruelty, dogfighting, and political corruption) produce inconsistent support for undercover investigations that depend on one's political party.

Exposure to a dogfighting investigation correlates with increased support for undercover investigations relative to the baseline only among Democrats. Likewise, learning about a farm animal cruelty investigation increases support for undercover investigations only among Democrats and Independents. And political

TABLE 6.8. *The importance of undercover investigations by type of investigation relative to baseline*[a]

| | Very important for revealing unknown truths | (n) |
|---|---|---|
| Baseline | 50% | (751) |
| Dog fighting | 65%*** | (228) |
| Farm animal cruelty | 62%** | (228) |
| Political corruption | 62%** | (216) |
| Sex trafficking | 64%*** | (222) |
| Abortion, selling fetal tissue | 51% | (271) |

[a] Statistical significance: *$p < .05$; **$p < .01$; ***$p < .001$. As noted above, $p$ values are based on logistic regression models. The models control for the respondent's gender, age, race, education, and political party. The baseline condition serves as the comparison group. A similar pattern emerges when it comes to the public perception of the integrity of persons who conduct undercover investigations. Compared with the baseline in Survey 1, the odds of seeing investigators as persons of high integrity increase in four of the five conditions: dogfighting, farm animal cruelty, political corruption, and sex trafficking. Again, abortion is the lone exception to the rule. Interestingly, compared with the baseline support for making undercover investigations illegal, the support for doing so drops in all five scenarios. In other words, providing a person with any investigative scenario, including one relating to abortion, tends to reduce the support for outlawing undercover investigations.

corruption investigations do not correlate with increases in support of investigations among either major party, but they do correlate with an increased support for undercover investigations among Independents.

Table 6.9 illustrates the basic reality that in most circumstances support for undercover investigations increases regardless of the topic of the undercover investigation across party lines. The exceptions are notable. For example, Republicans tend not to have increased confidence in undercover investigations when the topic of the investigation is factory farming. Likewise, Democrats do not have increased confidence in undercover investigations when the investigation is of political corruption or of an abortion provider.

In the aggregate, Surveys 3 and 4 provide a rather striking rebuke to the conventional wisdom that the perception of an investigation is contingent on the content of the message or the political affiliation of the investigated person. A number of commentators who have looked at investigative journalism and whistleblowing have posited that persons will be much more receptive to messages that further their cause (or political orientation), and more skeptical of investigations that challenge their own allies or values. But our research suggests much broader and more entrenched support for undercover investigations than previously assumed. There is certainly evidence of the partisan, motivated cognition, more so among Republicans than Democrats, but much less so among either party than had been anticipated by prior scholarship. Likewise, there is remarkable consistency among public perceptions of investigations across all of the randomized types of conduct that was investigated. More often than not, a person of *any* political orientation is

TABLE 6.9. *The importance of undercover investigations depends on type of investigation and respondent's political party*[a]

| | Very important for revealing unknown truths | (n) |
|---|---|---|
| Respondent is a Democrat | | |
| Baseline | 51% | (353) |
| Dogfighting | 73%*** | (106) |
| Farm animal cruelty | 67%* | (105) |
| Political corruption | 62% | (99) |
| Sex trafficking | 67%** | (107) |
| Abortion, selling fetal tissue | 46% | (134) |
| Respondent is a Republican | | |
| Baseline | 45% | (139) |
| Dogfighting | 61% | (38) |
| Farm animal cruelty | 45% | (42) |
| Political corruption | 49% | (41) |
| Sex trafficking | 60%+ | (47) |
| Abortion, selling fetal tissue | 50% | (38) |
| Respondent is an Independent | | |
| Baseline | 51% | (249) |
| Dog fighting | 57% | (79) |
| Farm animal cruelty | 65%* | (77) |
| Political corruption | 69%** | (73) |
| Sex trafficking | 64%* | (64) |
| Abortion, selling fetal tissue | 57% | (94) |

[a] Statistical significance: $^+p < .10$; $^*p < .05$; $^{**}p < .01$; $^{***}p < .001$. As noted above, $p$ values are based on logistic regression models. The models control for the respondent's gender, age, race, and education. The baseline condition serves as the comparison group.

likely to respond to *any* type of investigation by indicating a strengthened confidence in the importance of undercover investigations.

### 6.4.3.4 Study 5: Politically Motivated Nonprofits and Clear Consequences for the Entity Investigated

Prior research emphasized that the public reaction to investigative journalism is very likely shaped in large part by questions about whether the investigator is perceived as biased, politically motivated, or seeking financial benefits or fame. It has long been assumed that public confidence in an investigation is contingent on the public viewing the investigation as neutral and apolitical. To the extent an investigation is "viewed as more self-interested," commentators have asserted that the confidence in the investigation declines.[67]

---

[67] Heumann et al., *supra* note 22, at 19. *Id.* at 20 (noting that any acts that "tainted the[] sense of the purity of the employee's motivation" resulted in a reduction in the positive view of the

The hypothesis that undercover investigations by nonneutral, or cause-oriented, organizations will have diminished public value is highly relevant to the question of whether investigations by activists, as opposed to professional journalists, can serve a role in influencing public opinion. We therefore designed an experiment to test this theory.

Survey 5 started with the same general definition of undercover investigations and asked each participant the same set of survey questions we used for all the studies. The study also uses the same fact patterns from Survey 4 (sex trafficking, dogfighting, political corruption, farm animal cruelty, and abortion), but with three additional facts inserted into each randomly assigned investigative scenario: (1) the investigator was not neutral, but rather worked with an activist organization with an interest in the conduct investigated (e.g., an animal rights group or pro-life organization); (2) the investigation was expected to lead to donations and public fame (or positive attention) for the activist group that conducted the investigation; and (3) the investigation's target was at risk of civil and criminal liability because of the conduct exposed by the investigation. Based on the prior research about investigative journalism and whistleblowing, our hypothesis was that the support for undercover investigations in these circumstances would be significantly diminished.

Below are two examples (farm animal cruelty and abortion) that illustrate how we modified the fact patterns from Survey Four to add the suggestion of nonneutrality and motive to obtain fame and fundraising.

> An animal rights nonprofit organization recently sent someone undercover to investigate farm animal cruelty by a prominent politician who is the mayor of a large city. During the course of the investigation, the investigator used deceptive practices, including posing as a prospective intern with the mayor's office and secretly recording coworkers while training for the new job. The investigator learned that the mayor owns an industrial pig farm and personally approved animal husbandry practices that caused intense suffering. It was discovered that female pigs were impregnated and then kept in cramped cages that do not allow them to turn around. Baby piglets were separated from their mothers and the males were castrated without pain medication. At campaign events the mayor frequently talks about being a farmer and uses it as evidence of their good character. The investigator left the mayor's office and provided this footage to the nonprofit to air on national television as part of an exposé revealing the mayor's involvement in farm animal cruelty. The investigation could lead to criminal charges for the politician and could provide a high-profile fundraising opportunity for the animal rights nonprofit that sponsored the investigation.

> A pro-life nonprofit organization recently sent someone undercover to investigate a prominent politician (the mayor of a large city) who previously ran a local abortion

whistleblower). Again, we saw this concern raised in the debates over journalism ethics described in Chapter 2.

clinic. During the course of the investigation, the investigator used deceptive practices, including posing as a prospective intern with the mayor's office and secretly recording coworkers while training for the new job. The investigator learned that the mayor, while acting as head of the abortion clinic, may have violated federal and state laws. It was discovered that the clinic had been selling fetal tissue to research laboratories in other states, which is against the law. While this was happening, the mayor (who was then a candidate) focused their campaign on protecting young children and improving the health of infants. The investigator left the mayor's office and provided this footage to the nonprofit to air on national television as part of an exposé revealing the mayor's involvement in illegally selling fetal tissue. The investigation could lead to criminal charges for the politician and could provide a high-profile fundraising opportunity for the pro-life nonprofit that sponsored the investigation.

Our findings on this point are particularly novel. For the most part, our data show that even investigations done by politically motivated entities with an expectation of positive publicity and financial gain *increase* public confidence in undercover investigations relative to the baseline.

Compared with the baseline support for undercover investigations from Survey 1, support for undercover investigations went up in each case except for an abortion investigation. Persons randomly exposed to any investigation were generally more likely to find undercover investigations important to revealing underlying truths about society, and more likely to find that undercover investigators were persons with high integrity. Notably, however, those persons exposed to an abortion investigation by an activist group indicated a lower level of support for investigations than the baseline level of support.

Table 6.10 shows that the belief that undercover investigations are very important is lower in the abortion condition than in the baseline condition. Likewise, the odds of believing that the people who conduct undercover investigations have high integrity are lower in the abortion condition than in the baseline condition. Nonetheless, this conclusion should not be overstated because it tends to say more about an idiosyncratic feature of Democrats than perhaps anything else. As Table 6.11 shows, the downward-trending support for undercover investigations that this study reveals is overwhelmingly driven by Democrats (and to a lesser degree Independents) who make up a disproportionate number of the persons in our study pool. Just as Republicans appear to have idiosyncratic views about investigations of factory farming, Democrats are more likely to think that investigations done by partisan groups in support of a pro-life agenda are not to be trusted.

Something else that might explain these results is that persons on the political left may view investigations of abortion facilities as categorically different and entitled to less protection for a number of reasons. First, although it has not been linked to any of the reported investigators or, so far as we know, their organizations, physical violence and murder has been inflicted on persons working to provide access to

TABLE 6.10. *The importance of undercover investigations: Baseline versus partisan investigator with the risk of a criminal charge*[a]

| | Very important for revealing unknown truths | High integrity | (n) |
|---|---|---|---|
| Baseline | 50% | 43% | (751) |
| Dogfighting: Partisan investigator, risk of criminal charge | 65%*** | 64%*** | (225) |
| Farm animal cruelty: Partisan investigator, risk of criminal charge | 60%* | 58%*** | (230) |
| Political corruption: Partisan investigator, risk of criminal charge | 63%*** | 65%*** | (228) |
| Sex trafficking: Partisan investigator, risk of criminal charge | 67%*** | 69%*** | (242) |
| Abortion: Partisan investigator, risk of criminal charge | 42%* | 33%** | (226) |

[a] Statistical significance: [+]$p < .10$; [*]$p < .05$; [**]$p < .01$; [***]$p < .001$. As noted above, $p$ values are based on logistic regression models. The models control for the respondent's gender, age, race, education, and political party.

abortions by persons who oppose the practice. The potential for violence in this context unquestionably makes abortion different from any of the other fields we studied. Whether this violence justifies a lesser degree of protection for investigations in this realm, whether the threat of violence trumps the legal and moral arguments in favor of transparency, is of course beyond the scope of this project. Second, in some of the widely reported investigations of abortion organizations, there have been claims that the published videos misrepresented what the investigations actually uncovered.[68] But we would note that it is also commonplace for those who oppose undercover investigations of factory farms to raise claims about safety, privacy, integrity, and misrepresentation.

Specifically, by directly comparing Surveys 4 and 5, we were able to show that the presence of a partisan investigator makes very little difference to the public perception of any investigation, except for investigations of abortion providers. Our research shows that there is no statistically significant difference between investigations done by neutral entities and investigations done by partisan, activist investigators.

[68] Editorial, *The Campaign of Deception against Planned Parenthood*, N.Y. TIMES (July 22, 2015), www.nytimes.com/2015/07/22/opinion/the-campaign-of-deception-against-planned-parenthood .html (asserting that the edited version of the Planned Parenthood video conveyed inaccurate information to the public regarding the legality of organization's acts).

TABLE 6.11. *Democrats drive abortion findings: Baseline versus partisan investigator and the risk of a criminal charge*[a]

| | Very important for revealing unknown truths | Very important for informing people | High integrity | Should be illegal | (n) |
|---|---|---|---|---|---|
| **Respondent is a Democrat** | | | | | |
| Baseline | 51% | 44% | 47% | 12% | (353) |
| Abortion investigation: Partisan investigator, risk of criminal charge | 35%** | 34%+ | 34%* | 14% | (111) |
| **Respondent is a Republican** | | | | | |
| Baseline | 45% | 38% | 37% | 16% | (139) |
| Abortion investigation: Partisan investigator, risk of criminal charge | 52% | 44% | 34% | 26% | (50) |
| **Respondent is an Independent** | | | | | |
| Baseline | 51% | 45% | 43% | 10% | (249) |
| Abortion investigation: Partisan investigator, risk of criminal charge | 45% | 37% | 29%+ | 12% | (65) |

[a] Statistical significance: $^+p < .10$; $^*p < .05$; $^{**}p < .01$; $^{***}p < .001$. As noted above, $p$ values are based on logistic regression models. The models control for the respondent's gender, age, race, and education. Despite the prior literature's suggestions that indicators of nonneutrality or bias would shape the public's perception of whistleblowing and investigative journalism, our research focusing more narrowly on the more controversial practice of undercover investigations shows that this may not be the case. Table 6.12 shows that support for undercover investigations does not drop off when the public is told that the investigation was done by a partisan activist investigator.

Again, the one exception to the finding that investigations by nonneutral activists do not diminish confidence in undercover investigations is abortion, and as noted above this finding seems to be driven by the Democrats in our study population. Democrats approve of undercover investigations in the abstract and for every other investigative scenario. But confidence in undercover work drops sharply for Democrats who are exposed to an investigation about abortion clinics by a partisan investigator. We compared the different abortion conditions across both studies – the regular abortion investigation by a major news network (Survey 4), and the partisan investigation condition (Survey 5) – and this confirmed that the degree of support for undercover investigations in the abortion condition, particularly among Democrats, depends on how the scenario is framed. The numbers here are mostly too small to tell a story of statistical significance; however, it is striking to see the drop in support for an investigation in this realm when it is revealed that the investigator is a partisan activist.

TABLE 6.12. *Does the presence of a partisan investigator and the risk of a criminal charge change the importance of undercover investigations?*[a]

| | Very important for revealing unknown truths | Very important for informing people | High integrity | Should be illegal | (n) |
|---|---|---|---|---|---|
| Dogfighting investigation | 65% | 61% | 65% | 12% | (228) |
| Dogfighting investigation: Partisan investigator, risk of criminal charge | 65% | 64% | 64% | 5%* | (225) |
| Farm animal cruelty investigation | 62% | 58% | 61% | 9% | (228) |
| Farm animal cruelty investigation: Partisan investigator, risk of criminal charge | 60% | 57% | 58% | 10% | (230) |
| Political corruption investigation | 62% | 56% | 53% | 14% | (216) |
| Political corruption investigation: Partisan investigator, risk of criminal charge | 63% | 61% | 65%** | 8%* | (228) |
| Sex trafficking investigation | 64% | 60% | 63% | 8% | (222) |
| Sex trafficking investigation: Partisan investigator, risk of criminal charge | 67% | 61% | 69% | 9% | (242) |
| Abortion investigation | 51% | 46% | 42% | 11% | (271) |
| Abortion investigation: Partisan investigator, risk of criminal charge | 42%+ | 37%+ | 33%* | 16%+ | (226) |

[a] Statistical significance: $^+p < .10$; $^*p < .05$; $^{**}p < .01$; $^{***}p < .001$. As noted above, $p$ values are based on logistic regression models. The models control for the respondent's gender, age, race, and education and political party.

One final caveat about our findings that is worth considering is that in all of the hypothetical undercover investigation scenarios we included, the vignette states that the journalist or activist did, in fact, find the information they suspected they would uncover. In reality, of course, undercover investigators do not know *ex ante* what, if anything, they will find. It is conceivable that results might be different if we had

TABLE 6.13. *Democrats drive abortion findings: Abortion investigation versus abortion investigation with partisan investigator and the risk of a criminal charge*[a]

| | Very important for revealing unknown truths | Very important for informing people | High integrity | Should be illegal | (n) |
|---|---|---|---|---|---|
| **Respondent is a Democrat** | | | | | |
| Abortion investigation | 46% | 42% | 41% | 10% | (134) |
| Abortion investigation: Partisan investigator, risk of criminal charge | 35%[+] | 34% | 34% | 14% | (111) |
| **Respondent is a Republican** | | | | | |
| Abortion investigation | 50% | 45% | 42% | 13% | (38) |
| Abortion investigation: Partisan investigator, risk of criminal charge | 52% | 44% | 34% | 26% | (50) |
| **Respondent is an Independent** | | | | | |
| Abortion investigation | 57% | 50% | 45% | 11% | (94) |
| Abortion investigation: Partisan investigator, risk of criminal charge | 45% | 37%[+] | 29%[+] | 12% | (65) |

[a] Statistical significance: [+]$p < .10$; [*]$p < .05$; [**]$p < .01$; [***]$p < .001$. As noted above, $p$ values are based on logistic regression models. The models control for the respondent's gender, age, race, and education.

included a scenario with facts that either did not include any information about what might have been discovered or did not discover any evidence of wrongdoing. That is something future researchers may wish to explore (Table 6.13).

## 6.5 CONCLUSION

Taken together, these findings about undercover investigations across all five surveys both confirm and unsettle some of the key findings or assumptions from prior scholarship about investigative journalism, whistleblowing, and undercover investigations. Our studies tend to show overwhelming public support for investigations on matters of public concern, even when it is specified that lies or nonconsensual recording will occur, and overwhelming opposition to the criminalization of such investigations. Our findings also show that, overall, an investigation by any entity (news or nonprofit) tends to increase the public confidence in investigations. This suggests that when confronted with actual facts of potential malfeasance, no matter who uncovers it, confidence in investigations and support for them increases. Prior assumptions about public perception varying depending on whether the investigation was done by an entity that is friendly or oppositional (the *New York Times* or Fox News) or whether a Democrat or Republican was investigated are not supported by our findings. Overall, persons of all political parties support investigations by all entities on all topics, and often without regard to whether it is a neutral party or activist who conducts the undercover investigation. This information may be important moving forward as policy makers and judges make decisions governing the law surrounding undercover investigations.

# Conclusion

## C.1 INTRODUCTION

As the material in this book explains, undercover investigations using investigative deception and nonconsensual recording have been an important part of the eco-sphere of information gathering, speech production, and communication in the United States for well over a hundred years. These investigations continue to be an effective means of promoting transparency and exposing unlawful and otherwise objectionable conduct by powerful actors and institutions. And as our empirical research has shown, undercover investigations enjoy broad public support in nearly all political contexts and across a diverse range of demographic groups.

At the same time, at least in some contexts, undercover work has also become increasingly controversial as the targets of certain investigations seek public condemnation and legal remedies against investigators. As we write this book, we are at an interesting moment in the history of undercover investigations. Targets of investigations and their allies are gaining momentum in their efforts to prohibit or at least to limit and deter these investigative tactics, and policy makers and the courts are increasingly called on to address the related legal and policy implications. Even outside of government actors, moral philosophers and profes-sional ethics experts will likely always disagree about the permissibility of under-cover investigations.

In some areas, such as law enforcement operations, civil rights testing, and union salting, while the investigations are by no means universally accepted, their legality and ongoing legitimacy will probably remain unchanged.[1] In other areas, such as undercover investigations by journalists and political activists, there will likely

---

[1]  Alan K. Chen, *Investigative Deception across Social Contexts*, KNIGHT FIRST AMEND. INST. (Dec. 16, 2022), https://knightcolumbia.org/content/investigative-deception-across-social-con texts [https://perma.cc/Y3LN-7CKZ].

continue to be legal battles over their legitimacy. States continue to pass ag-gag laws to limit investigations on factory farms. Some states and provinces in Canada appear open to a broad range of recording or access bans that will greatly curtail investigations in all fields. And increasingly, there is litigation against right-wing investigative entities such as those seeking to expose misconduct in abortion facilities, and those investigating left-leaning groups. In public statements, the targets of these investigations tend to emphasize that the right-leaning investigators are mischaracterizing what they observed or unfairly editing the footage. But interestingly, the litigation challenging these investigations almost never includes defamation claims, which indicates that the primary concerns relate to privacy-type intrusions, and not false revelations or deceptive editing.

For example, as we have touched on in previous chapters, recent developments in these actions for civil liability against undercover investigators seem to suggest a trend toward punishing such investigators through sizable damage awards. As we discussed previously, the Ninth Circuit recently affirmed a $2.425 million verdict against the Center for Medical Progress and its agents for conducting undercover investigations of reproductive freedom organizations.[2] Though CMP may seek Supreme Court review of that decision, this level of financial exposure could certainly deter undercover investigators of all types and from all ideological perspectives across the country from carrying out investigations.

Similarly, as we discussed in Chapter 2, Democracy Partners, an umbrella group of left-leaning political consulting firms, successfully sued the conservative group Project Veritas after the latter conducted an extensive undercover investigation, and was awarded $120,000 in damages. The Project Veritas operation involved one of its representatives using a false identity and making a $20,000 donation to one of the consulting firms, helping to secure an internship for another Veritas representative posing as his niece. The "niece," also using a false name and background, then secretly recorded two consultants who worked with Democracy Partners making statements that suggested some unethical campaign tactics, such as pursuing strategies to provoke violence at Republican rallies. Project Veritas published a series of stories including the undercover videos that documented these conversations, allegedly causing Democracy Partners to lose some of its contracts.

The Democracy Partners suit was not for defamation (because the videos apparently depicted these conversations accurately) but for privacy intrusions, unlawful interception of oral communications and fraudulent misrepresentation, and civil conspiracy. The trial judge had earlier dismissed their claims of trespass and breach

[2] Planned Parenthood Fed'n of Am., Inc. v. Newman, 51 F.4th 1125 (9th Cir. 2022); Planned Parenthood Fed'n of Am., Inc. v. Newman, No. 20-16068, 2022 WL 13613963 (9th Cir. Oct. 21, 2022).

of fiduciary duty, including the duty of loyalty.[3] The court issued a $120,000 judgment against Veritas for their investigative tactics.[4]

Shortly after the verdict, the *Washington Post* ran a featured opinion piece celebrating the judgment against Veritas. The author was Erik Wemple, the *Post's* media critic, who claimed that the verdict "upends" the claim that undercover investigations are "old fashioned journalism," and comes very close to categorically condemning undercover investigations.[5] Wemple tells readers that media is "falling out of love with undercover tactics," and creates an image of undercover investigations as disfavored, and of investigations predicated on misrepresentations as particularly unseemly and out of fashion. Investigations that use lies are characterized as presumptively suspect, or unjournalistic. Under this telling, it as though lies have become the insuperable line when it comes to journalistic ethics, a transgression that is almost unforgivable. Such a framing of lies by media critics like Wemple is at odds with public sentiment, as our research in prior chapters shows, and if the position were enshrined in law it would support governmental efforts to make many undercover investigations a crime.

Indeed, as we write this chapter, the state of Iowa has once again appealed a lower court judgment invalidating one of its many iterations of an ag-gag law that criminalizes access gained by deception. Legal challenges to laws in Arkansas and North Carolina that allowed civil tort claims to be brought against undercover investigators are still pending.

We have argued throughout this book that such a cramped approach to undercover investigations is bad for transparency, and by no means required by the law. As we have contended, we believe that the First Amendment to the US Constitution in many cases should protect the activities of undercover investigators across a range of contexts because the tactics they engage in are critical to the promotion of transparency and free expression. They lead to the revelation of information that promotes democratic self-governance, facilitates the search for many different types of truth, and advances the autonomy of those who engage in such investigations. As we have outlined, only in cases where the government can identify a tangible, compelling interest in preventing such activity should the state be able to punish or prohibit undercover investigations. And the prevention of de minimis, technical legal harms should not suffice to overcome such freedoms if they lead to neither tangible nor material harms to the targets of such investigations. Nor should the law recognize

---

[3] Democracy Partners v. Project Veritas Action Fund, 453 F. Supp. 3d 261, 278, 283 (D.D.C. 2020), *reconsideration denied*, No. CV 17-1047 (ESH), 2020 WL 5095484 (D.D.C. Aug. 27, 2020).

[4] Adam Goldman, *Jury Rules against Project Veritas in Lawsuit*, N.Y. Times (Sept. 22, 2022), www.nytimes.com/2022/09/22/us/politics/project-veritas-lawsuit.html.

[5] Erik Wemple, *Journalism or Political Activism? Project Veritas Is on Trial over 2016 Sting*, Wash. Post (Sept. 13, 2022), www.washingtonpost.com/opinions/2022/09/13/project-veritas-trial-lawsuit-sting/.

the self-inflicted harms that such targets suffer when the public learns of their misconduct as a reason to shut down undercover investigations.

## C.2 WHAT TO EXPECT NEXT

### C.2.1 *Continuing Developments in First Amendment Doctrine*

We cannot with great confidence predict the direction that the law governing undercover investigations will turn. It is certainly foreseeable that the US Supreme Court will further clarify the meaning and scope of its decision in *United States v. Alvarez*, in which it first recognized that the First Amendment prohibits the state from punishing lies unless those mistruths cause a legally cognizable harm.[6] That may come in the context of a challenge to criminal or civil sanctions against undercover investigators, but it may arise in a different context. In either case, the Court will likely need to clarify what counts as a "legally cognizable harm," which serves as the legal standard for differentiating lies that are covered by the First Amendment and those that are not. Should that phrase encompass any technical legal violations of the common law, even if that harm is not recognized under all states' laws? Even if it includes all technical legal harms, may the state intervene to regulate activity if those harms do not lead to any meaningful, actual financial harm to the victim?

As we have already elaborated in Chapter 3, a broad reading of *Alvarez*'s harm requirement could lead to an unprecedented amount of state power to regulate an incredibly broad swath of human interactions, such as artificially puffing up one's own enthusiasm to work for an employer or lying to a friend to get a dinner invitation. And, of course, lower courts may continue to issue post-*Alvarez* decisions to clarify the scope of the First Amendment right to lie, both in and outside the context of undercover investigations.

In addition, the Supreme Court and other courts may continue to develop First Amendment doctrine as it pertains to the right to record, to produce speech by electronic media. Although several of the Court's other precedents certainly provide a solid doctrinal foundation for the right to record, the Court has thus far been reluctant to tackle that issue even in the context of video recordings of police officers carrying out their duties in public. A large consensus of lower federal courts has recognized such a right, which could be one reason that the Court has not taken this up. It seems that a decision about public recordings would be the likely first step, but perhaps later the Court would accept a case dealing with nonconsensual recording on private property, a tactic common to many undercover investigations.

---

[6] United States v. Alvarez, 567 U.S. 709, 719 (2012); *see also id.* at 734 (Breyer, J., concurring) (indicating that lies can be regulated only where they cause "specific harm to identifiable victims").

## C.2.2 *Prosecuting Investigators*

Some jurisdictions have attempted ag-gag–like prosecutions even in the absence of specific targeted statutes. Those who seek to conduct an undercover investigation in a setting where abuse is patent may risk prosecution if they do not report the misconduct to the government within the timeline established by the local authorities. For example, there have been examples in the United States and Canada where overzealous prosecutors brought charges against undercover investigators who exposed horrific abuse on factory farms.[7] The prosecutors sought to charge the investigators either for engaging in the types of practices that they sought to expose or because the investigators did not take actions to prevent others from engaging in the practices. Although charges were dropped in all of the cases the authors are aware of to date, the approach could certainly chill future investigations that are focused on exposing long-term, systemic suffering.

We think that prosecutions in these contexts are inconsistent with encouraging public debate on matters of concern, and tread too close to a policy of punishing the messengers. But we understand the intuitive appeal of requiring that misconduct or abuse be reported immediately. If a person went undercover at a childcare facility or hospital and quickly discovered acts of child abuse or neglect, many would recoil at the idea of an investigator not immediately reporting the abuse and waiting to expose additional abuse against other victims. Perhaps the instinct that delay in these settings is inappropriate would be less clear if the investigation was revealing fraud or financial misconduct or employee mistreatment; perhaps in such circumstances the investigation is viewed as more valuable if it reveals patterns as opposed to discrete acts of harm. For our purposes here, we simply note that when investigations are politically unpopular, there is a risk that prosecutors will seek to bring charges against the investigator who goes undercover. Laws specifically protecting investigations in some (or all) contexts from criminal prosecutions might be a necessary way to balance privacy and protection in this context.

---

[7]  Professor Marceau has personal knowledge of this occurring through his legal representation of clients, but the information is privileged or attorney work product and therefore cannot be publicly documented. But some states have tried to codify mandatory disclosure laws, which could substantially disrupt undercover investigations, which tend to take some time to set up and develop. *See, e.g.,* Mo. Ann. Stat. § 578.013 (2012) ("Whenever any farm animal professional videotapes or otherwise makes a digital recording of what he or she believes to depict a farm animal subjected to abuse or neglect under sections 578.009 or 578.012, such farm animal professional shall have a duty to submit such videotape or digital recording to a law enforcement agency within twenty-four hours of the recording"). Interestingly, the Tennessee legislature enacted a similar bill, but it was vetoed by then-Governor Bill Haslam, a Republican, after the state's attorney general issued an opinion declaring that the law was "constitutionally suspect." Andy Sher, *Tennessee Governor Bill Haslam Vetoing "Ag Gag" Bill,* Chattanooga Times Free Press (May 13, 2013), www.timesfreepress.com/news/2013/may/13/tennessee-governor-bill-haslam-vetoing-ag-gag-bill/. For the attorney general's opinion, see Tenn. Att'y Gen Op. No. 13-39 (May 9, 2013).

### C.2.3 *Developments under State Law: The Private Law Conundrum*

As we have discussed throughout the book, the key limits on investigations to date have been ethical concerns with investigations and legislation criminalizing undercover investigations. As the Wemple op-ed discussed above suggests, it is possible that major media outlets will become more averse to classic undercover investigations (if they have not already done so), thus limiting the number and potentially the public perception of investigations. In addition, beyond constitutional limits on legislation limiting investigations, future legal developments regarding undercover investigations may not be limited to constitutional doctrine. Even if the Court were to recognize a First Amendment right to engage in investigative deception and a limited First Amendment privilege to engage in nonconsensual video recording, opponents of undercover investigations might then turn to private law mechanisms to ban such speech activities.

### C.2.3.1 Contract Law

We have discussed the fact that many undercover investigations are employment based. Most investigators who secure jobs with the targets of their investigations are typically hired into at-will employment positions. Under the common law in most jurisdictions, an employer can fire an at-will employee for any reason, or no reason at all, so long as the basis of the discharge is not one prohibited under statutory law, such as race and gender discrimination. Such positions are typically not the type of jobs that result in formal written employment contracts, but that does not preclude employers from requiring new employees to sign such contracts. And employers could insist on terms under that the employees/investigators agree not to engage in an undercover investigation, perhaps exposing that employee to a lawsuit for breach of contract should they go forward with the investigation. Even short of an employment contract term, employers might require all employees to sign nondisclosure agreements, binding written contracts under which the employees agree not to divulge any information about their employment that is obtained or learned during the course of their employment.[8] It may be that even such private law mechanisms will not deter investigators from carrying out investigations because many of them might be judgment proof, not having sufficient assets to make it worth the employer's while to sue them. But such policies could certainly have an impact on how centralized or organized the investigations could be because institutional sponsors of

---

[8] The problems of nondisclosure agreements and their impact on transparency in other contexts have been well documented. *See, e.g.,* Maureen A. Weston, *Buying Secrecy: Non-Disclosure Agreements, Arbitration, and Professional Ethics in the #MeToo Era,* 2021 U. ILL. L. REV. 507 (2021).

investigations may be exposed to liability. And the harassment value of such litigation could still be a substantial deterrent.

Even in contexts short of employment, it is possible for potential investigative targets to deploy a similar strategy. For example, reproductive choice groups that were targeted for an undercover investigation by CMP have invoked private law methods to suppress undercover investigation methods. Recall that CMP's agents posed as representatives of legitimate businesses who, among other things, attended conferences to gain access to the reproductive choice groups' officials, whom they secretly recorded. One of the arguments in their successful litigation against CMP was that the latter's agents had signed contracts as part of their participation in such conferences under which they agreed that they would not make recordings, disclose recordings, or disclose any information received from their participation in the conference. Thus, the reproductive choice groups sued them in part for breach of contract and sought a federal court injunction against CMP's use of their secretly recorded videos. Their argument was that the CMP's agents waived any First Amendment rights they may have had when they signed those private nondisclosure agreements. A federal trial court judge issued the requested injunction, and the US Court of Appeals for the Ninth Circuit recently upheld that injunction on the grounds that CMP had indeed waived any First Amendment rights they might have otherwise enjoyed.[9]

### C.2.3.2 Tort Law

Another form of private law enforcement that investigative targets might employ is lawsuits under state tort law. Regardless of the existence of a contract, we can imagine that some targets may sue investigators for trespass, invasion of privacy, fraud, or breach of the duty of loyalty. We have already discussed these types of tort claims and cases that have been previously litigated, including the *Food Lion* case, the *Desnick* case, the CMP litigation, and the Democracy Partners suit against Project Veritas. While we do not think that the activities of most undercover investigators would violate legal duties under state tort law, that would not necessarily prevent targets from filing lawsuits, or at least threatening to file such lawsuits to shut down investigations. It also does not mean that investigations that extend beyond what we regard as reasonable action might not expose them to substantial tort liability.

In addition to common law tort claims, some states have responded to undercover investigations by creating new statutory tort claims, laws that enable the subjects of such investigations to sue the investigators and their sponsors for money damages. In

9   Nat'l Abortion Fed'n v. Ctr. for Med. Progress, No. 21-15953, 2022 WL 3572943 (9th Cir. Aug. 19, 2022).

the context of undercover investigations, at least two states have adopted laws that create such claims.

The North Carolina legislature enacted a new law in 2016 that states: "Any person who intentionally gains access to the nonpublic areas of another's premises and engages in an act that exceeds the person's authority to enter those areas is liable to the owner or operator of the premises for any damages sustained."[10] Among the acts that count as exceeding the scope of the person's authority are an employee recording images or sound occurring within an employer's premises and using the recording to breach the employee's duty of loyalty to the employer. Thus, unlike other laws targeting undercover investigations, the North Carolina statute targets *existing* employees, not just those seeking employment or access to property. Moreover, the North Carolina law applies to all industries, not just agricultural ones. If the property owner or operator prevails, it can secure an injunction, compensatory damages, costs and attorneys' fees, and punitive damages of up to $5,000 for every day that a violation of the law occurs.

In 2017, the Arkansas legislature enacted a similar law, which authorizes the owner or operator of commercial property to sue "any person who knowingly gains access to a nonpublic area of a commercial property and engages in an act that exceeds the person's authority to enter the nonpublic area."[11] The statute goes on to define an act that exceeds a person's authority as including the owner's own employees, and prohibits anyone from using information obtained because of their access and allow a suit against any person who "Records images or sound occurring within an employer's commercial property and use[s] the recording in a manner that damages the employer." Thus, undercover investigators may be sued for potentially significant amounts of money under this law, which would likely deter such activity. Although not exclusively limited to apply to animal rights investigators, the definition of commercial property under the Arkansas law includes, somewhat redundantly, "Agricultural or timber production operations, including buildings and all outdoor areas that are not open to the public."[12] Successful plaintiffs may obtain injunctive relief, compensatory damage, costs and attorneys' fees, and, even where there are no *actual* damages, up to $5,000 for every day that a violation of the law occurs. As we discuss below, both of these laws were initially enjoined by federal courts as violating the First Amendment, but a federal judge recently dismissed the lawsuit challenging the Arkansas statute and although the injunction against the North Carolina law was upheld, there may be other ways that state legislatures might craft new laws to avoid future legal challenges.

The issue of state-created legal claims to sue people who are trying to exercise their constitutional rights catapulted to the headlines when Texas enacted S.B. 8, its notorious law outlawing abortions whenever a fetus has a detectable heartbeat,

[10] N.C. Gen. Stat. Ann. § 99A-2.
[11] Ark. Code Ann. § 16-118-113.
[12] *Id.*

which most experts agreed would be around six weeks into a pregnancy.[13] This law was enacted well before the US Supreme Court decided *Dobbs v. Jackson Women's Health Organization*,[14] which overruled *Roe v. Wade* and pronounced that the Constitution does not prohibit states from banning abortions. But *Roe*'s overruling is not pertinent to the remedies dilemma created by laws like S.B. 8.

What was unique about the Texas abortion law was not only that it did not authorize enforcement by any state official, but it instead placed enforcement exclusively in the hands of private parties.[15] It authorized lawsuits by "any person" other than a state or local government official to sue any person who "performs or induces an abortion" in violation of the law's restrictions or who "knowingly engages in conduct that aids or abet the performance or inducement of an abortion," and authorizes statutory damages in the amount of $10,000 "for each abortion" that the defendant performed or helped facilitate.[16] It also asymmetrically allowed the prevailing plaintiff to recover costs and attorneys' fees from the defendants, but not for prevailing defendants to recover from plaintiffs.[17] Texas lawmakers clearly designed the law to avoid the traditional methods of constitutional enforcement. Typically, when a state enacts a law that is subject to constitutional challenge, plaintiffs may file suit in federal court to stop the state official responsible for enforcement of that law from enforcing it.[18] By placing enforcement in the hands of private actors instead of state officials, Texas created a loophole that allowed it to avoid such a suit.

The problem of whom to sue confronted those who sought to invalidate Texas's S.B. 8. The plaintiffs brought a constitutional challenge in federal court seeking to bar the law's enforcement before it went into effect, and named as defendants the Texas Attorney General, a state court judge, a state court clerk, the executive directors of the Texas Medical Board and the Texas Board of Nursing, the Texas Board of Pharmacy, the Texas Health and Human Service Commission, and a private person who had publicly declared his intent to sue under the new law. The Supreme Court took the unusual step of granting certiorari before judgment to evaluate this legal challenge. In *Whole Woman's Health v. Jackson*,[19] the Court issued a narrow ruling allowing the suit to proceed only against the four executive directors of the state agencies, whom the Court believed had the power to discipline or otherwise take disciplinary action against actors under their jurisdiction for violating S.B. 8's limitations on abortion.[20] Later in the same litigation, however,

---

[13]  TEX. HEALTH & SAFETY CODE ANN. § 171.204.
[14]  142 S. Ct. 2228 (2022).
[15]  TEX. HEALTH & SAFETY CODE ANN. § 171.207.
[16]  TEX. HEALTH & SAFETY CODE ANN. § 171.208.
[17]  Rebecca Aviel & Wiley Kersh, *The Weaponization of Attorney's Fees in an Age of Constitutional Warfare*, 132 YALE L.J. (forthcoming 2023).
[18]  Ex parte Young, 209 U.S. 123, 159–60 (1908).
[19]  142 S. Ct. 522 (2021).
[20]  *Id.* at 535–36.

the Texas Supreme Court ruled as a matter of state law that those four officials did not, in fact, have the power to issue sanctions against those who violated S.B. 8, ending the lawsuit and leaving S.B. 8 intact.[21]

The US Supreme Court found the suit to be improper with respect to all other defendants. With respect to the Attorney General, it held that although *Ex parte Young* authorizes suits to enjoin state officials from enforcing unconstitutional laws, the Attorney General had no enforcement authority under S.B. 8, and therefore could not be sued.[22] The Court also held that the suits against the state judge and state court clerk were impermissible because the Court interpreted *Ex parte Young* to categorically prohibit injunctions against state judges.[23] The Court also found that the suits against the judge and clerk could not proceed for a second, independent reason – they were not suitably adverse parties to the plaintiffs and plaintiffs therefore did not have Article III standing to sue them.[24]

Turning back to laws that impede undercover investigations, one might ask why similar impediments did not block those suits from going forward. One might reasonably ask, Why does (or might) the Constitution protect people from criminal laws enforced by the state, but not from private law claims that similarly burden their rights? That is, S.B. 8 raised similar (though not identical) questions to the ones relating to laws creating tort claims against undercover investigators. Why, then, does the First Amendment protect undercover investigators from criminal prosecution, but not from a state private law claim? There actually seem to be at least two distinct potential hurdles in suing private parties to enjoin them from suing under state-created tort laws that burden others' constitutional rights: the state action doctrine and the doctrine of standing.

The state action doctrine is a constitutional principle that limits constitutional rights to protect us from the actions of the government, not from private actors, who are generally not bound by the Constitution. For example, a public school could not fire a teacher for engaging in political speech during their own free time away from campus, because that would violate the First Amendment. A private school *could* fire a teacher for such activity if it chose to, absent any other legal or contractual protection for that conduct. In the North Carolina litigation, this was not a central issue because the plaintiffs sued the Chancellor of the University of North Carolina and the state's Attorney General on the grounds that some plaintiffs had previously investigated animal testing laboratories at the university, and that their future efforts to do so would subject them to a tort claim under the law by state officials. Though it

---

[21] Whole Woman's Health v. Jackson, 642 S.W.3d 569, 573 (Tex. 2022).
[22] *Whole Woman's Health*, 142 S. Ct. at 534.
[23] *Id.* at 532.
[24] *Id.* The suit against the private party, Mark Lee Dickson, was dismissed based on his sworn declaration that he had no intention of suing the plaintiffs under S.B. 8, *id.* at 537, though he had previously declared in several Facebook posts that he intended to do so. *See* Complaint, Whole Woman's Health v. Jackson at 16 n.4, No. 21-cv-616 (W.D. Tex.) (July 31, 2021).

was not directly addressing a state action issue, the Fourth Circuit found that there was a sufficient threat of such enforcement that the case could proceed.[25] On remand, the federal district court granted partial summary judgment to the plaintiffs and invalidated much of the North Carolina law. In doing so, it found that the law involved state action in two ways. First, the court noted that "while the Act operates in the private sphere, it is state action to the extent the State has identified speech (or in some cases, conduct which can include speech) it wishes to allow to be proscribed and has empowered private parties to enforce the prohibition."[26] Second, as already discussed, the plaintiffs specifically targeted a state entity that would have to use state actors to enforce the law.[27]

As with S.B. 8, the Arkansas law does not provide for enforcement by a state official. There, animal rights and labor groups sued to challenge the Arkansas law, naming as defendants the owners of two of the largest commercial poultry and pig farms in the state, one of whom was also a member of the Arkansas legislature who sponsored the law. Although the defendants raised state action issues in the trial court, the court never reached those issues because it dismissed the case for lack of standing, which was later reversed by the Eighth Circuit and remanded back to the trial court. Recently, however, the trial court did dismiss the case on the basis that there was no state action.[28]

But there are at least two things that could count as state action in these circumstances, even where there is no state official who can bring a claim. First, the very enactment of a law that targets free speech, albeit one that hands over enforcement to private actor, is itself state action that violates the Constitution. Second, even when there are no government parties to a private contract or tort lawsuit, the case is still adjudicated by a state court, which hears the case, rules, and enforces the judgment. The Court has recognized the latter as sufficient state action in a couple of different circumstances. For example, in *Shelley v. Kraemer*,[29] the Supreme Court held that the state courts' enforcement of racially restrictive covenants in real estate sales contracts constituted state action even though the private contracts themselves did not violate the Fourteenth Amendment. The Court acknowledged that "[i]t has been recognized that the action of state courts in enforcing a substantive common-law rule formulated by those courts, may result in the denial of rights guaranteed by the Fourteenth Amendment, even though the judicial proceedings in such cases may have been in complete accord with the most

---

[25] People for the Ethical Treatment of Animals, Inc. v. Stein ("PETA"), 737 F. App'x 122, 132 (4th Cir. 2018).

[26] People for the Ethical Treatment of Animals, Inc. v. Stein, 466 F. Supp. 3d 547, 565 (M.D.N.C. 2020), *aff'd in part and rev'd in part on other grounds*, 60 F.4th 815, (4th Cir. 2023).

[27] *Id.*

[28] Animal Legal Def. Fund v, Peco Foods, Inc., No.4:19 CV00442 JM, 2023 WL2743238 (E.D Ark, Mar.31 2023).

[29] Shelley v. Kraemer, 334 U.S. 1 (1948).

rigorous conceptions of procedural due process."[30] Under *Shelley*, although the plaintiffs were trying to enforce covenants attached to private real estate sales, the Court recognized that by enforcing those covenants, the state courts were effectively facilitating racial discrimination against those who refused to heed the covenants' racial restrictions. Similarly, in *New York Times v. Sullivan*, the Court held that even though the Constitution is limited to constraining state action, where a "state rule of law ... impose[s] invalid restrictions on [plaintiffs'] constitutional freedoms of speech and press," the existence of the law itself is sufficient "state action" to raise First Amendment concern.[31]

In addition to the state action question, plaintiffs seeking to challenge a state law that creates a solely private enforcement mechanism must have Article III standing to challenge the law. The doctrine of standing is a limitation on the powers of federal courts to adjudicate disputes unless the plaintiff has a personal stake in the outcome of the case. Generally, under Article III, a plaintiff can establish standing only if it can be shown that the plaintiff has suffered an injury in fact that is fairly traceable to the defendant's conduct and for which a court could provide a meaningful remedy.[32] With respect to the standing issue, the challenge for the plaintiff is to find the party responsible for the cause of their injury. One can imagine that there might be generalized threats by private citizens to sue anyone who violates the state law, thus presenting a potential harm that would allow the investigators to sue for an injunction. Plaintiffs must show that there is a reasonable threat that they will be sued, but defendants will quite likely argue in such cases that they have no intent to sue the plaintiffs under the state law and that there is therefore not threat of such enforcement.

But in both the North Carolina and Arkansas cases, two different federal courts of appeals rejected such arguments and found that the plaintiffs had standing. In both cases, the courts found that because the plaintiffs had conducted such investigations in the past and had present intentions and capabilities to do so again, they were under sufficient threat of enforcement that they had standing to proceed with the litigation. Although the defendants in both cases argued that the plaintiffs' alleged harm was too speculative, the courts disagreed. As the Eighth Circuit held, "A formal threat, however, is not required to establish an injury in fact. The question is whether the plaintiffs have an objectively reasonable fear of legal action that chills their speech."[33]

---

[30] *Id.* at 17. *See also Whole Woman's Health*, 142 S. Ct. at 548 (Sotomayor, J., concurring in the judgment in part and dissenting in part) ("S. B. 8's formidable chilling effect, even before suit, would be nonexistent if not for the state-court officials who docket S.B. 8 cases with lopsided procedures and limited defenses. Because these state actors are necessary components of that chilling effect and play a clear role in the enforcement of S.B. 8, they are proper defendants").

[31] 376 U.S. 254, 265 (1964).

[32] Clapper v. Amnesty Int'l USA, 568 U.S. 398, 409 (2013).

[33] *Vaught*, 8 F.4th at 720. *See also PETA*, 737 F. App'x at 130 ("We cannot say that the claimed 'chilling' effect of the Act is objectively unreasonable or that Plaintiffs' claims of injury are too speculative to satisfy the First Amendment standing framework at the Rule 12(b)(1) stage"). Similar to the private defendant in *Whole Woman's Health*, the private defendants in the

A full exposition of these questions of federal courts law is beyond the scope of this book, but we raise these issues here to acknowledge that we might see developments in the law here that affect the future of undercover investigations.

### C.2.4 *Political Developments*

Constitutional law is not the only possible source for the protection of undercover investigators. It is at least possible that in some jurisdictions, we might see the future political will of state legislatures to codify some protection for such investigations (or to limit investigations where the Constitution permits it). States can protect speech even if is not protected by the First Amendment. For example, today thirty-nine states have enacted shield laws protecting journalists from having to reveal confidential sources[34] even though the Supreme Court declared that there is no First Amendment exemption for journalists from having to testify under subpoena.[35]

We cannot predict the likelihood of such legislation. However, given our research showing that undercover investigations enjoy widespread, bipartisan support, Congress would seem to have a strong basis for considering broad legislation protecting undercover investigations across the country, and some states could do so as well.

### C.3 SOME STANDARDS AND GUIDANCE FOR THE FUTURE

Without regard to constitutional or other legal limitations, those who choose to conduct undercover investigations may find themselves subject to a plethora of criticisms about the ethics or legitimacy of their behavior. We think it is worth considering the adoption of a set of best practices to guide those who conduct undercover investigations. While not necessarily insulating such investigators from legal claims, following good practices may at least help in terms of achieving both professional and public acceptance. Following such practices may also help investigators demonstrate good faith attempts to limit potential harms or abuses that might flow from an investigation. We offer the following as one potential approach to a statement of best practices.

#### Best Practices for Conducting Undercover Investigations

1. Before conducting an undercover investigation, investigators and their sponsors must have some specific evidence that their investigation will reveal misconduct, illegality, or wrongdoing on the part of investigation's

---

*Vaught* case successfully moved to have the claims against them dismissed on remand after they stipulated that they would not bring suits under the Arkansas law against the plaintiffs.
[34] *See, e.g.*, N.Y. Civ. Rights Law § 79-h (1970).
[35] Branzburg v. Hayes, 408 U.S. 665, 681 (1972).

target. Undercover investigations should be conducted only to gather information that is of a public concern.

2. If the information sought, in terms of both quantity and quality, is readily available and easily obtained through other sources, those sources should be used first. But to the extent an undercover investigation can provide more detailed evidence of the misconduct, it is permissible to conduct an investigation to supplement and corroborate other fact-finding techniques.

3. It is permissible to use deception, including deception by omission or affirmative misrepresentation, about the investigator's identity, political affiliations, and motivations for gaining access to the investigation site. Such deception may not be used for any other purpose than gaining access to an investigation site, conducting an investigation, and remaining undercover. When conducting employment-based investigations, the investigator should not exaggerate or inflate their credentials; only lies that omit affiliations, understate qualifications, or conceal one's identity should be tolerated. And investigators must be able to competently perform their assigned job functions.

4. Any still photography, audio recording, or video recording must be reproduced truthfully in reports to the public. No alterations or editing to mislead the listener or viewer are permissible. Editing for brevity, coherence, and to protect the privacy interests of the individuals recorded is permissible. But any editing that is reasonably likely to mislead or misrepresent is not permissible.

5. Investigators must not cause physical harm, theft (including intellectual property), or other harms to the property of the investigation's target or to any person on the premises during the investigation. The investigator should not induce, solicit, or entrap others to engage in misconduct or actively celebrate or engage in misconduct themselves. However, investigators need not report misconduct to government officials immediately if doing so would compromise the success of the investigation.

6. Investigators must not deprive individuals who are associated with the investigation site of their dignity, privacy, or autonomy unless that is the direct result of those individuals' participation in the suspected misconduct being investigated. Investigations targeting highly vulnerable individuals are discouraged. Undercover investigations in which investigators gain access to commercial properties are preferable to investigations that involve access to private homes or spaces, but the latter are acceptable if the information sought is of a public concern and investigators limit their investigation only to that information.

✽ ✽ ✽

In this book, we have attempted to provide a comprehensive account of the state of undercover investigations in the United States as we approach the end of the first quarter of the twenty-first century. We anticipate that such investigations, after having endured for over a hundred years, will continue to be part of the information and speech landscape in the next generation, and probably beyond. New technologies, such as data scraping software, may even expand the scope of what types of undercover investigations are even possible. The ubiquity of high-quality video recording devices is likely to enhance the possibilities of undercover work to even greater levels. Given that such investigations are most likely here to stay, it is important to flesh out the constitutional, legal, ethical, social, and political ramifications of undercover investigations, as well as to understand what conditions make them more likely to occur and more likely to be successful.

We don't think that undercover investigations alone are likely to catalyze social change. But we think that the revelation of otherwise secreted facts on matters of public concern will often be a necessary element of efforts by emerging social movements to challenge the status quo. Facts, as Hannah Arendt recognized, have a stubbornness that makes them difficult to argue with, and thus undercover investigations will often serve an important role in promoting transparent, public debate of the sort that is and should be celebrated in democracies.

# Index

For EU product safety concerns, contact us at Calle de José Abascal, 56–1°, 28003 Madrid, Spain or eugpsr@cambridge.org.

www.ingramcontent.com/pod-product-compliance
Ingram Content Group UK Ltd.
Pitfield, Milton Keynes, MK11 3LW, UK
UKHW020307140625
459647UK00006B/75